BLACKBIRD

Music shapes our world more powerfully than any other cultural product. To fully understand America, we must learn the complex, diverse history of American musical life. The books in this series tell the stories of the artists, forms, and innovations that define the musical legacy of the United States and fashion its ideals and practices.

BLaCKbiRd

How **BLACK MUSICIANS** Sang **THE BEATLES** into Being—and **SANG** **BACK** to Them **EVER AFTER**

Katie Kapurch AND **Jon Marc Smith**

THE PENNSYLVANIA STATE UNIVERSITY PRESS | UNIVERSITY PARK, PENNSYLVANIA

NATIONAL
ENDOWMENT
FOR THE
HUMANITIES

The National Endowment for the Humanities: Democracy demands
wisdom.

Library of Congress Cataloging-in-Publication Data

Names: Kapurch, Katie, 1983– author. | Smith, Jon Marc, author.
Title: Blackbird : how Black musicians sang the Beatles into being and sang
    back to them ever after / Katie Kapurch and Jon Marc Smith.
Other titles: American music history.
Description: University Park, Pennsylvania : The Pennsylvania State
    University Press, [2023] | Series: American music history | Includes
    bibliographical references and index.
Summary: "Presents a history of the influence of Black musicians on the
    Beatles, exploring musical and storytelling legacies full of rich but
    contested symbolism and the transatlantic circulation of African
    diasporic arts, tropes, and symbols"—Provided by publisher.
Identifiers: LCCN 2023021744 | ISBN 9780271095615 (hardback) | ISBN
    9780271095622 (paperback)
Subjects: LCSH: Beatles. | Beatles. Blackbird. | Popular music—African
    American influences. | Popular music—History and criticism. | African
    Americans—Music—History and criticism. | Music and race. | Birds—
    Songs and music—History and criticism.
Classification: LCC ML421.B4 K39 2023 | DDC 782.42166092/2—dc23/
    eng/20230517
LC record available at https://lccn.loc.gov/2023021744

The Pennsylvania State University Press is a member of the Association of
University Presses.

It is the policy of The Pennsylvania State University Press to use acid-free
paper. Publications on uncoated stock satisfy the minimum requirements
of American National Standard for Information Sciences—Permanence of
Paper for Printed Library Material, ANSI Z39.48–1992.

Dedicated to the people of Victory Baptist Church at the corner of East Forty-Eighth and McKinley in Los Angeles, California

And to the memories of Robert Palmer and Clarence "Mac" McDonald

Contents

Foreword

Across oceans and nation-states, racial and cultural barriers, how long does it take any one voice to reach another? The voice of Paul McCartney, an illustrious son of Liverpool (a former outpost of the transatlantic slave trade), has been reaching me, as an African American listener, for precisely six decades: as a riveted first grader, I marveled at the Beatles' legendary first US appearance on *The Ed Sullivan Show*. Despite the "Queen of Soul," Aretha Franklin, being a longtime family friend, I mostly associate elementary school with the sound of the Beatles. In my boyhood brush with that Dionysian freakout known as Beatlemania, the local girls on my Air Force base screamed so loudly before the premiere of the Beatles' first film, *A Hard Day's Night*, that the flustered theater manager threatened to cancel the matinee. The response from the voluble female fans was lightning-swift and dramatic: absolute movie-house silence!

I'm delighted to salute my Texas State University colleagues Katie Kapurch and Jon Marc Smith for the eclectic, far-reaching scholarship on display in the wonderfully titled *Blackbird: How Black Musicians Sang the Beatles into Being—and Sang Back to Them Ever After*. "Blackbird" is, for so many of us, a poignant, indelible song, one that, since the release of that hippie treasure chest the White Album, has become an international anthem of comfort, encouragement, and stick-to-itiveness—a true courage song. Following the authors' discerning lead and diligent research, I'm thrilled to reassess this essential song and its central image's relevance to Black activists battling for civil rights in the United States.

Besides absorbing fascinating musical and cultural history, you can dip into this richly informative meditation on "Blackbird" for wonderful tidbits ("the Beatles didn't read music or do formal [Western] musical notation—which helped them respond spontaneously to one another") and for the joyful "homework" of relishing an expressive (even inventive) gallery of covers by hallowed Black musical acrobats, like Bettye LaVette and scatting god and Grammy winner Bobby McFerrin.

As Kapurch and Smith so ably document in these pages, in the visions of a formerly trammeled people, the still-moving and emoting blackbird remains a perennial figure of hope and liberation: "The ubiquity of birds, especially black ones, in arts of the African Diaspora goes back centuries. That tradition never died, and it was continued by the Black musicians who have interpreted and reinterpreted 'Blackbird,' simultaneously celebrating and resisting the cultural ubiquity of the Beatles."

I recently discovered, courtesy of a useful DNA kit, that I am 26 percent Nigerian, 22 percent English, 17 percent Scottish, 8 percent Welsh, and so on, so the transatlantic music and diasporas traced in this remarkable new book are rooted in the very building blocks of my being. It's a balm to me, as an African American poet and professor, to reflect on music as a form of cross-cultural ambassadorship and loving alliance—beyond the brutal, centuries-long legacy of colonialism and the Middle Passage.

I believe savvy jazz and blues artists continue to embrace the Beatles' cosmopolitan "Blackbird" because, in its inspiriting strains, Black singer-interpreters detect the arc from slavery, disillusionment, and despair to readiness. It is the soaring, all-systems-go pivot of decision: the first refusal to move seats on a segregated bus, the first defiant steps across the bridge at Selma: "You were only waiting for this moment to arise."

Cyrus Cassells
Mexico City, April 17, 2023

Acknowledgments

We are deeply grateful to the artists and other witnesses and experts who shared their stories for this book. The oral histories shaped ongoing research questions, song selections, sequencing, and the emphasis on storytelling itself. Musicians discussed their recordings and performances of "Blackbird," but we talked about so much more than this one Beatles song. Artists shared compelling stories that led to a richer understanding of popular music history and their roles in it.

One of these singers is Bettye LaVette, whose delivery of "Blackbird" in a live 2018 performance in San Antonio influenced this project early on. We are grateful to LaVette and her manager and husband, Kevin Kiley.

We are also grateful to the generosity of Martha Wash, whose voice defined the pop music zeitgeist of the early 1990s, and her manager, James Washington. Wash put us in touch with Eric Robinson, to whom we are grateful for providing additional key information about the history of Sylvester's "Blackbird."

With gratitude for their contributions, we dedicate this book to the memories of Robert Palmer, Billy Preston's lead guitarist for most of the 1980s and into the 1990s, and Clarence "Mac" McDonald, pianist, composer, arranger, producer, and Grammy winner. McDonald put us in touch with Palmer, and both provided a wealth of insight into Preston's musicianship and the LA music scene. Kapurch spoke to Palmer and McDonald early in the research process, so their stories and suggestions shaped the book's subsequent directions. She had planned to interview them again: McDonald mentioned a "Black Wrecking Crew" in Los Angeles in the mid-twentieth century and asked her to "come back and write about old Clarence next." Palmer also had more material to share, especially private sound recordings and other personal holdings. Both Palmer and McDonald died in 2021; their recollections were indispensable to this project's recovery of Preston's history. The correspondence of David T. Walker, who arranged the rhythm section for Billy Preston's *Music Is My Life*, was also very helpful in this regard.

We offer this book in dedication to the community of Victory Baptist Church in Los Angeles. As we mention in the chapter about Preston, Victory's physical structure was destroyed by suspected arson on September 11, 2022, just as this book was entering production. The loss of the building involves more lost music history, although the spirit of the church survives. We are deeply grateful to the generosity of the congregation and its leadership, especially the Reverend Dr. W. Edward Jenkins, his wife and First Lady of Victory, Kimberley Jenkins, and their son, Jahi Jenkins, along with Sister Johnnie Pearl Knox, Brother Will Yancy, and others. Individual contributions are specified later in this book, though Victory's loving welcome has affected us beyond the writing of this narrative.

Special thanks to the following: Kenneth Womack, series editor, for his unflagging advocacy, support, and expertise; Walter Everett, especially for his early suggestions related to Lead Belly and bird songs, insight into Nina Simone's "Blackbird," and help with many other musical inquiries; Mike Alleyne for generously supporting and advising on the project and for his expertise on Bob Marley and the Wailers, Jimi Hendrix, and Prince. We are grateful for their ongoing friendship, too.

Many thanks to Cyrus Cassells, Texas Poet Laureate and our colleague, for writing a beautiful foreword to this book.

Gratitude also goes to Kenneth Campbell for his support of and suggestions for the manuscript, as well as to the advisory board and editorial staff at Penn State University Press, including Patrick Alexander along with Josie DiNovo, Ryan Peterson, Archna Patel, and other members of the production team. We appreciate copyeditor Nicholas Taylor's astute editing and comments.

Thank you to many others who helped with the research of this book: Tim Kinley (Parliament-Funkadelic archivist and historian), James McGrath (pioneering scholar of the Beatles and Liverpool's Black community), David Bedford (local Liverpool historian, whose oral histories were of great service), Leslie J. Pfenninger (A&M Records historian), the public services department of the Library Special Collections at the University of California–Los Angeles, as well as other research librarians and staff at UCLA's Charles E. Young Research Library, where we reviewed holdings related to A&M as well as SOUL Magazine's press holdings. Materials from these collections are not explicitly referenced in this book, but they shaped a background knowledge. Similarly, Kapurch interviewed members of the band Blac Rabbit (Amiri Taylor, Rahiem Taylor, Patrick Starr, and Justin Jagbir), who shared their insight into the Beatles' relevance and impact. Along with this interview, we have other evidence and analysis that will appear in forthcoming publications.

We are grateful for the support we have received from our institution, Texas State University. This includes an award from the Research Enhancement Program and a research award from the College of Liberal Arts as well as access to Department of English travel funds that made primary research in Los Angeles possible. We appreciate the support of our students, colleagues, administrators, and staff at Texas State University, especially those (former and current) in the Department of English and the College of Liberal Arts. Special thanks to department chairs Daniel Lochman and Victoria Smith, deans Michael Hennessy and Mary Brennan, associate chairs Steve Wilson, Robert T. Tally Jr., and Miriam Williams, Lindsey Literary Series directors Tom Grimes and Cecily Parks, Associate Dean Aimee Roundtree, as well as department staff, including Taylor Cortesi, Brian Solis, and Deanna Voigt, and college staff, especially Jessica Schneider and Meredith Williams, who were instrumental in the NEH application and implementation processes. Thank you to our colleagues Nancy Wilson, Susie Tilka, Debra Monroe, and Whitney S. May for their friendship, cheer, and help while we were away doing research, and to Kathleen McClancy, who accessed records related to the Tobin Center for the Performing Arts in San Antonio.

Thanks to Smith Henderson and Chris Sanders for living in Los Angeles. And to Tomás Q. Morín, friend and wordsmith.

The authors would also like to thank their parents, Julie and Tommy Kapurch and Judy and Bobby Earl Smith. Thanks also to Eric Smith and Darra Rightmer.

Earlier versions of this book's argument and some corresponding evidence appear in "Blackbird Fly: Paul McCartney's Legend, Billy Preston's Gospel, and Lead Belly's Blues," an article published in *Interdisciplinary Literary Studies* 22, no. 1 (2020): 5–30, published by Penn State University Press. This article was based on a presentation delivered at a 2018 academic conference devoted to the Beatles' *White Album* at Monmouth University in West Long Branch, New Jersey. We appreciate our fellow panelists David Thurmaier and Kathryn B. Cox as well as others in attendance, including Walter Everett, Richard Mills, Matthias Heyman (who later helped with a grey-goose melody), Jeffrey Roessner, Matthew Schneider, Tim Riley, and Pete Compton. Special thanks to the conference's keynote speaker, Mark Lewisohn, who corresponded with Kapurch about subjects related to this book.

Selections from correspondence and interviews conducted by Kapurch appear throughout. They are edited for length and reordered for flow, but many selections are quoted in full. Selections from interviews with LaVette and Wash appear in different forms on *CultureSonar*'s website; special thanks to Cindy Grogan and Al Cattabiani for supporting the publication of this NEH-related research on the *CultureSonar* platform.

Blackbird has been made possible in part by a major grant from the National Endowment for the Humanities: Democracy demands wisdom. Any views, findings, conclusions, or recommendations expressed in this book do not necessarily represent those of the National Endowment for the Humanities. In 2019, Kapurch received the NEH's Award for Faculty at Hispanic-Serving Institutions, meaningful support that provided the time for research and writing. Special thanks to NEH staff members and administrators for their help, as well as to the project's reviewers and other supporters of research in the Humanities.

When research for this book began, the aim was to tell a wide-ranging story about Black artists' varied responses to the Beatles, but painting that picture with broad strokes did not serve the complexity of the music or its history. For this book, a blackbird is our guide, but there are many more musicians and songs relevant to this subject, and we invite readers' continued conversation.

Change the History

The Blackbird in Song, Story, and Transatlantic Flight

"I guess the man's saying, 'Go ahead, take my damn song, change the history of it and everything!'" Bettye LaVette was laughing as she imagined Paul McCartney's reaction to her first-person interpretation of "Blackbird."[1] The Blues Hall of Famer said this in an interview preceding the release of her 2020 album *Blackbirds*, which includes her take on the Beatles song. LaVette's approach to "Blackbird" is informed by her awareness of civil rights–themed stories McCartney himself has circulated, especially in concerts.

Close to the fiftieth anniversary of *The Beatles* (commonly known as the *White Album*), the Beatles' double record on which "Blackbird" first appeared, McCartney headlined the Austin City Limits Festival in 2018. Prefacing the song, he included an unusual tangent about how "mid-century modern" refers to the 1960s and not the mid-nineteenth century; it was a self-deprecating attempt to joke about his age at a youth-oriented event. Then, McCartney got to the point he makes consistently about "Blackbird": "Back in the sixties, there was a lot of troubles going on, seriously, about civil rights, particularly some of the southern states, like Alabama and places like Little Rock. We heard about this back in England, and I wanted to try and, uh, write a song, which, if it ever got back to those people going through the struggles, it might have some effect, it might just help them, give them a bit of hope."[2] For most people, McCartney's explanation is now the story of the song, a coded message of support that the Beatles sent to Black people fighting for civil rights in America. But the blackbird is a very potent image, one that defies McCartney's easy explanation; he himself has not been able to tell consistent stories about the metaphor.

Blackbirds are not easy to pin down. LaVette's comment thus introduces a fundamental irony: she talks about changing McCartney's history, but the blackbird's racialized symbolism does not originate with the song released on the *White Album* in 1968. Well before the Beatles and ever since, Black artists have imagined flight to claim freedom and to reclaim community. McCartney's song becomes a part of this centuries-long story partly because of the dissemination of his civil rights tales, but they are really just one small part of the equation. Since its release, "Blackbird" has been a vehicle for Black musicians to continue the legacy of flying in arts of the African Diaspora. During the last three decades of the twentieth century (a time when McCartney wasn't introducing "Blackbird" with a civil rights–themed story), Black musicians were realizing the song's liberatory potential in their recordings and live performances. LaVette does this when she, inspired by his stories of the song, repositions McCartney's "Blackbird" with a first-person perspective. This point of view shift calls back Aretha Franklin's memorable take on "Eleanor Rigby,"[3] and likewise renders LaVette the protagonist of the song.

Introducing Black Music and the Beatles: Vee-Jay and the Black Woman Who Brought the Beatles to the United States

From the Beatles to LaVette to Franklin and back to the Beatles: this circularity, rooted in "Blackbird," is characteristic of the broader dialogue between Black musicians and the Beatles. In the landmark study *The Music of Black Americans: A History* (1971), Eileen Southern described the relationship, pinpointing the inauguration of the "British Invasion": "The year 1964 brought a wave of English groups to the United States, first the Beatles, then the Rolling Stones, and others who made a tremendous impact upon rock 'n' roll and all of whom warmly acknowledged their indebtedness to black blues artists, rhythm 'n' blues figures, and rock 'n' roll stars, whose songs they covered and whose styles they emulated."[4] As we show throughout this book, the Beatles went on to draw inspiration from Black music throughout their entire tenure as a band.[5]

The Beatles' 1964 arrival in the United States was preceded by their records' release on the successful Black-owned label Vee-Jay, founded by Vivian Carter and her husband, Jimmy Bracken. The Chicago label's representative, Barbara Gardner Proctor (who went on to become the first Black woman to own an advertising agency), flew to London to trade songs with EMI Records, which included the Beatles' label Parlophone, in December 1962.[6] Proctor retrospectively noted that Vee-Jay and its stable were "hot"—unlike the Beatles, then unknown to the American market. The Vee-Jay releases didn't have any notable success in the United States when they were initially issued, but the Beatles' association with the label put the band's music in a physical vicinity to many of the very Black artists they admired and would go on to meet: Billy Preston, for example, recorded with Vee-Jay in 1964 and 1965.[7]

Decades later, Proctor was asked about the Beatles' legacy:

> I think the fact that the Beatles were not American white artists made a difference . . . because they weren't bringing along American baggage. When they came, they expressed a tremendous respect for the Black music. They were not ashamed of it. They did not feel threatened by it. They simply expressed it, and that made it okay for a whole generation of other people to do that. And once you have people recreating together, enjoying together, sharing common experiences together, they cannot ever again hate in that same way that they can when they are ignorant of each other. And knowledge reduces the level of hatred tremendously.[8]

Not everyone is as optimistic about the band and its impact,[9] and we take up the Beatles' identities as white British men from Liverpool later in this book. Worth noting here, however, is how Proctor's assessment echoes in the recollection of George Clinton, innovator and popularizer of funk music. Clinton says he heard in the Beatles "a great respect for American rhythm and blues," which "gave most of the English groups their legitimacy." His self-described "love affair with British rock" started in 1964, when Clinton heard "I Want to Hold Your Hand" on the radio, after weeks of disc jockey Murray the K's teasers.[10]

"A Black Woman": McCartney's "Blackbird" Inspiration?

Months before Proctor made the Vee-Jay–EMI trade and two years before the Beatles broke into the US charts with Capitol's release of "I Want to Hold Your Hand," LaVette had a hit on Atlantic with "My Man—He's a Lovin' Man." It was an auspicious beginning for the up-and-coming Detroit singer, but LaVette didn't achieve the consistent success enjoyed by the Beatles, Franklin, and many of her Motown friends. Still, LaVette never gave up in a career marked by many decades of starts and stops. Accolades and recognition finally came her way this century, and she is now a Verve recording artist. Through it all, LaVette has consistently harnessed, as she puts it, a will "to fly."[11]

Like McCartney, LaVette is still performing for live audiences into the second decade of the twenty-first century; both sing "Blackbird" as an anthem of liberation, though the message is perhaps more persuasive as such coming from LaVette. In addition to magnetizing the bird's struggle to her own, LaVette harnessed the blackbird concept to celebrate the Black women forerunners of rhythm and blues referenced by the title of *Blackbirds*. We expand on her artistic choices vis-à-vis blackbirds in the chapter devoted to LaVette after exploring numerous other examples of collaboration and callbacks,[12] especially representations of flight that advance a community of singers, musicians, and listeners. Tracing the blackbird's racialized history throughout popular song reveals that this musical icon does not belong to McCartney, though its "transatlantic flight" is, ironically, the story of the dialogue between Black musicians and the Beatles. All of that musical history—of birds in Black artistry and of the interracial musical exchange—has been overshadowed by stories that bind the bird's racial symbolism to the former Beatle.[13]

Whenever McCartney delivers "Blackbird" in twenty-first-century live performance, he typically does so alone onstage; the rest of the band exits, and the lights go down. Encircled by a spotlight, McCartney and his acoustic guitar, along with the chiaroscuro of the set design, reenact his song's imagery, which he explains before each performance. Out of a dark night, he sings to the blackbird *and* is the blackbird, a correlation with major significance in Black music. But McCartney did not wake up one day to find himself transformed into a blackbird, or, more accurately, branded with one.

McCartney's anecdotes began to emerge in the public arena after he spoke to Barry Miles for a biography published in 1997. Before that, the former Beatle had been consistently performing "Blackbird" in concerts, but with no civil rights–themed preface. The song was included in his 1991 *MTV Unplugged* appearance, where McCartney added a jokey bit about the song's title being mistaken as "Blackboard"; he was not taking the song too seriously as he attempted to seem cool for the largely Gen X audience. But in McCartney's discussion of "Blackbird" with Miles he cited the following inspiration:

> I had in mind a black woman, rather than a bird. Those were the days of the civil rights movement, which all of us cared passionately about, so this was really a song from me to a black woman, experiencing those problems in the States: "Let me encourage you to keep trying, to keep your faith, there is hope." As is often the case with my things, a veiling took place so, rather than say "Black woman living in Little Rock" and be very specific, she became a bird, became symbolic, so you could apply

it to your particular problem. This is one of my themes: take a sad song and make it better, let this song help you.[14]

A Black woman, not a bird. By making this distinction, McCartney drew focus away from his poetic conceit and toward its supposed meaning. He literalized the metaphor and insisted on a historical source, laying the groundwork for the melodramatic setting he eventually gave the song in concert.

The Beatles' "Blackbird" does contain multitudes, but it is a rich song only because it is so empty. McCartney intimated to Miles that he knowingly cloaked the civil rights message in order to make the song relevant to any listener who could "apply it" to their "particular problem." When it comes to his compositional process, the reverse is probably more likely: he wrote a broadly applicable song, the product of many inspirations and song traditions, about an injured blackbird transcending darkness to fly into the light *and only after* did he realize its more specific application to civil rights. Later in this book, we explore the particular emergence of "Blackbird" in 1968; this context presents multiple accounts about the song's provenance (including one civil rights explanation) and immediate uses in a chronological trajectory related to the late 1960s. Throughout these chapters, we also find many other unacknowledged or underacknowledged predecessors of "Blackbird" in Black music relevant to the Beatles; these associations enrich the song while revealing unseen depths to the dialogue between Black music and Beatles.

Inspiring Birds and Birdsong in Pop: A Book of Birds, Bobby McFerrin's *a cappella* "Blackbird," and Bob Marley's "Three Little Birds"

Whatever the inspirations and symbolic applications of "Blackbird," at a basic level the lyrics are about a bird and its characteristic actions: flying and singing. A blackbird is also the visual McCartney assigned the song in 1968. McCartney and fellow Beatle John Lennon were prompted to write down ideas for visuals to accompany *White Album* song titles that had been typed in advance.[15] Next to "Blackbird," in McCartney's handwriting, appears the following: "Blackbird from bird book."[16] This suggestion wasn't random or a matter of convenience. McCartney has been a birdwatcher since childhood, his musical aviary (including his post-Beatles band Wings) a testament to his love of the creatures.[17] In his recently released annotated collection *The Lyrics*, McCartney mentions his bird book in relation to "Jenny Wren," a 2005 song he compares with "Blackbird." Recalling his childhood in Speke, just outside of

Liverpool, McCartney remembers, "I had a little pocket book, *The Observer's Book of Birds*, and I used to go on my own for a walk, for a bit of solitude. . . . Pretty soon I started being able to recognize the birds."[18] Here, McCartney has come close to realizing something important about the central image of "Blackbird" and his many other bird-themed songs, whose hopeful messages are inspired by and recall actual birds.

Bobby McFerrin's extraordinary *a cappella* version of "Blackbird"—in which he vocalizes both the lyrics and the instrumentation of a jazz ensemble—encourages the listener to imagine a bird. More specifically, he re-creates the lone blackbird's song in a multidimensional arrangement. The aural layering of sounds, issued by a single singer, parallels the multiple meanings allowed by the song itself. At the end of a filmed performance of the 1984 song, McFerrin replicated the sound of wings while performing a corresponding gesture with his hands, accentuating the bird and the freedom that his virtuoso singing actualized.[19] Over the years, McFerrin has brought his improvisational technique, distinguished by a "four-octave vocal range" and "childlike sense of play,"[20] to a range of music including Johann Sebastian Bach—to whom, as the next section reveals, McCartney has retrospectively connected "Blackbird."

The encouraging birdsong McFerrin creates via "Blackbird" parallels the hope he whistled four years later in "Don't Worry Be Happy," whose massive popularity distanced McFerrin from the jazz roots he had planted in collaborations with Herbie Hancock and others. Inspired by the optimistic mantra of Indian guru Meher Baba, the refrain anticipates an uplift McFerrin brought to *Spirityouall*, his 2013 record of traditional gospel and other spirituals. These include the flight-oriented "Swing Low" and other songs that McFerrin witnessed his father, the first Black man to sing at the Metropolitan Opera, sing in church.[21] The faith-oriented message in "Don't Worry Be Happy" has also led to long-standing confusion about who penned the 1988 song. Bob Marley is often the misassigned as the composer for several reasons, especially because the refrain of "Don't Worry Be Happy" resembles that of Marley's "Three Little Birds" (1977). Considering McFerrin's earlier take on "Blackbird" adds interest to this Marley comparison, especially because Marley's song offers more evidence for why avian inspiration can prove so meaningful in Black music.

For his song of hope, Marley took inspiration from canaries that visited him on Hope Road.[22] Along with the Wailers and the I-Threes vocal group,[23] Marley became the encouraging singer of birdsong in "Three Little Birds," whose popularity is on par with both "Blackbird" and "Don't Worry Be Happy." Celebrating "the joy of being alive,"[24] Marley's song could be tempting to read as his own song of hope because it appears on *Exodus*, an album he finished in London after the attempt on his life in Jamaica. But Marley's music was broad in its intention and reach. Whether he was singing explicitly political critiques or pop ditties like "Three Little Birds," Marley's encouragement served the listener, especially for purposes of Black uplift. Reflecting his deep investment in biblical themes, the "Don't worry about a thing" reassurance of Marley's chorus—the three birds' message—also recalls "His Eye Is on the Sparrow." A standard in Black churches, this spiritual is derived from Jesus's Sermon on the Mount. Sparrows fly because God wants them to. If he has counted and cared for all the sparrows, won't he do the same for people? Have faith, Jesus tells his listeners, and don't worry.

On *Exodus*, "Three Little Birds" is preceded by songs about war, the struggle for freedom, and, in the title track, an explicit call to leave Babylon, conceived by Rastafarians as the capitalist and imperialist power structure that dominates the world. The final track on the album, "One Love / People Get Ready," includes references to and images of Armageddon, as well as the call to action of "Let's get together and feel alright." The latter word, frequently used to witness and motivate in Black vernacular, appears as well in the chorus of "Three Little Birds." Even though he maintains hope extended through song to a community of fellow sufferers, not everything is rainbows for Marley. In his music, he doesn't shy away from death-as-release, a motif in line with the trope of Flying Africans, which we introduce later in this introduction.

The optimistic message of "Three Little Birds" might appear simple enough for the casual listener, and its fungibility is the hallmark of a good pop song.[25] But anyone familiar with Marley's spiritual and philosophical background, as well as the postcolonial and anti-racist critiques he consistently communicated in his music, can see the lineages we have just pointed out. You almost have to mishear Marley's songs deliberately to not understand the rebellion in them. The Beatles, by contrast, were consciously apolitical on the advice of their manager, Brian Epstein; their songs' generic emptiness has made their music transferrable across time and place. And although "Blackbird" is a product of a relentlessly optimistic composer, it does not immediately warrant the profundity that Marley's persona grants his songs. Perhaps this is why McCartney has attempted to provide that legendary depth himself.

The Bach Stories: McCartney as Author-Composer

The story McCartney told Miles might have stayed tucked in the pages of the biography but for the fact that the former Beatle "needed" a tale to add interest to readings of *Blackbird Singing: Poems and Lyrics, 1965–1999*.[26] Positioning song lyrics as poetry on the advice of the poet Adrian Mitchell, who edited the collection, this 2001 book made a case for McCartney as author and thus a serious artist—with the blackbird as unifying emblem for his career to date. The practice of prefacing lyrics during poetry readings led to prefacing songs, especially "Blackbird," during the Driving USA Tour of 2002, when McCartney got more colloquial with his bird. Referencing civil rights as "troubles in the southern states," his word choice alluded to the ethnic-religious-political conflict in Northern Ireland—the very conflict addressed in his anthem "Give Ireland Back to the Irish" (the first single he released with his post-Beatles band Wings). McCartney then explained "Blackbird" as Britspeak: "I dunna if any of you know, but in England sometimes we call girls 'birds.' You know? I kinda wrote this song with that in mind."[27] The concert legend was born.

With Miles, McCartney acknowledged the Beatles song's essential emptiness, generic light-dark constructs that listeners could fill with their own meaning. This openness didn't last: in the twenty-first century, "Blackbird" has become a *McCartney* tune, a displayed bird stuffed with meaning—one that he keeps stuffing. Over two decades, McCartney's legend of "Blackbird" has continued to evolve,[28] culminating in the recent iteration appearing in *The Lyrics*. That account, whose details we mention when relevant to certain chapters in this book, includes other concert stories McCartney has used to explain "Blackbird," especially one about the song's roots in a Liverpool-era "party piece" that riffed on Bach,[29] which was a teenage effort to attract girls[30] and more evidence of McCartney's baroque inspirations ("Eleanor Rigby" and "Penny Lane" are others).[31]

McCartney's Bach party piece is usually identified as Bourrée in E minor.[32] McCartney gave a version of the Bach story to Miles when discussing "Blackbird," too, expanding on the appeal of stories about the composer: "For some reason we thought his music was very similar to ours and we latched on to him amazingly quickly. We also liked the stories of him being the church organist and wopping this stuff out weekly, which was rather similar to what we were doing." McCartney described the party piece, explaining how "its structure is a particular harmonic thing between the melody and the bass line" and works as the "original inspiration" for "Blackbird." In this telling, the party piece was a joint effort with fellow Beatle George Harrison, who could play it (i.e., the Bach piece whose name Paul and George didn't know at the time) "better than me actually."[33]

These classical lineages bind "Blackbird" to the Beatle's youth, making the song important to his biography and therefore amplifying his authorship and agency over the song's symbolism. In the "Blackbird" entry in *The Lyrics*, McCartney also adds a reference to Chet Atkins as an early "fingerpicking" influence, especially his song "Trambone."[34] But McCartney's exposure to Donovan's guitar-picking style (in Rishikesh, India, in 1968) is much more contemporaneous to McCartney's composition of "Blackbird."[35] The Atkins reference is meaningful for another reason, too: "Chet Atkins did in fact record Bach's Bourrée in E minor for an album called *Hi Fi in Focus*, released October, 1957."[36] But McCartney does not make the connection between Atkins's take on Bach and his own—even though the former Beatle does maintain the focus on Liverpool, moving from the subject of fingerpicking to stories about specific Black people, new variations of the civil rights explanation, which we take up throughout this book.

Between the publication of Miles's biography and *The Lyrics*, Harrison has been mentioned on and off when McCartney talks about the Bach lineages of "Blackbird" in concerts, where Paul also started asking audiences if they had tried to learn "Blackbird" on guitar. After they cheer, he proceeds to tell them that they are doing it "wrong" (apparently, he has seen their YouTube videos); it's a joke that gives McCartney the opportunity to prove the song's technical complexity, which defies imitation. The classical credentials bolster the seriousness of the song, serving the civil rights story, which now dominates popular and scholarly readings of "Blackbird." Meanwhile, in the twenty-first century, LaVette and others have continued to interpret the song, revealing untold histories—and more relevance.

The "Blackbird" Legend: An Ironic Motor for This Book

Whether they predate or postdate his concert stories, Black singers' and musicians' interpretations of "Blackbird" are often heard in relation to McCartney's authorial insistence on the song's civil rights meaning because he has successfully packaged and disseminated that message. McCartney's "Blackbird" legend is, then, an ironic motor for the chapters that follow: his repetitive insistence on the song's motivation foregrounds the memory of civil rights in the United States, specifically calling attention to the 1960s and hinting at racist structures Black people have long worked to dismantle. McCartney simultaneously compels listeners to hear *his* symbolism and the effects he *wishes* the song had. But the fact of the matter is this: Black Americans had songs of hope during the civil rights movement—and "Blackbird" was not one of them.

When he turned his blackbird into a carrier pigeon with a message for Black Americans, McCartney unknowingly tapped into a vibrant narrative legacy. For centuries, Black Diasporans have been telling stories and singing songs about birds and flying into freedom. And they have done so within traditions that are radically collaborative. Bird symbolism is by no means simple, especially because not all black-colored birds are signs of support for Black people. As racialized constructs with dual meanings and contradictory applications in popular culture, birds, especially black ones, have been used by white people to denigrate and dehumanize. Jim Crow was, after all, a black-colored bird flying in the dark night to which McCartney alludes.

Because of the stories McCartney has attached to "Blackbird," the song allows for the unfolding of layers and layers of history, especially related to Black artistry and, as it turns out, Black music relevant to the Beatles. Such historical multivalence is—again, ironically—currently eclipsed by the Beatle's insistence on concrete meaning by a singular creator. "Blackbird" is, as it happens, a Lennon-McCartney composition, and it was released on the Beatles' self-titled record, but over time McCartney has bound the song to himself alone. Discovering the lineages of the central image of "Blackbird" reveals unseen depths to his and all of the bandmembers' broader obligations to Black music. Black musicians' interpretations of "Blackbird" and other responses to the Beatles, in turn, evidence the ongoing potency of flight, a ubiquitous and robust metaphor in arts of the African Diaspora.

Like the legend of "Blackbird," the Beatles' musical obligation has been largely shaped by its members' own stories about the influence of Black American music. Since the early 1970s when the band broke up, the known and oft-repeated stories about how the pre-fame Beatles loved Black American music have resulted in a "canon" of sources: Chuck Berry's poetic wordplay and guitar work, Little Richard's scream and sass, Fats Domino's boogie-woogie piano-playing, Ray Charles's soulful crooning, and the group singing of the Coasters. Beatles drummer Ringo Starr and a friend were so enthralled with Lightnin' Hopkins that the boys looked into getting jobs in Houston. These legends loom in the band's biography, especially as told by the multimedia *Anthology* project—but they are still only fractions of a partially told history of the Beatles and Black music.

This book introduces many new stories. We consider some of the well-worn stories and their associated music, too, but situate them in a new history that sees the Beatles in relation to a broader legacy of Black cultural production, which includes some regions outside the United States. The narrative and musical legacies unraveled here are deeper and richer than the sound bites Beatles fans (and critics) have digested for all these years. With flight as a touchstone, *Blackbird: How Black Musicians Sang the Beatles into Being—and Sang Back to Them Ever After* presents a new history of the dynamic conversation between Black artists and the Beatles. Attention to this exchange reveals that the Beatles belong to a transatlantic conversation they neither began nor ended. It goes on, like a nest still being feathered.

Blackbird Fly: Introducing the Flying Africans, Afro-Atlantic Flight, and More Inspiring Birdsong

A blackbird's message of hope and liberation has a rich provenance in American popular song, rooted in an even older tradition of flight in folk arts of the African Diaspora. Gathering together representative texts and scholarship illustrative of the trope of Flying Africans, Henry Louis Gates Jr. and Maria Tatar distinguish between psychoanalytic readings of "flight as a universal expression of rapturous transcendence" and Diasporic representations of flight "as a strategic means of escaping the bodily degradations and spiritual humiliations of slavery and its toxic legacies."[37] The historical circumstances that gave rise to folklore of Flying Africans warrant more explanation. In chapter 1, we continue to explore the trope's attendant features and motifs, which have evolved over time in their expression and application. In short, when Black artists draw on this trope, they intervene in the "afterlife of slavery," asserting the existence of a tradition connecting "to specific diasporic pasts in order to enliven those pasts and drawn from their political force in the present."[38]

Especially in the post–civil rights era, contemporary representations of what Michelle D. Commander terms "Afro-Atlantic flight" are proof that "Black Americans have been perpetual travelers enraptured by the promises of flight since the Middle Passage. Flight is transcendence over one's reality—an escape predicated on imagination and the incessant longing to be free."[39] Along with many bird- and flight-oriented songs that precede hers, LaVette, for example, interprets "Blackbird" to tell of her own struggles and to elevate other Black women, reflecting the liberatory and collectivist themes available in folklore about Flying Africans. Significantly, LaVette's interpretation also participates in the ongoing resurgence of Black artists' flight rhetoric.[40]

Considering the Beatles within the frame of Black musical innovation warrants a sustained focus on flight. This touchstone brings to the fore Black musical forerunners sometimes (but not always) named by the Beatles themselves. The trajectories of musical influence that we discover are not straightforward: they zigzag through the air like birds. One Black US American musician involved in this indirect conversation with the Beatles even gave specific credit to birdsong. Legendary singer R. H. Harris of the Soul Stirrers (the gospel group that eventually launched Sam Cooke) observed the birds that populated the landscape of his rural home. Harris remembered his small farm in Texas: "I used to listen to the birds sing. Whatever tune they'd make, I trained myself to make. So my tunes and my vocal control, I just impersonated the birds."[41] With his birdsong musical education, Harris staked a claim for inaugurating falsetto with the singing group he formed at age ten, adding, "Even women didn't sing falsetto in church back then."[42]

Anthony Heilbut's characterization of Harris's techniques, lauded for their impact on gospel quartet singing, provides a sense of where impersonating birds led: "Harris' limpid melancholy tenor with its frequent flights into falsetto evoked several musical forms: a bit of cowboy yodeling, some traits of pop crooners like Bill Kenny, above all a relentless fervor and melismatic fluency that sprang wholly out of the Dr. Watts hymns he heard as a child in his family's Methodist church. To these elements he added his unique rhythmic sense, what he calls 'delayed time,' a capacity to sail across bar lines, to bounce irregularly off a syncopated background, to be at once rhythmically playful and deadly serious."[43] Along with the Soul Stirrers, Harris's innovations also included "switch leads," which "would allow two or even three-way conversations within the quartet format"[44]—kind of like birds moving within a flock. Heilbut, who interviewed Harris about his bird inspiration, continues to capture that influence in his description of Harris's take on "His Eye Is on the Sparrow," the hymn we introduced in relation to Marley's "Three Little Birds" and that appears more than any other in this book:

> He can take the old hymn "His Eye Is on the Sparrow" and, like he says, sing all around the barbershop "clang-a-lang-a-langs" of his group. It's all, as Harris knows, in accenting the right words and syllables. He'll sing a line, "whenever I am tempted, whenever clouds rise," and simply by pausing after the first "when," and then, by proceeding the second

"when" with a "sad uh," syncopate the whole line. Then he'll bisect the word "clouds," lifting to a slur resolved by the next word, "rise," and instruct all gospel singers how to swing lightly and moan at the same time. Later he'll let loose his falsetto "I sing because I'm free, ohhh," and convey the elements of Sam Cooke's style.[45]

Harris was with the Soul Stirrers from the late 1930s until 1950, when he left to form another group. Harris's legacy thus continued in the Stirrers—and into rock 'n' roll—via his "acolyte" Cooke, whose "Nearer to Thee" vocally enacts the movement the lyrics describe, "When I get lonely I can sing, nearer." This song, Cooke's arrangement of a nineteenth-century hymn by Sarah Flower Adams, is also notable for its explicit correlation between song and story: "There's a story in every song we sing." But Cooke is just one benefactor of Harris's innovations. Although "falsetto was as old as field hollers," Heilbut acknowledges the significance of Harris's assertions about his birdsong-inspired falsetto: "If Harris is right, the falsetto sound that traveled from gospel to soul to the Beatles began as a Texas birdsong mimicked by [Harris,] a latter-day Mozart."[46] These examples underscore the complexity of the Beatles' indebtedness to Black music while demonstrating the correlation between birds and Black singers in techniques and stories of song.

As symbols in and of song, birds are often figurations of Black musicians when they assume avian subjectivity to claim their freedom flight and lift others up, too. Black artists give voice to birdsong via lyrics[47] or instrumentation, often identifying birds with a color. These are powerful acts of recognition, belonging, and redress in African American and Diasporic arts. To people stuck on the ground and forced to labor in miserable conditions, the free flight of unbound birds surely appears limitless. Seeing an image of freedom can be a personal comfort, no doubt, but it can also provide a liberating flightpath for collectives. Birds aren't only above us in the sky and, while they can sometimes be caged and confined, many birds still find a way to fly.

Blackbird Signifyin(g)

In terms of racialized musical discourse, the blackbird is a more complicated figure than the one McCartney has made emblematic of his legacy. In fact, you could say that when LaVette and other Black artists vocalize his lyrics, the blackbird's singing is Signifyin(g).

Black artists who cover, interpret, answer, and otherwise converse with the Beatles are often being deeply ironic, Signifyin(g) on the band with "double-voiced" wit and other rhetorical techniques that Henry Louis Gates Jr. has theorized as characteristic of Black vernacular.[48] Exemplified by folktales about a punning monkey trickster-hero who bests his opponents with indirection and wit, Signifyin(g) is a system of speech acts born out of slavery and passed down and learned within Black communities, especially in the United States and the Caribbean.[49] The Signifying Monkey is the rhetorical meta-trope: "Unlike his Pan-African Esu cousins, the Signifying Monkey exists not primarily as a character in a narrative but rather as a vehicle for narration itself."[50] The Signifying Monkey *uses* the relevant figures of speech and *is* the figure of Signifyin(g)—the trope of a trope that will continue to trope and be troped.[51]

The multiplicity of meaning is accomplished through circumnavigation: "black double-voicedness" involves "formal revision and an intertextual relation."[52] Through repetition, especially the troping of tropes, "texts seem to address their antecedents."[53] Addressing the antecedent, whether a minstrel trope or the title character of "Blackbird," involves other relevant speech tropes, especially exaggeration, metaphor, rhyming, and irony, along with witnessing, testifying, name-checking, and others. With these tools, the Signifying Monkey "tropes-a-dope," a pun that references Muhammad Ali's rope-a-dope strategy. The boxer's rhyming phrase exemplifies the creative, generative nature of the competition inherent in Signifyin(g), as well as its capacity to topple authority.[54]

Birds are effective vehicles for pecking and poking at the status quo, so it's no coincidence that they abound in hip-hop braggadocio. The Migos' "Birds" (2014) is full of double meanings, including Black vernacular use of "fly" as a synonym for "cool" or "amazing." The chorus announces, "I'm too fly, I spread my wings and I'm soaring / Used to trap them birds, now I'm fly like a bird." These lines get right to the heart of the tension between confinement and freedom in representations of Afro-Atlantic flight, as well as the polysemy of birds as instruments of denigration and liberation. Although "Birds" does not reference the Beatles, the Migos inspired the hashtag #MigosBetterThanBeatles in 2013. Ever since, the fires of this internet controversy have been periodically stoked, notably in 2017 by Donald Glover, whose hip-hop persona Childish Gambino has his own trickster legacy. Glover Signified on the Fab Four, claiming the Migos were his generation's Beatles,[55] and others have continued making comparable claims about the Migos's popularity and hip-hop's dominance, drawing attention to the Beatles' appropriations from Black culture in the first place.

Similar to how rappers like Rae Sremmurd claim to be "Black Beatles," the Migos Signify on the Beatles, boasting and exaggerating to reclaim musical territory. Hip-hop's favorite bird pun might be on grey goose, usually a reference to the vodka brand, an irony considering the bird's appearance in both minstrel songs and the prison work song Lead Belly recorded and popularized. As they trope the bird trope, contemporary artists make all sorts of assertions for the ongoing relevance of flight. Especially in the case of "Blackbird," Black artists' interpretations claim the bird's freedom while simultaneously revealing the unknowability or unattainability of that flying creature.[56]

As is typical of Signifyin(g) in Black music, artists simultaneously acknowledge and upend "antecedents," performing multiple kinds of intertextual revisions at once.[57] Imagine a song as an image reflected in a hall of mirrors: when mirrors refract against one another, they create a visual echo chamber that makes locating the original impossible.[58] This lack of ownership is radically collective, especially when contrasted with McCartney's earnest efforts to direct the meaning of "Blackbird." The potency of irony, wit, and wordplay in songs that maintain a belief in the freedom flight of Black people is a source of individual and communal uplift, and one that elevates the Beatles, too.

Transatlantic Flight: In-Flight Music and Musical Flows

In this book, "transatlantic flight" is a way of characterizing the musical dialogue as well as song imagery. This includes the Beatles' blackbird and other birds, which are positioned in relation to the legacy of birds and flight in arts of the African Diaspora. The chapters that follow include numerous examples of Black artists taking inspiration from winged entities, singing as or to a bird, or otherwise assuming the position of the bird they sing about, often in relation to a flock that flies together.

As a descriptive phrase, transatlantic flight recognizes the ongoing vitality of the Flying Africans trope *and* characterizes the exchange between Black musicians and the Beatles. The bird central to the Beatles' "Blackbird" is always about to fly, but, by 1968, blackbirds (and so-called blackbirds) had already spread their wings in numerous tunes illustrative of earlier transatlantic musical dialogues. These conversations often occurred between Black musicians and white audiences in musical genres that shaped the pre-fame Beatles, who continued to engage in a back-and-forth dialogue with Black musicians during the 1960s and in the decades that followed.

Our use of transatlantic flight is influenced by Commander's aforementioned conception of "Afro-Atlantic flight"[59] along with earlier theoretical conceptions of the "Black Atlantic." In the 1990s, Paul Gilroy theorized the Black Atlantic "in opposition to . . . nationalist or ethnically absolute approaches," encouraging "cultural historians . . . [to] take the Atlantic as one single, complex unit of analysis in their discussions of the modern world and use it to produce an explicitly transnational and intercultural perspective."[60] Gilroy's influential formulation has since been contested, especially for its Eurocentricity, but he nevertheless characterizes a broad site of musical conversations relevant to the history told in this book. Gilroy highlights the special function of music[61] and invokes a sense of uplift when he articulates "the desire to transcend both the structures of the nation state and the constraints of ethnicity and national particularity."[62]

Even in its recognition of uplift, especially the persistently joyful qualities of Black music, transatlantic flight is not an attempt to idealize all manners of exchange. The term positions the Atlantic as an often-fraught site of inquiry: the triangulating consequences and echoes of the transatlantic slave trade; the interconnectedness *and* diversity of Black experiences in the African Diaspora; the vitality of Africa in the imaginations of diasporans; and the dynamic influences on and by African and African-descended people in politics, culture, and the economy in the places they were forced to and then went forth from. In addition to the Americas, these places include the United Kingdom, with its centuries-long history of profiting from slavery and the slave trade as well as subsequent racist policies and practices that continue into the present day.

Transatlantic flight includes a key prefix to understand cultural exchange in the Atlantic during the centuries after the transatlantic slave trade. Christina Sharpe theorizes "trans," Kevin Wynter explains, "as a mode for conceptualizing the conditions of contemporary Black life."[63] This is illustrated by the following: "translation, transatlantic, transgression, transgender, transformation, transmogrification, transcontinental, transfixed, trans-Mediterranean, transubstantiation (by which process we might understand the making of bodies into flesh and then into fungible commodities while retaining the appearance of flesh and blood), transmigration, and more."[64] These, "all ways of conceptualizing Black being" in relation to a "range of trans*formations," have been imposed on Black people.[65] Building on Sharpe, Kevin Wynter brings up Jamaican writer and critic Sylvia Wynter's notion of "transplantation";[66] he adds "trans/plantation," a concept he distinguishes and applies to the 2017 film *Get Out*: "Where 'transplantation' refers to acts of Black re-booting, trans/plantation describes the uprooting and replanting of white substitutions *in* Blackness; it is a form of slave life (social death) where white oppressors not only possess the Black body materially, they enter into a substitutive relation with the Black body so as to possess it subjectively from *within*."[67]

How does the blackbird function as such a vehicle for transplantation and trans/plantation? This question is implicitly addressed again and again in this book whenever we point to the bird's polysemous functions. When enslaved Black people and their descendants imagine flight, they can enact transplantation: imagining flight via song and story is a re-booting of Blackness in response to the plantation system, a "process of 'transplanting' Black cultural roots in the soil of the New World as a way of domesticating the destructive, alien territory of the plantation." The use of bird tropes in blackface minstrelsy is relevant to trans/plantation—although, as Wynter convincingly argues, "color-blind neoliberalism" is another "white *into* black" transformation, which "seeks to dissolve the slave's inner life to make way for whiteness."[68]

In popular music, the blackbird is a symbol that responds to the ongoing slave economy, alternately navigating the afterlives of slavery and perpetuating the plantation system. As a transitional port that played a key role in the transatlantic slave trade, Liverpool is a recurring meeting place in this book's history of musical conversations and flight imagery. Just as music was routed through Liverpool prior to the Beatles, transatlantic flight accentuates the "flows"[69] of music by African-descended people, especially those who moved between the United Kingdom, the United States, and the Caribbean in the twentieth century. Similarly characterizing the Beatles' physical movements and aural inspirations, transatlantic flight also involves the bandmembers' encounters with Black artists traversing the Atlantic. And, although the Beatles were certainly indebted to specific Black Americans in the United States, the attention paid to these inspirations has draped an invisibility cloak over Black people of other nationalities, especially Caribbean-born musicians in the band's home city.

Our use of "transatlantic" is not intended to disregard or minimize the Black Pacific, which has recently animated approaches to transoceanic studies and theories of the Global South.[70] Given our subject matter and the still-lacking attention to Black genres directly affecting the Beatles, we center the Atlantic even though the US West Coast, and especially California, emerges frequently across the chapters to come. We thus conclude this book with a clear look toward the Pacific, proposing directions for the study of more interrelated musical conversations involving or adjacent to the Beatles.

In sum, the formative presence of Black musicians in the "borrowing"[71] that gave rise to American popular genres is central to the notion of transatlantic flight. Similar to how they reworked British and English-language folklore in and prior to the nineteenth century, Black artists revised and continue to revise the Beatles. These revisions reinvest the Beatles' songs with themes pervasive in arts of the African Diaspora. Black Americans also recover those artists who influenced the Beatles in the first place or along the way, as well as those who previously or contemporaneously sang as and about birds.[72] That reinvestment and recovery work happens in the music itself—in melody, arrangement, lyrics, and sound effects—but it also occurs in the stories that frame the music.

Storytelling, Selection, and the Soaring, Circling Blackbird

Broadly, this book is about storytelling and music, an association made often in music and other discourse of the Black Church, and one we find repeatedly in this book.[73] As our emphasis on folklore and narrative theory suggests, we also use a literary-historical approach to consider the dialogue between Black musicians and the Beatles. For these aims, "Blackbird" is an ideal touchstone. McCartney has claimed a civil rights motivation for the song, but he only begins to tell a *story* for public circulation in the 1990s, decades after the song's release. If his song were always intended as a message for Black people in the United States (a question we take up in this book), he was working, knowingly or not, within a storytelling tradition: the ubiquity of birds, especially black ones, in arts of the African Diaspora goes back centuries. That tradition never died, and it was continued by the Black musicians who have interpreted and reinterpreted "Blackbird," simultaneously celebrating and resisting the cultural ubiquity of the Beatles.

Using the central image of "Blackbird" as a touchstone, we relate new stories about how Black artists sang the Beatles into being and sang back to them ever after. The stories that have been shared with us involve heretofore untold connections between Black musicians' interpretations of "Blackbird" and other allusions to the Fab Four. We show how this contemporary music calls back to major forerunners who meaningfully employed the blackbird and other flight imagery. They include the most famous Black American woman on Broadway in her day, the Queen of Happiness Florence Mills; King of the

Twelve String Lead Belly; the Grandmaster of Calypso Lord Kitchener (whose colleague, Lord Woodbine, was mentor to the Beatles); and the High Priestess of Soul Nina Simone. Many other musical forerunners, such as Louis Armstrong, Little Richard, and Fats Domino, and contemporaries, such as Aretha Franklin, Jimi Hendrix, and Diana Ross, are incorporated throughout; their bird-centric music and other flight-related discourse offer new context for exploring the Beatles' "flight" to the United States as well as McCartney's 1968 "Blackbird."

Post-Beatles interpretations of "Blackbird" (and other songs), in turn, reveal significant sequences of musical influences, and we focus deeply on Billy Preston. He wasn't the very first Black artist to cover "Blackbird" (that distinction goes to Ramsey Lewis in 1968), but Preston's interpretation evokes a gospel sensibility and calls back to his formative interactions with the Beatles. Preston, the so-called Fifth Beatle, inspired disco queen Sylvester's 1979 "Blackbird," an interpretation that also addresses liberation. Another sequence deals with Bettye LaVette's recuperation of underappreciated Black forerunners of rhythm and blues via "Blackbird" on the album *Blackbirds*. While all this music involves the Beatles in some way, what we repeatedly discover is that lines of succession are not straightforward. Instead, they are more like the movement Preston sang about in "Will It Go Round in Circles."

As a metaphor for transatlantic flight, the soaring and circling blackbird is a literary and historical lens through which to view conversations between the Beatles and Black music before, during, and after the 1960s. Always returning to these central motifs, we tell a mostly chronological history with context from oral histories, as well as memoirs, published interviews, and the analysis of lyrics. The available evidence shaped this book, which is not comprehensive to, for example, all bird precedents or all covers or interpretations of "Blackbird" by Black musicians.[74] Certain songs and artists are the focus on their own chapters, and we thread in references to others whenever relevant.

Building on existing studies of the Beatles and Black music,[75] we seek to add to these conversations, focusing our attention on a history that has been shaped and obscured by McCartney's storytelling related to "Blackbird." As white scholars and university professors, our perspectives are shaped by our identities, education, and racial privilege, along with our professional and institutional access. We are deeply appreciative to the Black people who shared their stories with us and welcomed us into their lives and communities; these stories changed the shape of the book we initially planned, necessitating a sharper focus on birds, flight imagery, and their theoretical underpinnings.

Learning new stories about Black artists' interpretations of "Blackbird" led to our reevaluation of the Beatles, especially Paul McCartney, whose mythologizing warrants critique. These stories offer new insight into Black music that converses with the band in other ways beyond this one song, especially tunes that include themes in line with or adjacent to the bird and flight-oriented focus. So, although we keep returning to "Blackbird," we reference other songs to offer a thorough (although not definitive) history of the multidimensional musical dialogue involving Black music and the Beatles.

CHAPTER I

Flee (Free) as a Bird

The Legacy of the Ring Shout, Flying Africans, and Gospel in Black Music and the Beatles

When he was a teenager in New Orleans during the second decade of the twentieth century, Louis Armstrong loved marching in the brass band; from these humble beginnings he went on to become an essential architect of twentieth-century popular song. Armstrong's "Hello, Dolly!" was, in fact, the song that bumped the Beatles from their unprecedented occupation of the number one position on the American charts in spring 1964. The Beatles also trace their beginnings to a parade—although the one that featured Lennon playing with his makeshift skiffle band in 1957 was not nearly as impressive as Armstrong's coterie. Funeral parades were, according to Armstrong, "really something to see," and he remembered the marchers playing "beautiful music," specifically the hymn "Flee as a Bird."[1]

Published in the mid-nineteenth century by a white woman named Mary Dina Shindler, "Flee as a Bird" was a frequently anthologized hymn that became popular in the Black Church.[2] Armstrong and the other musicians in funeral processions would play it "from the heart" on the way into the cemetery, their "instruments singing those notes the same as a singer would."[3] Parades gave these Black bandmembers the ability to play music in public— and to move more freely throughout the segregated city. Although there was still a threat of violence, together and with this purpose they benefited from a degree of security.[4] Playing "Flee as a Bird," a hymn about the freedom flight of death, Armstrong imagined himself along with bandmates and funeral celebrants to be as free as birds.

The lyrics of "Flee as a Bird" are derived from Psalm 11, in which fleeing like a bird is something one doesn't need to do if God is the refuge. In the hymn, however, flying to the mountain is synonymous with going to the Lord. The mismatch between lyric and biblical verse in "Flee as a Bird" can be compared to the disconnect in the Beatles' similarly named swan song. Derived from a fragment Lennon recorded before he was assassinated, "Free as a Bird" was finished by the three surviving Beatles and released in conjunction with the *Anthology* project. Lennon's parts imply that being home, "safe and dry," is actually better than being free as a bird; this is why he relates himself to a "homing bird." McCartney's and Harrison's verses, however, correlate being free like a bird with being Beatles, wondering what became of "the life that we once knew." Remembering prompts them to enter the chorus about being free like a bird. "Free as a Bird" is an ironic take on the glory days of Beatledom, when Lennon was still alive, because fame's consequences led to their bandmate's murder and, before that, the end of the Beatles.

Stories about "Flee as a Bird" and "Free as a Bird" are entrances into the Beatles' dialogue with Black music, helping us see that conversation as transatlantic flight: with the help of studio technology, the Beatles' swan song reprised the band's former cooperation, which was indebted to Black music, whose collective impulse can be traced to the ring shout. Although "Free as a Bird" almost certainly has nothing to do with "Flee as a Bird," the Beatles' celebratory reunion song is also haunted by death, particularly a dead Beatle's vocals. The ironies surrounding "Free as a Bird," whose music video takes the bird's own perspective, align the song with Black music in which flight is double natured, especially when it comes to hope and death.[5] This duality stems from folklore about Flying Africans, a trope that is still nourished in the Black Church and, by extension, popular music. Armstrong's association with "Flee as a Bird," which he released as an instrumental in 1957, exemplifies how "the story of the flying Africans flashes out to us from the words of a spiritual . . . as well as from novels, films, and musical productions."[6] Tracing flight through these mediums introduces Black musicians' persistent adaptations of British song content—more transatlantic exchange.

The Legacy of the Ring Shout: Community, Collaboration, and Birdsong

The mental and aural images of Armstrong's band playing "Flee as a Bird," free as they parade together in commemoration of death, point to themes of cooperation and flight in Black music. The community orientation in flight-oriented texts, in fact, runs parallel to the persistent collaboration that characterizes Black music of all genres. This legacy is rooted in the ring shout, a musical form that Thomas Brothers situates as predecessor to the cooperation he studies in Duke Ellington's Orchestra—and the Beatles.

The ring shout, a "circle ritual," was developed and refined among enslaved people in the Americas and involved music produced by vocalists and dancers. Hand clapping, finger clicking, walking, stomping, and stamping created complex syncopated rhythms.[7] This "deeply communal" music was informed by African techniques that encouraged (and even demanded) participation, especially through call and response. Allowing for "ecstatic outbursts," the ring shout also maintained "a sense of continuity and togetherness." As a mechanism for reclaiming lost cultural networks and for supporting the present community's survival, the ring shout included songs that encoded avenues for resistance within the plantation system. Given these uplifting aims, and their socializing functions, precision and perfection were not goals nor are they the prized objectives of, say, the gospel singing still happening in many Black churches today. Rather, the ring shout prioritized "interaction among those present. . . . Participants standing outside the inner circle formed the 'base' [whose] predictability" allowed leaders to create and contribute embellishments, both verbal and nonverbal.[8]

The ring shout echoes throughout Black musical genres, finding poignant expression whenever a community's survival is at stake, whether in a church service, a prison setting, or a demonstration for civil rights. Within this collaborative art form, "creativity" and "improvisation" reigned, the small parts accumulating and adding up to a larger whole. Brothers points to these dynamics, making a compelling case for how Beatles "generated material" in a similar fashion.[9] Referencing "Day Tripper" and "We Can Work It Out," Brothers cites Lennon's approach to songwriting, which John described as "doing little bits which you then join up."[10] Indeed, the Beatles' collaborative disposition, which also includes productive competition, might be the band's most important inheritance: "The Beatles embraced a collaborative image partly because of the egalitarian nature of the vernacular tradition, partly because of their closeness, and partly through an intuitive sense for how commercially appealing this model could be. People went nuts over the idea of a democratized rock-and-roll band saturated with creative camaraderie. Collaboration became part of what their music meant."[11] With their cooperation in mind, the individualistic thrust of McCartney's post-Beatles agenda becomes more apparent.

Over the years, McCartney has defended the Beatles, but he has also worked to solidify his own legacy, now emblematized by "Blackbird" and "Yesterday," his "solo" Beatles songs. On two of his live albums (*Wings over America* [1976] and *Back in the U.S.* [2002]) and in *The Lyrics*, McCartney has even reversed the songwriting credit on these and other "Lennon-McCartney Originals." That nickname is how the teenage lads labeled their compositions in Paul's schooldays notebook,[12] and alphabetical ordering was maintained when they started to publish songs. But McCartney worries people will forget or never know that he was the primary composer on certain tunes. As we showed in the introduction, McCartney's stories about "Blackbird" assert lead authorship on that song, a tendency found elsewhere when he offers who-did-what explanations (as in McCartney 3, 2, 1, a 2021 Hulu documentary series). Rhetorical maneuvers that delineate individual contributions (both his own and those of the other Beatles) stand in opposition to the communal values that characterize the band's roots as well as their own music and its appeal. In McCartney's efforts to recapture what he has lost (i.e., his band of brothers), he keeps enacting the source of his loss again and again.

John is probably the first to blame for designating certain tunes as "Paul's," usually to disparage them. Lennon's early 1970s insults spurred McCartney's insecurity, a defensiveness still on display (in *The Lyrics*, Lennon is like a specter haunting McCartney's memory). Soon after the Beatles disbanded, *Rolling Stone* cofounder and longtime editor Jann Wenner reminded Lennon about the Beatles' former representation of themselves as "four parts of the same person."[13] For a time, Lennon said, the Beatles believed their own "myth" but then "remembered that they were four individuals."[14] Even though he was being negative, Lennon's subsequent critique actually represented their groupness, with their contributions sliding into one another: "We were four guys, that—I met Paul and said, 'Do you want to join me band?' and then George joined and then Ringo joined. We were just a *band* who made it very, very big—that's all."[15] If it weren't for Western culture's emphasis on lyrics and melody—the parts of a song that can be copyrighted—Harrison and Starr might have received credit for their essential contributions to nearly every Beatles song. In fact, as all the "Fifth Beatle" talk illustrates, the band was reliant on many others who formed what Brothers terms "the creative collective," especially their producer, George Martin; their manager, Brian Epstein; the EMI engineers who worked out how to make the sounds the band requested; and all the other workers and members of their entourage.

Lennon's assessment of the Beatles included another bold proclamation that underscores the Beatles' indebtedness to Black music and to the ring shout in particular: "Our best work was never recorded." Lennon was specifically referring to the "straight rock" they played in Liverpool and Hamburg clubs, where they were playing many rhythm and blues covers. Lennon blamed the repetitive, rehearsed, and compressed twenty-minute performances, which came later as the Beatles toured the globe, for eliminating improvisation and artistic freedom.[16] Lennon goes overboard, but his exaggeration is apt for another reason. Also like the Black folks who developed the ring shout, the Beatles didn't read music or do formal (Western) musical notation—which helped them respond spontaneously to one another.[17]

The highly adaptable and inventive ring-shout singing defied replication and notation, a slipperiness that could be, and was, compared to that of bird-song: "Offering an apology for their musical transcriptions of *Slave Songs of the United States*, William Francis Allen and his coauthors wrote that black singing was 'as impossible to place on score as the singing of birds or the tones of an Aeolian harp' (1867)."[18] Though this sentiment could be read as a compliment, it also reflects comparable Romantic "perceptions of the ineffable in black song."[19] While some, such as Emerson and Whitman and later Du Bois, praised Black music's birdlike resistance to charting as authentic musical expression, not everyone agreed on whether birdsong qualified as music. According to a study of post-Enlightenment scientific and musicological discourse surrounding birdsong and evolution, "[debates concerned] personhood, for to be a musician—human or animal—was to be a person."[20] In the nineteenth century, admitting that "animals uttered musical notes," as Charles Darwin daily observed of birdsong, meant recognizing it as evidence of culture, a source of aesthetic value, and proof of artistic ability.[21] Here again we find birds at the nexus of competing discourses about the humanity of Black people.

Questions about musical authorship dovetail with the ring shout's capacity for appropriation, adaptation, and revision. As so-called folk arts do generally, the ring shout reflects a profound lack of personal ownership when it comes to creative enterprise. This community orientation is likewise available in the form and function of tales about the Flying Africans' birdlike escape.

The Trope of Flying Africans: Bird Metaphors and Life/Death

"Once upon a time, the people could fly." So begins Virginia Hamilton's take on the folktale "All God's Chillen Had Wings." The narrator continues, and the story gets more specific: "Say that long ago in Africa, some of the people knew magic. And they would walk up on the air like climbin up on a gate. And they flew like blackbirds over the fields. Black, shiny wings flappin against the blue up there."[22] Way before McCartney sang of a blackbird and connected its message to civil rights, Black folks were correlating their flight with black-colored birds. And songs about flying away are still being sung today.

For hundreds of years, Black people have represented flight out of bondage, a "trope" rooted in the lore of Flying Africans. Olivia Smith Storey explains that "the Flying Africans specifically refers to African born slaves flying from slavery in the Americas. Traditions of flight in Africa, such as shape-shifting, continue into the present in several African nations and potentially extend its range into an even larger territory and time period."[23] Also informed by African myths and rituals underscoring the special qualities of birds,[24] tales of Flying Africans often go like this: "A group of slaves is in a field and an overseer attempts to coerce them into heavier labor with a whip or a gun. The African born speak in a strange language and then fly away. The Creole or American born cannot fly away because they do not know the language."[25] An African, often a shaman figure,[26] can also return to teach the African-descended the speech that instigates liftoff, elevating a community who then fly like a flock of fleeing birds.

The association between Black people and birds, who become correlational through specialized speech that elevates individual and community, is rooted in the trope of Flying Africans. Soyica Diggs Colbert recognizes the inherent disembodiment, arguing that it stems from the trope's rootedness in "the slave system," which actively sought to dehumanize Black people.[27] Throwing the voice, especially via song, enacts a disconnect between the body and the soul or mind; flying would appear to be an inhuman function since it is not the province of unassisted mortals. But when they told (and tell) stories of people flying away, the enslaved and their descendants made (and make) a case for their humanity,[28] an ironic effect of the bird correlations. Voice-throwing, in fact, has sacred provenance in Yoruba mythology,[29] while flight itself "suggests . . . the power to interrupt the finality of death"[30] and, as Jason R. Young argues, reflects enslaved people's "cultural beliefs" in the ability to fly.[31]

Flying, especially that of birds, is not limited to Black creative expression and cultural production. Folk traditions often intersect with each other, especially in North America, where Indigenous myths and lore about ravens and crows can feature trickster and shapeshifting dynamics relevant to the Signifyin(g) blackbird previously introduced. Especially for the Tlingit peoples of the Pacific Northwest, the Raven is a trickster-hero who traverses different landscapes, giving rise to bodies of land and water as well as the features and functions of other animals.[32] Even more broadly, birds are ubiquitous in music and culture, unbound to one genre, generation, or geographical region. Their prevalence in music is not surprising since birds themselves are creatures of song. Across time and place, flying entities have inspired art in all mediums, and they have long been associated with physical survival. Birds' migration patterns evidence the seasons, predict the weather, and mark the passage of time, all major concerns for premodern people, whether hunter-gatherers or farmers.[33] Around the globe, wings have long been sacred metaphors for sustaining oneself.[34] Icarus, whose father, Daedalus, crafted wings from feathers and wax in order to escape imprisonment in Crete, ignores his father's caution and flies too close to the sun. The wax melts and Icarus falls into the sea and drowns. When Flying Africans take off, bound for Africa, their flight can be a hope-fueled escape, too. But, as with Icarus, flying away may involve death, literal or figurative, especially when travel takes place over a body of water.

Take, for example, a story of Yank'o the buzzard told among the Dombi clan who lived in what is now Suriname: the slave Sabaku promises his people "If we do not meet again in life, we shall meet in death," before running away with the help of the buzzard, whose back then becomes Sabaku's home. Addressing the black-colored bird, Sabaku speaks a language that initiates flight: "You who fly high, who fly over water, and over the high bush, carry me to safety."[35] The name itself, Yank'o, is "specialized religious vocabulary for evoking a spirit": "When the Granman prepares the Herskovitses for their journey, he touches them with a buzzard feather that will protect them with 'buzzard obia.' . . . The Saramacca in the text evoke his [deistic] presence with the song 'Obia-yo Yankoro Obia-e Yankoro.' They also imitate the buzzard's movement in a ritual dance that leads to a state of increased strength or possession." Ralph Ellison's short story "Flying Home" references such buzzard folklore, putting it in dialogue with the Icarus myth: "Challenging the idea of univocal meanings or messages, Ellison gives us symbolically charged fields, with a buzzard turning into the avian savior of African lore but also into the lethal force that brings the pilot's plane down."[36] Ironically, crashing the plane enables the protagonist to sort out internalized racism that could not be solved with flight, a coming-to-terms imaged by the buzzard's flight toward the sun.[37]

Bird symbolism is thus distinctive when calling attention to structures of oppression, especially when it refers back to the consequences of the transatlantic slave trade during which "suicide was not an uncommon practice among captive slaves on ships embarked on the Middle Passage."[38] The horrors of slavery, which bound enslaved people to land and owners across generations, prompted stories that imagined release into the sky through magical means. The institution of slavery was, after all, predicated on killing familial, community, and cultural networks. Flight, however, allowed those bonds to be reclaimed: "The Flying Africans narrative is fundamentally about the theft of life from the social and physical death of slavery. By stealing away individuals that slavery stole, flight reverses the theft of bodies."[39] Emphasizing the "resurrection" motif inherent in accounts of Flying Africans, Colbert points to their "triumph over black death [and over] the reduction of black people to only death bound materiality."[40]

The Flying Africans trope, as theorized by Smith Storey, is "a vehicle of expression" with many possibilities for textual application, then and now. Flight is its dominant feature, but the trope is at once more complicated and open-ended in application. As "a system of rhetorical devices that facilitates the possibility of expressing the diasporic predicament," the Flying Africans trope is "a highly fluid form that does not convey rigid meaning but that provides the basic structure and imagery for authors and speakers to adapt to their own purposes."[41] For example, Commander's study of Afro-Atlantic flight in post–civil rights cultural productions finds that "literal and figurative flights closer to Africa are indicative of the ceaseless reconfigurations of resistance to elide racism and its attendant systems of domination." Resisting a totalizing theory of how "African-descended people" conceive of Africa, Commander shows how flight-related impulses can be "celebratory and romantic" but also "disappointing."[42] The dual functions of flight parallel the lexical ambiguity of birds as song imagery.

McCartney's "Blackbird" includes key imagery relevant to the Flying Africans trope. The night's death is a hovering specter in the Beatles song *and* in flight-themed folklore. In arts of the African Diaspora, wings facilitate escape, but this does not necessarily mean bodily survival or, as Commander suggests, fulfillment.[43]

"All God's Chillen Had Wings": The Gifts of Speech and Ambiguity

The Flying Africans trope is elastic, but Smith Storey outlines key features: "a literal use of the word 'flying' or its variants, flight from a human representative of a coercive culture, and flight towards a place of refuge or home."[44] Along these lines, narratives about Flying Africans can be further classified by two major "twists": the first depicts an immediate departure as "newly arrived Africans . . . take wing and fly back across the ocean."[45] The second involves escapist flight from the lived brutality of slavery and oppression when "an African shaman or some other charismatic figure chants verses to physically depleted slaves laboring in the fields and enables them to fly. Like the lead bird in a migratory formation, he brings them home."[46] Clearly illustrating the trope's defining features, along with the second narrative twist, is "All God's Chillen Had Wings." In this folktale, enslaved Africans, though beaten and terrorized, speak the right words to reclaim their ancestral wings and fly away when a spiritual leader rises to direct the community.

As told by John's Island, South Carolina, resident Caesar Grant to John Bennett, the story begins with the correlation between birds and humans, a fairy-tale invocation in the first word: "Once all Africans could fly like birds; but owing to their many transgressions, their wings were taken away." The newly enslaved people suffer as they are forced to labor on a plantation, but they escape when an old man speaks a language they recognize: "All the Negroes, old and new, stood up together; the old man raised his hands; and they all leaped up into the air with a great shout; and in a moment were gone, flying, like a flock of crows . . . behind them flew the old man." "All God's Chillen Had Wings" insists that salvation is possible when a leader speaks and the people respond, or, as Gates and Tatar put it, "Language—charged, incantatory, and active—becomes a tool of collective liberation."[47] The ending underscores a vital moral about an individual's deliverance predication on lifting up the community.

When the logic of this folklore is translated to music, a song leader can perform the shaman's magic, celebrating the talents of others and inviting singers and musicians to signal their affirmation and participation in community transcendence. In "All God's Chillen Had Wings," "the master, the overseer, and the driver" are impotent in face of the Africans' taking flight to escape.[48] This "narrative logic" is further representative of the Flying Africans trope, which includes "three figures": "the *African* armed with a 'password,' the African American *Slave* as witness or participant, and the white *Overseer*, generally armed with a whip."[49] The persistence of these character types records the memory of slavery in subsequent texts that may not be set on plantations but nevertheless retain the trope's structure, positioning, for example, a prison guard or police (or even racist concepts) in the role of Overseer.

Stories of Flying Africans often involve chosen death and a soul's return home to Africa, with or without its body; the story bears witness, even if the storyteller was not present to observe the flight. These dynamics are rooted in legends related to Ebo Landing in Glynn County, Georgia, the site of an Igbo slave revolt that resulted in the mass drowning deaths of approximately seventy-five slaves brought to Savannah, Georgia, from what is today Nigeria: "The Igbos . . . either jumped overboard and drowned or 'took to the swamp' and committed suicide collectively. . . . The Igbo mutiny has powerful symbolic importance as an act of resistance and as the first freedom march in African American history."[50] Flight-themed accounts are further documented in *Drums and Shadows*, a collection derived from interviews performed by the Georgia Writer's Project in the 1930s and the first to name "Flying Africans."[51] Although some tales of Flying Africans are particular to the southeastern United States, accounts of enslaved people flying are present throughout the country and the rest of the Americas, including and especially the Caribbean.[52]

While at times seeming triumphant, especially in its Africa-bound target, Afro-Atlantic flight does not always have a clear destination, nor does it promise life (on earth at least).[53] Reflecting the "double meaning of flight as ascent and escape, with escape haunted by the specter of death,"[54] the birds of US author Toni Morrison's oeuvre are "often disruptive and unconventional" because they regularly "represent not freedom but lack of freedom, not life, but death."[55] In her novel *Song of Solomon*, Morrison's protagonist, Milkman, realizes why he is so interested in flying when he discovers that an ancestor, his great-grandfather Solomon, is related to a "flying African" and compared to a "bird." One character uses language evocative of "All God's Chillen Had Wings" to describe his sudden flight, whose destination is unclear, though it is back to "wherever it was he came from."[56]

Morrison's birds and other depictions of people flying are derived from the author's exposure to, as she put it, "the folklore of my life," as well as "African myths, cosmologies, and cultural practices" and her knowledge of the aforementioned *Drums and Shadows*.[57] The author also acknowledged the persistent and ubiquitous presence of flying people in the imaginations of Black people she knew, characterizing flight as "one of our gifts."[58] As Morrison's novels make clear, flight is a gift because it is a mechanism for addressing hardship even if the flightpath itself is obscured.

More recently, in Texas Poet Laureate Cyrus Cassells's *The Gospel of Wild Indigo*, the poem that gives the collection its title associates a bird's flight with salvation from slavery and death. Cassells's opening line situates the poem in the biblical tradition: "from the gospel according to wild indigo, / in which death and defiling / bondage are transformed / into foam and fish-scale blue, / a heron's swoop, / and bold-fisted hurricanes dismantle / the masters' belligerence." Birds appear throughout his collection, frequently sprinkled with references to biblical images as well as myth and folklore: Titus Sparrow teaches the speaker to "revere . . . the spirits of winged slaves," and "the agile sorcery" of "dusk-sharing blackbirds" glide into the poem "I'll Take You to Africa." Still more blackbirds, this time "gloom-banishing," are a "locomotive" energy, further correlating imagery consequential to Black American arts, that of the train and the bird.

As with Morrison, Cassells's bird imagery suggests that hope and doom are flipsides of each other, recalling the very duality that Gates and Tatar observe of the Flying Africans trope: "Embedded in the notion of flight back to Africa is a double pathway, a realistic route leading to a suicidal plunge into the ocean that separates Old World from New and a mystical one enabling a spiritual journey back home. Legends about flying Africans often capitalize on both possibilities, leaving the question of survival open, perhaps in part because tragic plunge, like redemptive ascent, means release from the punitive labors of slavery."[59] Morrison's and Cassells's are representative examples of many other literary works that deal in comparable bird imagery and themes, specifically the ambiguous nature of survival in relation to the ocean. When flight takes place over water, it's often a haunting reminder of the Middle Passage; such reminders have long been transmitted through the music of the Black Church.

Flying Africans in the Black Church: Hymns and Transatlantic Flight

Along with its clear view of mortality and life's suffering, music of the Black Church offers comfort through witnessing uplift. After all, a sweet sound saves the speaker in "Amazing Grace." Still, death is on the horizon in this song, sung so often at Black American funerals. Even though "Amazing Grace" does not feature flight proper, the concept is bound to the song's use in these "homegoing" ceremonies. Interestingly, in "Amazing Grace" blindness becomes, after the speaker is saved, sight; this appears to be a precedent for the learning-to-see blackbird's sunken eyes in the Beatles' "Blackbird," whose composer has a penchant for polar contrasts (e.g., "Hello, Goodbye," "Ebony and Ivory"). Explaining "Amazing Grace," William T. Dargan recognizes "the black rhetorical penchant for paired opposites (lost-found, blind-see),"[60] an observation that adds immediate depth to the depiction of sight in McCartney's "Blackbird" and the songwriter's numerous other pairs.

In the music of the Black Church, flight motifs continue to take on a tragic yet still relentlessly hopeful character.[61] Indeed, going home via a chariot or the soul's wings is about the journey of soul released from body. Like "Flee as a Bird" and "Amazing Grace," "Swing Low, Sweet Chariot" was not authored by a Black person, but the song's association is primarily with the Black Church, popularized by the Fisk Jubilee Singers gospel choir; the spiritual's instrumental role in the civil rights movement further bound the song to community uplift.[62] As these songs evidence, spirituals and gospel music are informed by abundant examples of bird-as-means-of-deliverance in the Bible, including Noah's dove returning with the olive branch, the Holy Spirit as a dove, and many winged angels; Ezekiel's flying wheel is another productive flight metaphor. But Heilbut also emphasizes revision, asserting that enslaved people "created our greatest national music" when they reworked hymns encountered during the Great Awakening, "combin[ing] the revival hymns of eighteenth-century England with an African song style."[63]

Illustrating the persistent infusion of British texts in Black Americans' artistry, many of these hymns were sourced from songs credited to English Dissenter Isaac Watts. The "Dr. Watts hymns" were "sturdy . . . hymns depicting amazing grace, Jordan's stormy banks, and fountains filled with blood." They were also among "the first songs slaves sang on this continent." Their form allowed for the application of the African technique of call and response, as well as a vocalist's flourishes: "Traditionally a leader would recite the line, after which the congregation sang in a slow, languorous manner called long or common meter, which allowed for intricate embellishments by each singer."[64] Referring to this practice, Dargan theorizes the "lining out" of Watts hymns: "Often such 'blackened' performances result in exquisitely extended renditions of the hymns." Dargan points to Richard Wright's short story "Long Black Song," which recognizes the consequence of length, both a "literal" description of lining-out performances *and* a metaphor "for the length and breadth of contested spaces between descendants of Africa and Europe living out a common American destiny." Consistently emphasizing the collaborative nature of lining out as a process of adaptation, Dargan shows how "the English hymns and the African ring shout became complementary elements in a core African American worship tradition."[65]

In Black American worshippers' "blackening" of the Dr. Watts hymns, we can also see the appeal of birds as metaphors.[66] Just as a bird relies on the flock, so too does the gospel singer fly within a formation, soaring while never losing home. Indeed, "under the shadow of thy wings" is one of the "recurring phrases from [Watts's] hymns that have been most popular among black Baptists." This example, another illustration of the textual revision that characterizes Signifyin(g), underscores a larger point that Dargan makes about the futility of determining "originality" in the enslaved Africans' reworkings of Watts.[67]

Noting how certain "components become their own," Dargan draws a line from the dissemination of Watts to the very musical features that will shape rock 'n' roll:

> When Baptist missionaries brought gospel to the masses of slaves, more than two centuries after the slave trade had begun, the latter grafted texts by Watts onto living oral traditions, which were by default grounded in an admixture of African orientations toward the universe, human existence, and family relations, as well as the ritual celebrations embracing these perspectives. It is no wonder that the continuing song-and-hymn-singing traditions still emphasize florid and stylized forms of speech intonation, that, through repetition and variation, initiate collective and individual responses, beginning with speech-song, progressing toward dance movements, and culminating in shouting as an embodiment of divine inspiration.[68]

As an emanation of the gospel shout, McCartney's imitation of Little Richards's yell, whose own predecessor appears in the next section, is, then, a technique rooted in the adoption and revision of the Dr. Watts hymns, a key precedent for this book's conception of transatlantic flight.[69]

Flying Africans: Spirituals, Gospel, and Rock 'n' Roll

Flight-themed biblical hymns such as "I'll Fly Away" do, of course, appear in all manner of Christian churches, but they take on special profundity within the context of the Black Church. The "fly away" word choice reappears often in Negro spirituals, such as "Sing A-ho That I Had the Wings of a Dove." Referencing Psalm 55 and its dove, the chorus of the spiritual promises, "I'd fly away and be at rest."[70] (Notice the "I would," rather than "I will," construction: "would" suggests constraints, the "coercive culture" Smith Storey identifies as definitional to the Flying Africans trope.)[71] One version of this spiritual, documented in Tennessee, was the product of a great many reworkings; its call-and-response form allowed preachers to "break off and extemporize."[72] This song was also revisited and reworked in the secular realm later in the twentieth century: "Wings of a Dove" gained traction in Afro-Caribbean popular music, first as a calypso and later in ska and reggae. Desmond Dekker—name-checked by the Beatles in "Ob-La-Di, Ob-La-Da"—recorded the song with the English band the Specials.[73] Adding to their own birds and biblically inspired songs, Bob Marley and the Wailers also recorded "Wings of a Dove."

The bridge from gospel to rock 'n' roll and later pop genres specifically involves the aptly named Swan Silvertones, a group dubbed "the Beatles of gospel" for their genre-crossing influences on Black and white pop artists.[74] Making an explicit connection between slavery and gospel's uplifting orientation, lead singer Reverend Claude Jeter explained, "Our music goes clean back to the days of slavery. They'd be tired, they'd be exhausted from the heat and everything, but they'd look up toward heaven, and they'd say, 'Jesus, I'm going to be there someday.' We've been living on hope for 200 years."[75] Although he doesn't mention the Flying Africans here, Jeter's understanding of enslaved people's sky-bound hopes shows how the trope's logic would apply to Christian belief, exemplified by Jesus's suffering and resurrection. Descriptions of the ensemble's singing also relate these motifs: Jeter's "ascents into falsetto singing lifted the group's music toward otherworldly realms. For most of [the 1940s to 1970s], his smooth lead vocals were balanced by a hard gospel shouter."[76] During that time, from the late 1950s to early 1960s, the Swan Silvertones recorded on Vee-Jay, the Chicago label that was the first to release Beatles' records in the United States.

The Swan Silvertones were celebrated for their memorable take on a spiritual predating the Civil War, "Mary Don't You Weep" (Roud 11823),[77] which Jerry Zolten describes as follows: "Against the backdrop of electric guitar, handclapping, and what might be the beat of feet stomping on the floor, Connor's bass voice pumps out a driving rhythm as Owens and Myles in a supercharged vocal exchange spur Jeter on to falsetto heights. . . . As it peaks, Jeter throws out the line, 'I'll be your bridge over deep water if you trust in my name,' which years later inspired Paul Simon to write . . . 'Bridge over Troubled Water.'"[78] The Silvertones' performance exemplifies how mid-twentieth-century gospel musicians continued to rework spirituals, which are folk texts often informed by tales of Flying Africans and enchanted objects that enable flight. Spirituals converted "the destination into Heaven rather than Africa."[79] Lorna McDaniel explains that "the Negro Spiritual adapts the Christian vision of the soul's ascent to heaven, of its flight 'to Jesus and to rest'" but also recognizes another vital function: "Some spirituals, though religious in practice, held a double function as signal songs of slave escape."[80]

Even if they were not featured in spirituals "used as 'alerting' songs," wings and other fly-away motifs evidence "structural depictions of flight."[81] In a famous example, "All God's Chillun Got Wings," wings are one of the mechanisms possessed by the speaker and the addressee: "I got-a wings, you got-a wings / All o' God's chillun got-a wings."[82] According to this song, these wings will be fully revealed once the speaker is in heaven; the other three verses apply the same logic to a robe, a harp, and shoes. A variation, "Going to Shout All Over God's Heav'n" (also known as "Everybody Talkin' About Heaven Ain't Goin' There"), includes those objects, too, except that instead of wings the speaker has a crown and a song.[83] In another variation, "Travelling Shoes," Death comes looking for the speaker (or a Sinner), a Gambler, and a Preacher.[84] Traditionally, the Preacher has shoes, so he is the only one ready to answer Death's call of "Come en go wid me,"[85] reflecting the Christian believer's "affirmative, realistic attitude" toward mortality.[86]

The legendary gospel singer Marion Williams performed her rendition of "Got on My Travelling Shoes" as part of a medley for a live (majority white) studio audience in 1965. As we suggested above, Williams's vocal technique is important to this book's history. Little Richard credited her as the source of his iconic woos—the ones McCartney continues to emulate. This particular trajectory of influence was a noted cause of some ridicule and frustration in the Black gospel community: "Singers would laugh dryly at the Beatles imitating Little Richard imitating Marion Williams, or Mick Jagger emulating Tina Turner. 'See them white boys,' I used to hear, 'doing everything those poor girls figured out for themselves—and making all the money.'"[87]

In a 1965 performance, Williams (who talked about divine musical inspiration as "the anointing") and her supporting vocalists reveal the transcendent and joyful possibilities of "Got on My Travelling Shoes," the spiritual rooted in the flight motif. With a rapturous delivery, the ensemble enacts the call and response and the "walking rhythms of the chorus,"[88] kicking up their feet to emphasize their shoes. During the next song, Williams's hit "Packin' Up," the singers' circular walking formation keeps building physical momentum, and Williams's black robes includes a split drape that evokes wings. Near the end, she retrieves her purse from under an audience member's seat, really selling the concept of travel and packing up for the Lord. These objects are significant, especially the shoes, a reminder of their "rarity" among enslaved people; shoes are vehicles of "transcenden[ce], symbols of salvation and Christian practice, fit for travelling to the other world."[89] Again, though, this uplifting journey comes only through death, signaling the social reality of Black people in America, one from which the Black Church does not turn away.

Many other bird-themed songs and sermons in the gospel tradition reveal the ongoing vitality of flight-oriented discourse among Black Christians. Perhaps the most famous bird-themed sermon was recorded by Aretha Franklin's father, the Reverend C. L. Franklin, who popularized "The Eagle Stirreth

Her Nest" with his best-selling Chess record (1953). This recording documents Franklin's take on the famous sermon originally written down by Sir Charles Lyell, a British observer of the Reverend Andrew Marshall and his six hundred congregants at the First African Church in Savannah, Georgia, on January 10, 1846.

For a decade prior to his 1953 recording, the young Reverend Franklin had been delivering the "demanding sermon," known for "require[ing] a maturity of thought and faith, coupled with a superior musical delivery."[90] With God figured as the eagle and history as the nest, the Deuteronomy-inspired metaphor directly addressed slavery—although "four hundred years is just a little while with God."[91] The sermon affirms divine oversight of living beings (all equal in the eyes of God), the purpose of suffering, *and* the promise of redemption.

As in "His Eye Is on the Sparrow," Franklin's sermon reaffirms divinity's oversight of living beings, who are equal in front of the Lord, while asserting that suffering has meaning, and redemption is a promise. B. B. King related this message in his memory of the sermon: "Reverend Franklin would remind me that God's angels made the lions lie down like lambs. Like an eagle, God is swift and strong in healing our hearts."[92] The final part of Franklin's sermon is delivered in the traditional chanted/sung style of African American preachers and involves more call and response between preacher and congregation, amplifying the co-creation of communal meaning.

Franklin's ending introduces a new story, which then applies new meaning to the central metaphor: a chicken farmer ends up raising a bird that is eventually identified as an eagle. This eagle keeps growing too large for his cage and is eventually freed by the farmer; the eagle inches toward full flight, finally soaring "to yonder's mountain." Then Franklin reveals, "One of these days, / One of these days / My soul / Is an eagle / In the cage that the Lord / Has made for me."[93] Now, the eagle is the *human* soul, whose wings are waiting for the time to "fly away / And be at rest,"[94] the shared fate of the preacher and his congregants.[95] Here again is the Flying Africans logic of freedom in death, as well as the leader-directed community rising as a flock through exposure to the Word—and Signifyin(g) that reverses the meaning of words.

The Ring Shout, Flying Africans, and Gospel Go to Space with George Clinton and P-Funk

The Black Church's profound influence in the spiritual, political, economic, and social lives of Black Americans helps explain why bird and other flight imagery appears so frequently in the work of artists raised in the Church.[96] Distinguished by its deeply affective, communal experiences, the music of the Black Church is also born out of the legacy of the ring shout. Gates points to a wider reach: "The Black Church has influenced nearly every chapter of the African American story, and it continues to animate Black identity today, both for believers and nonbelievers."[97] The Flying Africans trope has been nourished in the religious sector, which, in turn, influenced secular music's flight rhetoric, especially in the post–civil rights era. From Stevie Wonder's "Bird of Beauty" (1974) to Kendrick Lamar's "Black Boy Fly" (2012), the examples are too numerous to name, although one funky take on Flying Africans offers clear illustration of the legacy.

With the group Parliament (part of his Parliament-Funkadelic collective), George Clinton's *Mothership Connection* (1975) brings these threads—ring shout, the trope of Flying Africans, and the gospel sensibility—together in a record on which "Clinton's group claims liberation by technological innovation and manipulation of space."[98] Premised on flight, *Mothership Connection* is "a concept album based around a crazy alien funk mythology," whose inspiration comes, in part, from "imagin[ing] a black man in space."[99] Clinton was continuing in the tradition of Sun Ra, the pioneering cosmic jazz musician who imagined Black (and some white) people as angels and whose "Astro-black mythology . . . reinvents Africa and African Americans for the Space Age."[100] While some involved in the making of *Mothership Connection* saw "a black-liberation dimension," Clinton relates flight to creativity, as well as to Jimi Hendrix, whose own bird imagery is considered in chapter 7: "Space was a place but it was also a concept, a metaphor for being way out there the way that Jimi Hendrix had been. Imagining a record in space was imagining artistry unbound, before it was recalled to Earth."[101]

With "highly layered, otherworldly grooves"[102] that aurally manifested themes in the lyrics and album imagery, Parliament's funky journey is doing the serious work of reclaiming pyramids on *Mothership Connection*. Drawing on Gilroy's explanation of seafaring ships, Colbert argues for spaceships' difference: "The imagery of the Mothership attempts to recoup Africa by returning the continent to black Americans through the air, thereby avoiding the brutal Middle Passage." Seeing Parliament's project as "extend[ing] the web of the Flying Africans narrative," Colbert makes a case for their cultural innovation: "The conflation of Africa and space associate the continent with a region free from the alienating effects of being a black person in the United States. The desire to land the spaceship and incorporate the sound it produces into American black culture distinguishes Parliament's politics from that of other artists of the Black arts movement, who . . . tend to idealize Africa."[103]

The song "Mothership Connection (Star Child)" further draws a line between folklore about Flying Africans, spirituals, and contemporary music. The repeated line "Swing down, sweet chariot / Stop and let me ride" alludes to a playful variation of the well-known spiritual "Swing Low, Sweet Chariot." In "Swing Down, Sweet Chariot," an angel-driver stops to fix the chariot's wheel, and Ezekiel takes a spin (using logic from the spiritual "Ezek'el Saw the Wheel").[104] Popularized by the Golden Gate Quartet in the 1940s, "Swing Down" was also covered by Elvis Presley (1960) and Billy Preston (1971). Along with the refrain, "Mothership Connection (Star Child)" includes a line about being ready "when Gabriel's horn blows," another significant allusion: "Without polemics, militarism, or racially charged code words, Clinton's P-Funk placed the African-American sensibility at the center of the universe, and ultimately at the center of *history*."[105]

Clinton's P-Funk collective is a contemporary expression of the ring shout; in concerts, Clinton is the leader, but he presides over a musical party, with each member doing their own thing; individual talents (singing, playing instruments, and dancing) are allowed to flourish, but only inasmuch as they serve the whole. As we mentioned in the introduction, Clinton was influenced by the Beatles and other British rock 'n' rollers, appreciating their appreciation for American rhythm and blues. The Beatles group dynamic also appealed strongly to Clinton. The Beatles (along with the crew of *Star Trek*'s starship *Enterprise*) thus became role models for Clinton's concept of a band as a cooperative, cohesive unit in which each member is allowed to thrive.[106]

Punctuating his own respect and admiration for the Beatles while on a UK tour with Funkadelic in 1971, Clinton and his group made an excursion to Liverpool, where he remembers being "like any other Beatles fan."[107] When he recalls Liverpool, Clinton lists the stops now required on any Fab Four Taxi Tour (except that the Cavern he visited was still the original, not today's re-creation): "We went to the Cavern Club on Mathew Street, where Paul McCartney's uncle carpentered the stage. We went to Mendips, John Lennon's childhood home on Menlove Avenue."[108] We don't have to imagine the grandmaster of funk-strolling Liverpool with his crew: the inner gatefold of *Maggot Brain* (1971) includes a photograph from the trip. Clinton, Eddie Hazel, and three other bandmembers look funky and cool in jackets, flared jeans, and fringe. Guitarist Tawl Ross holds a brick that came from the slightly crumbling wall behind them, evidence of the working-class city's still under-revitalized postwar status. Clinton, however, saw an "energy" in the place: "This was less than a year after *Sgt. Pepper's Lonely Hearts Club Band*, so there wasn't the same sense of distant nostalgia there is now. There was a real energy around those sites, because the band was still a going concern."[109] Clinton's memory involves the Beatles still being together even though they were broken up by 1971, when Funkadelic was touring England.[110] But he anticipates how a post-Beatles Liverpool would be characterized by its Beatles' past, a point we will take up below.

Clinton's musical output with P-Funk, especially *Mothership Connection*, exemplifies the musical conversation that we trace in the coming chapters. There is, for example, specific precedent for Black Americans taking inspiration from English texts, found elsewhere in Clinton's allusions to nursery rhymes, such as 1977's "Sir Nose d'Voidoffunk (Pay Attention—B3M)," which interpolates "Baa, Baa, Black Sheep" (Roud 4439) and "Three Blind Mice" (Roud 3753). The title track of Funkadelic's *Let's Take It to the Stage* (1975) interpolates African American folk rhymes about pig-hunting as well as "Little Miss Muffet" (Roud 20605). Funkadelic's verse represents the girl getting high; she isn't scared away by the spider, who asks, "What's in the bag, bitch?" That refigured confrontation serves the song's larger goal, figuratively igniting a musical competition between Funkadelic and Sly and the Family Stone (Signified on as "Slick Brick" and "Slick and the Family Brick") and a host of other well-known Black artists and groups.

Similarly, Parliament's earlier single, "The Goose," draws on the Aesop fable about the bird that laid a golden egg. Addressing the goose as a lover, the speaker appreciates her abilities, comparing himself to a monkey with a peanut machine and a mole with eagle eyes, punning and playing with those images throughout the song. Cowritten with Eddie Hazel, "The Goose" is derived from a version Clinton performed in the 1960s with his doo-wop group, the Parliaments, illustrating another musical flightpath reliant on British and European folk content, Black Americans, and transatlantic exchange.

CHAPTER 2

Sing a Song of Blackbird

Pre-Twentieth-Century Transatlantic Flights in Black Music, the Beatles, and Liverpool

When the Beatles were on the cusp of losing one another in the 1969 *Get Back*–turned–*Let It Be* sessions, they jammed on a McCartney composition, "The Palace of the King of the Birds," whose title announces the bird branding he continued throughout the next six decades.[1] As an instrumental, the song also hearkens back to 1967's "Flying," the first of several songs to credit all four Beatles. It's really no wonder the Beatles have so many birds in their songs. Given their professed love of Black music, in which birds proliferate, the British Isles' folkloric penchant for birds,[2] and birds' general convenience as song objects, the presence of birds in Beatles' tunes is perhaps overdetermined before throwing their city of birth into the mix.

Long populated by "Liver birds," Liverpool's fixation with winged creatures goes all the way back to a fourteenth-century crest and King John, who registered the borough in 1217. Looking like duck-ish cormorants with sprigs in their beaks, Liver birds aren't an actual species of bird even though they enjoy a definite presence throughout Liverpool. Notable examples include the metal sculptures (dubbed Bertie and Bella) perching atop the Royal Liver Building and facing the River Mersey since 1911. The Beatles' musical contemporaries, the girl band who dubbed themselves the Liverbirds, made direct reference to the city's mascot, and Liver birds are Liverpool Football Club's official logo. And when lifelong bird lover McCartney was knighted, his crest included—what else?—a black-colored Liver bird. While this might seem like an appropriate nod to his hometown and "Blackbird" (and all his other winged imagery), a step back into Liverpool's history reveals a much more complicated story—another one McCartney has unknowingly stumbled into with his storytelling.

Birds abound in the folk arts of the British Isles, the subjects of some of the very texts that Black singers reworked in the Americas, especially when they Signified on blackface minstrelsy and Jim Crow apartheid in the blues tradition. Both ubiquitous and complicated, birds are polysemous imagery in the history of popular song, which also involves the interpolation of nursery rhyme content in early rhythm and blues and rock 'n' roll. Birds can be many things: a vehicle of liberation or an instrument of oppression, depending on who is doing the singing or assigning. That complex legacy is also shown in English uses of the word "blackbird," documented in Liverpool in conjunction with the transatlantic slave trade, and in the name of the most famous Black concert singer of the nineteenth century, Elizabeth Taylor Greenfield, the "Black Swan."

Transatlantic Birds: Folk Songs and Country, Chuck Berry and Rhiannon Giddens

Writing in the mid-twentieth century, the pioneering Black scholar Sterling Brown recognized how enslaved Africans and their descendants preserved English tunes such as "Barbara Allen" (Roud 54), "Lord Lovel" (Roud 48), and "Pretty Polly" (Roud 15), which then became part of the Black American folk repertoire.[3] Another British folk song known to be reworked by Black Americans prior to the twentieth century is "The Fox" (Roud 131), also called the "The Fox and the Goose." This very old song cycle is a significant predecessor in our history of transatlantic flight.

The earliest renditions of "The Fox" exist in the documentation of two fifteenth-century folk songs written in Middle English.[4] These songs feature a fox who comes into town to threaten a gaggle and is soon found out by a farmer and his wife; they try to thwart the animal with injury and chase him away. A defining "phrasing" feature of this song is the goose's own birdspeak of quacking in protest.[5] Despite her resistance, the bold fox, a repeat offender, usually gets away with this bird (or a hen), who is often brought to his den for a meal with Mrs. Fox. The version known as "The False Fox" ends with the reappearance of the goose's voice, a cry of "wheccumquek'" imploring her captor, "Take of my feders but not of my to."[6] Offering a moral about predation "within limits" for its medieval human audiences, the goose beseeches the fox to take her feathers ("feders"), which can grow back, though not her un-regenerating toe ("to"), a metonym for her life.[7]

The gender designated by "goose" involves a colloquialism older than the fifteenth century. The first written use of "bird" to refer to a young woman occurs in 1325.[8] Centuries later, the Beatles invoked the bird-as-girl slang in "Norwegian Wood (This Bird Has Flown)." McCartney later used that Britspeak to explain the meaning of "Blackbird," prompting Bettye LaVette to refer to this word choice when explaining her take on the song.[9] In the Anglophone tradition, hens and geese are also associated with women, the latter bird with female sex workers, a memory recorded in the nursery rhyme "Goosey, Goosey Gander" (Roud 6488).[10] This association explains the bawdy directions "The Fox" could take and is a reminder of the ubiquity of birds in English nursery rhymes and other folk texts.[11]

With a repetitive form indicating communal creation,[12] oral versions of "The Fox" were still circulating in England when first documented by nineteenth-century folklorists.[13] At the same time, variations of the folk song circulated in the United States, too, with "some evidence that it was known as early as the Civil War."[14] Southern variants of "The Fox" were observed to have particular relevance to Black men, who often identified with the trickster fox. Even though this association is further complicated by the song's presence in the blackface minstrel tradition, Black Americans' variations of "The Fox" recurred with the most frequency in folklorists' documentation.[15] Significantly, the goose in this folk song cycle is most often identified as "grey," a color that returns in our discussion of "Grey Goose" (Roud 11684), a prison work song that celebrates a bird who escapes the clutches of its captor.[16]

The gender dynamics between the rascally he-fox and a vulnerable she-goose are consistent with other British Isles folk ballads, such as "As I Roved Out" (Roud 3479),[17] whose speaker is accused of being "false" by the "true love" he let down. This folk song was one of McCartney's inspirations for "I Saw Her Standing There," as he remembered: "There was an old folk song about a guy who meets a girl on her 17th birthday. He tries to chat her up but she is having none of it. He ends up having to admire her from a distance. Most of The Beatles' audience were young girls and 17 was, let's say, a significant age. So I borrowed from that old song to make my own—that and a dash of [Chuck Berry's] 'Sweet Little Sixteen.'"[18] McCartney was bridging two musical influences, but they weren't unrelated. Berry was deeply informed by country and western music, itself very much indebted to folk songs like "As

I Roved Out" and to "black fiddle and banjo styles and . . . plantation songs composed by Black people." As Palmer explains, "From the time of the Civil War until the early twentieth century, the music of the songsters and musicianers shared a number of traits with white country music, with musicians of each race borrowing freely from each other."[19]

Berry inherits this dialogue. Exemplifying his knowledge of country, Berry transformed Bob Wills and His Texas Playboys' western swing song "Ida Red" into "Maybellene"; the new name was inspired by the brand of mascara, a box of which was sitting in the studio where Berry was recording. "Ida Red" centers on one of country and western's favorite tropes, a man turned into a "plumb fool" by his love for a cheating woman. With reference to a pecking chicken, the speaker realizes he's not the only one in the parlor and encourages dancers to lock down their partners. "Maybellene" picks up and extends that theme, making the sexual dynamics even more explicit with additional wordplay and rhymes, along with a car chase; these tropes will end up defining rock 'n' roll.

Berry's penchant for witty wordplay endeared him strongly to Lennon, who called Berry a "rock poet."[20] That talent reflected Berry's habituation to British and American poetry, an effect of his schoolteacher mother's influence. Berry was hero to all of the Beatles, whose songs reflect numerous ties to his music (be they lifts, allusions, or tributes).[21] In addition to the many musical Berry-isms, such as motoring rhythms that match lyrical content, the guy-chasing-girl scenario in "Maybellene" finds voice in "Ticket to Ride," "Day Tripper," and "The One After 909," songs with women who dupe or otherwise leave the speaker behind.[22]

But the persistent multiracial "borrowing" that resulted in country and western music prior to Berry has not always been adequately understood or appreciated.[23] In 2021, Rhiannon Giddens brought attention to the legacy of Black Americans' engagement with British Isles folk content, releasing the bird-full *They're Calling Me Home*, a collaboration with partner and collaborator Francesco Turrisi, an Italian multi-instrumentalist. His Dublin home was the site of their prerecorded NPR Tiny Desk (Home) Concert in May 2020, which opened with the Appalachian banjo song "Black as Crow." Giddens introduced the song, also known as "Blackest Crow," as "one of the earliest songs [she] learned in traditional music." She explained it goes by other names, too, including "As Time Draws Near" and "Dearest Dear," titles that underscore the song's longing for a return home.[24] At the center of the song is the image of the crow, whose black feathers will "surely turn to white" if the speaker proves "false," a promise of transformation that reverses the values conventionally attached to black-white symbolism.[25] Giddens personalized the song's longing, homebound themes, explaining that even though they were both in Ireland during the earlier periods of pandemic-related lockdowns, she and Turrisi had been unable to see each other, too—a reminder of a key feature in the Flying Africans trope.

With *They're Calling Me Home*, Giddens musically demonstrated what she explained in Ken Burns's 2019 documentary series *Country Music*. Black Americans innovated the genre, especially through the use of the banjo, while remixing the British Isles musical content ubiquitous in the Appalachians and Ozarks. In the 2020 Tiny Desk concert, Giddens mentioned that they wouldn't be playing any of her "original songs," explaining that "with these kinds of emotions [during the COVID-19 pandemic], the old songs say it best."[26] The latter seems a riff on W. B. Yeats's "Ancient salt is best packing," a phrase often used to characterize the Irish writer's reliance on folklore and myth. Giddens's insight evokes the Irish setting of the recording, which distanced both her and Turrisi from their home countries and even from each other. Celtic themes are evoked elsewhere on the album, especially in Emer Mayock's Irish flute and in one of the original songs, "Avalon," a ballad of loss that hopes for reunion in the someday of that mythical isle of plenty, themes also available in "Black as Crow." Given the persistence of its lost-found motifs, the album unsurprisingly closes with "Amazing Grace," another song with a white authorship but whose legacy resides in the Black Church.

The persistent circularity of these transatlantic flight songs from the nineteenth century to today highlights an important fact: Black people in the Americas have long been revising and reinterpreting European discourse, mediating through music and other forms the experiences of slavery and its consequences, as well as African storytelling content and techniques. That remixing has also involved the negotiation of blackface minstrel content, too.

Signifyin(g) Crows: Blackface Minstrelsy and the Blues

Within the musical milieu in and just following the nineteenth century, Black musicians and other artists Signified on minstrel subjects, naming Jim Crow and other sources of oppression.[27] They reappropriated the very birds and other animals that were sometimes appropriated from Black folk culture for minstrel content in the first place.[28] They also re-reappropriated the birds of British Isles folk songs that they might have already once appropriated. The goose, for example, is one bird whose freedom and fortitude have been unequivocally articulated in folk songs circulated among and recorded by

Black musicians like Lead Belly. We address this and other examples in the chapters that follow, but introducing this minstrel context further establishes the polysemous functions of birds.

Crowing and black-colored crows often featured in early to mid-twentieth-century blues because of the homophonic association with Jim Crow. This term derives from the moniker of famous blackface minstrel performer Thomas Dartmouth "Daddy" Rice, a white man who performed "Jump Jim Crow" in the nineteenth century. Rice's vulgar blackface performances became synonymous with laws and other practices used to disenfranchise and discriminate against Black people in the United States. Meanwhile, crows and other birds made visual appearances on minstrel posters and covers of the genre's widely distributed sheet music in addition to being named in nineteenth-century minstrel songs.[29] These include "The Old Grey Goose" (published as "De Ole Grey Goose" in 1844), which was performed by the well-known white blackface performer Dan Emmett.[30] In 1844, Emmett also published "Wild Goose Nation," whose title page dedicates the song to Rice, the "original" Jim Crow.[31] Illustrating one Black American family's understanding of crows in this context is the recollection of Margo Jefferson, who went on to become a critic at *Newsweek*. In the context of her review of Toni Morrison's *The Black Book*, Jefferson remembered, "As a young girl I was taught that black surgeon Daniel Hale Williams had performed the first successful heart operation; that blacks were shipbuilders, inventors and landowners; and that I was never to sing a song that used the words darky, coon, or crow."[32] Here, Jefferson refers to songs with an obvious blackface minstrel heritage, not the crows in songs such as "Strange Fruit," which we later discuss in conjunction with Dr. King's use of crows and others that Signify directly on Jim Crow injustice.[33]

Like the Signifying Monkey that represents Gates's theory, birds can be both a sign as well as the speaker of Signified speech, especially when correlated with the singer's persona. This is because Monkey immediately Signifies back onto himself, an "ironic reversal of a received racist image of the black as simianlike."[34] We find such metatextual reversals happening with birds in Black music, too. Black-colored birds are thus relational to the Monkey for this major reason: in the hands of white people employing them for racist ends, birds often mean something very different than when they are employed by Black people.

Birds are particularly useful animals to Signify on in English because of their availability for punning and wordplay. Birds' flying, soaring, singing, and pecking (or the plucking done to them) encode other boast-worthy actions. Sexual bird puns exist in classical Greek and Roman texts,[35] but erotic birds really abound in British folk songs. For example, in "My Gentle Cock," a medieval English ballad, a speaker regales the listener with verses that celebrate the nobility and grace of his early-rising cock, who "every nyght he perchit hym / In myn ladyis chaumbyr."[36] Even in Middle English, these final lines leave little doubt as to the central metaphor. It's the same one Willie Dixon employed in writing "The Red Rooster" (or "The Little Red Rooster"), a song that draws on comparable rooster symbolism in the blues tradition to Signify on sex and work.

Recorded by Howlin' Wolf in 1961 (and later by Sam Cooke and the Rolling Stones), "The Red Rooster" is about the speaker's bird, who is too tired to "crow" for daybreak, thus upsetting the balance of things at home in the backyard. The reason he can't or won't crow is because he's been "on the prowl," presumably all night. The blues song is basically a humble brag about sexual exhaustion. The reference to crowing, something the speaker's bird is not up to doing, also Signifies in another way. In "The Red Rooster," crowing is synonymous with working or domesticating in the correct way—something the speaker's bird can't or won't do. In addition to sexual innuendo, the refusal to "crow" is a significant word choice in "The Red Rooster," especially because the action is synonymous with acceding to another's demands.

The Beatles never covered "The Red Rooster," but a rooster's crow ushers in the rest of "Good Morning Good Morning," whose animal sounds return at the end, evoking the horses and dogs of an English hunt. Directly inspired by the Beach Boys' pet sounds on "Caroline, No" and a Kellogg's cereal commercial, the Beatles song is often read as Lennon's commentary on his own domestic boredom. The speaker recounts the hum drum of life's demands but is finally enlivened by "watching the skirts," leading to a flirtation that may become something more.

The Beatles' Birds

Recalling the decorative Liver birds in their home city, the Beatles' own bird language is often wallpaper. In "Cry Baby Cry," the local shop is the "Bird and Bee," and the children's enjoyment is a "lark." In this way, the Beatles' birds are also indebted to the British Romantic tradition,[37] whose poets used birds as vehicles of pathetic fallacy reflecting a speaker's emotional state. The chirpy birds of their cover of the "Till There Was You" (from *The Music Man*) seem to be the same ones feeding on the ground in "Good Day Sunshine," evoking the kind of "joyance" Coleridge wants to hear in the nightingale's song.[38] In

Richard Avedon's series of psychedelic headshots, a white dove perches on Starr's hand, perhaps a nod to Ringo's get-along affability. In 1969, Lennon and Yoko Ono gave an interview holding paper doves, symbols of their "War Is Over" peace slogan; that image also appears on Lennon's "Man of the Year" *Rolling Stone* cover in February 1970.

Never ones to take themselves too seriously (when they were together at least), the Beatles used birds to joke around. During the 1962 performance at the Star Club in Hamburg, Lennon inserts a ridiculous-sounding pelican into McCartney's intentionally saccharine preface to "Till There Was You." When Ringo, in the film *A Hard Day's Night*, accidentally threw a dart into a bird's cage, the squawking is preamble for the drummer getting kicked out of a pub. The silliness continues in the famous 1968 Mad Day Out photoshoot, which resulted in multiple photographs of the band in which a parrot perches on their shoulders while they look earnestly into the camera or play a grand piano.[39]

The sounds of wings flapping introduces and closes "Across the Universe," accentuating imagery of flow and concepts that defy containment. This avian sound effect was reprised in "Free as a Bird." As we mentioned in relation to the band's swan song, the Beatles' birds are sometimes vehicles to explore loss: the sunken-eyed blackbird sings in a dead night, after all. "Blue Jay Way" is the place Harrison's speaker waits for his friends who, like off-track birds, have lost themselves in the foggy material world of Los Angeles, an irony in the "City of Angels." On the *White Album* and contemporaneous with "Blackbird," the eagle tormenting Lennon in "Yer Blues," whose title and content invokes the Black American genre, turns him into a modern-day Prometheus, favorite Greek god of the Shelleys.[40] Ironically, when the Beatles alluded to nursery rhymes on this double record, they were also calling back to their rhythm and blues predecessors, who were themselves continuing folk precedent.

Rock 'n' Roll Nursery Rhymes

The year 1968 witnessed the Beatles revisiting multiple nursery rhymes, plucking them for inspiration like passed-down toys stored in a toybox. Ray Charles's 1960 version of Titus Turner's "Sticks and Stones" is one such example. The Beatles' take on this song is captured in the recordings of the *Get Back / Let It Be* sessions in January 1969, when they were jamming old, remembered tunes to recapture a spirit of yesteryear.[41] The fact that Billy Preston had served as Charles's organist no doubt contributed to his piano-playing on this number and gave the song what it needed. Lennon even announced that "Ray Charles was here" during these sessions.[42] Charles, like other Black Americans the Beatles idolized, was singing the Beatles throughout the 1960s, covering "Something" and "The Long and Winding Road," both inspired by him, on 1971's *Volcanic Action of My Soul*.

Similarly, Fats Domino's take on "Lady Madonna"—a song for which he was muse—was his last charting hit.[43] As McCartney later remembered, "'Lady Madonna' was me sitting down at the piano trying to write a bluesy boogie-woogie thing. It reminded me of Fats Domino for some reason, so I started singing a Fats Domino impression. It took my voice to a very odd place."[44] Perhaps McCartney was realizing something about his interpolation of British nursery rhyme content. In addition to lines beginning with days of the week, the standard line about Sunday's child having grace[45] becomes, in McCartney's "boogie woogie," Monday's child's ability to "tie his boot lace." The song's refrain also uses "see how they run" from another nursery rhyme, "Three Blind Mice" (Roud 3753).[46] These allusions add whimsy to otherwise serious and adult subject matter: the song's Lady Madonna is a struggling single mother with children to feed. The juxtaposition is not unlike the one in Fats Domino's hit "I'm in Love Again," which made a big impression on the Beatles: it was the first rock 'n' roll song Harrison ever heard,[47] and they lifted its speaker's promise for "All My Loving."[48]

The chorus of Fats Domino's "I'm in Love Again," begins "Eenie meenie and miney-mo," a line derived from a popular counting rhyme (Roud 18278). By the end of the nineteenth century, variations of this rhyme were found in Scotland and Ireland, but they were even more ubiquitous in the United States, where the opening line was most often followed by "Catch a n—— by his toe."[49] This line, a racist "American corruption,"[50] did not become popular in the United Kingdom and, of course, did not appear in Domino's song. Still, his chorus seems to be in conversation with versions of the counting rhyme that called for the pursuit of Black people running away. The chorus of "I'm in Love Again" ends with "Don't let your dog bite me," voicing resistance to those who would pursue and catch. The vestiges of slavery and the still-continuing oppressions of Jim Crow were woven into a song about sexual teasing.

When the Beatles drew on nursery rhymes, they were playing with the kinds of folk texts long reworked by Black people in the Americas, although, as white British men, the Beatles weren't articulating Black subjectivity. The Beatles' penchant for nursery rhymes also corresponded to the revival of British kitsch in the late 1960s. Relics of a white colonial past were available to fashionable Londoners in vintage shops like I Was Lord Kitchener's Valet that pedaled military and other garb. This Notting Hill store commemorated an earl decorated for his leadership in the Boer Wars and World War I. In the 1940s, when Trinidadian-born Aldwyn Roberts adopted Lord Kitchener as a sobriquet, the calypsonian was Signifyin(g) on British imperialism.[51] But white rockers of the late 1960s weren't engaging in same kind of critique when they donned neo-Edwardian accoutrements and rejected the sleek modernity of tailored mod suits. Announcing their playful, escapist agenda with *Sgt. Pepper*'s uniforms in 1967, the Beatles retreated via style into an idealized past, where the sun never set on the British Empire.

A royal estate is the setting of another nursery rhyme *White Album* track, "Cry Baby Cry." This song borrows from "Sing a Song of Sixpence" (Roud 13191), which features the most well-known of all blackbird choruses in the genre. The singing, escaping creatures' vocal insistence on their freedom in a rhyme traced to the sixteenth century has been read as a thumb at the king's authority.[52] One of those fleeing blackbirds gets revenge by pecking the nose of a maid "in the garden" (a phrase Lennon used for his king's location). This maid could have been Anne Boleyn, revealing the song's provenance in folklore about Henry VIII, one of the world's most famous divorcers of wives.[53] Perhaps not coincidentally, this song's composition, recording, and release coincided with Lennon's own divorce proceedings, which made his union with Yoko Ono possible.

In British folk culture, birds and pies are connected for another reason: vestiges of bird heads were once routinely carved into pie dough; after baking, escaping steam made the birds appear to sing.[54] Pies, still so beloved among the British, have long been useful objects, whether for hiding things, such as secret correspondence,[55] or doubling meaning, like the sex joke McCartney includes in the "fish-and-finger pie" line of "Penny Lane." Pies abound in the Beatles' oeuvre. Lennon even fabricated a story about "a man on a flaming pie" as the source for the spelling of "Beatles with an A."[56] In "Cry Baby Cry," Lennon tweaks the royal scenes of "Sing a Song of Sixpence" depicting his king and queen in various domestic spaces while leaving out the pie-escaping blackbirds. With this nursery rhyme context in mind, others have assumed that the pie-fleeing blackbirds of "Sixpence" do show up elsewhere on the *White Album*. As Ian MacDonald observes, "The ['Sixpence'] rhyme's reference to blackbirds suggest that Lennon heard McCartney singing 'Blackbird' in Rishikesh and free-associated his own ironic and sinister train of thought."[57]

When McCartney urges his blackbird to fly, he actually recalls a direction given to the title characters in a different nursery rhyme, "Two Little Blackbirds," also known as "Two Little Dicky Birds" (Roud 16401). These two birds were initially Jack and Gill but were renamed after the apostles Peter and Paul in the nineteenth century. The title characters are told to "fly away" and "come back"; the lilting rhyme's associated fingerplay has made the song popular among British children "for at least two centuries."[58] One of these youngsters was almost certainly McCartney, who probably enjoyed his own name's presence in the rhyme and eventually used its related colloquial expression for saying nothing. "Not a dickie bird," chirps McCartney in 2001's "She's Given Up Talking," whose short rhyming lines and playground scenes evoke a nursery rhyme sensibility as well as the most mockingbird-featuring folk lullaby, "Hush, Little Baby" (Roud 470).

In the twenty-first century, McCartney used a lesser-known bird-girl image from "Sixpence" when he named a song character "Jenny Wren"; in the nursery rhyme, she sweetly restores the maid's pecked-off nose. This happens to be the nursemaid function of McCartney's "brave" title character in "Jenny Wren" (2005), a song he, ever the birdwatcher, credited to his affinity for actual wrens and to Charles Dickens's so-named character in *Our Mutual Friend* (Paul's favorite book).[59] For McCartney, the Dickens character is synonymous with the actual singer Jenny Lind. He explains that he imagines his Jenny Wren as "a great singer," adding a caveat: "The kids may no longer have heard of her, but my parents' and grandparents' generations knew of the great Swedish opera singer Jenny Lind, whom they used to refer to as Jenny Wren."[60] The latter applies the name of the Dickens character from *Our Mutual Friend* to Lind, even though her more ubiquitous nickname was the "Swedish Nightingale."

In *The Lyrics*, McCartney also compares "Jenny Wren" to "Blackbird," relating them as optimistic bird songs; elsewhere in that book, he mentions Liverpool's function as a slave port when discussing "Blackbird."[61] He has thus come close to realizing a very deep and complicated history he *could* attach to these songs, especially when it comes to singing women and bird names. Lind's nickname, the Swedish Nightingale, was a progenitor in the nineteenth-century practice of giving women singers bird-related nicknames, including that of Elizabeth Taylor Greenfield, the Black Swan. But Lind's nickname was also the inspiration for a notorious slave ship that embarked from Liverpool. So, when McCartney mentions Lind in relation to "Jenny Wren," a bird song he compares to "Blackbird," he broaches other events in the nineteenth century, when blackbirds and nightingales converged in the transatlantic slave trade.

Blackbirds and Nightingales in Liverpool

With its system of river and canal access points, the Beatles' home city has been long characterized by its function as a transitional port, especially for merchant sailors and immigrants bound to America from England, the Continent, and other places. The explorer Richard Burton, in fact, sailed from Liverpool to West Africa on a steamship named the *Blackbird* on August 24, 1861.[62] The city also headquartered the White Star Line, the company that launched the RMS *Titanic* from the city's docks in 1912. That sunken ship was an extremely popular topic for early twentieth-century folk songs, especially among Black Americans who recognized the ironic dimensions of the ship's fate in light of its rejection of Black passengers.[63] Lead Belly, for example, began to sing his ballad "The Titanic" in 1912.

A century before, Liverpool established itself as a major port by becoming a dominant outpost in the transatlantic slave trade. West Africans who survived the horrors of the Middle Passage were exchanged in the Americas for sugar and other raw materials brought back to England to be milled in bourgeoning industrial towns. The eighteenth-century Liverpool gentry, including a string of mayors, garnered wealth by investing in these ships.[64] The Beatles themselves were not descended from the Liverpool elite,[65] but the slave trade helped build infrastructure and industry that shaped the city. Lennon alluded to this legacy while remembering his many musical influences:

> Liverpool is a very poor city, and tough. But people have a sense of humor because they are in so much pain. So they are always cracking jokes, and they are very witty. It's an Irish place, too; it is where the Irish came when they ran out of potatoes, and it's where black people were left or worked as slaves or whatever. It is cosmopolitan, and it's where sailors would come home with blues records from America. Liverpool has the biggest country & western following in England besides London—always besides London because there is more of it there. I heard country & western music in Liverpool before I heard rock & roll.[66]

Lennon recognized the port city's association with the slave trade, but his offhanded reference glossed over the complex history of Black people in Liverpool, where a "Black presence" was "multidimensional."[67] Still, the former Beatle acknowledged a necessary truth: some enslaved Black people were brought to Liverpool, which has continued to grapple with its foundations in the slave trade.[68]

The twentieth-century city Lennon described was preceded by earlier transatlantic crossings in the nineteenth century, when the term "blackbirder" was used for "men who kidnapped laborers from plantations."[69] More evidence of this appears in conjunction with the voyage of the *Nightingale* in

1860, when the word "blackbirding" was used in the Liverpool press in reference to the act of kidnapping Africans and the role that Liverpool waterways played in that illegal activity.[70]

Even though the international trade was made illegal at the beginning of the nineteenth century, some outgoing slave ships were still being outfitted in Liverpool.[71] Formerly a cruise ship, the *Nightingale* was one such vessel, and its eventual interception was a major headline.[72] In the United States and the United Kingdom, newspapers repudiated the ship's mission as if it were a singularity, despite widespread awareness of such illegal ship makeovers. As Marika Sherwood explains, "The *Liverpool Mercury* and the *Liverpool Post* [were] both in a position to have been well aware of what was happening on the city's River Mersey." The Liverpool papers nevertheless speculated about whether the *Nightingale* was even outfitted in Liverpool, reasoning that, if this were indeed the case, "there can be no doubt but that the Government will cause inquiry to be made, and if possible, teach those interested in the trade that 'nightingales' cannot go a-blackbirding with impunity."[73] The pairing of these two birds—the nightingale and the blackbird—to refer to the kidnapping of Africans is a grim irony. The mythic provenance of the nightingale's call in Western culture is the Greek Philomela's sorrowful song, a remembrance of her assault.[74] The association between nightingale and blackbird is also ironic if we consider another pairing, that which involves the aforementioned nineteenth-century women singers.

Nineteenth-Century Women Singers: From the Swedish Nightingale, Jenny Lind, to the Black Swan, Elizabeth Taylor Greenfield

When the *Nightingale* went "a-blackbirding," it did so with a vestige of Jenny Lind at the helm. Her likeness had been made into a bust that graced the stern of the ship, paralleling "the many white male expressions of longing littering Lind's press." Around the same time Lind was being promoted to global fame by P. T. Barnum, Elizabeth Taylor Greenfield was a well-known Black American concert singer popular among white and Black listeners in the northern United States. Celebrated for her extraordinary alto-to-soprano vocal range, Greenfield's repertoire included "opera, arias, sentimental parlor songs, ballads of the British Isles, and the occasional hymn," songs that were conventionally the domain of upper- to middle-class white women.[75] These gender and class dynamics intersected with Greenfield's Blackness, which white listeners were simultaneously fascinated by, fixated on, confused by, and anxious about, both in America as well as abroad in England.

Comparing women to birds enabled an "elite white male" press to render women's singing effortless; but when reviews of Lind and Greenfield occupied the same papers, Lind "suddenly possesses far more agency and scientific control when the white press pits her against Greenfield."[76] So, even though the "[Black Swan] sobriquet exemplified the nineteenth-century practice of referring to female singers with bird nicknames," "the obviously racialized [nickname] also called attention to Greenfield's former slave status and thus simultaneously distanced her from these European contemporaries."[77]

Greenfield's 1851 performance debut came at the zenith of blackface minstrel shows. For some reviewers, the nickname "Black Swan" was a way of interpreting and positioning her within that genre even though Greenfield's style was inconsistent with minstrel tropes.[78] She did eventually adopt it as a symbol of her artistry,[79] but the assignment still marked her as Other, more historical evidence of the racist applications of black-colored birds for Black people. The swan association carried with it implicit doubts and even insults. Honking swans are not known for sweet songs, a swan song has a fleeting connotation (last heard before death), and black swans are long-standing symbols for rarities or impossibilities.[80] She was indeed lauded by many, but the Black Swan moniker was a vehicle for white reviewers to diminish a Black woman performing "white" musical genres. One paper called her the "African Crow."[81]

The Black press and prominent Black figures, such as Frederick Douglass, also paid attention to Greenfield and her name, but with mixed feelings. Even though some reviewers writing for his paper praised "the magnificent quality of [Greenfield's] voice,"[82] Douglass's once-favorable opinion changed when he perceived "her seeming lack of a public voice in the antislavery fight."[83] He Signified on her nickname, critiquing her "white mimicry," and assigned another bird name: "The Conduct of the Black Swan (if not exaggerated) should be reprobated by the colored people. She should no longer be called the Black Swan, but the White Raven.—F.D."[84]

Greenfield had notable white supporters, including Harriet Beecher Stowe, who helped sponsor Greenfield's ongoing musical training in England. In 1854, Greenfield performed for Queen Victoria—the first Black American to do so. Just as it had in the States, the blackface minstrel tradition informed Greenfield's reception in London because, as Eric Lott notes, British audiences were also predisposed to that genre's racist tropes, which led to more misinterpretation. The Fisk Jubilee Singers, for example, encountered similar assumptions related to minstrelsy in the 1870s.[85]

The product of transatlantic exchange in the nineteenth century, minstrel songs popular in America had found firm footholds in the United Kingdom, too, something Greenfield's critic, Douglass, witnessed firsthand. Fifteen years after receiving a welcome reception in England, Douglass returned to the United Kingdom and was deeply troubled by the rise of "American prejudice" he encountered in "the streets of Liverpool" circa 1860. He connected the rise of racism in Britain with "that pestiferous nuisance, Ethiopian minstrels," who "brought here the slang phrases, the contemptuous sneers all originating in the spirit of slavery."[86] Minstrel performances and song content were popular in Ireland, too, and into the twentieth century, when blackface minstrel themes and imagery are found in James Joyce's modernist fiction, including his novel *Ulysses*.[87]

Given the Irish makeup of twentieth-century Liverpool (evidenced in the Beatles' own ethnic heritage), the Irish association with blackface minstrelsy bears noting. Back in the 1820s and 1830s, "blackface performance began with mostly Irish and English working-class American men darkening their faces with burnt cork, wearing tattered clothing, using stereotyped 'black' dialect, and cavorting on stage to tunes that were mostly adopted from blackface sheet music."[88] Emphasizing the role of Irish American working-class men in blackface performance, Matthew D. Morrison references (and revises) Lott, pointing to the anxieties and racism on display in minstrel theater.[89] These origins, Morrison argues in his recent theory of "Blacksound," are necessary to understanding "the political implications of embodying, making, and commercializing popular music in the United States," whose "music industry, which developed out of blackface, has remained one of the most influential markets of popular music worldwide."[90]

Within the nineteenth-century minstrel milieu, Greenfield's legacy as the Black Swan further establishes the profoundly polysemous nature of birds as song imagery prior to the twentieth century. In the 1920s, still before the Beatles, Florence Mills announced herself a "little blackbird." Mills and her fellow Black performers continued to navigate minstrel tropes in the United States and abroad—including London and Liverpool.

CHAPTER 3

I'm a Little Blackbird

Florence Mills, Blackbirds of the Harlem Renaissance, and the Beatles' Jazz Age Predecessors

Before she became the blackbird of the Harlem Renaissance, Florence Mills was charming audiences in 1890s Washington, DC, as the child performer "Baby Flo." One relative described the eventual Broadway star as if Mills were a bird: "Florence loved to dance, to spread joy and happiness. Why, her eyes would light like ship flares when she heard music. . . . She would throw out her little limbs, and her arms would go waving, swaying, flying. It didn't seem to us children as if she touched the sidewalk."[1]

Years later, when a twenty-eight-year-old Florence unveiled "I'm a Little Blackbird Looking for a Bluebird," she publicly dazzled with a song that catapulted her to international stardom—and forever linked her with the blackbird. The song stands as testament to how she "made racial equality integral to her star persona."[2] Two generations removed from a maternal grandfather who was a freed slave,[3] Mills performed her blackbird-centric number fully aware of its lyrical appeals for equality, heightening that theme with her sympathetic delivery. In doing so, Mills has the original claim on the blackbird both as a singer's internationally distributed brand and an image of racial equality in twentieth-century popular song. A persistent sense of uplift is palpable in Mills's identification with the blackbird, still a symbol of her artistry in the work of those celebrating her contributions.

Even though many racist modes from the past century had remained in place, there is no doubt that the Jazz Age brought change, and Harlem Renaissance performers elevated Black arts to new heights.[4] Mills's blackbird persona also calls back to the previous century's tradition of bird-named women singers, particularly the "Black Swan," concert singer Elizabeth Taylor Greenfield. Like Greenfield, Mills performed for audiences that included British royalty in England, where the lineages of blackface minstrelsy still haunted the reception of Mills and her fellow "blackbirds" three-quarters of a century later. The correlation between Black singers and blackbirds is further ironic when we consider other Jazz Age songs, such as "Bye Bye Blackbird," a known influence on Paul McCartney and the other Beatles. The use of blackbird-as-song-image, whether in Mills's "I'm a Little Blackbird Looking for a Bluebird" or its contemporary "Bye Bye Blackbird," is double-edged, recalling W. E. B. Du Bois's notion of "two-ness" as the state of Black people in America.[5] Du Bois himself interacted with Mills, whose own writing and other discourse was also influenced by Du Bois. His insight applies to hers and other blackbirds, which are similarly paradoxical, both caged *and* free, trapped *and* liberated in American popular song. As a symbol of transatlantic flight, the blackbird traverses but does not transcend: history lives within it, as the background relating to Mills and her song illustrates.

"I'm a Little Blackbird Looking for a Bluebird": Florence Mills, Broadway, and Lew Leslie's Revues

Florence Mills was the most popular Black woman on Broadway in the 1920s. She was the requisite triple threat with superb comedic timing, signature tap-dancing ability, and a showstopping soprano voice. In the absence of recordings of Mills, Stephanie Doktor has theorized Mills's vocal abilities and characteristics based, in part, on written reviews (which often reflect racial bias). In the following passage, Doktor's analysis elucidates persistent tensions in Mills's performances,[6] which were sweet and strong, inviting and assertive, so skillful as to appear effortless:

> American critic Paul Rosenfeld said her voice was so pure "it was not a human voice at all." Mills was a soprano, and many listeners commented on her "sweet," "pure," and "delicate" voice, indicating that she did not have noticeable passaggi and relied mostly on her "head voice" register— or what is now more commonly referred to, among vocal pedagogues, as CT dominance. Critics wrote about Mills's wide range and the ease with which she navigated it. Like the flute to which she was compared, her attack was gentle, her vocal weight was light, suggesting her pitch was precise, and florid vocal lines came easily.[7]

Celebrated (and objectified) for her sweet voice, adorable mannerisms, slim build, and expressive eyes, Mills's breakout role was in *Shuffle Along* (1921), whose music was written by Eubie Blank with lyrics by Noble Sissle. That revue was the first Black-authored, Black-composed, Black-produced musical with an all-Black cast in Broadway history. *Shuffle Along* was a milestone for the Harlem Renaissance and African American theater, but the show still grappled with colorism in both casting and content.[8] Mills did not stay with the production long, soon joining producer Lew Leslie's *Plantation Revue*, a 1922 show modeled on cabaret performances at his "swanky, up-market, up-town" Plantation Room.[9] As Mills biographer Bill Egan explains, "Once fame arrived, after *Shuffle Along*, [Mills] saw the opportunity to use her new status to benefit her fellow black performers. Lew Leslie shrewdly used this to persuade her to stay with him rather than take up Ziegfeld's historic offer to make her the first black woman to star in the *Follies*."[10] With Leslie, Mills continued to garner more appeal across racial lines all over the United States and abroad, especially in the next London-based revue, *Dover Street to Dixie* in 1923.

Leslie's revues were distinctive for their promotion of all-Black talent. This unprecedented representation was lauded by Black critics, who recognized Mills's skillful performances, too. But as the plantation-themed names and titles suggest, the Leslie-produced revues in which Mills performed traded in blackface minstrel tropes, to which Mills was no stranger given her years on the vaudeville circuit, where she met her husband, fellow performer Ulysses "Slow Kid" Thompson. This background shaped her perspective from an early age: as a three-year-old, Mills started crying onstage when she saw a white man wearing cork on his face.[11] Zakiya R. Adair recognizes an adult Mills's polysemous performances, which often Signified on racist content, appealing to Black audiences while entertaining white audiences, too: "Mills' comedic performances used African American song and dance styles like the *Cake Walk* and the *Charleston* to perform racial identities that when presented for an international audience conflated varied African-derived populations. Although white audiences may not have understood the satirical aspects of Mills' performances, the parody would not have been lost on African American audiences."[12] Florence's performances routinely Signified on blackface minstrelsy and other stereotypes of Black artists, ironizing racist tropes with comedy and critiquing their effects with pathos—especially when she became the little blackbird.

On October 29, 1924, Mills introduced "I'm a Little Blackbird Looking for a Bluebird" to New York City theatergoers as part of the musical revue *Dixie to Broadway*, again produced by Leslie.[13] The song (music by Arthur Johnston and George W. Meyer and lyrics by Grant Clarke and Roy Turk) was written specifically for her. It was, as Egan explains, "the vehicle through which Mills sought to project her passionate plea for racial tolerance." The seemingly "simple" song was complicated by her "extraordinary blend of pathos and humor . . . [as well as] the sincerity with which she sought to project its message."[14] Mills's performances were socially conscious and deeply affective; when she sang about aspiring to a better life, the lyrics recalled her own journey from impoverished beginnings in Jim Crow Washington, DC. Poor treatment was not limited to the American South, though. In her theatrical career in vaudeville and later on Broadway, Mills was no stranger to racism (and sexism) given the "color bar" that kept casts segregated.[15]

When she performed her signature tune, Mills delivered the song as "an anthem of racial tolerance and a plea for justice," which was "widely understood and appreciated by her own people and by audiences generally."[16] The song's lyrics, especially as Mills sang them, made the racial dynamics clear: bluebirds enjoy what forlorn blackbirds—doomed to loneliness and tears—are denied. Bluebirds are also desired objects, comparable in the verses to other whimsical objects. The song's avian content and other imagery was an occasion for Mills to Signify on "stereotypes of Black musicians with a direct confrontation of one of the most pejorative terms associated with her profession: jazzbo, a racial slur used to mark Black musicians, in particular, and Black Americans, in general, as vulgar and less human. Verse two challenges reigning concepts of racial difference: 'Tho' I'm of a darker hue, I've a heart the same as you.'"[17]

As Mills herself explained, "There is a little song I sing on the stage that indicates the Negro's attitude toward life. He is very much a small boy flattening his nose against a pastry-cook's window and looking for all the good things on the other side of the pane."[18] She added, "[The boy] wants so badly to 'belong'—and as yet there is no place for him."[19] Connecting this imagery to the song's opening verse, Mills elaborated about the lonely bird: "'Never had no happiness. Never felt no one's caress. I'm just a lonesome bit of humanity. Born on Friday, I guess. . . . If the sun forgets no one, why don't it shine on me. I'm a little blackbird looking for a bluebird, too."[20] Mills's critique, Doktor explains, "extends a tradition of Black women intellects such as Ida B. Wells, Gwendolyn B. Bennett, and Zora Neal Hurston. Mills used both her singing and writing voices to express 'the higher and more modern ambitions of Negro Youth.'"[21] When Mills correlated her blackbird to a small boy, she might also have been referencing some of the song's source material.

Drawing on existing connections between looking for bluebirds and the search for happiness (especially as health and material comfort), the conceit of "I'm a Little Blackbird" was immediately legible to theatergoers, whose associations were fostered by the popularity of Belgian poet and playwright Maurice Maeterlinck's 1908 play *The Blue Bird* (*L'Oiseau bleu*). The title referred to the play's "Blue Bird of Happiness," which, along with a fairy named Berylune, accompanies a boy and girl (Tyltyl and Mytyl) on a journey to learn about happiness. Rather than being envious of the rich, whose wealth doesn't really make them happy, the children learn that true joy comes from appreciating the meager comforts one has—and in giving them away. At the end of the play, Tyltyl is made to give a sickly girl his bird, which suddenly flies away just as the play draws to a close. Tyltyl vows to catch the bluebird again, and the stage directions call for him to move downstage, breaking the fourth wall to enlist the audience's help in locating his bird: "If any of you should find him, would you be so very kind as to give him back to us? . . . We need him for our happiness, later on."[22] Despite everything that has happened throughout the course of the play, happiness remains a dream to recover. The play's little boy is very much like the one Mills mentioned, the one pressing his face against the pane in hopes of getting his piece of the pie.

"I'm a Little Blackbird Looking for a Bluebird" is an individualist spin on the play's themes: Mills's song requests access to the American dream white people have aspired to, a dream troped as a pursuit of the bluebird, whose feathers Mills sang about wanting for her nest. Another lyrical comparison parallels the logic of the bluebird-blackbird inequality: "I'm a little jazzbo looking for a rainbow, too / Building fairy castles, just like all the white folks do." Mills popularized the song during a cultural moment in which Black people's artistry—particularly in jazz-inflected music and dance—was being fetishized and co-opted by whites, who were still legally disenfranchising, segregating, and oppressing the very same Black Americans they mimicked and desired. Mills even addressed this in an interview. After denying that she had purchased a Park Avenue home, she explained, "In America we [Black people] have our own restaurants and cabarets and theatres, and your people come to see our shows. The white people say, 'Let's go slumming,' they seek us out."[23]

According to Maeterlinck's play, no person is guaranteed the bluebird of happiness, but "I'm a Little Blackbird" acknowledges that white people are, at the very least, allowed to look for it. Unlike almost all other Black Americans, Mills—with her talent, Broadway success, and widespread fame—was able to enact that search and apparently achieve its goal. One of Mills's nicknames, the "Queen of Happiness,"[24] even transposes the bluebird's key attribute onto her, the self-proclaimed blackbird. But Mills was also conscious of her obligation to the community, as she told the London press: "I want to help the colored people. . . . I realize that, in my line of work, I am doing much to help them. The stage is the quickest way to get to the people. My own success makes people think better of other colored folk. . . . I must say that I have found in London nothing but kindness and friendliness. . . . I have met lots of wonderful people, willing to help us in our great struggle. We have been given a chance to prove our worthiness and to feel that we are free."[25] Here, Mills associated performing on stage with freedom, underlining the correlation between singers and birds. She is encouraging, like the "wise old owl" who appears at the end of "I'm a Little Blackbird" to motivate the blackbird (i.e., Mills).

Through her bird-centric song, Mills thus "subverted the racist subtext," as Adair points out: "The song's comparison of African Americans to animals, in particular black birds, exemplifies dominant and racist attempts to construct African Americans as essentially savage and wild. Mills' reinterpretation of the song shifted the songs' racist overtones to focus on racial injustice."[26]

Singing the Blackbird: Mills's Transatlantic Reception in the 1920s

Mills's association with the blackbird was nourished by critics' reliance on such metaphors: "Descriptions of Florence Mills appeared frequently between 1921 and 1927 in the Black and white press, in US and European publications, and in personal accounts and works of literature. Writers most often compared her voice to birds and sometimes flutes—highlighting both her high range and pure timbre." Recognizing that Mills's reception was "rife with gendered and racialized stereotypes," Doktor provides a sampling of descriptions emphasizing birds and air:

> For Alberta Hunter, Mills "was a hummingbird and dainty and lovely. Her little voice was as sweet as [Bessie Smith's] was rough." Some listeners describe a "bubbling" sound in [Mills's] voice—a "little pulse in her throat, throbbing like a bird," which I interpret as referring to her vibrato. One critic claimed she had "heart-taking bubbles of sound thronging out of her throat like champagne from a bottle." These descriptions imply that her vibrato was fast and narrow. Since Mills's voice was quiet, she would naturally have a smaller vibrato. Hers did not disturb the pitch but rather enhanced it, giving her flute-like voice depth and warmth. British author Beverly Nichols said her voice was "distinctly silvery" and described her singing as "high silver notes like beams of light, floating

into the dark auditorium." Such a description elucidates the way in which her vibrato created a luscious tone.[27]

This documentation survives but Mills's recorded voice does not. In this absence, Doktor has theorized the "sonic properties" of Mills's voice, considering the aforementioned critics' written accounts, but also reconstructing sound through music written for Mills by William Grant Still's *Levee Land* (1925) and Edmund Thornton Jenkins's *Afram* (1924). These African American composers, Doktor argues, "imagined a much more musically complicated and politically powerful voice than that found in the racialized and gendered stereotypes permeating both her vaudeville and Broadway repertory and the language of her reception."[28]

When made by white reviewers, Mills's bird comparisons are double-edged: they reflect racist tropes related to primitivism[29] while also taking Mills up on the blackbird identity she fostered as a plea for equality. The avian vocal associations were also linked to visual and other aesthetics. One French reviewer described Mills as having a "nightingale voice and brilliant eyes."[30] A London reviewer complimented her "lovely voice with its haunting cadences and flutelike quality," along with her "wonderful sense of humour." British journalists paid frequent attention to her size, especially her "slender" and "slim" wrists, hands, and ankles, rendering her weightless in both physicality and affect.[31] As Adair notes, Mills had already been functioning as a "blank slate" onto which the British press could project "their pseudo-scientific and hierarchal racial and ethnic demarcations. In a 1923 theater review in the *London Mail*, Mills was described as appearing 'not Negress' but more like 'a very sunburnt Italian.'"[32]

Correlations with birds were amplified when Mills wore feathery costumes as she did in a publicity photograph for Leslie's *Black Birds* of 1926. In this black-and-white picture, she faces the camera directly; she is inviting but assertive in her white feathered headdress with dangling white feathers that brush her collarbone. As a fashion columnist described, "Curiously fascinating, I assure you, is the contrast between dusky skin and shimmering white satin embroidered with diamante and a foam of white ostrich feathers over chiffon. Florence Mills wears this feather-skirted gown, and has a white wig, too."[33] This description belies audience fascination (and fixation) with her racial identity, as well as Mills's sex appeal and sexual objectification during a historical moment when feathers were read as signifiers of women's sexuality. Relevant here is the complicated legacy of gendered and racial (and racist) associations between birds and women singers that we encountered with Greenfield, whose bird name was not always a compliment, especially among white reviewers.

Also associated with flappers, feathers remained popular on the vaudeville circuit, a reminder of persisting nineteenth-century minstrel tropes. More specifically, the white ostrich feathers mentioned in the above description of Mills were a *Ziegfeld Follies* aesthetic for the dancing girls in the revues produced by Florenz Ziegfeld Jr. In 1930s-era film costuming, feathers were later used to communicate implicitly about sex to get around the Hays Code—such was the shared meaning of feathers.[34] So, although she was cute and youthful, when Mills sang about wanting a bluebird feathering her nest, she was also voicing some desire. Songs such as "I'm a Little Blackbird" and "Mandy, Make Up Your Mind" capitalized on her multifaceted appeal with the latter song an occasion for Mills to wear a formal tuxedo, illustrative of her gender-bending performances.

Illustrating the circulation of one of the looks described above, as well as her broad stardom and visibility, Du Bois himself dictated a letter asking that she send him a picture of herself, "that photograph with the white wig."[35] Du Bois's letter, which threatens to cut Mills off if she does not comply with his request,[36] is not the most significant evidence of their association. As Doktor explains, "Just before her death, [Mills] wrote an article, 'The Soul of the Negro,' addressing the effects of white supremacy on the day-to-day realities of Black lives. Echoing W. E. B. Du Bois's 'double consciousness' theorized in his similarly titled book, *The Souls of Black Folk* (1903), Mills wrote: 'It is the eternal burden of the coloured people—the penalisation for an accident of birth—to be made to feel out of focus with the rest of humanity. . . . How absurd it all is—how utterly unfair!'" The statement is another example of how Mills's spoken and written discourse "directly confronted white supremacy, reflecting the political tenor of the New Negro movement."[37]

As the singer of a bird-centric song, the "Harlem Jazz Queen"[38] exemplified themes consistent with the trope of Flying Africans when she named the sources of Black people's oppression (in the song itself as well as interviews) and spoke about community uplift. Mills frequently discussed her personal artistry as bound to the collective: "I belong to a race that sings and dances as it breathes. I don't care where I am, so long as I can sing and dance. The wide world is my stage and I am my audience. If I didn't feel like that I wouldn't be an artist. The things you do best for other people are the things you would do just as well for yourself."[39]

Mills's "I'm a Little Blackbird" thus reveals the irony of the song's medium and message. When Mills and her castmates (as well as those in Leslie's subsequent revues) sang under the guise of a blackbird, the issue of race was explicit: Black performers gave voice to causes and ongoing conditions of their inequality. Mills enumerated these conditions in interviews, mentioning examples of "mammies [who] bring up white babies" as well as educated Black men who, despite their training, couldn't get hired as lawyers and doctors.[40] As Doktor notes,

> Beginning in 1924 [the year she debuted "I'm a Little Blackbird"], Mills became increasingly vocal about racial inequality after spending time in London, where, like many Black artists, she laid claim to greater freedom and less discrimination. Stories circulated in the Black press about her courageous challenges to Jim Crow segregation in the music theater industry. For example, she declined to take the lead in a play that reportedly "degraded the race." At an after party celebrating *Blackbirds*, she also refused to leave her Black cast members at dinner to join the white guests, saying "I am coal Black and proud of it."[41]

At the same time, performances of white-authored songs in a white-produced show capitalized on the Otherness of Blackness and white audiences' fascination with it. Even though Mills spoke highly of her experiences in England,[42] her British audiences were certainly inclined to fetishize Black Americans as well.[43]

Blackbirds in Liverpool and Mills's Legacy

The persistence of nineteenth-century blackface minstrelsy in popular culture stretched well into the twentieth century in both the United Kingdom and United States: "Even as late as the Depression, the Federal Theatre Project of the Works Progress Administration was sponsoring minstrel shows." Bing Crosby (whose film oeuvre includes other minstrel content) actually played Dan Emmett, wearing "occasional blackface" in the 1943 film *Dixie*. And "in Britain, blackface minstrelsy lasted even longer—the *Black and White Minstrel Show* was on TV every Saturday night through 1978."[44] More than a hundred years after blackface minstrelsy originated, music and artwork founded on it continued to facilitate the association between Black people and black-colored birds for racist ends, a legacy found in early Walt Disney animation, such as the crows in 1941's *Dumbo*.

The Beatles, who loved American films (especially by Disney) when they were kids in the 1940s and coming of age in the 1950s, were not immune to the minstrel milieu. Their parents' generation was definitely familiar with these tropes as well as Black jazz-age music. Although all of the Beatles were habituated to music through their families, McCartney was especially attuned to that of his father, James, a self-taught pianist and trumpet player. In addition to leading the jazz-oriented "Jim Mac's Band," the elder McCartney was also known to play ragtime tunes around Liverpool.[45] During the late 1920s, when Jim Mac was in his twenties and still enjoying his bachelor days, Liverpool had, in fact, hosted Mills and her fellow Black American Broadway performers, who performed under the moniker *Black Birds*. So, even as Florence Mills embraced the bird's subjectivity to issue an explicit plea for equality, she was still navigating racist holdovers of minstrelsy in her reception at home and abroad.

Dixie to Broadway turned out to be the launch of what became a series of blackbird-centric revues, starting with *Black Birds* in 1926; each subsequent revue was distinguished by its corresponding year (i.e., *Blackbirds of* [insert year]). The inaugural revue sought to capitalize on Mills's growing popularity as encapsulated by "her" song, and so with *Black Birds* Mills brought the message of equality to England, where she told Londoners that she "never felt slighted" according to the same *Daily Express* interview cited above.[46] She had previously performed abroad, but *Black Birds* further catapulted Mills to international stardom. The popularity of this revue was confirmed by the repeat attendance of Edward, Prince of Wales; as Mills's husband remembered, "[the prince] sat right in the front row and sang songs with Florence."[47]

The European tour in which Mills sang her ode to equality turned tragic, however. During the summer of 1927, she gave her last performance in *Black Birds* at Liverpool's Empire Theatre, which also hosted her goodbye party[48] (this theater would later be the venue in which McCartney saw a life-changing Lonnie Donegan concert). Mills had contracted pelvic tuberculosis, and she died following an operation in October 1927. Her death devastated Harlem's Black community while dashing Leslie's plans to make her the centerpiece of later revues; he eventually tried to get Lena Horne to sing like Mills, who was also in talks for film projects before she died.[49]

Mills's funeral amplified her correlation with the blackbird: reports claimed that an actual flock of blackbirds flew overhead. Egan doubts their release was planned, insisting that the red-wing variety "is common to the eastern regions of the United States and forms large flocks." At the time, a *New York World* journalist made the bird association in his tribute: "Florence Mills played to her last 'house' yesterday. It was the greatest show Harlem has had, or is likely to have again until another blackbird dances and sings her way from the tenements to such far-flung popularity."[50] After she died, many musicians soon composed and recorded tributes, including Duke Ellington, who commemorated Mills in "Black Beauty," an instrumental he dedicated to her.[51] This song, "recorded . . . as a piano solo and in a full-blown orchestration," "captures her fleeting stardom in the most enchantingly beautiful melody ever conceived in the stride idiom."[52]

The blackbird stood for Mills back then and is still invoked to characterize her look and legacy now; multiple attempts have been made to tell her story in various musical revues, always with "blackbird" in the title.[53] Renée Watson's 2012 award-winning children's picture book *Harlem's Little Blackbird* makes poignant and specific connections to the civil rights consciousness Mills brought to her signature number. Christian Robinson's attendant illustrations capture the cute mannerisms, slight build, and expressive eyes on which critics constantly remarked. This artwork reinforces the connection between singer and bird: in the book, Mills looks upon blackbirds as a source of inspiration and dances like a bird in the air. Similarly, in 2014, Jonelle Allen mounted the one-woman show *Blackbird: The Florence Mills Story*, in which she took audiences on a journey through the Broadway star's life. She projected photographs of Mills and performed signature numbers such as "I'm a Little Blackbird," dancing in the style of Mills, whom, Allen reminds everyone, was taught to tap by Bill Robinson, better known as Bojangles.[54]

Given the popularity of Mills during the Harlem Renaissance and her association with the blackbird, the relative dearth of US cultural memory about her and "I'm a Little Blackbird" may seem surprising. The song's sympathetic appeals for racial equity, which Mills described as coming "from her soul," were "edited out in more recent performances." Writing in the early 2000s, biographer Egan notes, "The words 'just like all the white folks do' are nowadays typically rendered with the word 'white' changed to 'other' or 'rich.' Furthermore, the second verse, starting, 'Tho' I'm of a darker hue, I've a heart same as you,' is generally omitted completely."[55] Such changes explain why the song's anti-racist intent isn't better preserved. On top of this, Mills's memory is also obscured because no recordings, audio or audiovisual, of her survive.

Months after Mills's initial October 1924 debut, her friend, singer Eva Taylor, did record a version of "I'm a Little Blackbird" in December 1924 with (her husband) Clarence Williams and his Blue Five, which, at this time, included Louis Armstrong and Sidney Bechet.[56] Here, Armstrong's contribution is an occasion to consider another artist who simultaneously tapped into and resisted racist tropes. Armstrong was a master at code-switching, which he learned as he came of age as a dark-skinned Black child in New Orleans.[57] Armstrong's presence on the recording of "I'm a Little Blackbird Looking for a Bluebird" evidences the popularity of blackbird- and bluebird-themed pop standards, especially American tunes written by white authors and performed by Black performers or white performers in and out of blackface. Another such tune, trailing in the wake of Mills's signature song, was "Bye Bye Blackbird."

"Bye Bye Blackbird": Another Double-Voiced Bird

One of the best-known blackbird-titled pop standards, published in 1924 and presented onstage in 1926, is "Bye Bye Blackbird." Its two dominant images—a blackbird and a bluebird—echo those in Mills's "I'm a Little Blackbird Looking for a Bluebird." The white performer Eddie Cantor, a contemporary of Mills on Broadway, popularized "Bye Bye Blackbird" (music by Ray Henderson and lyrics by Mort Dixon). But Cantor's associations with minstrelsy were more obvious: a first-generation Jewish American, he often performed in blackface and introduced the song on the vaudeville stage.

In "Bye Bye Blackbird," the speaker shuns the blackbird's winter night, opting for a journey home to the bluebird's sunshine. The speaker intends to leave the blackbird, who sings "the blues all day right outside of my door," a detail reinforcing racial associations designated in "I'm a Little Blackbird." The speaker of "Bye Bye Blackbird" then promises to go home to the bluebird where "dreams will come true." If we read the blackbird-bluebird associations as Mills articulated them, the song can be read as the rejection of a Black lover or of Blackness more generally. But such a reading becomes more complicated when the song is performed by Black performers. Although Cantor first made it famous, "Bye Bye Blackbird" has been covered by some of the most iconic twentieth-century Black musicians, including Josephine Baker, John Coltrane, Miles Davis, Sammy Davis Jr., Ella Fitzgerald, and Nina Simone, all artists with crossover appeal to white audiences.

Black artists continued to riff on "Bye Bye Blackbird" in other media, too, such as *Pie, Pie Blackbird* (1932).[58] This short film featured the phenomenal tap dancing of the Nicholas Brothers with a premise that merged the logic of "Sing a Song of Sixpence"[59] with "Bye Bye Blackbird." The song does not actually appear in the film, but the movie's spin on its title illustrates the association between Black performers and blackbirds. In the opening number, Nina Mae

McKinney sings a tune about blackbirds in "a master's pie." The rest of the film plays with that gimmick. In fact, the Nicholas Brothers are such "hot" dancers that they end up setting the whole pie on fire by the film's end, their dancing skeletons both proof of their talent and a racist caricature. Along the way, the Brothers perform a friendly dance-off—their tapping evoking flight— in front of gigantic, fabricated pie containing an orchestra led by Eubie Blake and Noble Sissle, who were responsible for the film's music.

Longtime collaborators Blake and Sissle had, in fact, composed the music for *Shuffle Along*, the revue that provided Florence Mills's breakout role prior to her performances of "I'm a Little Blackbird." *Shuffle Along*'s hit, "I'm Just Wild About Harry," was performed by Mills to great acclaim;[60] President Harry S. Truman even adopted it as his campaign slogan, a testament to the song's popularity.[61] Had Mills not died in 1927, it's possible she would have been cast to perform in *Pie, Pie Blackbird* given her association with the blackbird and these musicians. Fats Waller, after all, titled his recorded tribute to Mills "Bye Bye Florence" in 1927, bridging her song with "Bye Bye Blackbird." That year, in "Blackbird Blues" Lonnie Johnson also seemed to riff on the blues-singing blackbird image from "Bye Bye Blackbird." The speaker asks a blackbird why his "baby" left, then imagines the freedom of that bird: "If I was a blackbird / I'd pack my troubles on my back." With the speaker lonely and rejected, the song's ending is conventional to the blues tradition: "Because these black-bird blues," Johnson sings, "Lord, it sure burned me," making it clear just how dangerous the blackbird can be.

"Bye Bye Blackbird" and the Beatles

When the Beatles' caravan to Hamburg departed the English coast (bound for the Hook of Holland) in 1960, they sang "Bye Bye Blackbird" at the ship's stern to punctuate their departure.[62] "Bye Bye Blackbird" had been featured in Cantor's 1953 biopic, amplifying the song into the mid-twentieth century, when the young Beatles encountered this and comparable tunes via their parents and other relatives.[63]

McCartney, reinforcing his ever-present nostalgia, brought this musical education to everyone's attention on his record of covers, *Kisses on the Bottom* (2012). He singles out "Bye Bye Blackbird," situating it in the context of family gatherings: "A lot of these songs, like 'Bye Bye Blackbird,' were ones that I'd sung along with. They're quite complicated, the chords and things. I'd have a bash, and I did eventually become the sort of family piano player, at New

Year, as my Dad got a bit older and I got a bit more capable. But I was always busking it; he knew the real chords, and I had to busk my way around. But it was good enough for the family sing-song."[64] In addition to being a favorite in the McCartney household of Paul's youth, "Bye Bye Blackbird" was well-known among the other young Beatles.[65] Ringo Starr recorded a version of it for his first solo album, *Sentimental Journey* (1970), a tribute to his mother and stepfather.

The extent to which the Beatles understood the racial connotations of "Bye Bye Blackbird" is unclear although we should remember the persistent popularity of blackface minstrelsy in England into the twentieth century. During the 1960s, echoes of "Bye Bye Blackbird" appear in the Beatles' "Baby's in Black" via the pairing of blue and black, whose connotations are swapped: the beloved baby wears black and the speaker feels blue.[66] Later, "Blackbird" uses the basic light-dark motifs available in "Bye Bye Blackbird," although the Beatles song encourages the blackbird to come out of the darkness rather than altogether discarding it for a bluebird's light. The lingering presence of "Bye Bye Blackbird" in 1968 coincides with other McCartney songwriting impulses in the late 1960s, when Paul doubled down on vaudeville nostalgia, recalling his father's style of music in "When I'm 64" and "Honey Pie"—*Kisses on the Bottom* certainly wasn't the first time he got musically wistful.[67]

During the 1960s, "Bye Bye Blackbird" was almost like an inside joke among the Beatles, a reference its members understood. That function comes through McCartney's recollection about the lyrics of "Bye Bye Blackbird," which became "You Never Give Me Your Money" and, before that, "Here, There, and Everywhere": "Then it goes, 'Pack up all my cares and woe' and you go, 'Oh, I know this song!' You finally recognise it. John and I liked that. We used to talk about that as one of things it would be good to do. We gave a kind of nod to it on 'Here, There and Everywhere': 'To lead a better life, I need my love to be here . . .' Whereas in the old days they would have extended that: 'She was here, and I was there, and I think she's everywhere.'"[68] The *Abbey Road* medley, which includes "You Never Give Me Your Money," is often read as an expression of McCartney's desire to keep the band together. This interpretation is aided by the allusion to "Bye Bye Blackbird," which reminded the Beatles of their shared musical and cultural roots in Liverpool.

McCartney continued to reprise the birds and the blue-and-black color pairing from "Bye Bye Blackbird." After the Beatles broke up, Paul and Linda McCartney soon recorded the whimsical "Bluebird," a song about becoming the happy bird and flying away with a lover, who also becomes a bird; together they find sanctuary, an obvious metaphor for McCartney's new musical partnership with his wife. He then performed "Bluebird" back-to-back with "Blackbird" on a television special with Linda.[69] During the 1970s, the two bird-themed songs also made appearances (with one or two songs separating them) during Wings tours.[70] A domestic context, which introduced McCartney to "Bye Bye Blackbird," is the setting of another story about the origins of "Blackbird," one told by his stepmother, Angie McCartney, whose memory we consider in chapter 7. The crows at McCartney's door in "I Don't Know" from his 2018 record *Egypt Station* continue to suggest the memory of "Bye Bye Blackbird."

"Bye Bye Blackbird," Jim Crow, and Selma, 1965

Even though the Beatles weren't invoking blue and black to make a point about race in "Baby's in Black," the memory of those colors' racial connotations in pop standards lingered elsewhere in the 1960s. In March 1965, segregationists amplified "Bye Bye Blackbird" to harass marchers beginning their trek after a rousing speech from the Reverend Dr. Martin Luther King Jr., who also invoked black-colored birds in his Selma address. Signifyin(g) on Jim Crow as a bird metaphor for Black people's unwanted and abused status, King related segregation to "eating crow" to show how "poor white" people have been fed a diet of racism that further compounded their own poverty while unjustly scapegoating Black people.[71] Here, King echoed the many Black musicians who have Signified on Jim Crow in song.[72] In the 1940s, for example, Lead Belly recorded "Jim Crow Blues," motivated by his observation of the mistreatment of Black veterans returning from the war.[73] The song is about ever-present roadblocks ("You're gonna find some Jim Crow every place you go") and concludes with a final request ("Please get together and break up this old Jim Crow").[74] Simone also co-composed a song, released in 1964, addressed to the title character of "Old Jim Crow,"[75] letting him know his day was done. Simone also makes an important distinction: "It ain't your name / It's the things you do."[76]

Signifyin(g) on Jim Crow, the blackface minstrel character whose name came to stand for segregation laws and de facto practices, both Lead Belly and Simone situate the figure as an antagonist. This is also how Billie Holiday's "Strange Fruit" renders crows that come after lynched bodies. In these songs, as in King's speech, "crow" is named and thus caught, its power or mystique dismantled by the act of recognition. Naming, especially when coupled with characterizations of Jim Crow as decrepit, weak, and unhealthy, is a rhetorical device that makes a seemingly insurmountable injustice knowable and therefore able to be taken apart. This context makes the appearance of "Bye Bye Blackbird" all the more ironic because the song was amplified at a planned *counter*protest in Selma.

In a letter to the *New Yorker* documenting the events, Renata Adler wrote, "On Broad Street, which is also US Route 80 to Montgomery, they turned left, and as segregationist loudspeakers along the way blared 'Bye, Bye, Blackbird' and the white onlookers began to jeer, the marchers approached and crossed the Edmund Pettus Bridge."[77] The segregationists were enacting the song's racial symbolism, applying the blackbird-bluebird symbolism to their dismissal of those marching. Correlating the blackbird with Black people, the segregationists jeered at the kind of plea for equality that Mills had made as the blackbird four decades earlier. The 1965 appearance of "Bye Bye Blackbird," then, illustrates how white people kept using that song and its central image—the black-colored bird—as a vehicle for racist antagonism. At the same time, twentieth-century Black artists were performing this and other bird-centric songs, troping a racist trope and reclaiming the very image used to mock and exploit them.

A Few More Birds in the 1920s and 1930s

Florence Mills's blackbird anthem for racial equality is a major touchstone in a profound legacy of that bird's association with Black Americans' artistry. Still, blackbirds and other black-colored birds have served racist ends in the twentieth century, too, paralleling Greenfield's reception in the nineteenth century. Following Mills's performances of "I'm a Little Blackbird Looking for a Bluebird" and the popularity of "Bye Bye Blackbird," there appear many more bird-centric songs and media, more historical context for the transatlantic conversations involving the Beatles and Black music.

From aeronautical acrobats to stage actors, Black people in the early to mid-twentieth century frequently performed as and sang about birds, such as the Dixie Hummingbirds gospel group, founded in 1928. One member, James Davis, explained how their name, adopted in the early 1930s, was inspired by actual birds: "I came up with the Dixie Hummingbirds because I saw how the hummingbirds were down there in South Carolina. I figured that was the only bird could fly both backwards and forward. Since that was how our career seemed to be going [*laughs*], I figured that was a good name, and the guys went along with it."[78] The "Dixie" of Dixie Hummingbirds Signifies on "the minstrel song of the same name" while also designating a regional association with South Carolina (the latter too cumbersome for a group's name). After World War II, many other vocal ensembles took the names of birds, but Davis claimed they were told the Dixie Hummingbirds were "first."[79]

Referencing those who became the Beatles' musical forerunners, Jerry Zolten situates subsequent Black singing groups' penchant for bird names in a trajectory that begins with the Dixie Hummingbirds: "The Wrens, Crows, Cardinals, Swallows, Quails, Parrots, Robins, Penguins, Flamingos, and even the plain old Five Birds were some of the best known, and all would be part of the first great wave of the music that came to be called 'rock 'n' roll.'"[80] Notably, the Penguins' hit "Earth Angel (Will You Be Mine)" (1954) centers on a winged image, and the Flamingos' "sha bop sha bop" callbacks mimic birds in their hit cover of "I Only Have Eyes for You" (1959). The bird-naming tradition among musical professionals parallels the names of recording labels, especially for "race records," such as RCA Victor's Bluebird Records, founded in 1932.[81] Nearly a decade later, that label (sans Bluebird at that point) released one of Lead Belly's many recordings of "Grey Goose," whose title character is another avian vehicle for ironic double meanings. The goose's journey over the ocean speaks to another transatlantic flight, the movement of Lead Belly's music into the Liverpool skiffle scene.

CHAPTER 4

Flying Across the Ocean

Lead Belly, "Grey Goose," and the Beatles' Liverpool Skiffle Scene

George Harrison was remembered to say, "If there was no Lead Belly, there would have been no Lonnie Donegan; no Lonnie Donegan, no Beatles. Therefore no Lead Belly, no Beatles."[1] Harrison was referring to the influence of an influence: the Black American "King of the Twelve String" and the white British "King of Skiffle," the latter a known hero of the future Beatles and the Quarry Men, Lennon's own skiffle band. As Harrison says, Donegan's major source was Lead Belly (né Huddie William Ledbetter),[2] who was born in 1888 (probably): he "always said that he entered the world on the fifteen of January, but never said exactly where."[3] The question of Lead Belly's birthplace would become a later point of contention when, given his legendary status, Texas and Louisiana would lay claim to his remains, an irony considering his earlier prison stints in both states.[4] Lead Belly's prison experience is noteworthy because it was integral to the persona that John and Alan Lomax cultivated when they marketed the self-titled "musicianer." The prison setting was where the father and son folklorists met Lead Belly, witnessing his magnificent talent and extraordinary musical knowledge.

Harrison's equation becomes more profound when we consider the rebellious spirit of prison work songs, such as "Grey Goose" (Roud 11684), as precursors to rock 'n' roll. "Grey Goose" exemplifies the narrative logic of Flying Africans, illustrating the trope's ongoing relevance to Black people in the twentieth century, especially those incarcerated in the southern United States. "Grey Goose" features a bird who won't be broken, a theme that also applies to Lead Belly's musicianship and artistic perseverance. After his death, the transatlantic flight of Lead Belly's music then becomes an entry point into skiffle's (and the Beatles') indebtedness to him and other Black Americans, especially through the mediation of Donegan. Now, in the second decade of the twenty-first century, McCartney has drawn an even straighter line to Lead Belly, claiming him as a hero.

"Grey Goose" and the Flying Africans

"Grey Goose" exists prior to its association with Lead Belly, so we first look at the song's key features, especially in relation to the trope of Flying Africans, and then trace its flightpath into Lead Belly's oeuvre and legacy, which can be characterized by the bird's perseverance. "Grey Goose" is a folk ballad about an indestructible bird whose wings and body can't be broken. The goose, a "he," is shot down by hunter; this man is sometimes a daddy on a Monday and other times (with Lead Belly) a preacher who skips church on Sunday. Throughout the song, the trickster goose evades this man's control: it takes six weeks for the goose to fall from the sky, six weeks to be found, six weeks to be de-feathered, and six weeks to be boiled. Even when the goose is served up for dinner, he continues to outsmart everyone: they can't cut into him, so they throw him into the hog pen, where the goose breaks both a sow's jaw and then the saw used to cut him. The speaker of the song is a witness to the goose's un-breakability and testifies that the goose was last seen flying across the ocean—site of the Middle Passage—with a trail of goslings behind him, all of them honking in mockery of the failed man.

"Grey Goose" is a secular song that ends with a soaring bird bolstered by a community of other birds. Though not a spiritual, it nevertheless responds to systemic oppression in a similar way as religious songs do, with the imagery of liberation through collective winged flight even if that freedom can only be found in death. No being could survive so much breaking, but the grey goose's indefatigable spirit lives on, haunting the man who tried to eat and otherwise punish the goose. That theme is accentuated by the song's "leader-chorus form," the call-and-response design, originating in West Africa, that is so essential to gospel.[5]

In its opening line, lyrical motifs and themes, word choice and use of verb tense, and repetitive structure, "Grey Goose" bears a striking resemblance to "'Twas on One Sunday Morning," a Negro spiritual that witnesses Jesus's Easter resurrection.[6] In addition to details like the opening invocation and the verb construction, "Twas On One Sunday Morning" reflects the "three-step process" of the "gospel impulse": "(1) acknowledging the burden; (2)

bearing witness; (3) finding redemption."[7] Those elements are present in "Grey Goose," whose title character's suffering is acknowledged and witnessed by the song's speaker, its addressee, and their wives; by the song's end, all are entreated to hail the redeemed goose whose ascension into the sky is a source of hope. If the roots of "Grey Goose" are in a spiritual, then the "*Lord*, Lord, *Lord!*" lament,[8] which is the chorus's response to the leader, Signifies on the religious refrain. In the case of "Grey Goose," "*Lord*, Lord, *Lord!*" commiserates, yet also double-speaks, bestowing a bit of mockery on the man for exerting so much impotent effort to destroy the bird. (This becomes even more apparent when Lead Belly specifies that the church-skipper is a "preacher.")

In theme and imagery, "Grey Goose" is indebted to stories of Flying Africans, especially the narrative thread in which laboring slaves regain their ability to fly as in the folktale "All God's Chillen Had Wings."[9] As a folk song collected in the twentieth century, "Grey Goose" also resembles the folktale of "The Flying Man," whose title character escapes the police. Like the grey goose, the flying man's physical strength saves him, a metaphor for spiritual salvation: "the faster they walked the faster he walked, until he just spread his arms and sailed right on off"; he is later compared to a plane, his memory inspiring others "throughout the South."[10] In addition to reflecting the rise of aviation technology,[11] "The Flying Man" positions the police in the role that slaveowners occupied in earlier folklore. Similarly, in "Grey Goose," the goose's refuge-seeking flight is away from oppressive circumstances, and the song's characters correspond to the following: "the *African* armed with a 'password,' the African American *Slave* as witness or participant, and the white *Overseer*, generally armed with a whip."[12] All three are present in "Grey Goose," though Signified in code.

The quacking grey goose, with its trailing goslings, is the African, who "can give the magic password to those who believe in its power."[13] In this case, birdspeak—the "quank" that is the goose's particular call or noise—functions as that password.[14] There is also the speaker's telling reference to "my wife and your wife," who are tasked with the de-feathering, implying that they all work for the daddy/preacher, the Overseer. The daddy/preacher character thus stands for the Overseer exerting the traditional means of authority, "the blunt instruments of power,"[15] afforded by his gun, saw, laborers, and even his domestic animals like the hog. The Slave, who is denied these technologies, "is left with nothing more than ordinary words to tell his odyssey of withdrawal,"[16] which is the song itself. The second-person shift to "you" in the "wife" lyric positions the listener of the song as a fellow Slave. And the

Slave—both singer and listener—can become correlational with the goose when they sing those magic words at the end of the song, the "quank quank."

Aside from "daddy" Signifyin(g) on master, why else might "Grey Goose" position the Overseer figure in the guise of a daddy or a preacher? Perhaps because white listeners—whether they are the overseers, prison guards, police, or even seemingly benign audience members—could then assume that the song's transgressor is Black. Meanwhile, Black performers, claiming bodily fortitude, freedom of spirit, and community solidarity, could codify their resistance in the face of white oppressors. The goose's quanking flight, after all, reveals the daddy/preacher's ridicule-worthy impotence.

"The Mighty Blue Goose" and "Grey Goose": From Iron Head to the Lomaxes

With its admiration for physical strength, resistance to authority, and potential for call and response, "Grey Goose" was a valuable song for mitigating the miserable experiences of prison work.[17] The Lomaxes heard the song among incarcerated men in Texas, where they documented "Grey Goose" at three separate prisons: in 1933, James Baker "Iron Head" sang it at Sugarland and Washington Lightnin' sang it at the Barrington State Farm; and in 1934, Augustus Haggerty "Track Horse" sang it at Huntsville Unit.[18]

"Grey Goose" is about the public recognition of physical resilience, a quality that applied to Iron Head, "a sixty-four-year-old trusty [prisoner with relative freedom and other privileges], whose deep knowledge of songs led John [Lomax] to proclaim him a black Homer. Baker lived his songs, feeling their emotions viscerally."[19] In a 1933 manuscript titled "Negro Material: The Story of the Mighty Blue Goose by Iron Head Assisted by Alan Lomax," Alan took notes before Iron Head sang. The younger Lomax's written text explains how and where Iron Head received his nickname: even though the other men yelled "Timber!" multiple times, Iron Head was singing so loudly he didn't hear them, so a live-oak tree fell on his head and broke. "The tree broke, not Iron Head's head," Lomax clarifies. Iron Head "went right on chopping down his live oaks and singing his song" and the rest of the men "for ever after called him Iron Head."[20] Iron Head's unbreakable head is a rallying point for other incarcerated men, paralleling the inspirational goose's toughness.

In the post-Reconstruction era and into the twentieth century when Iron Head was singing, Black men's incarcerations were often the result of insignificant infractions, trumped-up charges, or false accusations, a system akin to slavery, especially because these men were used as unpaid forced labor—work needed for essential infrastructure such as irrigation ditches, lumber, and the railroad. Significantly, the younger Lomax's notes represent Iron Head, who was punished for petty theft and given an exorbitant sentence because of recidivism, as the opposite of boastful. When it comes to the tree, "he was not proud about this," noted Alan, and the other prisoners kept the story alive by asking Iron Head to use his head "to break down a wall." In response, he remained cool: "Iron Head would light his pipe as if he didn't hear them." Afterward, though, he turned thoughtful and reflective, remembering the blue-goose song: "You know boys, last night after I lay down, I began to study about that tree falling on me. Somehow it reminded me of the time my daddy went hunting the blue goose. Would you like to hear about that time?" Lomax describes Iron Head's next action: "So Iron Head lighted his pipe and began to sing. He always smoked his pipe when he sang. This is what he sang."[21]

Iron Head's unbreakable goose is blue in Alan Lomax's written documentation of that otherwise undated 1933 rendition of "The Mighty Blue Goose" (or "The Blue Goose"). The title character is grey in their Library of Congress entry for the December 1933 performance, titled "The Grey Goose."[22] In October 1934, the Lomaxes returned to Sugarland to record Iron Head backed by a group, a recording subsequently released and referenced in other Library of Congress documentation.[23] In addition to the goose's apparent color change, a significant difference exists between Alan's representation of Iron Head in his 1933 manuscript and the Lomaxes' later descriptions of Iron Head.

The rallying function of Iron Head's unbreakable head and his personal association with "Grey Goose" is deleted in the stereotyping preface for "De Grey Goose" in the Lomaxes' *American Ballads and Folk Songs*. Instead of using the story about the tree falling on him, the introduction reads, "Iron Head grinned, very literally like the Devil, while he sang this saga of the grey goose. It has the feel of the Paul Bunyan tales and of Uncle Remus."[24] In that book, the Lomaxes also change the gender of the goose at the very end of the song: it inexplicably becomes a "she" even after being a "he" in earlier lyrics. Other Lomax documentation about Iron Head's 1934 version maintains consistent masculine gendered pronouns for the grey goose.[25]

The elder Lomax was known to sensationalize Black respondents, trading nuance for the value of a dramatic story. Contrast the pipe-smoking sage that Alan draws in the 1933 blue-goose manuscript with the one the elder Lomax describes in a 1941 radio transcript for his Library of Congress series *Ballad Hunter*. Prefacing "Grey Goose," John presents the opposite of the thoughtful man Alan described: "[Iron Head] once described himself to me as 'the roughest colored man who ever walked the streets of Dallas—in the pen off and on thirty-four years."[26] At the same time, Lomax characterizes "Grey Goose" as "a wonderful song for children,"[27] thus diminishing its political implications. This contradiction—it's a silly song by a seriously bad man—turns "Grey Goose" into a kind of minstrel number reminding audiences of grey-goose songs known to have circulated in that context.[28] One such blackface minstrel number is "The Old Grey Goose" (Roud 3619), which also appears in the aforementioned Lomax collection, *American Ballads and Folk Songs*.

The lyrics of "The Old Grey Goose" derive from a folk song, "On Saturday My Wife Died," collected in Scotland in the late eighteenth century (also Roud 3619). Minstrel-style sheet music for "De Ole Grey Goose" was published in 1844,[29] and the banjo tune was a standard in subsequent nineteenth-century traveling blackface minstrel shows in the American West.[30] Although the lyrics correlate the goose (and a cow) with the dead wife, the minstrel context forces an association between grey feathers and blackface (and Black faces). This also suggests, however, that the title character of Iron Head's "Grey Goose" *resists* the fate of grey geese so often killed off in folk songs circulated in America. These examples reinforce the complicated legacy we find throughout this book: birds are racist caricatures *and* vehicles for Black people to sing their freedom while voicing specific causes of its denial.

The value of the Lomaxes' recovery and preservation of folk music for the Library of Congress is immeasurable, but the Lomaxes (John in particular) have been rightly criticized for sensationalizing accounts as well as exploiting Black singers and respondents when it came to claiming joint copyright and royalties. These relationships, though certainly exploitative in many ways, were complicated. Lead Belly and Iron Head each worked with John, traveling with him upon their respective releases from prison. Even though both musicians fell out with the elder Lomax, disappointed with representation and compensation, they kept in contact with him and other members of the family, especially Alan, who continued to promote and support Lead Belly's musical career. Alan Lomax, a committed leftist, was more progressive than his conservative father and more socially conscious, especially about inequities related to race (along with class and gender).[31]

The younger Lomax's attention to systemic racism is apparent in his "Grey Goose" documentation for the Library of Congress. Alan points to structural conditions of disenfranchised and oppressed African Americans, acknowledging the ubiquity of survival lore like "Grey Goose," but making a case for the song's particularity to the Black people in the South: "The folk have always loved humble heroes who were absolutely invincible, who could endure any hardship or torture without fear or harm. For the southern Negro, faced with the problem of sheer survival under slavery and later as the sub-standard economic group, this pattern has dominated his ballads and folk-tales. The ballad of the heroic goose, who, after being shot, picked, cooked, carved and run through the sawmill, was last seen with a large, derisively honking flock of goslings, flying over the ocean, epitomizes the Negro's belief in his own ability to endure any hardship."[32] Lomax then points out key features: "The design of the song is the African leader-chorus form, and this version is used on the Texas prison farms for hoeing—a whole gang moving forward together, their hoes flashing together in the sun, across an irrigation ditch."[33] Lomax's description, albeit romantic, recognizes the artistry of synchronous movement and voices, which occurred alongside strenuous, often inhumane labor in the brutal heat, work that Lead Belly knew from experience.

Meet Lead Belly

In March 1935, Lead Belly laid down his first recorded version of "The Grey Goose" for the Lomaxes and the Library of Congress.[34] Two years prior, at age forty-two, he met the Lomaxes during the same year that Alan documented Iron Head's blue-goose variant. In 1933, Lead Belly was serving one of several prison sentences at Louisiana's Central Convict Sugar Plantation, which had forbidden prisoners from singing while working.[35] That injustice is consistent with others at the prison, a "sweatbox" that was formerly a plantation. This legacy was even preserved in the institution's nickname, "Angola," after the African location from which so many of the plantation's enslaved people originated.[36]

At Angola, Lead Belly was singular, immediately impressing the Lomaxes: "[Lead Belly] spoke with confidence, pride, and an undisguised intelligence, none of it part of the standard prisoner's repartee. . . . He played with an aggressiveness that suggested the Texas Mexican guitar bands and two-fisted juke-joint piano, and sang in a declamatory tenor that, like his guitar, could cut through the noise of street traffic and crowded bars. Singing with his eyes closed, rocking his body as he kept the rhythm with his feet, he seemed to draw inspiration from some distant, undisclosed source, or perhaps just from memory."[37] Biographers Charles Wolfe and Kip Lornell make an important distinction between the public perception of Lead Belly, especially as filtered through the Lomaxes, and his "intensely personal" side. "Casual fans," Wolfe and Lornell note, often had the wrong impression of his musical dexterity because of his marketing as a convict: "He had a rather high, gentle voice when he talked and was capable of singing with great expression and restraint. He could sound at times like an Irish tenor, at times like a radio crooner, at times like a child on the playground."[38]

Lead Belly, the self-titled King of the Twelve-String Guitar, had a storied life before the Lomaxes. He spent time in the red light district on Fannin Street in Shreveport, Louisiana, traveled as an itinerant musician, and in 1912 started performing with (and learning from) Blind Lemon Jefferson in Dallas and around Texas, functioning "as his eyes."[39] Lead Belly also experienced repeated violence that led to repeat incarcerations, where he "develop[ed] a large and diverse repertory of songs that stretched from church music to blues, folk songs to popular favorites."[40] In addition to his own compositions, Lead Belly's preservation of the oral tradition and his arrangements of songs later encountered via the Lomaxes (like "Grey Goose") demonstrate how Black American innovation is the foundation for American popular music.

As Pete Seeger put it, "[Lead Belly] bequeathed to us a couple hundred of the best songs any of us will ever know."[41] Lead Belly's musical ability was also not limited to oral exposure; he told one interviewer that "as a young man he occasionally did listen to records, and even learned songs off pieces of sheet music."[42] These details unsettle romanticized and presentist notions of Black music as unadulterated and raw folk material,[43] while also highlighting the many dimensions of Lead Belly's artistry. Along with his extraordinary musical talent, versatility, and recall, Lead Belly's personality made him a compelling figure in popular culture, although, during his lifetime, he did not achieve the level of recognition to which he aspired.

In the 1930s and '40s, Lead Belly's Blackness made his transgressions more titillating for white people both afraid and in awe of Black people,[44] something John Lomax capitalized on when he had Lead Belly perform in convict stripes.[45] Those stripes appear on film in 1935, when Lead Belly was the subject of the second-ever *March of Time* newsreel.[46] The short film also featured John Lomax in a reenactment of prison life in Angola: the pair are surrounded by other prisoners for whom Lead Belly, wearing the prison garb, sings "Goodnight Irene" (Roud 11691) as Lomax records (or pretends to). The newsreel's narrative then situates Lomax as a white savior and Lead Belly as a willing slave who, upon release, pledges himself to Lomax ("You be my big boss and I'll be your man"). This oversimplified representation is bluntly racist but consistent with the version of events that both Lomax and Lead Belly presented for public consumption.[47]

According to the newsreel, Lead Belly continually freed himself using the tools of his guitar and voice and the power of his song. In the film, Lead Belly asks John Lomax to take a recording of a song he composed about Louisiana governor O. K. Allen to the chief state executive, explaining that this strategy had previously worked with Texas governor Pat Neff. The liberation-through-music narrative was the story the Lomaxes circulated about their intervention, as well as the tale Lead Belly would later tell: "One day [the Lomaxes] took [my records] to old Governor O. K. Allen and played them for him. And what do you know? I'm out of prison again."[48] The truth of Lead Belly's 1934 prison exit is less dramatic; he did record a song for Allen, but he was released from Angola under Louisiana's "good-time laws."[49] As John Szwed explains, "It was a good story, a very old and maybe even universal story—the victim who saves his life by keeping his captor amused by telling a tale or riddling, or singing, and it brought the attention of the press."[50] The Scheherazade-like legend nourished Lead Belly's mythology, which also tapped into the Byronic archetype. This sexy literary character is a singular artist with a mysterious and dangerous past but is (eventually) brought back into the social fold by the love of a good woman; Lead Belly's Blackness accentuated these sensational qualities.[51] The newsreel thus concludes with Lead Belly's marriage to his wife, Martha, and the conferring of his songs to the Library of Congress, where they receive a place next to the Declaration of Independence.

Lead Belly associated with the Lomaxes for periods of time during the 1930s, driving for John and helping the folklorists with the transcription and documentation of prison work songs for the Library of Congress, while singing from his extensive repertoire and traveling to other prisons to collect and learn more songs. The Lomaxes devote an entire book to transcriptions of Lead Belly, *Negro Folk Songs as Sung by Lead Belly* (1936), but this publication punctuated the end of his working relationship with John; Lead Belly and his family were not pleased with his portrayal in the book.[52] Citing insufficient payment in the year preceding publication, Lead Belly broke with the elder Lomax in 1935 but kept working with Alan.[53]

Lead Belly was briefly incarcerated again in Texas before moving to New York City, where he linked up with key members of the progressive folk music movement, which would eventually precipitate the Beatles' exposure to his music. Much of Lead Belly's public exposure was helped by Alan's efforts to get more compensation for him by arranging paid appearances and recordings. In 1939, Alan dropped out of Columbia University to raise money for Lead Belly's legal costs,[54] and the younger Lomax and Lead Belly continued to record into the beginning of the next decade.

Lead Belly and "Grey Goose"

During the 1940s, Lead Belly's subsequent recordings of "Grey Goose" document his variations on the song. The 1941 recording produced by Alan Lomax for RCA's Victor label features Lead Belly as vocal lead accompanied by the gospel-style Golden Gate Quartet, who "had become the nation's best-known black quartet"[55] but whose "polish conflicted with Lead Belly's rawness."[56] Learning the song in one rehearsal and avoiding "too much precision,"[57] their "Lord, Lord, Lord" is slow, solemn, and deliberate. Given their disparate styles, Lead Belly and "the golden gate boys" (his name for them) were skeptical about the collaboration. Overall, however, Lead Belly was pleased, "swell" as he put it, adding that their take on "Midnight Special" was "a killer."[58] Later, Moses "Moe" Asch produced multiple versions of "Grey Goose" with Lead Belly on his own and with others, including a loose, folksy one with Woody Guthrie and Cisco Houston in 1946.[59]

Throughout the 1940s, Lead Belly's song prefaces habitually added detail appealing to his white, often academic audiences.[60] In one 1947 recording, Lead Belly sings both call and response, speeding up the tempo so as not to protract the "Lord, Lord, Lord." As Lead Belly often did during later performances, he identifies different voices present within the song and makes the preacher's transgression clear: "Down in my home, Baptist people go to church on a Sunday." The preacher violates his obligation to hunt the grey goose, who "is still laughing at him." This laughter is compounded by the sisters, Lead Belly explains, who discover the failure: "That's where that 'Lord, Lord, Lord' come in."[61] In this explanation, Lead Belly offers a motivation for the goose's honking laughter and makes clear the Signifyin(g) potential of the Lord response, a lament-turned-taunt in the hands of the sisters, who also judge the ineffectual preacher.

Given the marketing of Lead Belly as a "very mean boy," the racist diminutive John Lomax used in the 1935 newsreel,[62] it might be surprising to discover that Lead Belly was later presented to children as a kind of Mother Goose. On the one hand, this presentation diminished the danger and sex appeal he garnered from the convict presentation, putting him into the kind of nurturing role that mid-twentieth-century audiences were comfortable seeing Black people play onscreen (think Sam in *Gone with the Wind*). On the other hand, Lead Belly's easy rapport with young listeners was testament to his versatility.[63]

Paralleling the English tradition of nursery rhymes and other folk tunes about birds in peril, "Grey Goose" was later included on *Negro Folk Songs for*

Young People (1960) and *Lead Belly Sings for Children* (1999). The latter gathers songs he performed for children in concerts and radio programs, as well as those released on the LP *Play Parties in Song and Dance as Sung by Lead Belly*. On that 1941 album, Lead Belly prefaces "Red Bird" with directions for an associated dance, which involves partner-changing and "everybody going round in the ring." "You swing my partner, then I'll swing yours," Lead Belly explains, concluding that the aim is to "get back home, then you settle down."[64] The lyrics recount the flight of the title character, who is caught by a cat and a hawk, and whose flight-to-home evokes a key motif of the Flying Africans trope. Lead Belly's abrupt stop makes the play dynamics clear: the winning dancers will have returned to their original partners, but the point of the cakewalk-style dance is to rehearse the intention and uncertainty of that return.

In the folklore of popular culture, Lead Belly himself becomes the unbreakable, soaring grey goose about whom he so famously sang. This correlation was nourished by filmic representations, including his performance of "Grey Goose" for what was probably intended to become a "Soundie," precursor to the modern music video that played on Panorama machines and cost a dime per song.[65] The filming took place in 1945, when two California filmmakers recorded audio and shot footage of Lead Belly performing "Grey Goose," along with "Pick a Bale of Cotton" (Roud 10061) "Take This Hammer" (Roud 4299), and a few other songs. All the settings were different, but "Grey Goose" seems to have been shot on a black screen. After some faint strumming, an announcement: "This is a work song." A bit of light begins to illuminate Lead Belly, his white hair against a solid black background. Impeccably dressed in a dark grey suit, he faces the camera and braces his guitar: "They gonna sing about a grey goose. When they sang, they *swang*." He draws out the last word, a reference to the hammering of chain gangs, before he begins to sing. Throughout this rendition of "Grey Goose," Lead Belly uses his signature twelve-string guitar as a prop to accentuate the actions of the song's characters, especially the title bird.

At the end of the performance, Lead Belly traces an arc with his arm and looks admiringly on an imagined sky as he hails the triumphant grey goose.[66] Perseverance, the grey goose's key attribute, is, in fact, what Lead Belly brought to Hollywood in the first place. He traveled there "on spec," aspiring to play himself in a movie version of folklorist-musicologist John Lomax's life, which had been optioned by Paramount Pictures.[67] That venture never got off the ground, and neither did the audiovisual footage that included "Grey Goose"— until Pete Seeger salvaged the materials.[68] His reedit, *Three Songs by Lead Belly*, is a testament to Lead Belly's ability to "play" versions of himself.[69]

Ironically, Paramount was the studio that produced director Gordon Parks's *Leadbelly*, the 1976 film starring Roger E. Mosley. "Grey Goose" does not appear on the soundtrack, but the song is mentioned in dialogue by the main character's child daughter; she lists it as one of the songs for which he is known. The film also depicts Lead Belly's grey-goose-like outwitting of a prison guard and escape from a chain gang, along with frequent close to mid-shot depictions of Lead Belly's head and torso against a blue sky like a bird, momentarily free from his prison uniform. In one such frame he delivers the last lines of the film, spoken to a guard, evoking the repetition of "six" and the motif of un-breakability in "Grey Goose": "Six more months, that's all, just six more months. And for seven years, you ain't broke my body, you ain't broke my mind, you ain't broke my spirit." Lead Belly swings his hammer to punctuate each line of dialogue. The intensity of the steel-on-steel sound recalls the folk hero John Henry (Roud 790) and "Take This Hammer," but the film's Lead Belly refuses to be broken: his ending is not death (in the film at least). This theme is evidenced by British rocker Van Morrison's tribute: "My message from the Lead Belly story is called survival."[70]

Lead Belly died in 1949, just before the folk revival of the 1950s saw an appreciation of his work. As Seeger put it, "If he could have lived ten more years he would have seen his dreams come through—young people by the millions learning and singing his songs."[71] Another irony of "Grey Goose" is that while the song's political potential seems to be weakened when relegated to children's culture (starting with John Lomax), many young people would go on to develop a political consciousness through their exposure to Lead Belly and other folk music.

No Lead Belly, No Beatles

After his death, Lead Belly's versions of "Grey Goose" are included in multiple compilations of his music, which includes many of the ingredients, such as dancing, sex, and resistance to authority, that became rock 'n' roll. While the Beatles were coming of age in the port city of Liverpool, their pre-fame lives were soundtracked by a variety of musical genres from abroad but also those homegrown, the latter of which included British skiffle. Unlike Van Morrison and members of the Rolling Stones (who were listening to Lead Belly himself), Lead Belly's music comes to the Beatles via the more immediate skiffle influences, particularly Donegan.

Harrison remembers "Leadbelly tunes" as material played by an early and infrequent bandmate Les Stewart, who "played banjo, mandolin and guitar."[72] McCartney mentions Lead Belly to highlight the importance of Donegan as an "accessible" guitar player:

> In the late Fifties, [Donegan] was virtually the only guitar player that you could see. He was the most successful person, and had the highest profile. He had a great voice, a lot of energy and sang great songs— catchy versions of Leadbelly tunes and things. I loved him. He was a big hero of mine. Everyone got guitars and formed skiffle bands because of him. Skiffle came out of the blues, but the way it was performed made it accessible to us white Liverpudlians. It was dead cheap—just a wash- board, a tea chest, a bit of string, a broom handle and a L3 10s guitar.[73]

Note that McCartney praises Donegan as his hero—not Lead Belly. Donegan's style of performing was informed by British music halls and comedic musical acts. The presence of those genres alongside American folk songs, some of them prison work tunes sung by Black American men like Lead Belly, helped make Donegan's song content more legible to a broad English audience.

Lennon mentions Lead Belly in passing, an example of a "blues" record he spun to appeal to the art-school "snobs" when he was trying to "con" teach- ers into letting him play rock 'n' roll.[74] Lennon also names "Leadbelly" in conjunction with Robert Johnson and Sleepy John Estes as evidence of his habituation to Black music; those references appear in the 1972 *Jet* interview in which he claimed, "Black music is my life."[75] The *Jet* spread features Lead Belly's headshot in the layout, an exaggeration of his impact on Lennon. Len- non's art school context is, however, still instructive for understanding the Beatles' other acknowledged musical loves.

When the Beatles retrospectively discuss their love of Black American rhythm and blues musicians, they often speak with awe and idealization, plac- ing them on "an exalted pedestal"; this is what members of the "trad jazz" subculture[76] (which Lennon encountered in art school) were wont to do with the American blues and jazz musicians they deemed "authentic."[77] Trad jazz, which gave rise to skiffle, is an ironic moniker: Trads' choice of music was actually a revival of the kind of hot jazz played by Louis Armstrong and oth- ers. The history of the trad jazz movement and skiffle in Britain is complex (even involving Alan Lomax at one point). The Beatles weren't Trads; in fact, the pre-fame Beatles identified more with the Teds when it came to style (the quaffed hair and leather gear) and their preference for rock—although the Beatles did not share the Teds' violent racist agenda.[78]

This overview (albeit simplified) of the British subcultural music scene helps to situate the reception of Lead Belly in the Beatles' mid-century Liverpool soundscape. Lead Belly was part of the trad jazz movement's obsession with locating "authentic" music, but then Trads ended up rejecting skiffle due to its commercialism. Prior to this, Decca, in an appeal to the trad jazz crowd, released "Rock Island Line"(Roud 15211) by the Lonnie Donegan Skiffle Group in November 1955.[79] This recording, which "still sounds like a song that is about to go off the rails,"[80] was likely based on a 1947 Lead Belly recording of "Rock Island Line."[81] Describing the song's content in the hands of Donegan, Mark Lewisohn relates the tempo of "Rock Island Line" to its powerful impact.[82] Perhaps helped by the inclusion of "rock" in the title (glimpsing the genre's future dominance), the subsequent slow-burning popularity of Donegan's "Rock Island Line" helped solidify the skiffle movement among teenagers in the United Kingdom.[83] For the Beatles and other boys, this Donegan recording was major, particularly for Harrison as his first-ever record.[84] McCartney also saw Donegan perform live in concert at the Empire Theatre in Liverpool in 1956; it was a life-changing experience, one that inspired Paul to trade in his trumpet for a guitar.[85]

Like those who would follow him,[86] Donegan "plundered" Lead Belly's oeuvre for other songs, including "Ol' Riley" and "Midnight Special" (Roud 6364), both which give voice to freedom's plight.[87] The Lomaxes attributed the latter, another train song akin to "Rock Island Line," to Lead Belly after he recorded it at Angola in 1934; the folklorists claimed this song was inspired by an actual train whose passing light shined onto the Sugarland prison outside Houston. Illustrated by the figuration of the Underground Railroad, trains are another potent metaphor for enslaved as well as incarcerated people, whose movement "away" from oppression on a train is comparable to that of the Flying Africans.[88]

The trains of "Rock Island Line" and "Midnight Special" would have been familiar to the British, but these were songs rooted in Black Americans' experiences. Today's listeners don't often think of the Beatles as indebted to prison work songs sung by Lead Belly and other incarcerated Black men in the American South; that is a legacy more legible in the oeuvres of the Stones and other British Invasion acts. But, in addition to his own recordings of "Midnight Special" in the latter decades of the twentieth century, McCartney has another relevant recollection.

At the Woolton Village Fete, where the future songwriting partners linked up on July 6, 1957, Lennon sang a particularly memorable ad lib with his skiffle band, the Quarry Men: "There was a guy up on the platform with curly, blondish hair, wearing a checked shirt—looking pretty good and quite fashionable—singing a song that I loved: the Del-Vikings' 'Come Go with Me.' He didn't know the words, but it didn't matter because none of us knew the words either. There's a little refrain which goes, 'Come little darlin', come and go with me, I love you darlin'.' John was singing, 'Down, down, down to the penitentiary.' He was filling in with blues lines, I thought that was good, and he was singing well."[89] This is a tidy illustration of how prison work song motifs were circulated by Black American balladeers and absorbed by British skiffle, which then launched the Beatles. Incidentally, what Lennon did with his improvised lyrics is the very thing Lead Belly had mastered with his fillers: "A talented improviser, Lead Belly had no compunction in extemporizing a few extra verses, borrowing from children's nursery rhymes and the blues tradition."[90] Billy Bragg's detail also points to Lead Belly's and other Black Americans' circulation and remixing of English-language nursery rhyme content.[91]

Near the end of their tenure as a band, the Beatles revisited their skiffle roots, rerecording "The One After 909" in January 1969. In doing so, they resurrected a train-themed song first composed prior to 1960 and in closer proximity to their Donegan listening than the other original music recorded during the Get Back / Let It Be sessions. The song owes a great debt to Chuck Berry in its "station"/"location" rhyme and other clever wordplay, along with a vehicular motif and the plot about a guy chasing a girl via a train. Unlike Berry's cars, though, the train was a vehicle "familiar to the Quarry Men's skiffle roots and Liverpool's own Lime Street Station." This station is significant to "909" and other Beatles' late recordings: "Lime Street—a terminal for travelers from throughout England and Scotland—is the workplace of sex worker Maggie Mae in the Liverpool folk song (Roud 1757) and skiffle number covered on 24 January in Get Back. . . . The first minutes of [Get Back] also show the Beatles rehearsing Lead Belly's train-based 'Midnight Special' on 3 January; this song had been a skiffle standby for Lonnie Donegan and others in the late 1950s."[92] Donegan's association with "Midnight Special" underscores how skiffle shaped the cues that the Beatles took from Lead Belly.

Bragg takes issue with how Harrison's equation is pared down to "no Lead Belly, no Beatles," a "snappier sound bite" that leaves out the essential skiffle ingredient of Donegan.[93] This shorthand reflects broader trends when it comes to histories of rock: "As pop became profound in the 60s, artists who had learned their chops playing skiffle tended to leave it out of their biographies. If you wanted to be taken seriously, better to claim you were initially inspired by Chuck Berry and Buddy Holly rather than Chas McDevitt and Nancy Whiskey. Thus skiffle became a bit of an embarrassment for Britain's sixties rock royalty, like an awkward photo from a school yearbook, a reminder of shabby realities of postwar, pre-rock Britain."[94] With Bragg's caveat in mind, Harrison's equation remains useful theoretical shorthand for recognizing the Beatles' indebtedness to Black music, which includes Lead Belly, even in the absence of a one-to-one influence. Donegan's own grey goose, in fact, continues to show how other selections remain indebted to Black American musical traditions even when the connection is less obvious.

Donegan's Grey Goose

Donegan never released a cover of Lead Belly's version of "Grey Goose," but he did record a goose-oriented song that exists in folkloric conversation with the song Lead Belly recorded. Donegan's 1959 single "Does Your Chewing Gum Lose Its Flavour (On the Bedpost Overnight?)" included the B side "Aunt Rhody (The Old Grey Goose)." The latter is a skiffle take on the American folk song "Go Tell Aunt Rhody (The Old Grey Goose Is Dead)" (Roud 3346). In the United States, this aunt has had multiple names, including Dinah, Patsie, Tabby, and Nancy. The latter name might substantiate a link to African Anansi folklore that came up through the Caribbean and into the Gulf states.[95]

Donegan's "Aunt Rhody" includes his characteristic skiffle embellishments with guitar and banjo, reworking a melody that derives from an opera composed by Jean-Jacques Rousseau having nothing to do with aunts or geese. But the lyrics are agreed to be American in origin, possibly deriving from African American folk tradition, where the song flourished.[96] A 1939 recording of "Go Tell Aunt Tabby," collected by John Lomax and wife Ruby T. Lomax from incarcerated women in Florida, is one example of the song's presence in Black Americans' folk repertoires.[97] Corine Jackson and Hasel Futch's delivery is evocative of the Negro spiritual "Go Tell It on the Mountain" (Roud 15220), whose documentation dates back to 1865.

Regarding the origins of the song Donegan covered, one early twentieth-century folklorist insisted on Black American invention in the southern United States and actively resisted other folklorists' attempts to claim the lyrics as derived from white people in the North.[98] Since then, others have continued to speculate about a connection between "Go Tell" and "Grey Goose,"[99] a relationship that could explain the presence of "my wife and your wife" who are doing the feather-picking in the latter song. The pervasiveness of "Go Tell" variants in the United States suggests parallel traditions about grey geese that involve Black American innovation. Even though Donegan reworked the lyrics, he maintained basic actions: the dead goose's feathers make the aunt's bed, and the gander mourns the loss with tears. But in some variants, the dead bird gets revenge by being impossible to eat and the harbinger of bad luck—a revenge akin to the "quanking" bird in Lead Belly's "Grey Goose."

"Grey Goose" and the Beatles' Tricky Birds

The birdsong added to the "Blackbird" track is a sound effect enriched by the quank-quanking in "Grey Goose." "Grey Goose," especially when situated in the Flying Africans trope, the folk genre of Black Americans' prison works songs, and Lead Belly's oeuvre, offers a thematic depth to an image that has puzzled some critics: how does a blackbird fly with broken wings?[100] "Grey Goose" answers that question. Oppressors can try to break a bird's wings, but ingenuity and fortitude are key to survival, figurative or literal. This hope can be extended to others, whether the trailing goslings or fellow incarcerated men who listen and respond to the song itself.

In addition to their bird gags in story and visuals, some of the Beatles' birds are also a little tricky, similar to the cheeky goslings trailing after the grey goose. On *Rubber Soul* (1965), "Norwegian Wood (This Bird Has Flown)" uses British slang to refer to the young woman in the song's title; she doesn't give the speaker what he wants and flies out of his reach, so he lights her nest on fire. He might have taken his revenge, but the speaker, like the preacher of "Grey Goose," still doesn't get the bird. Interestingly, the reverse is true on *Revolver* (1966). In "And Your Bird Can Sing," the speaker admits that the addressee of the song has a bird that sings, but this "you" doesn't possess the song's speaker, who is doing his own singing. Like the incompetent preacher of "Grey Goose," the know-it-all addressed by Lennon's speaker is made to look inept. This song recalls lyrics in Blind Lemon Jefferson's take on "Corrina, Corrina," a tune covered by the Quarry Man (and by Bob Dylan in 1963): "I got a bird that whistles, I got a bird that sings, but I ain't got Corrina—life don't mean a thing."[101]

This history adds irony and interest to McCartney's Wings-era grey goose in his 1978 *London Town* track "Morse Moose and the Grey Goose," a song about a warplane that keeps flying away. Perhaps the indestructible aircraft recalls Howard Hughes's famous *Spruce Goose*, motivating the pair of rhyming character names. McCartney's song also likens the wind to a fox, suggesting "The Fox," the English ballad dating back to the fifteenth century.[102] In that folk song, the fox and his wife usually eat the grey goose—yet McCartney's warplane stays in flight. Might Lead Belly's indestructible bird have influenced McCartney? A goose that endures does, after all, recall the surviving bird of "Grey Goose" more than the dead geese in so many other folk songs.

A "Hero" to McCartney, Keith Richards, and Kurt Cobain: Lead Belly Returns

The correlation between singer and bird is a rhetorical strategy McCartney lifts whenever his speakers imagine themselves as or in relation to birds.[103] He has acquired a veritable aviary throughout his career, and he once more becomes a bird on McCartney III. In the bird-oriented songs of this 2020 record, McCartney both sings about the bird and becomes the aging creature. As Kenneth Womack observes, "McCartney himself is the 'Long Tailed Winter Bird' who soars above the opening track, a spirited, largely instrumental number that is highlighted by one of the musician's niftiest acoustic guitar licks in years."[104]

In an interview that preceded the album's release, McCartney also revealed that he was "reading a book about Lead Belly" while composing songs for McCartney III.[105] McCartney does not identify the book, but he could be referring to the 2015 Smithsonian Folkways Lead Belly compilation, whose extensive and comprehensive liner notes are book bound. Perhaps not coincidentally, McCartney's explanation resembles one Keith Richards gave in 2015 when he was promoting *Crosseyed Heart*, his first solo record in more than two decades. Richards shared the anecdote on *The Tonight Show Starring Jimmy Fallon*, explaining that he chose "Goodnight Irene" because he "wanted to do a classic, old, American folk song." Even though Lead Belly is a known Stones influence, Richards said he was prompted to record "Goodnight Irene" after actor-singer Tom Waits, another devotee, sent Richards "this book on Lead Belly."[106] Five years later, McCartney echoes Richards to credit Lead Belly for inspiring a song on McCartney III.

With the song "Women and Wives," McCartney adds yet another example to more than a half century of imagining himself as specific Black musicians during the composition process:

I was looking at [Lead Belly's] life and thinking about the blues scene of that day. I love that tone of voice and energy and style. So I was sitting at my piano, and I'm thinking about Huddie Ledbetter, and I started noodling around in the key of D minor, and this thing came to me. "Hear me women and wives"—in a vocal tone like what I imagine a blues singer might make. I was taking clues from Lead Belly, from the universe, from blues. And why I'm pleased with it is because the lyrics are pretty good advice. It's advice I wouldn't mind getting myself.[107]

McCartney's revelation includes details related to what *he* hears in Lead Belly—D minor, vocal characteristics, thematic subject matter, and the advice-giving tradition.[108] McCartney's song addresses women, but he also calls upon "husbands and lovers," warning that "what we do with our lives" is consequential to others. Although these lines are more prescriptive and earnest than the irony and wit that so often characterized Lead Belly's delivery, the advice-laden "Women and Wives" may indeed recall "Goodnight Irene."

If McCartney did read a Lead Belly book, he encountered "Goodnight Irene," as Richards did, since Lead Belly recorded multiple versions of his extremely popular tune. He even called this his "theme song" during his last concert, held in honor of John Lomax, which took place at the University of Texas at Austin. In most versions, the speaker addresses Irene: she and the speaker are separated, but he hopes to be with her in his dreams. The speaker's advice about not staying out late to gamble—and to go home to the wife and children—seems be directed to himself or another rambler. In the 1949 performance in Austin, however, Lead Belly explains that this is *Irene's* advice, a point-of-view shift that considers her perspective.[109] This strategy is not unlike McCartney's penchant for songs that drop into the interiority of both men and women in the same tune. The parallels are even more interesting in this context because, throughout Lead Belly's 1949 performance of the song, he keeps explaining that Irene is "sweet sixteen" with you-know-what-I-mean Signifiers, the same kind of nudge Lennon gave McCartney for the seventeen-year-old in "I Saw Her Standing There."[110]

When McCartney claimed Lead Belly as a hero, he struck a chord that rings slightly hollow; most of the artists of McCartney's generation (Van Morrison and Keith Richards, for example) have been consistent about Lead Belly's formative influence over the course of many decades. In a different generation, Kurt Cobain was another avid admirer and student of Lead Belly, recording an instrumental version of "Grey Goose" in 1989 with the Jury, which included members of Nirvana and the Screaming Trees (Cobain, Krist

Novoselic, Mark Lanegan, and Mark Pickerel). They recorded three other Lead Belly tunes in the August 1989 sessions: "Where Did You Sleep Last Night" (released by Lanegan in 1990) and "Ain't It a Shame," "They Hung Him on a Cross," and "Grey Goose," all of which were released on the 2004 Nirvana box set *With the Lights Out*, released a decade after Cobain killed himself with a shotgun.

But Nirvana is also host to a meaningful convergence of Lead Belly and the Beatles, along with bird-centric song imagery, during the 1993 *MTV Unplugged* performance (released as an album the following year, six months after Cobain's death). Nirvana's show begins with "About a Girl" (a song Kurt Cobain composed after a day spent listening to *With the Beatles*) and closes with "Where Did You Sleep Last Night" (a retitled variation of Lead Belly's "Black Girl" [Roud 3421]). In between, they perform yet another song focused on a girl, "Polly." The first line, "Polly wants a cracker," resembles the interrogative/declarative used to prompt domesticated parrots to repeat after the human in order to receive food.

With references to clipped wings, the predicament of a caged bird forced to repeat a captor's words to survive underscores the abusive dynamics related by the speaker, who is holding Polly hostage while imagining her asking for the abuse. Inspired by the actual story of a fourteen-year-old girl kidnapped on her way home from a concert and tortured by her captor in 1987, the Nirvana song, especially its title, resembles a much older folk song cycle. "Pretty Polly" (Roud 15) is an English murder ballad recorded by many folk artists of the mid-1960s, including Bob Dylan, another Lead Belly admirer. In the folk song, after the wronged Polly (or Molly) is lured into a forest and murdered, she returns as a bird-on-fire (or ghost) to punish the man who ended her life for being pregnant. Cobain's composition thus reflects the folk tradition's ability to document and respond to real events, including and especially the dark and ugly sides of human nature, furthering a link between Cobain and Lead Belly, whose "Black Girl" (again, recorded by Nirvana as "Where Did You Sleep Last Night") is often understood with a similarly sinister edge— especially because its "pines" share forest imagery with "Pretty Polly."

The convergence of Lead Belly and the Beatles via Nirvana in the early 1990s is intriguing context for McCartney's twenty-first-century knighting of a new hero. McCartney's discussion of Lead Belly was not one of McCartney's oft-repeated stories during the marketing blitz of *McCartney III*. Even so, McCartney, whose preferences lean more pop than blues and folk, made Harrison's witticism about "no Lead Belly, no Beatles" come a little truer in 2020. A year later, the "Women and Wives" entry in *The Lyrics* conclusively bound the song to Lead Belly, who McCartney proclaims "is definitely one of my heroes."[111] Perhaps it is true that, if you live long enough, you can discover new heroes, prompted by those who admire and take inspiration from you, too.

Mediated through Donegan, Lead Belly's formative influences on the Beatles' skiffle scene illustrate transatlantic flight, the movement and exchange of music. But skiffle obviously wasn't the only music afoot in Liverpool. By the end of the 1950s, rhythm and blues was taking firmer hold—but contending with calypso as the next "it" genre. This convergence characterizes the Beatles' pre-fame soundscape. In fact, one of this musical scene's central players, Lord Woodbine, is another Black artist who, like Lead Belly, can be credited with bringing the Beatles into existence.

CHAPTER 5

You Can Fly Away

Lord Woodbine and Lord Kitchener, "Yellow Bird," and Calypso in the Beatles' Liverpool Club Scene

"The first thing I learned about Negroes was that they were swinging like mad and that they had a great beat. Only later did I start meeting some of them. I didn't know a single black person in England, and I *worshipped* black people in America," announced John Lennon in a March 1969 interview.[1] The Beatle was probably exaggerating to prove his solidarity with the US civil rights movement because by 1958, Lennon was certainly familiar with Black people in Liverpool. As Lennon himself told *Jet*'s Black US readership in 1972, "We'd [the Beatles] been hearing funky Black music all our lives" in a "seaport city" whose ports were still blighted by England's "earlier, racist colonial period," referring to Liverpool's role in the slave trade.[2]

Almost half a century later, McCartney echoes Lennon's thoughts in *Jet* but, like his former songwriting partner, still isn't specific about what they learned from Liverpool's Black community. In the "Blackbird" entry of *The Lyrics*, McCartney moves from the subjects of Bach and guitar-picking (discussed in the introduction, above) to the subject of Black people:

The other story has to do with "blackbird" being slang for Black girl. I am very conscious that Liverpool was a slave port, and also that it had the first Caribbean community in England. So we met a lot of Black guys, particularly in the music world. I'm thinking in particular of Lord Woodbine, a calypso singer and promoter who ran a couple of joints in Liverpool, including the New Cabaret Artists' Club, where he hosted The

Silver Beetles. Then there was Derry [Wilkie] of Derry and the Seniors, a band that had paved the way for us in Hamburg.[3]

McCartney goes on, offering yet another version about "Blackbird" being motivated by his investment in the US civil rights movement and one of its most important figures, the Reverend Dr. Martin Luther King Jr.[4] With this gathering of evidence in 2021, McCartney suggests that his consciousness about US racism in 1968 was rooted in his exposure to Black people and their music during his Liverpool youth—specifically Lord Woodbine.

Harold Adolphus Phillips, whose calypsonian moniker was Lord Woodbine, "was an all-rounder who recognised the need to find performance spaces and create scenes rather than go cap-in-hand to known venues and promoters with the hope of scoring a gig. There is a consensus that he ran several shebeens in Liverpool, and that he could easily switch roles from barman to security."[5] *The Lyrics* is not the first place McCartney has referenced Woodbine, but to our knowledge McCartney has never mentioned him in conjunction with "Blackbird." Unknowingly, McCartney opened a door for considering Woodbine in relation to the song's thematic content—the blackbird relegated to darkness—as well as bird- and flight-oriented calypsos.

As we mention in previous chapters, Liverpool's association with the slave trade, as well as Black performers, involves many ironic blackbird associations in a city long emblematized by birds; these ironies now also include McCartney's most recent "Blackbird" story. The new tale is an entry point into calypso, particularly the popular 1957 song "Yellow Bird" and Woodbine's colleague, Lord Kitchener. During this early postcolonial era, the musical conversation involving the Beatles and multiple genres of Black music was even more dynamic than band members' well-known tributes relate.

The Liverpool 8: Lord Woodbine, Calypso, and the Windrush Generation

By the late 1950s, calypso was having a moment in popular culture, rivaling rock 'n' roll as the next big thing. Calypso's origins as an Afro-Caribbean folk music are particular to Trinidad and Tobago, but the genre spread throughout the West Indies.[6] McCartney has mentioned Liverpool's large population of West Indian immigrants, who settled in the L8 district: "The big factor about Liverpool was it being a port. There were always sailors coming in with records from America, blues records from New Orleans. And you could get so many different ethnic sounds: African music, maybe, or calypsos via the Liverpool Caribbean community, which I think was the oldest in England. There was a massive amount of music to be heard. So with all these influences, Liverpool was a huge melting pot of music. And we took what we liked from all that."[7] McCartney frequently credits the Beatles' eclectic repertoire to Liverpool's port identity, fostering the impression that he and the other Beatles were standing on the dock catching records as they came in. But that is a romantic impression of the city.

Mid-twentieth-century Liverpool, while diverse and known for its residents' collective sense of humor, was a tough place. Lemmy Kilmister of the hard rock band Motörhead put it best when he made a distinction between the Beatles ("hard men") and the Rolling Stones ("mummy's boys"): "Brian Epstein cleaned [the Beatles] up for mass consumption, but they were anything but sissies. They were from Liverpool, which is like Hamburg or Norfolk, Virginia—a hard, sea-farin' town, all these dockers and sailors around all the time that'd beat the piss out of you if you so much as winked at them. Ringo's from the Dingle, which is like the fucking Bronx."[8] Within the L8, the Dingle bordered the segment now known as Toxteth, which was home to many Caribbean immigrants like Woodbine. The threat of violence, as Starr frequently remembers, often had to do with roaming, pipe-wielding Teddy Boys. These violent young men were a threat to white people, too, but they became notorious for anti-Black, anti-immigrant racism expressed in physical attacks on West Indians.[9] The irony is that the rocker Teds loved Black American rhythm and blues but hated Black people.[10]

Romantic notions of Liverpool's musical "melting pot" also flatten the impact of calypsonians such as Lord Woodbine and other Black musicians whom the pre-fame Beatles encountered firsthand. Indeed, the musical knowledge the lads gathered did not only come from NEMS Record Shop and Radio Luxembourg. The city's Black musicians—especially in live performance— were also rich and present sources. Additionally, their L8 clubs drew Black American servicemen stationed at Burtonwood, a US Air Force facility in the late 1950s; these men also helped circulate contemporary American music.[11] It's important to realize that West Indians and other Black musicians were exposed to and versed in rhythm and blues coming out of the United States, too. As a musical genre of the African Diaspora, calypso shares some features with rhythm and blues, especially the Signifyin(g) that happens in lyrics laced with wit and wordplay that subvert authority, encode sexual expression, and otherwise resist the status quo.[12]

Understanding the Beatles' exposure to Black Caribbean musicians in Liverpool involves the history of the Windrush generation, so named for the ship that brought the initial groups of West Indians to help rebuild the post-war United Kingdom.[13] Woodbine was a member of the first Windrush group, but his June 1948 arrival was, in fact, a return to England, where he had previously served in the Royal Air Force after using his brother's passport to enlist as a fourteen-year-old in 1943. In 1947, Woodbine briefly went back to Trinidad, where he "perform[ed] calypso on street corners; with few locals able to afford newspapers, his songs provided commentaries on topical events." Then, following his return-to-England *Windrush* journey, he formed Lord Woodbine and His Trinidadians, "among the first calypsonians to tour" the country, and eventually settled in Liverpool, continuing to work a variety of skilled-labor jobs in addition to performing music. In 1949, Woodbine married Helen "Ena" Agoro, whom he met at a talent show; she sang jazz and then served as lead vocalist for his next band, Cream of Trinidad. They settled in the Toxteth area and went on to have eight children.[14]

In 1955, Woodbine formed the All Caribbean Steel Band for which he "played tenor pan and made steel pans from oil drums and bamboo wood."[15] When he made his own instruments, Woodbine was continuing an important tradition in calypso. This was probably not lost on the Beatles, who got their start in a skiffle, another genre whose participants made (or appropriated objects to become) instruments, including the necessary guitar: "The instrument's appeal had kicked off with the Bill Haley records but Lonnie Donegan single-handedly propelled the guitar high into the consciousness of young British males. For many, getting a guitar—and singing with it—would become a fixation, albeit, for most boys, one frustrated by lack of funds and the paucity of guitars in the shops. Lots of boys made them, a nation of young can-dos getting down to work with wood, glue and strings."[16]

Woodbine's band performed at his own establishment, the New Colony Club in the L8, and had a regular evening gig at the Jacaranda club starting in 1958.[17] Owned by Allan Williams, who served as the Beatles' booking agent and early manager, the "Jac" "was *the* scene of the city's art students."[18] This coffee bar, located in the L1, was blocks from Lennon's art college and McCartney's Liverpool Institute for Boys. Williams, at this point Woodbine's frequent business partner, was a white Welshman married to Beryl, the daughter of Chinese immigrants. Allan and Beryl's mixed-race marriage was another factor in the Jac's progressive ethos—although the couple was also the target of racist harassment.[19]

Liverpool was not legally segregated in the manner of the Jim Crow United States, but segregation practices were in place, especially when it came to the city's musical venues: the teenage Beatles, for example, could wander into predominately Black clubs and listen in the L8, but Black people in Liverpool did not do the same vis-à-vis clubs like the Cavern in the L2. Founding member of the Shades (later the Chants), Joe Ankrah, lived in the L8 and, like other Black people in Liverpool, did not frequent the city center; Ankrah had never been to the Cavern before 1962, when the Beatles provided musical backing for the Shades. As Ankrah remembered, the all-Black group was initially denied entrance to the club, nervously waiting on Mathew Street before McCartney facilitated their entrance.[20]

The Cavern also hosted Derry and the Seniors, which featured a Black British leading singer in an otherwise all-white band, but the convergence of the Shades and the Beatles in the Cavern is significant. First, the Shades are singular in the Beatles' story, as they are the only group to receive instrumental backing by the Beatles. Second, the Cavern is a location at which the consequences of the Beatles' exposure to Black music comes through in more ways than their Chuck Berry covers, which when played "in a dance hall in Liverpool in 1962 was an open act of defiance." The Beatles "became 'part of the crowd,' as one musician described the Cavern. 'Or the crowd was part of them . . . all the jokes and all the shouting. They were very, very funny, and spontaneous, and the nearer the front you were the more evident it was.'" Brothers attributes this to the "phonograph," which transmitted the ring shout's legacy.[21] But the Beatles heard its vestiges firsthand in their contemporaries, the Shades—and years before from older and experienced Black musicians like Woodbine.

Woodbine's Boys

As McCartney mentions in *The Lyrics*, Derry and the Seniors preceded the Beatles in Hamburg, a booking facilitated by Williams and Woodbine. Hamburg is widely considered the Beatles' crucible, a testing ground that turned them into pros. Prior to this, the Jacaranda and L8 clubs afforded their exposure to steel-band music, especially that of Woodbine, who sang calypsos, played pans and guitar, and wrote his own songs.

For the Beatles (excluding Starr who joined later), Woodbine was a model of professional musicianship and an object of admiration because he was a singer-songwriter.[22] Such was their intrigue that Lennon and McCartney (and sometimes Harrison) were "briefly dubbed "Woodbine's Boys.""[23] Woodbine, reflecting on his time with the pre-fame Beatles in a 1998 interview, gave an honest assessment: "There was nothing to pick them out from any of the other groups hanging around Liverpool then. . . . They were just boys wanting to play music, living off their dole money which they pooled. John Lennon did all the singing. As a singer myself, I didn't think he sounded that good then."[24] Ever humble himself, Woodbine wasn't the one who dubbed the Beatles his "boys"; the nickname came from witnesses, retained in the cultural memory of Black people in Liverpool, including Woodbine's daughter.[25]

As the "Silver Beetles," Lennon, McCartney, Harrison, and Stu Sutcliffe sometimes gigged at the Jacaranda on Monday nights when the All Caribbean Steel Band had off.[26] The Trinidadian pannist Gerald "Gerry" Gobin (also credited with leading the steel band) was "unimpressed by [the Silver Beetles'] music" and "initially irritated by these hangers-on."[27] Gobin's then-partner, Candace Smith, was similarly wary of Lennon and McCartney as they followed the band from the L8 clubs to the Jac: "Bloody white kids, trying to horn in on the black music scene."[28] Another witness from Jamaica, Marylee Smith, remembered, "They was there all the time, you know, all the time, like they was looking for some black magic, pushing in, rough boys, unwashed sometimes. Jumping on to the stage, playing the pans like it was theirs. Some of us didn't like that. But the musicians, they didn't mind so much."[29] Woodbine's patience with the lads owed to his generosity and artistic sensibilities; he was "bohemian, free, left wing, incautious."[30] Lennon's sense of humor was particularly appealing to Woodbine, who remembered, "John could make jokes which had the whole room laughing. . . . But he would always keep a straight face. I liked that."[31]

Williams later credited Woodbine with the Beatles' entire existence: "Without Woodbine there would have been no Beatles."[32] Referencing this assertion, Alibhai-Brown and James McGrath describe the relationship using apropos bird imagery while also quoting Woodbine himself: "When the lads were just starting out, dreaming, green and crazy about music, they, said Woodbine, 'made themselves orphans, deliberately' and followed him like motherless chicks, hanging around the joints he either part-owned or played at, always trying to have a go on the steel pans."[33] Even though Mark Lewisohn's first installment of his biographical Beatles trilogy does mention Woodbine, the 2013 book includes no references to "Woodbine's Boys" to illustrate the musical mentorship. The earlier *Anthology* project, which was guided by the Beatles' own accounts, is similarly vague about Woodbine. But, especially if we take

McCartney's 2021 Woodbine-"Blackbird" correlation seriously, these authoritative texts severely understate his role.

In addition to his New Colony Club, where the lads sometimes played (and slept as needed),[34] Woodbine opened another venue in 1960. With Williams as "silent partner,"[35] the Cabaret Artistes Social Club (also known as the New Cabaret Artists' Club) hosted the Beatles, who have, over the years, selectively remembered this place. In an interview McCartney gave ahead of the release of McCartney III, a memory of Woodbine came flooding back to him when touring Liverpool with talk show host James Corden in 2018: "So I give the guided tour until I get into the city centre and I say, 'This is a little place where we used to play in the basement, a little illegal club run by this Liverpool black guy called Lord Woodbine. That's when it was just me, John and George. I was drumming as we didn't have a drummer at the time.'"[36]

It was, in fact, Woodbine who recommended the need for an actual drummer; he wasn't buying McCartney's excuse: "The rhythm's in the guitars."[37] Woodbine's recommendation understood what characterized rhythm and blues, "so named because a strong rhythm of accented backbeats was often applied to the twelve-bar blues form."[38] So, in the summer of 1960, Woodbine was the professional who did the boys—still novices—a favor by hiring them. George Harrison recalled that McCartney's drumming "seemed OK" but admitted, "Probably we were all pretty crap at that point."[39] Harrison continues, remembering Lord Woodbine as "a guy" who "owned a strip club," explaining, "We were brought on as the band to accompany the stripper [Janice], Paul on drums, John and me on guitar and Stuart on bass."[40]

Like McCartney, Harrison made it sound like Woodbine's claim to fame was a strip club, but his contributions to the Beatles' legacy were much greater than that. Woodbine was a partner in Williams's booking-bands-in-Hamburg ventures from the beginning, starting with Derry and the Seniors.[41] When the Beatles were tapped to go to Germany in August 1960, Woodbine, now in his early thirties, was an integral part of the entourage. Woodbine's presence is visually documented in a widely circulated early photograph at Arnhem War Memorial in the Netherlands, a stop along the journey. Harrison recalls Woodbine's presence[42] but does not elaborate on other important details: Woodbine secured and drove the van and, with his own history of passing for older to enlist in military service, helped to "smuggle" the seventeen-year-old Harrison and Pete Best into Hamburg since they were a year too young to work as foreigners in the German city. That operation involved maneuvering the sketchy van (which, at one point, got caught on some tracks with an oncoming train) into and through the Hook of Holland. This detour allowed them to enter Hamburg, as Woodbine remembered, "through the back door."[43] Once in Hamburg, Woodbine opened for the Beatles, too, perhaps to provide a professional polish ahead of the lads' rougher performance. In their capacity as promoters, Williams and Woodbine were, after all, invested in the Beatles making a go of this. Woodbine also recognized how eager the Beatles were for the opportunity, feeling protective of them.[44]

In the last decade of his life, Woodbine had the occasion to see himself "written out" of the Beatles' story at the Liverpool Playhouse in 1992; he was invited to see the tribute play *Imagine*, whose backdrop featured the aforementioned war memorial photograph—with Woodbine airbrushed out.[45] Woodbine, again famously modest, did not take credit for band's success, but in 1998 he admitted, "When I saw [the airbrushed photograph], it hurt me. That was the end of the Beatles memory and me."[46] The omission of Woodbine reflects his generation's broader history.

Elisions and oversights related to Woodbine's mentorship and presence in the early days speak to larger injustices and erasures. When Trinidadians like Woodbine and other Caribbeans arrived in England on the *Windrush*, many of them saw it as a "homecoming" but soon realized the country that had invited them to rebuild was entirely unequipped to offer housing, jobs, and other basic requirements. Characterized by their hardworking ethos, West Indians often took on multiple jobs and established cultural centers, doing so with pride even though they faced decades of discrimination and structural disenfranchisement. In 2018, the exposure of mismanagement and racist policies in the Home Office revealed how Windrush-generation immigrants and their children had been denied rightful citizenship and access to services, resulting in what has been termed the "Windrush scandal," which remains unresolved.[47]

Correctives related to Woodbine include efforts made by the Liverpool Beatles Museum, founded and operated by Roag Best, half brother to onetime Beatles drummer Pete Best. Roag is also the son of longtime Beatles road manager Neil Aspinall and Casbah Coffee Club owner Mona Best; Best is another important but often-uncredited influence on the Beatles' early career. Woodbine's hat and other belongings have been featured at the museum, which has also hosted events featuring Woodbine's daughter Carol Phillips. The on-display objects offer a glimpse of the man, but the Woodbine association raises many more questions about which songs John, Paul, and George encountered via Woodbine and other steel-band calypsonians. As McGrath notes, "Unlike his fellow *Windrush* calypsonians, lords Egbert and Kitchener, Lord Woodbine did not record his music."[48] In 2000, a tragic house fire killed Woodbine and his wife and destroyed their belongings, rendering any documentation related to Woodbine's own music unrecoverable.[49] But memories of steel-drum band members who played in L8 clubs[50] and the Jacaranda certify that these Black musicians were playing multi-genre songs of the day—including the calypso "Yellow Bird."

"Yellow Bird" at the Jac and in 1950s Pop Culture

By the very end of the 1950s, Woodbine's All Caribbean Steel Band turned into the Royal Caribbean Steel Band but retained its standing gig at the Jacaranda. Everett Estridge, the Royal Caribbean's lead pannist and musical arranger, described his process of interpreting and arranging music, illustrating the emphasis on textual revision that characterizes Signifyin(g): "I would listen to the songs and think how we could do it differently. I would think of the song and just put a different beat to it and that was that. Everybody loved it."[51] This observation lends support to Kevin Le Gendre's summation of the Beatles' exposure: "Time spent in the company of West Indian musicians was invaluable because they knew how to attack the beat of a tune with sufficient vigour to effect an audience. Calypso was able to teach pop all these things."[52]

Following the emergence of "Yellow Bird" in 1957 and its immediate popularity, the Beatles would have almost certainly heard this iconic calypso in live performance at the Jac (and on recordings elsewhere). The steel band's repertoire was diverse, but Estridge remembers "Yellow Bird" as one they were asked to play on repeat. When he recollected this song, Estridge also recalled the kind of eclecticism the Beatles would become known for:

We would be learning new songs, and practising others, too. The evening performance started around 8pm, and we would play on until about 2am, so we had to learn a lot of songs. It is hard to think of my favourite songs, as we played so many, but I was using classical music, jazz and pop music. I remember we did "Melody in F," "There's Always Tomorrow" and "Inchworm" and I enjoyed playing those. These tunes and melodies were great, but once I had listened to them a couple of times, I could do more with them, and put a rhythm behind them. After that, it was improvisation and arranging the song the way I wanted to play it. But I'll tell you this. If I ever hear "Banana Boat Song" or "Yellow Bird" again I will go crazy! Everybody wanted us to play those songs, but I hated them![53]

While it bored Estridge, "Yellow Bird" has a relevant backstory, resembling the broader movement of calypso into the mainstream.

"Yellow Bird" is derived from another song, "Choucoune," an 1893 composition by American pianist Michel Mauléart Monton. With music inspired by Monton's Haitian father's background, this song's French lyrics are drawn from a politically charged 1883 lyrical poem by Oswald Durand. Centered on the loss of a beautiful woman, "Choucoune" was extremely popular in Haiti. The song's melody then gained more traction, appearing in multiple songs (including "Yellow Bird") following calypso's "commercial highpoint" in the United States, marked by "actor-singer Harry Belafonte's 1956 sensation, 'Banana Boat Song.'"[54]

Given the political applications of its melody, "Yellow Bird" glimpses the history of Carnival's legacy in calypso,[55] as well as evidencing the genre's appropriations by white people in the late 1950s and into the early 1960s. Calypso was rooted in Black artistry and was well received when performed by Black artists, but the genre was subject to gimmicky exploitation, especially in the hands of white performers: "The calypso craze crested in 1957, when Belafonte had double-sided hits with 'Mama Look at Bubu' / 'Don't Ever Love Me' and 'Coconut Woman' / 'Island in the Sun.' Originally recorded by Trinidad's Lord Melody around 1955 as 'Boo-Boo' or 'Boo Boo Man,' the comic 'Mama Look at Bubu' was also recorded, in an assumed Trinidadian accent, by the white actor Robert Mitchum on his 1957 *Calypso Is Like So*. [Belafonte's] 'Don't Ever Love Me' borrows its melody from the nineteenth-century Haitian song 'Choucoune,' as does 'Yellow Bird,' recorded by the Norman Luboff Choir in 1957."[56] "Yellow Bird" made its album debut on *Calypso Holiday* (1957) as performed by the Norman Luboff Choir, whose white namesake is credited with the arrangement that then became popular; the song's English-language lyrics were also authored by a white couple.

Whereas Belafonte's lyrics for "Don't Ever Love Me" are closer in theme to "Choucoune," "Yellow Bird" picks up on other source material, namely the poet Durand's bird reference ("ti zwazo"). The calypso "Yellow Bird" thus addresses a lonely bird whose isolation reflects the speaker's own unfortunate status. On the surface, the scenario seems to be about being unlucky in love, a motif in line with the Durand poem. But the speaker of "Yellow Bird" is focused on the bird, recognizing its ability to fly away, a freedom the speaker does not share. The song was recorded by other white groups into the 1960s, but "Yellow Bird" has also been performed and recorded by many Black artists. The Mills Brothers (a group on McCartney's radar) had minor chart success with the song in 1959, paralleling Estridge's memory about how "Yellow Bird" became part of the repertoire (even if reluctantly) of some Black musicians in the late 1950s and beyond.[57]

"Yellow Bird" Remembered: The Beatles, the Paragons, and McCartney

The ubiquity of "Yellow Bird," in addition to "Banana Boat Song," underscores the broader commercialization and appropriation that led to calypso's fad status and mainstream near obsoletion—despite the genre's important connections to postcolonial resistance and its applications to West Indians' everyday lives.[58] Remembering sojourns to their Caribbean home and studio in the decades following the Beatles' tenure, Judy Lockhart Smith, producer George Martin's wife,[59] mentioned "Yellow Bird," illustrating its popularity among tourists even after calypso faded. Friends of Beatle George Harrison even include a joking reference to the song in a 1973 episode of *Monty Python's Flying Circus.*[60]

The flight motifs in "Yellow Bird" echo in "Blackbird," whose bird is encouraged to fly. Making the association between these two songs in 2011, Treasure Isle Records rereleased the Paragons' takes on these two songs together as one single—implicitly making a case for the Beatles' Caribbean provenance. The Jamaican group released "Yellow Bird" in 1967, giving the calypso a smooth rocksteady treatment, which is echoed in their "Black Birds Singing," featuring Roslyn Sweat, in 1973. The new title is significant: the two-word plural suggests racialized birds well before McCartney starts separating the words to achieve this affect; the plural emphasizes the collective—the Paragons with Sweat—over the individual.

Also in 1973, McCartney composed a tune even closer in theme to "Yellow Bird" following his family's sojourns in Jamaica, where he fell in love with reggae.[61] Though not overtly showing that musical influence, on *Red Rose Speedway* (1973), "Single Pigeon" addresses lonely birds, first a pigeon and then a seagull, both unlucky in love and relationships and subject to the rain because they were turned out of the nest by domestic partners.[62] Just like the speaker of "Yellow Bird," McCartney's speaker empathizes with birds, correlating himself with them to ponder his own lonely condition.

Lord Kitchener's Calypso and Lennon's Broken-Winged Bird

We can't be sure of the setlists at the Jacaranda or the calypsos that the Beatles heard Woodbine sing, but Lewisohn has documented Lennon's familiarity with Woodbine's calypsonian colleague, friend, and fellow traveler on the *Windrush* journey, Lord Kitchener (né Aldwyn Roberts). Lord Kitchener's ship-side performance of "London Is the Place for Me" (a deeply ironic song) was widely circulated in British Pathé News footage that became emblematic of the Windrush-generation immigrants and their "homecoming" hopes for England.[63] Kitchener's command of language, especially his ability to elicit a laugh while issuing an incisive critique, must have appealed strongly to Lennon, whose "political cynicism" was another point of commonality that Woodbine said he shared with John.[64] No doubt Lennon's consciousness was also raised by his exposure to Kitchener's calypso, which routinely Signifies on colonial power.

The first volume of Kitchener's 1955 *Calypsos Too Hot to Handle* (issued by British-based Melodisc) was one of two records Lennon owned by the beginning of 1959. Details surrounding the acquisition are unknown (though Lennon was known for stealing records from house parties).[65] Lennon's exposure to and affinity for calypso is reflected in the title of his first-ever composition, "Calypso Rock," in 1957.[66] His pairing of these two genres was, however, not novel: "Seriously living up to his new self-styled nickname of 'the Professor,' Kitchener used London's studios to their limit, pioneering both harmony and rhythms on recordings like 'Rock 'n' Roll Calypso,' 'Black Puddin,' . . . 'Nora and the Yankee,' and 'Ghana'—which was specially commissioned by the in-coming government of that newly independent African nation."[67]

Kitchener was a major player in the music scene of the latter 1950s. Recording on the Melodisc label from 1955 to the mid-1960s, Kitchener enjoyed "a phenomenally successful residency at London's jazz hotspot The Sunset" and opened his own nightclub in Manchester, down the River Mersey from Liverpool. Second only to Belafonte in popularity, Kitchener "pushed the profile of international calypso to new heights," performing in "New York City and Washington D.C. to rapturous applause" and for those who sought him out in London clubs: Queen Elizabeth II's sister, Princess Margaret was one of these fans, and she purchased one hundred copies of "Kitch (Small Comb, Scratch Me Head)" (also known by the subtitle "Come to Bed") when she visited Trinidad and Tobago in 1955.[68]

During the convergence of calypso and rhythm and blues in the Liverpool soundscape, a broken wing appears in the lyrics of an early Lennon song. In 1957, between "Calypso Rock" and "Hello Little Girl," Lennon's second-ever composition included this bird imagery. Lennon "remember[ed] just as little" about this song, saying "only once, some years later, 'I did one which had the line "My love is like a bird with a broken wing" which I was very proud of.'"[69] Unlike McCartney's "Blackbird," whose speaker addresses the bird,

Lennon's speaker compares his own feelings to that of an injured bird. The romantic content evokes "Yellow Bird" and its source, as well as another song by Kitchener. In "Kitch Take It Easy," first issued on a Lyragon single with "Redhead" in 1953, the speaker compares love to a "turtle dove." These associations alone are not enough to claim a one-to-one influence, but they begin to suggest Lennon's habituation to tropes available in calypso.

The generic musical qualities of Lennon's early bird song aren't clear—was it rock or calypso? Based on Lennon's recollection about his second-ever song, the broken-wing lyric sounds earnest. Lennon was, however, long familiar with the use of birds as points of humor and vehicles of wordplay via Edward Lear and Lewis Carroll, whose nonsense poetry is emulated in Lennon's *In His Own Write* (1964). In the Wordsworth-evocative "I Sat Belonely Down a Tree," a lady who is actually a pig perches on a twig and flies away; accompanying sketches depict birds perched ridiculously on people's heads.[70] Still, the wordplay of calypso was clearly influential, too. Kitchener's album is full of irony and puns, often sexual in nature, along with some of his characteristic boasts sprinkled with self-deprecating humor. In "Redhead," women are like birds to "catch." Significantly, "Muriel and the Bug," also included on the record Lennon owned, is an ode to a "clever" bedbug who finds Muriel's "treasure," also suggestively referred to as "that area." The humorous dimensions of the last verse are clear: "The bug apparently succeeded where many men previously failed, [which] adds a layer of comical irony and continues a theme in calypso lyrics . . . in which the animal world wreaks erotic havoc on women to the salacious delight of male calypsonian narrators."[71] Remember also that the Beatles' own name is a bug pun usually attributed to Buddy Holly's Crickets. You could, in fact, suggest that Holly's bugs enter an accidental dialogue with Kitchener's because of their sheer proximity to each other in Lennon's possession: *The "Chirping" Crickets* was the other record Lennon was said to have owned by the end of the 1950s.[72]

Kitchener's lifelong rival for the calypso crown, the Mighty Sparrow (or King Sparrow, né Slinger Francisco), frequently referred to his bird sobriquet by third-person reference. He does so on 1959's *King Sparrow's Calypso Carnival* in "Teresa," which also includes a first-person declaration of love: "I love you and I'm always thinking of you." This lyric is echoed in the Beatles' "Ask Me Why," recorded in 1962 and released in 1963 as the B side to "Please Please Me" prior to the song's inclusion on the Beatles' first LP that year. Associations like these deserve more attention, especially since McCartney mentioned calypso in a 1980 interview, identifying the genre as a sound the pre-EMI recording Beatles were chasing: "We were trying to find the next beat—the next new sound. *New Musical Express* . . . was talking about calypso, and how latin rock was going to be the next big thing."[73] In addition to McCartney's '70s-era fascination with Jamaica, Caribbean rhythms and beats bookended Lennon's musical career, from his teenage endeavor "Calypso Rock" to "Borrowed Time"[74] and "Beautiful Boy (Darling Boy),"[75] some of the last songs he would ever record. The latter includes the sound of waves—and steel pans.

Liverpool Legacies: The Black Christ and the Four Lads

The Black Christ rises, arms outstretched in a V, as though he is about to fly from Toxteth's Metropolitan Methodist Centre on Princes Avenue in the L8. Suspended in ascension, this Arthur Dooley sculpture has been colloquially known as the Black Christ since it was mounted in 1969. When unveiled, *The Resurrection of the Christ* (its official name) was controversial for its representation of a Black and emaciated Jesus.[76] Dooley—a white leftist activist, radical Catholic, and committed communist—tapped into the logic of Flying Africans with his sculpture, representing death-bound flight from bodily suffering.

Dooley modeled this sculpture on none other than Lord Woodbine.[77]

For the Black Christ, Dooley clearly took inspiration from Woodbine's facial features while exaggerating his long, lean limbs. Erected just one year after "Blackbird" was recorded and released, the Woodbine-inspired Black Christ is a Jesus who is not necessarily easy to gaze upon. The sculpture depicts bodily deterioration signaling a long period of starvation. As a representation of the human form divine, the art challenges onlookers. The sculpture's dominant black material is accented by other paint colors visible upon closer inspection—key among them the red, bloodlike lines. The Black Christ rises, but this is a man who has suffered and suffers still, anticipating one of Lennon's most profound lyrics: "God is a concept by which we measure our pain."[78] Lennon's "God," aided by Billy Preston's supportive, motivating piano playing, was released in 1970, the year after the Black Christ was erected.

Dooley grew up in the Dingle, Starr's neighborhood and the one bordering Toxteth's Black community. Given Dooley's habituation to the culture of Liverpool, it's possible that his flight-bound sculpture references the "Liver birds" emblematic of Liverpool, a city whose modernity is rooted in the slave trade.[79] In preserving Woodbine's memory, Dooley brought Woodbine out of the darkness and into a certain light—before the next decades would impose a shadow status. Dooley's art thus commemorates Woodbine's leadership in the community, which included the Beatles.

In 1974, Dooley turned his attention to the band, producing a provocative piece installed on Mathew Street. *Four Lads Who Shook the World* is dedicated to the Beatles and features a ghoulish Virgin Mary cradling four babies. Above her is a street sign for "Beatle Street." (Illustrating Liverpudlians' famous sense of humor, cherub Paul, distinguished by his wings, was kidnapped in 1975 and hidden in a Liverpool resident's garage for forty years. He has since been restored, returned in a plastic bag with an apology note.)[80] Haunting the road of the rebuilt Cavern Club and a number of Beatles-themed clubs, Dooley's installation today reads as an eerie comment on Liverpool's present-day identity as a Beatles' tourist playground, continually asking the viewer to consider the nature of remembering.

Dooley frequently dealt in religious iconography, but the Black Christ and the *Four Lads* link Lord Woodbine and the Beatles, providing a visual link when the musical one has been obscured for so long. And Woodbine wasn't the only Black musical mentor to the Beatles in Liverpool, as Le Gendre notes: "The input of other black Liverpudlian musicians, such as the guitarists Odie Taylor, Vinnie Tow and Zancs Logie, was also instrumental in widening their musical vocabulary, particularly a knowledge of chords, which later served their song-writing."[81] McGrath finds evidence of a "casual guitar lesson" that Lennon and McCartney received from Tow at the Cavern in 1961. A Somali Irish rhythm guitarist living in the L8, Tow, later known as Vinnie Ismail, instructed Lennon and McCartney how to play "the string-bard seventh chord" necessary to Berry. As with Woodbine's insistence on the Beatles' need for a drummer, here is another example of a Black musician in Liverpool providing the tools needed to play music in the style of US rhythm and blues. Citing this and other examples, McGrath summarizes the musical dialogue: "The Beatles, especially John and Paul, were always looking and listening for new sounds to use in their music. This began in Liverpool, and the city's black musicians were part of it. . . . [A] lot of time and encouragement was generously given to the Beatles by these local black musicians."[82] Indeed, Woodbine's generosity is a quality Dooley captures with the Black Christ.

Exploring calypsos such as "Yellow Bird" in the Beatles' late-1950s Liverpool soundscape, we have found an expanded provenance for "Blackbird." This also includes Lennon's early use of broken-wing imagery, available in early compositional efforts that corresponded with his exposure to Lord Kitchener's calypso. These associations are significant because injured birds are poignant symbols in arts of the African Diaspora. Nina Simone's "Blackbird" features one such bird, who is encouraged to give up her flight dreams—and who predates McCartney's by five years.

CHAPTER 6

You Ain't Ever Gonna Fly

Nina Simone's "Blackbird" and Revolutionary Responses to the Beatles

A blackbird called "little sorrow" struggles to fly.[1] Her song, like the mythic Philomela's sad nightingale call, is one of mourning.[2] She's an unwanted and unloved creature whose parents are named Lonely and Pain. Her future tears will be so numerous no vessel will be able to hold them, and from neither person nor place will she find love. She's always and already rejected, and this is why the song's speaker keeps telling her she shouldn't even bother trying. Her miseries and obstacles mean she'll never fly.

This earthbound blackbird is decidedly not Paul McCartney's. "Blackbird" by Nina Simone was first released in 1963 as the B side on a Colpix single featuring a live version of "Little Liza Jane." Five years before McCartney's 1968 "Blackbird," Simone's song uses the bird to address conditions of being Black in America. Similar to Jazz Age star Florence Mills, Simone identified personally with the blackbird, making this connection clear in interviews. In doing so, Simone's musical and other discourse exemplifies Afro-Atlantic flight; like her contemporaries, Simone recalled a historically contingent artistic legacy that imagined flying as a response to the bondage of slavery. This reading is supported by bird imagery appearing elsewhere in Simone's oeuvre, which also includes her answer to the Beatles' "Revolution." These texts also evidence transatlantic flight: she Signifies on the Beatles, though not only them, when she imagines or remembers flying, both in music and in autobiography.

Meet Nina Simone and "Blackbird" (1963)

Simone's "Blackbird" addresses a miserable creature, asking why she, so lonely and full of sorrow, would even want to fly. Read with the trope of Flying Africans in mind, the song exposes slavery's legacy. Folktales such as "All God's Chillen Had Wings" speak of an ancestral heritage that remains accessible for enslaved people forced to labor in the fields. They are still able to understand an old man's language—and this understanding is what allows them to free themselves and fly.[3] But Simone's blackbird is alienated, inheriting from her equally miserable parents the generational consequences of systematic post-Reconstruction oppression, as well as family separation and the erasure of ancestral knowledge. That immense and inarticulable loss is expressed in Simone's "Blackbird": this bird can't fly because her obstacles are too great for one individual to overcome.

In the early 1960s a black-colored bird was still synonymously evoked by "Jim Crow," the laws that segregated Tryon, North Carolina, the town in which Simone (then Eunice Waymon) grew up. Simone's daughter, Lisa Simone, remembered, "When [my mother] talked about Jim Crow and segregation, she rarely referred to it at that stage in her life, even though it did touch her. . . . She did tell me about the times when she was told her nose was too big, her lips were too full, and her skin was too dark. I assume she was told there are only certain things you'll be good for in your life."[4] This is the kind of rejected status known and communicated in Simone's "Blackbird" and, later, "Fodder in Her Wings," a song to which we return at the end of this chapter.

Simone learned the lessons of loss predicated on racism throughout her life. A major rejection involved Philadelphia's Curtis Institute of Music; in her memoir, she explains how she was later told the denial was due to her race. The Institute's decision barred Simone from achieving her intended goal, to be "the first black classical concert pianist," but the disappointment was not just a personal letdown. Both her family and the Black *and* white members of her segregated community in Tryon had invested in her education—and she felt her obligation to them: "I applied myself with great dedication and turned my back on everything but the fulfillment of our destiny."[5] The rejection ended up being a turning point in her career, changing its musical direction from classical to popular.

Prior to the Curtis audition, Simone was already studying at Juilliard following the training she received from a white Englishwoman living on the other side of Tryon. Muriel Mazzanovich ("Miz Mazzy") instilled in the girl a lifelong love of Bach (the composer McCartney claims to riff on in "Blackbird"). Explaining Bach's mathematician's approach, Simone insisted, "He is technically perfect. . . . Bach made me dedicate my life to music."[6] Before she fell in love with the composer and other classics, Simone's first formative musical experiences were playing piano in the church: "Gospel taught me about improvisation, how to shape music in response to an audience and then how to shape the mood of the audience in response to my music. When I played I could take a congregation where I wanted—calm them down or lift them up until they became completely lost in the music and atmosphere. Of course God, the church and His ministers provided the spiritual inspiration, but the music was part of it too."[7] Early on, Simone was developing a rhetorical musical disposition that attenuated her to others, which she then bridged with the discipline of a classical pianist. This translated into concert performances during which she was demanding of both herself and listeners, whose focus and attention she expected. Throughout her life, though, Simone had experience dealing with white audience members who did not give her the respect she deserved.

For Simone, the blackbird was a ready metaphor for discrimination she encountered, as well as the broader treatment of African Americans in the United States. A writer for *Jet* magazine also heard in "Blackbird" a desire "to express her feelings about the current racial crisis."[8] The September 1963 release of the Colpix single, in fact, coincides with the very month that Simone marked as the real beginning of her civil rights consciousness. Up to that point, playwright Lorraine Hansberry had been urging Simone to get more involved in the movement; Medgar Evers's assassination in June was also a catalyst. But the September bombing that killed four Black girls at the Sixteenth Street Baptist Church in Birmingham, Alabama, was Simone's epiphany: "I suddenly realized what it was to be black in America in 1963, but it wasn't an intellectual connection of the type Lorraine had ben repeating to me over and over—it came as a rush of fury, hatred, and determination."[9]

Perhaps because the composition and recording of "Blackbird" preceded or just coincided with that September 1963 turning point, critics seldom situate "Blackbird" in the trajectory of Simone's 1960s civil rights songs, such as "Mississippi Goddam" (1964),[10] which she remembered writing that very day.[11] But Simone also admits that her "ideas developed over months and years." Simone had, for example, met Stokely Carmichael in 1962, and her exposure to him and other leaders habituated her to the "question of where to go next." In her memoir, Simone reflects on this timeline of gradual awakening, a period during which she composed and recorded "Blackbird." Simone came to realize the importance of "separatism": "In the white man's world the black man would always lose out, so the idea of a separate black nation, whether it was in American or in Africa, made sense."[12] Africa's promise as a haven was long on Simone's mind, and, as we show in the next section, the instrumentation of "Blackbird" bespeaks an African musical sensibility.

Lacking the indignation of the soon-to-be-censored "Mississippi Goddam," "Blackbird" is not a rallying anthem. The low self-esteem[13] presented in Simone's "Blackbird" is also a far cry from the complex celebration of Black women's images in "Four Women" and the "Black is beautiful" message in the Hansberry-inspired[14] "To Be Young, Gifted and Black." But we don't need to see "Blackbird" in opposition to those songs; rather, they reflect different aspects of Black experiences in the United States, the kind so often negotiated in the dramatic and literary works of Simone's contemporaries Hansberry, Langston Hughes, James Baldwin, and Maya Angelou, who all wrote about the hopelessness and vulnerability of isolated individuals as well as the hopefulness and strength available in and with the recognition of the community.

Comparing "Blackbird" (1963) and "Blackbird" (1968)

Simone's songs, especially "Sinnerman," have proven effective choices for film and television soundtracks even when the accompanying visuals are a mismatch with the song's rich content; her take on "Ain't Got No, I Got Life" (from the musical *Hair*) recently scored a vitamin commercial. Compared to the popularity and longevity of these songs, Simone's "Blackbird" is an obscurity. The song is additionally peculiar in the Simone oeuvre because Colpix stuck "Blackbird" on *Nina Simone with Strings* (1966), one of the records issued after Simone left the label, even though this track does not have any added string arrangements.

Simone brought her characteristic intensity to "Blackbird," whose lyrics are relentlessly pessimistic.[15] The song's musical features reflect these themes and anticipate her interest in African music and her eventual move to Liberia. According to Walter Everett, Simone's track includes "very distinctive rhythms," involving "an African drum, the djembe, because of the same pitch bend on every downbeat."[16] Everett adds that "the Simone performance is also notable for having no suggestions of chord changes, which are very intricate in McCartney's "Blackbird."" Along these lines, "Simone's singing is entirely restricted to the minor pentatonic scale," which, coupled with the absence of chord changes, serves the lyrics' hopelessness and lack of flight. By contrast, McCartney sings his optimistic "Blackbird" almost entirely in the major pentatonic scale—except for one use of the minor pentatonic during "into the light of the dark black night."[17] The "blues scale" that accompanies this lyric is "the only material in 'Blackbird' with an exclusively African American origin."[18] Although the comparison helps draw a contrast between the two songs, no evidence suggests McCartney was familiar with Simone's "Blackbird." Paul did, however, admit to a Simone influence on the Beatles' "Michelle," although this was John's contribution: "Lennon offered a bridge (C) with a 'bluesy edge,' inspired by the intense spirit of a line from Nina Simone's scatted version of 'I Put a Spell on You.'"[19]

Unlike with McCartney's numerous explanations for his "Blackbird," we find much less evidence of Simone speaking about her "Blackbird." In September 1963, the month "Blackbird" was released on the Colpix single, Simone did give a backstage interview with *Newsweek* in which she strikes chords reminiscent of Florence Mills, except that Simone is even more blunt: "What I am and what I do are all involved with the underlying fact of color. . . . I'm the Blackbird of show business. . . . When I first sang that song, it made me sad. But I liked it, and it expressed the truth. That's how I perform. . . . I relate to people. My music is about what they feel. Others could tell the same story, maybe their talent is not as obvious as mine. Music is my medium."[20] When Simone compared herself to her title character, she claimed the blackbird's subject position in order to talk about her "sad" song. She was also accessing a particular tradition of Black women singers in the music industry, one that begins with Elizabeth Taylor Greenfield being labeled the "Black Swan," a sobriquet that often reflected denigrating attitudes by the white press.[21] And, like Mills, Simone used the blackbird as a symbol of her talent, which she saw as serving the Black community in the United States.[22] In retrospect, Simone's blackbird could be Mills singing her signature tune, whose speaker claimed to be a forlorn, crying, lonely blackbird—albeit one with hope.

Similar to how McCartney's "Blackbird" sounds like an optimistic response to Simone, Simone's "Blackbird" sounds like a pessimistic response to Mills. Simone's level of familiarity with Mills and "I'm a Little Blackbird Looking for a Bluebird" is unclear, and it goes unmentioned in her memoir. The memoir does not mention the composition of her "Blackbird" at all, in fact, providing no explanation for why Herbert Sacker is co-credited on the song. Simone also does not acknowledge sharing titles with the Beatles' "Blackbird," which appeared on the same double album as "Revolution 1," the latter a song Simone definitely knew.

Simone's "Revolution" (1969)

As an answer to the Beatles song, Simone's "Revolution" (cowritten with Weldon Irvine) was split into two tracks, "Revolution (Part 1)" and "Revolution (Part 2)," on her 1969 single and appeared on the album *To Love Somebody*. Citing Black Americans' past, current, and ongoing struggles, Simone's "Revolution" is a call to action, whose urgency is made especially clear with imagery of boots pressing on the backs of Black people.[23] Things in America were beginning to change (and escalate even), but, as she argues in the song, there's a long way to go in dismantling the white power structure. In Simone's answer to the Beatles, nowhere is there a suggestion that she or Black people have woken up to find themselves suddenly free in the last years of the 1960s—although this is what a twenty-first-century McCartney implies when he explains the symbolism of his 1968 "Blackbird."[24]

With her 1969 "Revolution," Simone (like others in the New Left at the time)[25] took the Beatles to task for their disaffected attitude about the need for radical change. The *White Album*'s "Revolution 1" "expresses ambivalence, quizzically telling the revolutionaries that they 'can count me out—in,'" because, as Lennon explained, "I wasn't sure."[26] The promotional film for the single version of "Revolution" maintains the indecision in the out-in lyrics, even though the record itself squarely refuses to participate in structural upheaval. In the filmed performance, McCartney's and Harrison's throwback "shooby doo wop" vocables are perhaps a bit too playful for the occasion, betraying a cavalier attitude in line with an unwillingness to donate. Everett explains the shift that had not yet come: "Despite Lennon's strong antiwar feelings, he was not against the establishment in 1968, as he would be a year later."[27]

The Beatles' "Revolution" specifically addresses political revolution and war, but the peace movement, as Dr. King argued before his assassination, was intertwined with civil rights. After all, Black men were disproportionately affected by the war. By the late 1960s, Simone had resolved to use her musical platform to talk about dismantling, not reforming, racist institutions. As she explained, "When I had started out in the movement all I wanted were my rights under the Constitution, but the more I thought about it the more I realized that no matter what the President or the Supreme Court might say, the only way we could get true equality was if America changed completely, top to bottom. And this change had to start with my own people, with black revolution."[28] The words ending in -*tion* quoted above also appear in Simone's "Revolution," creating rhymes that Signify on the Beatles. Simone lifts "destruction," "evolution," and the repeated alrights while transforming imagery like Lennon's "free your mind" cliché into "clean your brain." Simone additionally uses rhymes ending in -*ate* to underscore her desire to "communicate" a message she will cross an "ocean" to deliver. The use of the latter, which rhymes with all the words ending with -*tion*, calls back to the dangerous Middle Passage that robbed Black people of their freedom in the first place.

Pointing to the Atlantic's deadly history and lethal potential, Simone's function's is akin to the "African armed with a password" in the trope of Flying Africans.[29] Simone's "Revolution" positions the singer as minister to her community, especially with "alright" repeated throughout, Signifyin(g) on the word's appearance at the end the Beatles' "Revolution." Delivered in an ecstatic rock crescendo by Lennon's throat-ripping vocals, the Beatles' "alright" does reassure the listener that things will turn out, but they ask their "brother" to "wait." Simone's answer? She won't wait—*can't wait*—because the state's boot is on Black people's backs, figuratively and literally. Simone incorporates and repeats the alright refrain with the sensibility of a gospel song, recalling her musical roots in the Black Church, where that word is used as a salve, spur, and recognition. This is palpable in live performances of this song. At the Harlem Cultural Festival in 1969, Simone bound its revolutionary spirit to the Afro-American struggle. In her introductory delivery of David Nelson's poem "Are You Ready?" she directed its central question to "Black people," repeating variations to encourage the audience "to listen to all the beautiful Black voices," as well as asking them if they were "ready to smash white things" and to "build Black things,"[30] a metaphor for what she does to the Beatles' "Revolution."

Simone's recorded version of "Revolution" includes a cacophony of sounds—an aural experience of dismantling. This possible allusion to the Beatles' "Revolution 9" may suggest familiarity with the *White Album* and not just the "Revolution" single. This, once again, raises questions about Simone's knowledge of the Beatles' "Blackbird": Did she consider the Beatles' song, possibly hearing theirs as an optimistic response to hers? Perhaps she would have noted McCartney's blackbird's movement into the light and a motivation to sing. These motifs are familiar to an interpretation of jazz artist Billy Taylor's "I Wish I Knew How It Would Feel to Be Free," a song she released on *Silk & Soul* (1967). First recorded by Taylor in 1963 and released on Capitol as a single in 1964, "I Wish" was prevalent in the US civil rights movement and has since been covered by many other gospel-oriented Black artists, such as Mavis Staples, Bela Fleck and the Alabama Blind Boys, and John Legend.

Simone's potent version of "I Wish" has proven memorable, circulated by her recorded performances and via interviews in which she riffed on its lyrics, drawing attention to the song's parallels to her life (discussed in more detail below). The first-person perspective of "I Wish" evokes the logic of spirituals that express the desire to fly while recognizing present limitations through the use of "if" (as seen in "Sing A-ho That I Had the Wings of a Dove").[31] Likewise, flight is anticipated and imagined in "I Wish," which claims a right to personhood through a correlation with the bird. Waiting and hoping for flight are actions available in McCartney's "Blackbird," whose use of light and dark are also reminiscent of "I Wish." Its last verse connects would-be flight and the sun: *if* the speaker could fly, they would fly into its rays and "look down at the sea," at which point singing would be the proof of freedom. Notably, when "I Wish" references a body of water, the song positions the wished-for transcendence happening over the very space that motivated the trope of Flying Africans and that continues to animate expressions of Afro-Atlantic flight during and following civil rights.

The sea imagery of "I Wish" echoes in Simone's "Revolution" in which she promises to carry her message over the ocean—which she promptly did in 1969. She was disappointed that her answer to the Beatles' song hadn't received the notice enjoyed by "Ain't Got No, I Got Life" and her cover of the Bee Gees' "To Love Somebody," whose positive reception widened her appeal among British listeners.[32] At the end of 1970, when Jann Wenner asked Lennon to give his opinion on a selection of Black artists' covers, the former Beatle singled Simone out: "I think it was interesting that Nina Simone did a sort of answer to 'Revolution.' That was very good—it was sort of like 'Revolution,' but not quite."[33] Lennon gestures toward Simone's uniquely critical perspective. That perspective, radical in both form and meaning, did not necessarily translate to Top 40 success.

As Simone told London-based *Melody Maker*, "I'm sensitive about all my records but I'm concerned because this one ['Revolution'] isn't selling. I'd like the fans to find out why it's not being played, I want to know what they think. 'Revolution' means what's going on in the world. If you listen to the lyrics of the song you will see though it does mention the racial problem, there are numerous others—the young against the old, the black against the white, the poor against the rich, the new breed against the old establishment."[34] Like Dr. King, Simone was attuned to intersectional dynamics, and she continued her musical dialogue with the Beatles, recording other memorable interpretations of Harrison-authored songs, whose melancholy edges are well suited to Simone's rearrangements. In the early 1970s she brought to "Here Comes the Sun" and "Isn't It a Pity" her characteristic intensity of world-weary regret and recognition of past pain.

Nina Simone's Wings

Simone did not mention her "Blackbird" in her memoir, but she frequently mentioned the double-edged nature of actual flight via aviation. One such journey summoned "Four Women," whose title images parallel the four deceased girls who inspired "Mississippi Goddam": "They came to me while I was on an airplane. I wrote it and kept it to myself for a year before I was ready to share it. I had to make sure I was saying a whole truth."[35] When Simone reflected in her memoir about traveling, flying into the United States on a plane was frequently a harbinger of bad things.[36] Such apprehensions and anxieties are expressed in "Blackbird" and other bird or flight songs that appear throughout Simone's oeuvre.

When she headlined Carnegie Hall in April 1963, Simone performed the aria "Black Swan," the first track on *Nina Simone at Carnegie Hall*. The 2005 EMI reissue of that record lists "Blackbird" as the last bonus track, finally situating the song in its proper historical context. "Blackbird" is a fitting bookend to "Black Swan," in which a forlorn bride, who is searching for her lover, addresses the title bird; perhaps some of this lonesome bird imagery inspired Simone's 1963 "Blackbird." Prior to this, she had also recorded an instrumental version of "Bye Bye Blackbird," included on *Nina Simone at the Village Gate* (1962). Although she does not sing the lyrics, Simone certainly knew that in them a blackbird's darkness is spurned in favor of a bluebird's light, a rejection motif that shows up so clearly in her "Blackbird."[37]

Two decades after singing to and comparing herself with the blackbird, Simone rendered herself a bird who couldn't fly in "Fodder in Her Wings," a variation of the 1982 LP's title, *Fodder on My Wings*. "Fodder in Her Wings" is like Icarus in reverse, the image of a fallen bird, wingless on the ground. As Simone explained, "It's about a bird that fell to earth and was crippled when it landed in fodder and other human debris. Although it was able to survive, it couldn't fly. So it walks from country to country to see if people had forgotten how to live, how to give. As it went, the bird found that most of the people had forgotten."[38] With "Fodder in Her Wings," Simone linked her bird-oriented songs, binding them to her perspective on racial inequality and the unresolved status of the civil rights movement, themes reflective of

Afro-Atlantic flight. Ironically, "Fodder" offers another pessimistic dialectic with the Beatles when she sings, "She flitted here and there / United States, everywhere." Those lines would appear to allude to "Here, There, and Everywhere," a song McCartney has, in fact, connected to "Bye Bye Blackbird."[39]

"Fodder in Her Wings" can also be heard as a deeply personal reflection on Simone's post-1960s migrations—she traveled back and forth from the United States to Barbados, Liberia, Switzerland, and elsewhere—constant moves that, according to her memoir, rendered her placeless and vulnerable. In retrospect, "Blackbird" anticipates Simone's inability to find a stable home and lover, her in-between status determined in no small part by her race, gender, and nationality. Simone was unwilling to submit to controlling patriarchs at home and abroad.[40] Refusing to be subservient to men with their own political and social power in Barbados and Liberia, she then lost the homes she cultivated there. In Europe, she was frequently treated as a token outsider and was the victim of more acute acts of violence and exploitation in England. Meanwhile, America was no safe haven for Simone either: "I couldn't stay in my own country for more than a couple of weeks before I had to flee like a runaway slave."[41] Simone's take on the aforementioned "I Wish I Knew How It Would Feel to Be Free" similarly foresees the intersectional challenges she continued to face in this transatlantic context. The premise of that song was invoked when an interviewer asked her to explain freedom. "Just a feeling," she said, before comparing its ineffability to "tell[ing] somebody how it feels to be in love." Turning more definitive, she said adamantly, "I tell you what freedom is to me. No fear. I mean, really, no fear."[42]

Simone, Angelou, and Literary-Musical "Blackbird" Legacies

Looking back on the fall of 1963, Simone reached a breaking point that is either expressed or anticipated in her "Blackbird" and then reprised in "Fodder in Her Wings." In addition to apprehending her own story, Simone's 1963 "Blackbird" anticipates the rise of Afro-Atlantic flight in literature of the post–civil rights era, such as the work of Maya Angelou, who met and wrote about Simone in 1970.

Angelou called attention to Simone's associations with flight. In the "High Priestess of Soul," an article for *Redbook*, Angelou begins with imagery from a spiritual, "Ezekiel Saw the Wheel," reproducing lyrics about the air-bound wheel within a wheel, inspired by the biblical account of the prophet's vision. Angelou relates these metaphors for faith and God's grace—instruments of flight—to Simone's mother's belief that she was pregnant with "someone 'very special.'" With Angelou, Simone explained the technical relationship between Bach and the blues (both "structured like a good piece of architecture"), as well as her role as a Black artist committed to addressing "the needs of my people." Angelou's piece paints a complex portrait of Simone, concluding, "Life has left keloidal scars on her voice, and wells of angry tears lie beneath each spoken word. Here lies innocence betrayed, and the keening that is heard is a dirge for hope abused. She is loved or feared, adored or disliked, but few who have met her music or glimpsed her soul react with moderation. She is an extremist, extremely realized."[43]

After this interview, Simone and Angelou would each go on to pursue the racial haven they saw in Africa. The title of Angelou's *All God's Children Need Traveling Shoes* (1986) riffs on the so-named flight-oriented folktale and the spiritual that both communicate the homebound flight motif.[44] The autobiographical account of the author's "two-year exile" in Ghana reflects, as Michelle D. Commander argues, Afro-Atlantic flight's pessimistic outcomes: "Angelou makes the mistake of reading Ghanaians as kin because of their skin color, while most Ghanaians read her as simply a foreigner."[45] Commander situates Angelou's "familial longing" and resulting "disappointment" in the context of other "exiles [who] embraced the fantastic Pan-African ideal of working and producing together in Ghana to show their sincerity in returning; yet constant, dramatic refrains regarding reminders of slavery's past occur."[46] Simone had a comparable experience in Liberia, reinforcing the tragedy of homelessness appearing in her bird songs.

In stories and representations within the United States and elsewhere in the Diaspora, birds are often vehicles for negotiating pressing and present limitations when Africa is out of physical reach. Simone's wounded blackbird in 1963 is also precursor to the central image of Angelou's autobiographical *I Know Why the Caged Bird Sings* (1969).[47] Angelou's now-iconic cover features a black-colored bird taking flight, reinforcing the central image named in the title. Positioning authorship in relation to the bird's subjectivity, Angelou's coming-of-age account examines the consequences of the racism and sexual violence that she faced as a girl in the southern United States. Her title is lifted directly from Paul Laurence Dunbar's 1899 poem "Sympathy," which includes imagery of a "bruised" wing, another precedent for a blackbird's broken one. The singing bird's voice is a prayerful "plea" flung up to heaven for freedom; the speaker's knowledge of bird's message relates their shared experiences: "I know why the caged bird beats his wing / Till its blood is red on the cruel bars."[48] Angelou's singing bird is, then, another figuration for reclaiming voice.

On *Songs in A Minor*, the 2001 debut album that includes her hit "Fallin'," Alicia Keys alludes to Angelou in "Caged Bird." The speaker expresses discomfort with being caged and looked upon, revealing that the caged bird's song is one of joy and imploring others to recognize her "beauty" and let her "fly." With its allusions to a coming-of-age novel that has resonated with generations of young readers, the song also reflected the twenty-year-old Keys's own youth and relative inexperience in the industry. A decade later, in 2011, Keys, by then a well-established artist, performed a cover of the Beatles' "Blackbird."[49] Accompanying herself on the piano, Keys extends the song, using melisma and her vocal range to move between sensitivity and strength. Notably, she shifts the song into the first person toward the end, claiming herself to be the blackbird, the strategy that Aretha Franklin used with "Eleanor Rigby" and that Bettye LaVette had done with "Blackbird" during her 2010 Hollywood Bowl performance.[50] Along with these predecessors, Keys's bird songs dialogue with each other as statements about her own career, while also contributing to the poetic legacy of Dunbar via Angelou.

In retrospect, Angelou's novel seems to bridge the world-weary sorrow of Simone's "Blackbird" with the optimism of McCartney's song; although Maya is the victim of both sexual and racial trauma, she locates the tools of survival in literature and storytelling. This legacy continues: Larry Duplechan's use of the blackbird nods (albeit not intentionally) to Angelou's coming-of-age memoir while (intentionally) adding McCartney's "Blackbird" to the mix. Along with numerous other allusions, Duplechan invoked the Beatles when he titled his book *Blackbird* (1986), a novel "for gay men of my generation (who had, presumably, gone through similar experiences, and who might understand my pop cultural references)."[51] The Beatles' song appears in the novel during an impromptu performance at school; the protagonist, Johnnie Ray, sings while his friend plays guitar: "Todd slid his fingers into the intro and tapped the stiletto-point of his boot against the floor, head down, his yellow-gold hair nearly obscuring his face. I closed my eyes and sang. . . . Todd did the accompaniment without a single hitch, and when we finished there was some applause. And I felt so good, so warm, a feeling like Saturday morning in bed and pancakes for breakfast."[52] Johnnie's narration then considers the depth of Todd's feelings for his girlfriend, whose love of "Blackbird" motivated the boy to learn the song.[53] Even though the song certainly applies to the Black gay protagonist, who loves to sing but whose sexuality is relegated to the dark, Duplechan does not reductively bind the song only to race or sexuality; the coming-into-the-light awakening themes are fungible and broadly applicable to the adolescent subject matter.[54]

Simone's "Blackbird" Remembered in Visual Art

In addition to participating in literary and musical discourses of Afro-Atlantic flight in the twentieth century, Simone's "Blackbird" has inspired politically responsive art. "Why You Wanna Fly Blackbird," a 2020 art installation, called attention to Simone's song, further reclaiming its central image as one special to Black Americans, especially in relation to the loss of children. The Detroit-based artist Sabrina Nelson explained, "I got [the title and concept] from a Nina Simone song who talks about Black women, like, how dare you try and be happy in your life, how dare you not expect pain. Pain is gonna come; you have to move through it, and you have to live, but pain will be here." True to the double-edged nature of the Flying Africans trope, Nelson's art is not, as she explains, conventionally "pretty," and her large drawings and reliquaries have "girth" to depict the embodied experience of trauma and loss.[55]

With many representations of empty cages and unpopulated nests (such as hanging dresses with an empty cage where a womb might be), Nelson visualizes the flip side of Simone's "Blackbird": whereas Simone's title character has no home, here the homes have lost their children. These images are, as Nelson explains, a response to "homicides and death," the loss of individual Black lives that impact the entire community.[56] With Simone's "Blackbird" as antecedent, Nelson Signifies on Simone and her recurring themes, echoing a legacy comparable to that of Florence Mills, whose association with the blackbird has also been a source of artistic inspiration for others.

Motivated by her own political awakening, Simone's "Blackbird" and other bird and flight-oriented music participate in the identifiable legacy that Commander theorizes, that of Afro-Atlantic flight in a post–civil rights context. Also illustrating this book's concept of transatlantic flight, Simone was active in the back-and-forth dialogue with the Beatles, her music offering exemplary instances of other such conversations between Black musicians and the Beatles during the 1960s. Simone's "Blackbird" exists in a trajectory with predecessors such as Mills's "I'm a Little Blackbird Looking for a Bluebird" while complicating the easy optimism of McCartney's 1968 song, a tune whose provenance has more explanations than any other Beatles number.

CHAPTER 7

A Blackbird on a White Album

Aretha Franklin, Jimi Hendrix, Diana Ross, and Other Winged Inspirations in and around 1968

"Blackbird" creates a colorized contrast with *The Beatles*, more commonly known as the *White Album*. Here two favorite Paul McCartney tropes converge, birds and paired opposites. Some of the songwriter's most memorable songs are rooted in contrasting states: hello and goodbye, making love and taking love, Venus and Mars, living and letting die, Ebony and Ivory—the list goes on, evidencing, as we've suggested, a rhetorical impulse related to pairs also found in Black American culture (although here pairs are often more ironic).[1] In the case of "Blackbird," the black-colored bird flies out of the void of the album's white cover, a metaphor for the song's existence and longevity outside *The Beatles*—and the Beatles.

The central image of "Blackbird" characterizes transatlantic flight, but not simply because McCartney, a white British man, eventually mentioned an inspiration that involved Black people in the United States. To this point in this book, we have explored precedents that involve the bridge from gospel to rock 'n' roll, as well as the Beatles' penchant for interpolating nursery rhymes in the late 1960s, the latter an impulse inherited from their Black American rhythm and blues idols and folk traditions that precede them. McCartney's "Blackbird" can also be read in dialogue with 1920s pop standards, including "I'm a Little Blackbird Looking for a Bluebird" and especially "Bye Bye Blackbird." Lead Belly's "Grey Goose" offers a particularly compelling precedent for broken-wing imagery, and, as a song that addresses the bird's ability to fly, the calypso "Yellow Bird" is another precursor. In retrospect, McCartney also seems to converse with Nina Simone's 1963 "Blackbird" and her cover of "I Wish I Knew How It Would Feel to Be Free." In addition to these songs, we have mentioned numerous other examples, including blues numbers and spirituals, that evidence the potency of birds as liberation metaphors in the Black music. We begin this chapter with a few more bird precedents, especially those contemporaneous to the Beatles during the 1960s. Beginning with folk revivalists leads to Aretha Franklin's bird songs and then to the winged imagery of Jimi Hendrix, whose attenuation to flight corresponds with his association with Little Richard, who also referred frequently to angels.

Birds are, as we have also addressed, not always kind designations for Black people in American popular song. The polysemous functions of blackbirds parallel the multiplicity of explanations for McCartney's song. Different accounts situate McCartney's inspiration for the 1968 song in multiple geographical contexts; in addition to Scotland, they include his family's home in Liverpool and the Transcendental Meditation retreat the Beatles attended in Rishikesh, India, early in 1968. Following the *White Album*'s release, McCartney's conversation with singer-songwriter Donovan Leitch (known simply as Donovan) offers more clues about how civil rights came to be attached to "Blackbird," including the mention of Diana Ross. We consider the evolving uses of the words "Black" and "bird" in the United States and the United Kingdom, questioning whether white British men calling Black women "blackbirds" is wholly complimentary in 1968 and 1969.

It is because the title image of "Blackbird" is so double-edged that the polysemous symbol represents the broader nature of the Beatles' dialogue with Black music, especially during the postcolonial milieu of the 1960s. Alongside the composition and recording of "Blackbird," another 1968 song, "Ob-La-Di, Ob-La-Da," had its title appropriated from Nigerian-born musician Jimmy Scott. The immediate afterlives of "Blackbird" also involve wildly contrasting uses: on the one hand, the twisted interpretations and applications of Charles Manson; on the other, the innovative approach of Ramsey Lewis, the first Black American to reveal the song's liberatory meaning.

Blackbird Predecessors in the 1960s: From Folk Revivals to Aretha Franklin

The four-and-twenty blackbirds of "Sing a Song of Sixpence" and the going-and-coming birds in "Two Little Blackbirds" feature some of the numerous black-colored creatures that fly throughout English-language nursery rhymes, which made their way into Black people's folk songs and subsequent recorded popular music in the Americas. So many other folk songs feature blackbirds or black-colored birds, especially in the British Isles folk tradition. There are too many to name, but we might start with the blackbird of Delia Murphy. This Irish folk singer, who recorded songs she collected, released two singles that included "If I Were a Blackbird" (1940, 1949). Sung from the perspective of a maiden trying to regain a lost love, this folk song (Roud 387) is mentioned in passing in the memoir of Pattie Boyd, George Harrison's first wife.[2] The reference underscores the song's cultural ubiquity in British pubs; Murphy's tunes would have been otherwise known to the Beatles through their exposure to radio.

As we saw with Nina Simone's representation of her sorrowful blackbird in 1963, black-colored birds are often sad. This has a long precedent, seen in a "minstrel ballad" with "popular features" and whose documentation dates to the sixteenth century.[3] "Crow and Pie" (Child 111 Roud 3975)[4] is a cautionary song recounting the rape of a young woman whose assailant first tries to seduce her, but then refuses to marry her or provide financial restitution; the song's title and sexual bird puns reinforce associations between crows and scavenging and between magpies and sorrow, as evidenced by the magpie-centric nursery rhyme "One for Sorrow" (Roud 20096), the latter a counting nursery rhyme relevant to another McCartney song, "Two Magpies" (discussed near the end of this chapter).

In addition to Donovan's "The Magpie" (1967) many more folkie birds appear in songs by the Beatles' contemporaries, including Marianne Faithfull, who released her version of "This Little Bird" in 1965 on her self-titled record, which also included her take on Lennon and McCartney's "I'm a Loser." On her next album that year, *Come My Way*, Faithfull released "Black Girl," her take on Lead Belly's song. The latter song, like other bird-oriented folksongs mentioned here, centers on the title's subject to probe loss and fidelity—and is probably the most famous rock 'n' roll predecessor to feature a young Black woman in the title.

White musicians from the United Kingdom were, of course, not the only ones singing about sad birds as they revived traditional music in the early to mid-1960s. Aretha Franklin's "Tiny Sparrow," which she performed on television in 1964, is a case in point. Based on the arrangement released the previous year by Peter, Paul, and Mary, "Tiny Sparrow" is another name for the Appalachian folk song "Come All You Fair and Tender Ladies" (Roud 451). Composed in the style of a "Come All Ye" song, which gathers listeners to behold a lesson, maidens are called to witness the consequences of not protecting oneself from a false lover. After his betrayal, the speaker imagines herself as a sparrow, an instrument of redress whose flight is symbolic of reclaiming virtue. But the speaker realizes she is not a sparrow and cannot correct the past; her aim now is to warn fellow maidens about guarding their own hearts (and virtue).

Aretha's soulful delivery of the song stretches out the lines and reaches deeply for feeling, the techniques born out of her gospel background. The style positions the central image of "Tiny Sparrow" in relation to "His Eye Is on the Sparrow"—rendering the former song's speaker's inability to fly like a sparrow more profound, illustrative of the doubt with which human beings live. Remember that, in the gospel hymn, sparrows fly because they have faith in the Lord, who counts and thus values them all; that faith isn't always so easy for humans. When Franklin sings the last verse of "Tiny Sparrow"— in which the speaker realizes she does not have wings and cannot fly—she imbues the song with the kind of flightless sadness Simone expressed in her 1963 "Blackbird." The song's last lines, "And on this Earth, in grief and sorrow / I am bound until I die," likewise make a case for how a flightless bird is relevant to Black Americans' experiences. The lyrics are about being broken and bound, but in this case Franklin's powerhouse gospel register communicates a strength and will to survive, which are offered to the listener, too.

Franklin's "Tiny Sparrow" followed her success in 1963 with "Skylark," a jazz standard published in 1941 with music by Hoagy Carmichael and lyrics by Johnny Mercer. In a song full of lush, romantic imagery (a blossom-covered lane, a misty meadow), the speaker sings to the bird. She recognizes its loneliness and asks for guidance: "I don't know if you can find these things / But my heart is riding on your wings." Franklin added to her aviary with her take on "Mockingbird," released on *Runnin' Out of Fools* (1965) and rereleased as a charting single in 1967. The bird of this duet song, written and originally recorded in 1963 by siblings Charlie and Inez Foxx and based on the lullaby "Hush, Little Baby" (Roud 470), is involved in a barter: if the mockingbird doesn't sing, a diamond ring is required. With her bird imagery in "Tiny Sparrow" as well as "Skylark" and "Mockingbird," Franklin also called back to the central image of her father's bestselling Chess record, the sermon "The Eagle Stirreth Her Nest."[5]

Jimi Hendrix's Wings to Little Richard's Gospel

In addition to Simone and the bird songs addressed in the previous chapter, the birds of folk revivalists and of Franklin are instructive precedent for approaching the broken-winged blackbird on the Beatles' *White Album*. But no countercultural musician was more obsessed with wings—of birds, of angels, even of planes—than Jimi Hendrix, whose paths crossed with the Beatles on multiple occasions in 1967. Several years later, on the Isle of Wight on the last day of August 1970, Jimi Hendrix instructed the emcee, "Call [me] the blue wild angel. The wild blue angel."[6] He died shortly after this. Less than two months later at Dunlap Baptist Church in Seattle, Jimi Hendrix's October 1970 funeral service included the apropos gospel numbers "His Eye Is on the Sparrow" and "The Angels Keep Watch over Me."[7]

From an impoverished and broken home in Seattle, Hendrix was not raised in the church, but he nevertheless had a lifelong affinity for birds and winged entities, especially angels. Biographer Charles Cross emphasizes Hendrix's fixation on flight, foregrounding the history of his military service as a paratrooper in the 101st Airborne Division with a key detail: Hendrix was long fixated on their winged insignia, a "Screaming Eagle," which he drew in his notepad.[8] Wings and flight show up repeatedly in Hendrix's oeuvre, such as when he becomes a flying man kissing the sky in his second single, "Purple Haze," the 1967 song McCartney recognized in *Melody Maker* for pushing the limits: "So, Jimi freaks out and sounds all the better for it! It's breaking out all over the place, you know. I thought it would be one of those things that people might keep down but it's breaking through all over. You can't stop it. Hooray."[9]

In 1967, Hendrix also recorded "Little Wing," released on *Axis: Bold as Love* in December. The fairy-tale-obsessed girl in "Little Wing" is flighty but also offers protection, a gendered approach maintained in the posthumously released "Angel," which was titled "My Angel Catherina (Return of Little Wing)" in handwritten lyrics dated 1968. The appearance of Hendrix's bird imagery around this time coincides with the Beatles' reference to "Hey Joe" in "A Day in the Life" (1967), the culmination of *Sgt. Pepper's Lonely Hearts Club Band*.[10] Hendrix kept that conversation going with his live cover of Pepper's "hard-rocking" title track,[11] which he performed only three days after the album's release. The performance "thrilled" McCartney, in attendance at the Saville Theater, leased for the occasion by Beatles manager Brian Epstein.[12]

Hendrix's bird themes returned on *The Cry of Love* (1971), assembled after his death, which included "Night Bird Flying." This song promises to set the bird free—but only after she flies down at midnight to embrace the speaker, enclosing him in her wings. Hendrix's second verse shifts point of view to address the night bird, encouraging her to sweep the blues (and other unwanted objects) under the bed. With its blues-singing speaker at night and black-and-blue colors, the song includes motifs with a long legacy in twentieth-century bird songs sung by Black Americans.

In his bird songs, Hendrix both becomes the bird and imagines it as a feminine love object, and his stories about these compositions are similarly flexible. For example, when he was asked about "Little Wing," he explained, "I figured that I take everything I see around, and put it maybe in the form of a girl . . . and call it 'Little Wing,' and then it will just fly away."[13] He also told his brother that "Little Wing" and "Angel" were inspired by their mother, of whom he had visions as an angel after she died.[14] These associations sort of correspond to McCartney's much later correlation between the title image of "Blackbird" and the "black woman" he had "in mind."[15] Yet Hendrix's meaning is much more fluid, allowing the inspiration itself to fly away in his story.

Adding more flight to his repertoire, Hendrix's guitar of choice between 1967 and 1969 was the Gibson Flying V, whose name appropriately characterizes its shape, evocative of wings or a craft about to launch. Winged entities have continued to characterize Hendrix's legacy, defining how he is remembered and understood. Until recently, legend had it that Hendrix was responsible for the green parrots present in London parks because he released a pair of parakeets on Carnaby Street.[16] More verifiable, given his recognizable influence on guitarists, is the memory of Hendrix's winged imagery in Lenny Kravitz's hit "Fly Away" (1999). There are also the doves and purple imagery of another Hendrix devotee, Prince, whose birds were introduced in "When Doves Cry" on 1984's *Purple Rain* and remain paramount to his brand. Prince's gender play, a source of sex appeal, can also be seen in relation to Hendrix, whose hair was another preoccupation for the guitarist.

Hendrix's practice of curling and styling his hair during the mid-1960s recalls the preshow beauty rituals of Little Richard, with whom he toured in that decade (the Beatles observed these, too, when they met the 1950s pioneer).[17] Hendrix had initially encountered Little Richard "during a brief period when Richard renounced rock 'n' roll for the Lord." Hendrix may not have been raised with religion, but he did have at least one memorable experience in a church when he and his brother Leon went to see Little Richard preach in 1958. The brothers, who didn't have "nice clothes" to wear, "sat transfixed in a pew watching Little Richard's conk-styled hair bounce up and down as he preached of fire and brimstone."[18]

Little Richard is famous for his theatricality; he was always the center of attention. As one can imagine, Hendrix's eventual scene-stealing with his own antics did not sit well with the older performer, and Hendrix was inevitably kicked off Richard's tour. Hendrix was threatening to Little Richard, but

McCartney wasn't, even though he spent a career mimicking Richard's signature vocals. As McCartney remembered: "I could do Little Richard's voice, which is a wild, hoarse, screaming thing, it's like an out-of-body experience. You have to leave your current sensibilities and go about a foot above your head to sing it. You have to actually go outside yourself. It's a funny trick and when you find it, it's very interesting. A lot of people were fans of Little Richard so I used to sing his stuff but there came a point when I wanted one of my own, so I wrote 'I'm Down.'"[19] "I'm Down" is one of many Beatles' songs indebted to Richard.[20] Richard took ownership of his influence on the band, often taking credit for McCartney's screams. Richard frequently explained that he taught McCartney "everything he knows"—which McCartney admitted was correct.[21] The other Beatles were also transfixed by Little Richard, as Lennon remembered: "The most exciting thing about early Little Richard was when he screamed just before the solo; that howling. It used to make your hair stand on end."[22]

Although McCartney was imitating Little Richard long before they met, the Beatles played on the same bill with their hero in Hamburg in 1962. That year, Little Richard had just recently returned to secular music after the temporary return to gospel (when Hendrix had the opportunity to see him preach). Little Richard's hiatus was motivated by the doom he felt about *Sputnik* (whose sky-bound remnants he claimed to behold several days after the 1957 launch) as well as an anxious experience in a plane, which he imagined catching *Sputnik*'s fire while being held up by winged angels.[23]

Little Richard's rock 'n' roll flight imagery is born out of the gospel imagination. In the aptly titled 1970 *Rolling Stone* article "Little Richard: Child of God," the self-proclaimed architect of rock 'n' roll remembered the experience of going onstage following a riveting performance by Janis Joplin: "Oh my God, I said a prayer like I always do, and I know that He heard my prayer. And so I went on, leaped up on the piano with my wings high, talking to the people and spreading joy to them, and the kids just came, it was like magic power came over—[*whispers*] oh Lord, oh God, it was one of the greatest experiences."[24] Little Richard consistently took flight via the performance of song—whether on the piano or the falsetto soaring of his voice—providing yet more correlations between singer and flyer.

Blackbirds Singing in 1968: Liverpool, Rishikesh, and London

The ubiquity of black-colored and other birds, both in culture and in physical nature, along with the ubiquity of flight in Black musical discourse, makes futile any effort to locate a single influence on McCartney's "Blackbird." There was a single English blackbird, though, among all the metaphors, slang, and stories. This bird disturbed the sleep of McCartney's elderly step grandmother. According to Angie McCartney, her mother, Edie, heard it outside her window, and, when she couldn't sleep from the noise, Paul stayed up with her to record the bird sounds on his tape recorder. In an early studio recording Angie claims to have, he even dedicated the song to Edie. Paul's stepmother acknowledges the existence of the civil rights story but insists that "it was in our little back bedroom that he originally recorded the sweet singing blackbird (in the dead of night). It is one of the special flowers in my garden of memories."[25]

Before McCartney started mentioning to Barry Miles his Scottish farm as the site of writing "Blackbird,"[26] the February 1968 Indian meditation retreat was the location biographers frequently cited for the song's composition. The Rishikesh sojourn was intended to be a spiritual getaway, but that meant it also distanced the Beatles from media, which would have included civil rights–related news from America. In 1994, Ian MacDonald explained, "Beyond the reach of electricity in the Maharishi's retreat at Rishikesh during the spring of 1968, The Beatles could use only their Martin D-28 acoustic guitars, which meant either strumming or brushing up on the arpeggio patterns used by folk guitarists to sustain their chords."[27] Likewise, fellow retreat attendee Donovan, who saw his shared Irish roots with the Beatles as their point of connection, remembered, "John used to draw, we'd meditate and there was no press, no media, no tours, no pressure, no fame. I learnt new styles as they did and their songwriting changed just as mine did. We'd play for hours on end and so much of this became part of the *White Album*." Pleased that he could have an influence on the double record, Donovan also explained how he showed Lennon his fingerpicking guitar style (his "secret moves"), which McCartney picked up after overhearing the instruction.[28]

Given the association between freedom and birds, as well as their appeal to McCartney, could the Indian birds he encountered on the 1968 Rishikesh trip have given rise to "Blackbird"? Ajoy Bose mentions the "large black crows that started squawking from early in the morning, when it was still dark," as part of the "vagaries of ashram life" that might have inspired "Blackbird." McCartney also mentioned these birds to Miles, remembering that when meditators complained about the birds' distraction, the Maharishi explained they could only be eliminated if they were shot—perhaps a reason to imagine broken wings.[29] Harrison's then-wife and fellow retreat-goer Pattie Boyd is sure that McCartney could not have been singing about the extremely "noisy" black-colored birds in India, which she said are so unlike the familiar "sweet-sounding" blackbirds in England. (Her hearing of the song is clearly informed by its added sound effects, that of an English blackbird recorded by an EMI sound engineer in his backyard in Ickenham.)[30] When asked about Beatles' tunes that make her think of India, Boyd, however, immediately recalled "Blackbird"—hearing it as reflective of the rejuvenation the Beatles found in India following the death of Brian Epstein.[31]

Following their staggered returns from India, toward the end of May the Beatles together reviewed their "bumper crop of new compositions" at Kinfauns, the home Pattie shared with George in Esher and the site of rehearsals for songs that ended up on the *White Album*.[32] In between India and the Esher Demos, McCartney went to his farm in Scotland and then went to New York City on Apple Records business with Lennon on May 14. Lennon's presence warrants consideration: in an analysis of "And Your Bird Can Sing," Everett speculates that the broken-wing lyric in "Blackbird" might have come from Lennon, who said he contributed one line to the song.[33] In addition to the broken-wing imagery that appears in one of Lennon's earliest compositions ever,[34] more compelling reasons can be found vis-à-vis the "Revolution" series, specifically spoken additions recorded on June, 20 1968. In them, Lennon can be heard saying, "My broken chair / My wings are broken and so is my hair / I am not in the mood for wearing blue clothing."[35] While this postdates the studio recording of "Blackbird," it might suggest that, for Lennon, broken wings were a kind of fixed phrase, a formula he could insert into songs.

On the Esher Demo of "Blackbird" released on the 2018 reissue, "McCartney's double-tracked vocals and acoustic guitar picking get some help from Lennon, who enthusiastically contributes bird sounds."[36] The effect is some semblance of community. Another gathering cohered around the song in the summer, on the first night that Linda Eastman spent at McCartney's London home on Cavendish Avenue. As one fan remembered, "He must have been really happy that night. He sat on the windowsill with his acoustic guitar and sang 'Blackbird' to us as we stood down there in the dark."[37] Paul frequently sang this song in the company of women during the summer of 1968; before Linda's arrival, his girlfriend Francie Schwartz was present in studio when McCartney's rehearsed the song, which was filmed for some Apple promotional material.

McCartney recorded "Blackbird" in Studio 2 on June 11, 1968. Harrison and Starr were both in California, but George Martin and Lennon were present. Martin suggested the memorable "false ending," and Lennon offered some accompaniment on acoustic guitar and piano. When McCartney, Lennon, and

Martin discussed the arrangement, McCartney said his ideas involved "a string quartet after the second verse," and Lennon proposed "a brass band," an idea McCartney considered "lovely." McCartney then played "Mother Nature's Son," confirming that some brass would complement that song, too. Martin also offered one of his "sound pictures," the idea of "arranged sound coming from a distance [into the song after a solo acoustic McCartney reaches the false ending] like a bit of decoration you've got on the back of a painting."[38]

McCartney rehearsed the song many times on that June day, and Lennon didn't stay the entire time; the aforementioned blackbird sound effects were added four months later during the mixing process. In the final version of "Blackbird," the isolated singer is more like a lone troubadour singing to a bird, rather than a fingerpicking folkie warbling with and to friends. With "Blackbird" and "Mother Nature's Son"—neither of which get a brass band—McCartney is a Wordsworthian wanderer above a sea of fog on the *White Album*. With the exception of the bird effects, the vocals and instrumentation (down to the foot-tapping) of "Blackbird" are all credited to McCartney, foreshadowing the individual ownership the former Beatle went on to exert over his broken-winged blackbird in years to come. It was, in fact, a solo McCartney who became responsible for promoting the *White Album* at the end of 1968; he was on his own because the other Beatles were either engaged in other projects or, in Lennon's case, in the hospital at Ono's bedside following her miscarriage.[39]

Two days prior to the album's UK release, McCartney gave an interview to Radio Luxembourg on November 20, 1968, which took place at his home at 7 Cavendish Avenue. After he explained the *White Album* as "mainly the Indian batch that we've sort of finished," McCartney downplayed "serious" readings, pointing out, "I don't ever try to make a serious social comment, you know." Right after Paul mentioned the "Indian batch," Tony Macarthur brought up "Blackbird," complimenting it as "beautiful." McCartney responded by distinguishing it from the orchestrated numbers on *Sgt. Pepper*: "There's nothing to the song ['Blackbird']. It is just one of those 'pick it and sing it' and that's it. The only point where we were thinking of putting anything on it is where it comes back in the end . . . sort of stops and comes back in . . . but instead of putting any backing on it, we put a blackbird on it. So there's a blackbird singing at the very end. And somebody said it was a thrush, but I think it's a blackbird!"[40] Ever the birdwatcher, McCartney might be joking: a common blackbird is technically a thrush. Blackbirds and thrushes also appear side by side in two folk songs popular in the British Isles (Roud 2380; 12657). If he had been pondering a civil rights association, it was not mentioned; he also didn't distinguish "Blackbird" from the "Indian batch." Rather, he insisted on the song's simplicity, highlighting the stripped-back instrumentation and sound effects, while suggesting the sing-along quality he would later remember in his own family's renditions of "Bye Bye Blackbird."[41]

With no draft of the lyrics, "Blackbird" is "unusual" for the late 1960s Beatles.[42] This may validate Angie McCartney's story while also suggesting that Paul worked on the song over time in multiple places, with multiple influences, and no one specific inspiration. Hunter Davies, the Beatles' biographer at the time, doubts the current civil rights legend, suggesting that an "American writer" might have proposed the meaning to the Beatle. Davies concludes, "Creative people don't always know from whence inspiration comes."[43]

It's significant that this speculated-about writer would be American, someone habituated to the racialized significance of blackbirds in US popular culture, yet also perhaps familiar with flight-oriented spirituals and other songs serving as civil rights anthems—such as "I Wish I Knew How It Would Feel to Be Free"—during the 1960s. Presumably, McCartney would have spoken to this American writer shortly after the aforementioned Radio Luxembourg interview during other promotional gigs—when he was on his own, sans other Beatles to witness or contradict. If this writer planted the notion with McCartney (to be clear, this is Davies's suggestion and we find no other evidence that it happened), the meeting most likely occurred before another conversation that was captured on tape.

The McCartney-Donovan Conversation: The *Post Card* Sessions

Following the *White Album*'s release, Donovan visited the studio during sessions for McCartney's Apple label protégée Mary Hopkin, who recorded *Post Card* between November 1968 and January 1969. Donovan mentioned seeing "so many blackbirds now," and McCartney laughed, apparently getting the joke. Paul then added, "That's what I said to Diana Ross the other night," adding, "She took offense." Donovan giggles while a still-laughing McCartney says "not really" to absolve himself; neither are particularly concerned with the slight to Ross. McCartney chuckles, enjoying the innuendo about attractive young Black women before suddenly getting serious and insisting he "*did* mean it like that originally." Donovan might have made a gesture of disbelief, prompting McCartney to become earnest: he illustrates the song's intent by singing some lines. After this performance, McCartney mentions "the riots" he read about in the newspaper.[44]

With Donovan, McCartney does not mention any of the details he attaches to the song in the twenty-first century. One of those details concerns Rosa Parks, who refused to give up her seat on a Montgomery city bus in Alabama in 1955 and whose image McCartney projected during 2002 concerts when he performed "Blackbird." Later, McCartney started specifying "Little Rock" and "Alabama" in concert stories. In 2021, McCartney does not mention Parks or these places in *The Lyrics* but still references Little Rock, reproducing a picture of himself posing affectionately with two members of the Little Rock Nine. Thelma Mothershed-Wair and Elizabeth Eckford went backstage when he played the city in the spring of 2016.[45] These "birds" integrated Central High School in 1957, the year a baby-faced teenage Paul met John at the Woolton Village Fete in July; McCartney was otherwise on the prowl for romance that summer.[46] But details like a ten-year gap are, of course, often irrelevant in a myth.

Instead of identifying Little Rock or Alabama as he often does in concert, in *The Lyrics* McCartney tries to hit the big time: according to him, the "song was written only a few weeks after the assassination of Martin Luther King Jr."[47] King was killed on April 4, 1968. Perhaps McCartney noticed news of demonstrations that took place after the assassination, especially given his and Lennon's visit (albeit brief) to New York City for a day in the middle of May 1968. But Paul does not mention the civil rights leader's name to Donovan. Notably, the subject of Dr. King was raised during January 1969 recording sessions—by Lennon. He had just seen King's "I Have a Dream" speech, which had apparently reaired on television the night before, and praised King, saying he's "like Tennyson." Over the course of multiple days, Lennon repeatedly riffs on the speech's phrases, tone, and tenor in jams with Billy Preston and the rest of the band.[48] All the while, McCartney says not a dickie bird about King and "Blackbird."

During the *Post Card* sessions, McCartney and Donovan do not linger on the difficult, serious issue of US race relations, which were no laughing matter for Black Americans, as Simone's "Revolution" makes clear.[49] The musicians' conversation, in fact, turned to magpies—more black-colored birds. This topic shift is not coincidental: Donovan's 1967 ode "The Magpie" features a black-colored bird who lives in a diamond-encrusted tree, typical imagery in the singer-songwriter's oeuvre. In fact, when Donovan brought up the idea of multiple blackbirds, he might have been implying that McCartney's song bore a resemblance to his own—"so many blackbirds"—causing McCartney to distinguish the importance of his song in opposition to Donovan's seemingly apolitical, fairy-tale imagery.[50] Ironically, McCartney does not mention

Donovan's influence in *The Lyrics*, even though his fingerpicking style was eventually used in "Blackbird," hence McCartney's "pick it and sing it" reference in the Radio Luxembourg interview mentioned above.

McCartney's and Donovan's conversation during the *Post Card* sessions is the first known recording of this Beatle correlating the title character of his song with Black people. In it, Motown's biggest star and lead singer of the Supremes appears, bringing up associations that have heretofore been ignored in analyses of this song. Was Ross playful or serious when she took offense to "Blackbird"? Her reaction as filtered through McCartney isn't clear, but her role in this history warrants consideration, starting with the words "Black" and "bird."

"Black" and McCartney on Race Circa 1966–1968

In the years leading up to the *White Album*, the term "Black" was only beginning to emerge in England as a preferred term, and the lexicon did not change all at once. As British filmmaker, musician, and cultural historian Don Letts remembers, "British blacks—black British, easy to say now but in those days this was a confusing concept, trust me."[51] In his 1969 novel *Travels with My Aunt*, Graham Greene also represents the confusion when a white British character is corrected by another character, a white British woman who has spent time in Paris. She explains, "We call them coloured or black—whichever they prefer."[52]

Literary historian James Procter explains how the word became "a positive label of racial pride": "'Black' did not emerge as a category internal to the British nation, but was imported from America during the new social movements of the 1960s and 1970s."[53] The change in word choice took firmer hold in the United Kingdom in the decade that followed: "During the 1970s—and partly in response to both the rise of racial intolerance [following World War II] and the rise of the Black Power movement abroad—'black' became detached from its negative connotations and was reclaimed as a marker of pride: 'black is beautiful.'"[54] Could a 1968 McCartney have been sensitive and aware enough to understand the connotative intricacies in how "Black" was being used in both the United Kingdom and the United States, where it had been reclaimed and charged with at least some degree of political valence?

McCartney was certainly attuned to the treatment of Black people in the United States prior to 1968. As a collective, the Beatles had refused to perform for segregated audiences at the 1964 Gator Bowl performance, a stance documented in the 2018 film *Eight Days a Week: The Touring Years*.[55] McCartney himself articulated his views on US race relations in an interview first published in a March 1966 edition of London's *Evening Standard*. McCartney had no expertise in racial discourse, and his rather inelegant commentary used incendiary (but not unprintable in 1966) language: "And it's a lousy country to be in where anyone who is black is made to seem a dirty n———. There is a statue of a good Negro doffing his hat and being polite in the gutter. I saw a picture of it."[56] McCartney did notice racism and its attendant structures, bandying the use of offensive language to illustrate his point about the treatment of Black Americans; his argumentation projects a kind of aloof wit.

In 1966, McCartney comes across as if he were trying to sound smart to appeal to the British readership. His commentary about America's treatment of Black people actually served a broader critique about Americans' failure to appreciate the arts. Prior to the observation about race, he talked about the fact that US television stations did not broadcast plays (even though the 1950s were the golden age of theatrical drama on US television). He then followed up on the statue, saying, "We look after things a lot better over here"—but what he means by this is that England had preservation societies dedicated to "barrels of beer," the poet "John Betjamen," and "ban-the-bomb."[57] Whatever his insight into race, it is embedded among other concerns, one piece of evidence to support his case about Americans' lack of sophistication in the interview, which appeared in the same *Evening Standard* issue as Lennon's notorious "We're more popular than Jesus" comment. Both of these interviews, conducted by British journalist Maureen Cleave, were reproduced that year in the September issue of the American magazine *Datebook*. Ironically, the distribution of the interviews via this outlet (and subsequent press coverage) was a PR mistake for another reason: white Southern evangelical Christians perceived Lennon's description of religion's decline amid the Beatles' rising popularity as an attack on religion itself.

Two years after the publication of the *Datebook* interview, McCartney was probably more aware of changing labels in both countries, especially given his excursions to Los Angeles on Apple business in 1968. But even in the United States, widespread use of "Black" did not take hold until the end of the decade, a change advanced by songs including James Brown's "Say It Loud—I'm Black and I'm Proud," recorded and released in August 1968. Simone introduced "To Be Young, Gifted, and Black" to the Harlem Cultural Festival in August 1969 but did not release it until 1970. To provide some context for Simone's festival performance, one commentator in the 2021 *Summer of Soul* documentary explained that the reclamation of "Black" was bold: "It was a significant change, calling yourself Black. In the early '60s, if you called someone Black it meant you wanted to fight them because no one wanted to hear that mess."

"Blackbird" was recorded in June 1968, preceding the public distribution of the Brown and Simone songs. Even granting McCartney some degree of word-choice awareness, the way he and Donovan spoke, especially surrounding the reference to Ross, indicates a consciousness about the demeaning way "Black" *could be used* in the United Kingdom.

"Blackbird," Diana Ross, and Black American Girl Groups

Along with the use of "Black," historical context related to gender and sex informs how we should approach Ross's "offense." Compounding the issue of racial objectification in the McCartney-Donovan conversation, their use of "bird" reinforces a laddish atmosphere: "During the sixties, the expression 'bird' still meant a 'young girl,' but was deployed to imply someone sexually available; young men would go out in search of 'birds' but would not usually deploy the term to describe a steady girlfriend."[58] Even if Ross were being playful, her response might have signaled familiarity with the derogatory connotations of both "Black" and "birds" in the UK; quite probably it had to do with the overall jokey tone surrounding the blackbird application.

Ross's presence in McCartney's "Blackbird" story is ironic for a number of reasons. First, the inclusion of this Supreme calls attention to the Beatles' musical dialogue with Black American girl groups, whose discourse was fundamental to the early Beatles' appeal.[59] Significantly, on *Please Please Me* and *With the Beatles* a total of five tracks are covers of songs recorded by the Shirelles, the Cookies, the Marvelettes, and the Donays.[60] Emphasizing the influence of the former, Maureen Mahon concludes, "Following the musical model of the Shirelles helped both the Beatles and the Rolling Stones shift from being bands that covered African American music to becoming artists who created an original rock and roll sound."[61]

The Beatles were otherwise vocal about their admiration for girl groups in the early 1960s while they were "invading" the United States. Ahead of the pivotal *Ed Sullivan Show* appearance in 1964, a press release listed biographies for each lad; Lennon's favorite things were "steak, chips, jelly, curries, painting, modern jazz, cats, suede and leather clothing, Juliette Gréco, The Shirelles and blondes who are intelligent."[62] George Harrison also named Martha and the Vandellas (along with Smokey Robinson's Miracles) as a favorite in *Melody Maker*.[63] The Beatles producer George Martin also made the connection, characterizing the Beatles as "a male Shirelles."[64] The Beatles' tastes reflected a musical preference definitional to the mods, who often sought out lesser-known tracks by Black American girl groups. And, in addition to their girl-group covers, early Lennon-McCartney originals, such as "She Loves You" and "From Me to You," were using girl-group discourse to sing about romance and relationships, using direct address and playful vocables, while projecting intimacy and camaraderie between the members of the group itself.[65] These rhetorical strategies were instrumental to the band's appeals to girl listeners—but the band was conscious of their girl-talk, often using "you" to appeal directly to girls and to encourage a perception of individual specialness. Lennon specifically noted that "P.S. I Love You" was McCartney's attempt to write a song that resembled the Shirelles' "Soldier Boy."[66]

The Shirelles, Mahon notes, "took pleasure in their link to the band. Years later Shirley Alston Reeves told a reporter, 'Whenever anybody interviewed us, we were always proud to say, "Well, the Beatles said that we're their favorite group."'"[67] At the time, Black artists—especially women—also returned the musical "love" in records like Mary Wells's *Love Songs to the Beatles* (1965). Before that (and after the Beatles' successful US visit), in fall 1964 Motown responded to the Beatles' "invasion" with the Supremes' *A Bit of Liverpool*, released as *With Love (From Us to You)* in the UK.[68] The year 1964 was also when the Supremes, who had been recording since 1961, finally "crack[ed] the pop Top 20 with 'Where Did Our Love Go.' The song was the first in a string of number one hits that consolidated the pop cultural prominence of the Supremes, the only American group to rival the pop chart dominance of the Beatles during the 1960s."[69] *A Bit of Liverpool* included covers of five Lennon-McCartney compositions, contributing to the back-and-forth dialogue between Motown and the Beatles during the decade.[70]

But the friendship between the Beatles and the Supremes had a somewhat rocky start. The Supremes came to visit the Beatles in a New York City hotel room in 1965, a meeting that was, by all accounts, awkward because the Beatles expected three good-time girls. Supreme Mary Wilson remembered, "I guess there [was] a lot of grass being [smoked,] and so we went into their hotel room and it was dark and it was smelly. . . . And we went in there with our little gloves, all dressed up, with our little pillbox hats and . . . it wasn't a kind of thing we thought we were walking into. So we were very disappointed and we asked our publicist to please get us out of there."[71] They later became friends, and Harrison admitted to Wilson, "We expected soulful, hip girls like the Ronettes. . . . We couldn't believe that three black girls from Detroit could be so square!"[72]

that would inspire a "Negro Revolt." He heard in the *White Album* the Beatles' awareness of his lunatic prophecy and in "Blackbird" specific encouragement to "the Black man" waiting for this "moment" to "arise." The word "rise" was, according to one of Manson's followers, "one of Charlie's big words"; he also heard it in "Revolution 9," which Manson connected to Revelation 9 in the Bible. "Rise" was painted in blood at the LaBianca home, which, in addition to actor Sharon Tate's residence, was attacked "in the dead of night."[90]

Manson's twisted meaning-making amplified an unease that the Beatles, especially Lennon, had already voiced about tedious close readings of their songs.[91] Along with the other Beatles, McCartney was deeply troubled by associations that linked their music with the Manson Family's brutality. In fact, he considered "forever" avoiding live performances of "Helter Skelter," another *White Album* song Manson used to justify violence."[92]

For thirty years after the Beatles disbanded, McCartney generally eschewed the hidden-messages approach to songs—especially "Blackbird" since it was a Manson-made-fraught *White Album* song. McCartney did not tell the civil rights story again until the end of the twentieth century, when his concerted efforts to explain this and other songs started.[93]

The Joyful Possibilities of "Blackbird" in 1968: Ramsey Lewis, Aretha Franklin, and the Beatles

Prior to Manson's perverse interpretation and application, McCartney's blackbird was enjoying another joyful life outside of the Beatles' *White Album*. The very first Black American—and most likely the very first artist—to record "Blackbird" was Ramsey Lewis. His version foresaw the song's nearly limitless applications. Recorded in December 1968 and released that same month, Lewis's acclaimed jazz album *Mother Nature's Son* offers instrumental takes on ten *White Album* songs, including "Blackbird," all recorded live with musicians from the Chicago Symphony Orchestra. Lewis's interpretation of "Blackbird" reveals the song's possibilities: it opens with electronic oddities that make the song unrecognizable (Lewis was playing with the Moog synthesizer before the Beatles did the following year), but then the melody comes into the light and a drama ensues with Lewis's signature piano against orchestral backing.

With "Blackbird," Lewis presented the kind of revelation in line with his musical goals, to bring the audience along (often dancing) with a style of jazz that welcomes rather than alienates. Dizzy Gillespie once defended Lewis's approach, saying, "He's got gospel and classical and jazz all mixed up together,"[94] further praising Lewis as "a gust of fresh air on the musical scene."[95] On the cover of *Mother Nature's Son*, Lewis's approachability comes through; he is seated at a grand piano, facing and smiling at the listener. Amid lush greenery, Lewis is accompanied by white rabbits along with flying doves and perching parrots. The topological mismatch works as a visual representation of the ahead-of-his time fusion that Gillespie complimented, much like the "bouquet of tonal delight" Duke Ellington also described.[96]

Lewis reveals the musical richness of "Blackbird," aurally replicating images of hope connected to flying in arts of the African Diaspora. Beginning with Lewis, other Black musicians' interpretations continued to illustrate how "Blackbird" participates in a Diasporic musical and storytelling legacy whose applications to the civil rights movement do not always have to be overtly stated. Perhaps they would have been more obvious if, say, Aretha Franklin had added "Blackbird" to her collection of bird covers in the late 1960s or early 1970s, especially given her stature and association with the movement by that time. But "Blackbird" was not one of the Beatles' tunes Aretha covered. As illustrated in her performance of "Tiny Sparrow," Franklin's treatment of loneliness—which can also call for community—is relevant to her other takes on the Beatles.

"When Aretha sang any song, even a Beatle song, she claimed it as her own—and the Beatles knew it," writes Rob Sheffield, succinctly capturing the effect. By the end of the 1960s, Paul McCartney was particularly attuned to Aretha, sending her the demo of "Let It Be," sealed with his hope that she would record it. She did, including her gospel-infused version on *This Girl's in Love with You* (1970), whose sessions also saw Franklin covering "The Fool on the Hill." Whereas McCartney's ballad is wistful, observational, and accepting of the fool's isolated position, Franklin's version is a protest. She delivers the line "Nobody wants to know him" in the style of a gospel shout with an intensity that asks the listener to question the injustice of his rejection.

Similarly, when Franklin covered "The Long and Winding Road" in 1972, the listener believes she has seen that road before. In retrospect, it's easy to hear that song as a kind of prequel to her cover of "Eleanor Rigby" (1969), in which Franklin adopts the title character's first-person point of view.[97] She announces herself to be the song's title character, Eleanor Rigby, with the backing singers essentially name checking her throughout the song. Franklin-as-Eleanor might be one of the lonely people she observes, but her subject position means that she's a witness to other characters in the song like Father Mackenzie. By the end of the song, she shifts back into third person in order to tell the story of Eleanor's death; together with the backing vocalists, the fullness she offers makes a case for community as the antidote to individual suffering. This, of course, relates to the blackbird's problem, too: wouldn't it be better if this bird had a flock with which to fly out of the darkness?

The late 1960s context in which "Blackbird" emerges on the *White Album* reveals a song whose origin is not as simple as McCartney now wants us to believe. This does *not* invalidate the song's ability to serve the cause of civil rights; as forthcoming chapters show, its liberatory potential has been realized in interpretations by Black artists. This is especially true of Preston's take on the song, which involves one of many stories no one has yet heard about "Blackbird."

CHAPTER 8

Like a Bird Up in the Sky

Billy Preston Flies to the Beatles in London and Circles Back to Los Angeles with "Blackbird"

Once upon a time, Billy Preston picked up a guitar, a memory Robert Palmer, Preston's lead guitarist from 1983 to 1992, shared:

> I didn't know he could play guitar. I never knew he could play guitar. But we were sitting in a room one day. He said, "Hand me your guitar."
>
> I said, "You can't play guitar." But I handed it to him, and he plays "Blackbird"!
>
> I'd never seen him play the guitar in my life, but he knew how to play that song. He'd never played anything else, literally.
>
> When he finished, I was just staring at him. Billy said, "I think that is the only song I know how to play. Paul showed me one day."
>
> I thought, "'One day?' He didn't have to keep teaching you?" I don't think he realized what he had just said. You know what I mean?[1]

"Blackbird" was the only song Palmer ever saw Preston, an extraordinary organ, piano, and keyboard player (and singer-songwriter in his own right), play on the guitar.[2] Palmer's account of Preston's onetime strumming is a new "Blackbird" story, adding yet another remarkable layer to the song's history.

Preston recorded his full-band version of "Blackbird" in 1972, and it became a standard in his touring repertoire, always performed during a "Beatles set" that dedicated one song to each Beatle.[3] "Blackbird" was, as you might expect, Preston's tribute to McCartney. During his live "Beatles set" and elsewhere,

Preston habitually thanked the Beatles, an action consistent with the grateful disposition he publicly projected. This wasn't just performative: Preston was cooperative and generous, qualities nourished in him by the community of Victory Baptist Church in Los Angeles. Preston's own songwriting is likewise informed by spiritual-political themes that reflect Victory's approach to service (and, more broadly, philosophies of gospel music and the Black Church).[4] We can see this ethos in Preston's collaboration with the Beatles, which precedes his recording of "Blackbird," the B side to his hit "Will It Go Round in Circles." These 1972 songs reflect liberatory themes characteristic of Afro-Atlantic flight and the gospel music community in which Preston was raised.

Meet Billy Preston and Victory Baptist Church

Billy Preston played "the most exciting organ ever," according to the title of his second LP. He could hear a song once and play it back with flawless precision on the piano or keyboard. He also had, as Preston himself told the Beatles in 1969 and as Palmer reiterated, "perfect pitch."[5] Preston could join in on the keyboard, piano, or organ and immediately elevate a song, even a faltering work in progress. Citing George Martin's assessment of Preston as an "emollient," Thomas Brothers explains, "No musician knows how to fit in better than a gospel pianist."[6] Preston even fit into the Beatles' made-up band, becoming Billy Shears (first introduced in 1967) in the film *Sgt. Pepper's Lonely Hearts Club Band* (1978), which featured the Bee Gees.

In addition to playing with an incredible roster of artists from Sam Cooke to Aretha Franklin and others mentioned throughout this chapter, Preston's musical legacy includes his own chart-toppers: "That's the Way God Planned It" (1969); the flight-evocative "Outa-Space" (1971), a 1972 Grammy winner for Best Pop Instrumental Performance; "Will It Go Round in Circles" (1972); and "Space Race" (1973), another flight-titled song recalling George Clinton's Mothership Connection. The number 1 *Billboard* hit "Nothing from Nothing" (1974) was performed on the very first episode of NBC's *Saturday Night Live*. With Stevie Wonder's protégée (and former wife) Syreeta Wright, Preston had a hit with "With You I'm Born Again" (1979). He also cowrote "You Are So Beautiful," which his friend Joe Cocker popularized.[7] Preston's version of this hit song appeared on *The Kids & Me* (1974), on which he dubbed himself "Uncle Billy," another exemplar of his generosity and service via song.

Preston's virtuosity and talent were predicated on technical skill as well as diligent practice from an early age. He often explained the origins of his piano-playing with a story about sitting on his sister Rodena's lap to reach the keys from the piano bench. By age three, he was playing back what he heard from his organist mother, Robbie Lee Preston (later Williams).[8] After moving from Houston to Los Angeles during the Great Migration of the 1940s when Billy was little, the family of three soon found Victory Baptist Church at the corner of East Forty-Eighth and McKinley.

Authors' note: On September 11, 2022, Victory Baptist Church was burned down by suspected arson. We have chosen to keep the present-tense representation of the former building in the sections that follow to convey our experiences with the community of Victory and to underscore the living memory of Preston in this place. Illustrating the ubiquity of bird imagery, the church's pastor used the image of a phoenix rising out of a fire to encourage his congregation in the wake of the tragedy.

As present-day pastor, the Reverend Dr. W. Edward Jenkins confirmed this in his sermon when we first visited in January 2020: "Victory is the beginning of Preston's story."[9] Tellingly, when many congregants think about Billy, they immediately speak of his mother and sister, recalling, for example, that the family originally came to LA from Houston, where Preston was born in 1946. These three were influential and defining presences in the music ministry of Victory and its outreach, including the church's participation in gospel workshops.

Billy's sister, Dr. Rodena Preston, was an accomplished pianist in her own right and became the minister of music for the Gospel Music Workshop of America (GMWA), founded by the Reverend James Cleveland, with whom Rodena collaborated. Like Billy, Rodena credited her mother: "I was blessed to learn so much from my mother, Robbie Preston Williams. She was an incredible musician who played at Metropolitan Baptist Church in Los Angeles, then served 35 years as pianist at Victory Baptist, one of the first churches to televise their worship services. She exposed me and my brother, Billy Preston, to gospel music and many early pioneers in the field."[10] Likewise, Billy paid tribute to his mother in live performances, bringing her to the stage to sing the refrain of "That's the Way God Planned It" in a performance that aired on *The Midnight Special* on NBC in 1980. When he introduced her, Preston said, "She's the one who's prayed for me and kept me going."[11]

When Billy and his family went to church, they entered a gleaming white building with an elegant interior. In addition to the stained-glass windows, crystal chandeliers refracted light while golden accents highlighted the pulpit area, always full of lush floral arrangements. From the time Victory Baptist Church was built in 1944, the historical church has been impeccably maintained. There, as the standard story goes, the seven-year-old Preston was noticed mimicking the chorale direction one day, so he started conducting the choir in an official capacity. (The church still has the stepstool Billy used when he directed the choir.) When he was ten years old, Preston played with Mahalia Jackson when she visited Victory, singing from a pulpit that would later host the Reverend Dr. Martin Luther King Jr. in 1967 when the church celebrated its twenty-fourth anniversary. At age eleven, Preston also appeared on Nat King Cole's NBC program, trading off singing and organ-playing with Cole on "Blueberry Hill" after a solo performance of "Billy's Boogie."[12] In that performance, Preston seems to be a miniature adult, adopting the smooth crooner style of Cole during the televised show.

Preston grew up part of a congregation that instructed its congregants in joyful service. Gospel music was integral to this: "At its best, the gospel vision helps people experience themselves *in relation to others* rather than *on their own*. Where the blues offers reaffirmation, gospel offers redemption."[13] Victory Baptist Church gained national attention in 1950 when KTTV began airing its Sunday evening services; on Channel 11, the nationwide broadcast allowed television viewers across the United States to hear the Reverend Dr. Arthur A. Peters's sermons and the Voices of Victory choir.[14] Dr. Peters founded Victory in 1943, and the church's collective history continues to live on in the hearts and minds of the current members. Part of this continuity is owed to the fact that the church has had, following its founder, only two subsequent pastors, including Dr. Jenkins.[15] The musicians at Victory today include Dr. Jenkins's son Jahi, who is a gifted multi-instrumentalist. Offering a glimpse into Preston's past and the church of his day, he and Pastor Randy Allison are skillful in the art of responding to Dr. Jenkins's sermons, offering musical phrases that match or anticipate his message, sometimes picking up spoken fragments and turning that speech into song.

Victory's mid-century national broadcast served as a realization of the church's motto, "To serve the present age—my calling to fulfill," which is displayed in golden letters on the wood-paneled back wall of the worship space. Through his music, Preston also fulfilled that calling, regularly telling audiences that "God loves you" in concert and sharing other "Good News stories." The latter is a phrase Clarence McDonald, who arranged the horn section of Preston's "Blackbird," used throughout our interview. He attended Susan Miller Dorsey High School at the same time Preston did and, like Palmer, confirms the crucial role Victory played in Preston's life and art.[16]

Longtime, revered church elder Sister Johnnie Pearl Knox also confirmed Preston's origins at Victory. Now president of the New Voices of Victory choir, Knox witnessed Preston's musical development firsthand: she sang in choirs directed by Preston numerous times. Knox was there from the beginning, a member GMWA and lifelong friend to Billy's sister Rodena. GMWA's members backed Aretha Franklin in the recording of the 1972 live album *Amazing Grace*, whose companion documentary film features Rev. Cleveland and Preston's protégé, Kenny Lupper, on organ. Members of Rodena's workshop also appear in the film *Blues Brothers* (1980). (Watch either of those movies and you will see Knox).[17]

Knox described Preston's playing with reverence, noting its singularity. He was "smooth, so smooth," she said. Both Dr. Jenkins and Knox confirmed that Preston returned to Victory throughout his life. "Of course he did," Knox said. If you visit Victory today, you will see the spot where he honed his skills: the original Hammond B3 remains positioned at the far right, in front of the choir's pews and facing the pulpit. Knox and others remember Victory's Hammond B3 as "Billy's organ."[18] The church has made some renovations, but the dramatic stained-glass windows featuring biblical scenes, the white walls, and the wood paneling with gold lettering toward the back remain as they were. From the organ, Preston could see almost the entire space, which filters a beautiful light as the LA sun rises throughout the morning.

Especially when he was seated at the organ, Preston was responding spontaneously to the pastor, deacons, and singers issuing forth from the pulpit; as gospel musicians do, he encouraged or shaped the direction of their discourse, too, all the while observing the congregation. When he looked to his right, toward the choir, he would have been looking at a particular stained-glass window, one depicting a scene that characterizes Preston's ethos of musical friendship: John the Baptist pouring water over Jesus. This New Testament episode also documents Jesus's humility: in Matthew, John hesitates, unsure that Jesus even needs to be baptized.[19] Preston's "John the Baptist," cowritten with Bruce Fisher, calls John an exemplary "Christian man."[20]

Jesus's baptism is, in fact, one of the most iconic convergences of Jesus and a dove: to mark the occasion, the Holy Spirit descends in bird form, an embodiment witnessed by John the Baptist.[21] Coupled with the numerous birds and images of uplift that appear in the spirituals and hymns that Preston learned and played at Victory, the image of Jesus's baptism is a dramatic expression of joyful service and recognizes the inevitable suffering to come, dualities that are not shied away from in Preston's music.

With the Beatles

Preston's presence in the Beatles' story, as well as in their respective solo work, spans the past, present, and future like a bird flying across times and places. These collaborations are so substantial they warrant more detailed investigations; our survey here is designed to illustrate transatlantic flight. Preston was a bridge to the Beatles' Black American heroes; he recorded and performed with the Beatles and recorded albums on their label; and, as "Blackbird" illustrates, he covered their music while also writing his own songs that allude to the band.

Back in 1962, the Beatles (all of whom were in their twenties except for George, still nineteen) and their new friend Billy (also still a teenager) hung out backstage observing Little Richard's preshow rituals. These included his beauty routine as well as reading from the Bible. Preston later recalled that meeting:

> I was on tour with Little Richard, and we toured England. The Beatles were a supporting act on the show. We went to Hamburg, Germany, the Star-Club. And that's where we really became tight because we were there every day for a couple of weeks. They used to always come backstage because they wanted to know about Little Richard and America, so they'd come to me and say, "What's it like?!" So, you know, we got close. I used to get them free Cokes from the club. [*laughs*] So maybe that's why they remembered me so much! [*still laughing*] It was great, I always liked them. When I first saw them in Liverpool, I always liked them. They were different from all the other bands. Their harmonies were great, they looked different from everybody. I always knew—well, out of all the other English bands that were on the tour with us, they were my favorite. I used to always go in the wings and watch them perform.[22]

Preston's memory also nods to Little Richard's characteristic demands for the spotlight: "And one night in Hamburg, I was standing in the wings watching . . . my organ was sitting there because I was playing with Little Richard and he was the star of the show. . . . George said, 'Come on out and play!' I said, 'Yeah!,' but then I thought, well, I'm playing with Little Richard and he's the star and he'd probably fire me and leave me in England (which he did) [*laughs*]."[23] Seven years later, Preston would essentially take Harrison up on that invitation when he recorded with the Beatles in London. In between, Preston released his debut album, *16 Yr. Old Soul* (1963), and played on Sam Cooke's last album, *Night Beat* (1963). After releasing more solo records, Preston became even better known to American television viewers, teenagers specifically, as a dancing and singing house artist on the *Shindig!* variety show before touring with Ray Charles starting in 1967.

Preston reunited with the Beatles in 1969, starting on January 22. In the decades that followed, George Harrison took credit for inviting Preston to the January 1969 studio sessions, where the Beatles were being filmed by director Michael Lindsay-Hogg and his crew, who documented the band's struggle to record new songs while trying to conceive and plan a live performance. At the beginning of these dates—on January 3, the first day of filming—Harrison did tell the other Beatles' about seeing Preston play with Ray Charles in London, calling them "the best jazz band I've seen."[24] Harrison notes how the elder Charles had passed organ duties to the younger Preston in a concert that took place well prior to these January recording sessions. Still, in Harrison's retrospective memory, the Charles show seems to happen in tandem with him quitting the band, and Harrison long fostered the image of reuniting with the band with Billy by his side. Peter Jackson's 2021 film shows this is not the case (Billy arrives on his own), but the newer film still upholds the vibe Harrison later described: "I knew the others loved Billy . . . and it was like a breath of fresh air. It's interesting to see how nicely people behave when you bring a guest in, because they don't really want everybody to know they're so bitchy."[25] In the *Anthology* project, where Harrison tells this story, Preston's sun is a counterpoint to the Beatles' gloom because the winter 1969 Beatles were depleted and grumpy during the filmed recording sessions that became *Let It Be* (1970). Preston himself remembered this version of events, noting "They were kind of despondent. They had lost the joy of doing it all."[26]

Anthology upheld what viewers had seen in *Let It Be*, which includes fleeting shots of Preston laughing while whipping out funky licks amid four rather glum Beatles. That film culminates in the rooftop concert, a setting on which the Beatles finally manage to agree for their live show. Despite the chill (Billy is shivering, too), the Beatles are markedly more energetic here. Lindsay-Hogg's cameras do not focus on or habitually frame Preston, though, often edging him out of the frame. Beholden to the original footage, Jackson's *The Beatles: Get Back* does include many more instances of Preston but rarely includes audio of the keys player's conversations—and does not articulate the range of Preston's contributions. Audiences in 2021 did get to see more of the playing that reflects Preston's gospel background, especially when he leans over the keyboard toward whichever Beatle he is trying to help, even though sometimes audio and visuals are mismatched.

Even if the films did not or could not do him justice, Preston's role in the January 1969 recording sessions have made him distinctive in the Beatles' story. Other musicians had played on late 1960s Beatles records (such as Eric Clapton), but Preston is the only officially named: the "Get Back" single is credited to "The Beatles with Billy Preston." The "Get Back" grooves alone, producer George Martin observed, prove why Preston would be a welcome addition to the 1969 Beatles.[27] As a result, Preston is often anointed with the coveted "Fifth Beatle" label, though that title is legitimate for many other reasons as well.

Billy could hang with the Beatles because he was a musical equal; his playing could also be said to have surpassed the Fab Four, a point made adamantly by Palmer.[28] The films Let It Be (1970) and the reedit based on its footage, The Beatles: Get Back (2021), don't show viewers the extent to which Preston contributed. Preston's additions were also complex and require a trained ear, as Walter Everett explains:

> [Preston's] Rhodes [electric piano] work on "Stand by Me" is especially fine, as is his 12-bar boogie medley of Chuck Berry and Larry Williams songs. He changes their orientation in the blues; most of their January 12-bar jamming is squarely in the major mode (as in 1967's "Flying"), but he brings a stronger minor-pentatonic language to this format; this point has been anticipated [in] the #9 chord of "Get Back." Despite his soul and gospel roots, Preston also adds some Nashville "slip-style" keyboard work landing on downbeats in both John's verse and the Paul/John duet verse of "I've Got a Feeling," right off the bat on the 22nd (Nagra roll 428A). The next day, he adds a country-styled right-hand tremolo to his Rhodes solo in "Get Back" (Nagra roll 1026B).[29]

Remember that these Beatles' songs were works in progress. Preston's contributions did not simply involve falling into existing frameworks but shaping those very frameworks.

These sessions also saw the Beatles resurrecting an earlier Chuck Berry–inspired track, "The One After 909," on which Preston plays the Rhodes keyboard and later organ and piano, moving between instruments as the song developed.[30] To "Something," a song for which Harrison claimed a Ray Charles inspiration, Preston's Hammond organ seems to carry the insecure Beatle, who struggled with the lyrics to this song for months. "Something" and McCartney's "The Long and Winding Road" both achieve their Charles aspirations with Charles's own organist.

The January 1969 musical themes of "getting back" were aided by the real-life synchronicity of Preston's presence. As McCartney later recollected, Preston was "an old mate."[31] What's more, this "old mate," with his expertise in multiple American musical genres and their associated techniques, brought the skill necessary to complete the songs the Beatles were struggling to get off the ground. At the time, McCartney himself noted, "Coming from the north of England, it doesn't come through easy, you know, all, the *soul*."[32] Paul says this after "a particularly piquant contrapuntal riff on the Rhodes [that Preston added] to 'Let It Be.'"[33] As a Black American man in an almost exclusively white British studio, Preston was a link to the music the Beatles were trying to recover. This is initially evidenced by Beatles' persistent questions to Preston about Little Richard's whereabouts. Harrison admits to asking "everybody in LA if they knew where Richard was," and "nobody knew." Preston deflects; he understands a lot more about Little Richard than the Beatles do: "No. 'Cos he's kinda hard to find, you know . . . all over . . . everywhere." His answer appeases the Beatles for whom Little Richard is like a butterfly they can't catch, "trying to be hip all the time" as Lennon concludes.[34]

As Craig Werner notes, Preston's "straight-out-of-church organ helps make the Beatles' 'Don't Let Me Down' one of the greatest soul songs ever recorded by a 'white' group."[35] No wonder Lennon proposed formally adding Preston as fifth member of the band, a suggestion supported by Harrison but nixed by McCartney who feared another person would further complicate the group's decision-making, famously moaning, "It's just bad enough with four."[36] Perhaps five would have been the magic number after all.

Preston was not inducted into the Beatles, but he also didn't stray too far from them. As is also discussed in the January 1969 sessions, Preston was signed to the Beatles' new Apple label with Harrison serving as producer and often playing guitar on Preston's songs. (Billy even lived with George and his wife, Pattie, for a time, too.)[37] In the liner notes for *That's the Way God Planned It* (1969), Preston's first Apple LP, Derek Taylor proclaims, "Billy Preston is the best thing to happen to Apple this year. He's young and beautiful and kind and he sings and plays like the son of God."[38] Preston's Apple output is, once again, characterized by the spiritual uplift that comes from his church background. Playing the organ, singing, and choir-directing at Victory influenced Preston's listener-centered approach to music, which kept evolving. As Andy Davis's liner notes to a reissue of the next Apple LP, *Encouraging Words* (1970), explain, "Billy kept his songs alive by developing them over time. He'd play them live, he'd change the arrangements, he'd re-record them."[39] Preston offers a willingness to help his listeners, communicated clearly in the title of that record.

Preston's Apple LPs offer both visual and musical allusions to the Beatles. The cover of *That's the Way God Planned It* features full shots of Preston in quadruplicate, a playful parody of the four early Beatles, whose matching suits were themselves copying the uniformity of doo-wop and girl groups.

The four Prestons are in various postures of what Davis calls "gospel strutting,"[40] to which Preston later alluded with the title of his instrumental jam "Struttin'." On *That's the Way God Planned It*, the title track recalls "Let It Be," which Preston claimed was inspired by McCartney's song.[41] The spiritual quality of "That's the Way God Planned It," whose speaker relinquishes control to a higher power, clearly echoes that of "Let It Be," although the former is a bolder "testimony," which is how Preston often introduced the song in concert.

Similarly, the cover of *Encouraging Words* is a close-up shot of Preston's face, his eyes cast upward against a black background, an image somewhat evocative of the floating heads on the cover of *With the Beatles* (1963). *Encouraging Words* includes Preston's fun and funky take on Lennon and McCartney's "I've Got a Feeling." Preston also covered Harrison's soon-to-be-released solo songs "My Sweet Lord" and "All Things (Must) Pass," giving them a powerful spiritual charge, reconciling gospel Hallelujahs with Harrison's beloved Krishna chants. The Preston songs that open the album, "Right Now" and "Little Girl," also project the kind of joyful, romantic urgency heard at the beginning of *Please Please Me*.

This is just a sampling of Preston's Beatles-inspired work, anticipating how he continued to engage with the band in the coming years, including and especially with "Blackbird."

Billy Preston's "Blackbird" and "Will It Go Round in Circles"

Following his work with the Beatles and recordings on their label (which had entered a state of decline), Preston returned to Los Angeles and signed to the A&M label based there. His "gospel-tinged"[42] cover of "Blackbird" is the third song on *Music Is My Life* (1972), his second A&M album. As Clarence McDonald explained, "the opening of the song features playing typical of Preston during this period, beginning with a rousing riff on the organ run through two Leslie speakers to create an oscillating effect." Preston is the only vocalist credited on the album, but McDonald, who arranged the horn section, remembered "three other guys" who served as backing vocalists and helped create "the gospel vibe."[43] According to McDonald, "the vocal arrangement which Billy did was typical of the church gospel quartet. It was Billy alone doing all of the lead vocals."

McDonald, who would later become a Grammy winner himself, arranged the horns "to complement Billy's musical desires" because they are "basically following the leader, Billy Preston."[44] This point was echoed by David T. Walker, who arranged the rhythm section. Walker remembered that "everyone who was called to perform or record with Billy was free to play what they felt at the time on the music, including me." Walker was present during the initial recordings (but not later overdubs) and explained what having a gospel background meant to the studio process: "We only knew how to play and perform from the heart, nothing contrived or planned, that's how we did it. [Preston] trusted the people that he admired to be able to feel how he feels about what he was thinking and playing. [This was] based upon similar musical upbringing."[45]

That upbringing, of course, relates to the musical training ground of the Black Church, whose gospel discourse maintains the legacy of the ring shout, explored in detail in chapter 1. The Reverend Dwight Andrews offers an apt reminder of the collaborative circle ritual's significance: "The ring shout really becomes the cornerstone for understanding the nexus between African religion and emerging African American religion. It's the foundation of singing, worshipping, and praising, getting filled with the Holy Spirit in this circle, which is a way of also identifying the cycle of music, the cycle of life."[46] When Preston sings of songs and stories, birds and circles themselves, he is calling back not only to images with major relevance to gospel, but to the prior foundation of Black American music.

During the recordings sessions for *Music Is My Life*, Preston was the leader, but his process recalls the collaboration that characterizes gospel (the shared "musical upbringing" to which Walker refers) as well as the ring shout. What McDonald and Walker describe is a marked contrast to the Beatles' January 1969 recording sessions, especially prior to Preston's arrival; the Beatles' faltering and failing trust in one another and in the very concept of "The Beatles" affected their creative process, something visible in both the *Let It Be* and *Get Back* films. The rooftop concert required them to fall back on the kind of cooperation that had always gotten them through such live performances—when individual's choices couldn't be questioned, and the setting forced real-time responses, improvisation, and adaptation.

The participatory leader-chorus *collaborative* dynamic is audible in the vocals and instrumentation of Preston's "Blackbird." McDonald explained that the first two verses are separated by interludes played on the Hohner Clavinet D6,[47] which evokes the wannabe harpsichord instrumentation in the Beatles' "In My Life" from *Rubber Soul* (1965). Preston and the backing vocalists enter the chorus, repeating "blackbird fly," and only then does Preston's voice break out on its own "into the light of the dark black night." This vocal, reminiscent of a gospel shout, is the most powerful flourish in the song. The remainder of Preston's "Blackbird" includes more vocal improvisations, but these twirls are rather subdued and cool, with a "well, well" and the repetition of "sing on." The song, which lasts two minutes and forty-three seconds, ends rather suddenly: Preston and the backing vocalists sing "rise," evoking the feeling of liftoff just when the song is over.

Although Preston basically maintains the standard length of "Blackbird," he and his backing vocalists, in contrast to McCartney's vocal clipping, stretch out of the word "night." Kimberley Jenkins, Dr. Jenkins's wife and Victory's first lady, related the stretching out of notes to "singing from the soul," a performance by a singer that, in turn, reaches down into the souls of listeners, allowing them to be in the moment.[48] Preston's "Blackbird" arrangement suggests the soul style inherited from gospel while also being a little funky and somewhat restrained. This creates a contrast with "Will It Go Round in Circles," the A side of the single that featured "Blackbird" as the B side.

"Will It Go Round in Circles" showcases Preston's vocal range and virtuosic organ-playing. The song, as John Tobler's liner notes explain, was motivated by Preston's joke that becomes the opening lyric, "I got a song ain't got no melody."[49] The ring-shout evoking "Circles" is "an air-tight groove that, despite its protestations, has no shortage of melody or moral"; Sean Ross notes that cowriter Bob Fisher contributed a "philosophical bent" that he gave other Preston numbers as well.[50] Offering a metacommentary on music itself, Preston sings a song that asks questions about a song (the "it") going around in circles like a physical disc on a record player. Preston's speaker also wonders whether the song will soar, birdlike, to imagined heights. Unlike McCartney's blackbird, Preston's bird does not have broken wings, and it doesn't need to learn to fly, implicitly aware that confronting the unknown is a cyclical problem, not a straightforward one. Birds, after all, don't necessarily fly in straight lines either. The uncertainty, which relies on faith for support, recalls the premise of the ring shout, as well as the spiritual "Will the Circle Be Unbroken?" a Christian hymn first published in 1907 and popular throughout American churches. Whereas the hymn includes a question mark in its title, Preston's is not punctuated, so the recurring phrase functions, in its commentary on life's uncertainty, as both an interrogative and a declarative.

On an April 7, 1973, episode of *Soul Train*, Preston performed his bird-themed A and B sides back-to-back, binding these songs together, just as McCartney did with "Blackbird" and "Bluebird" on the *James Paul* McCartney *TV Special* in 1973. During live performances, Preston often highlighted the song's circularity with a lasso gesture for the audience to imitate, a gestural call and response. Palmer, Preston's lead guitarist, recalled their live performance of "Will It Go Round in Circles": "When we would play it live and he got to that hook part, we would turn around in a circle." For Palmer, Preston's lyrics may be understood in the context of this gospel physicality: the song "can also mean that despite the fact there's no melody, that his music has always been inspired by God. People in church jump up-and-down and turn around, being moved by the Holy Spirit. That's probably why we turned around during that [hook] part."[51]

When asked about the bird imagery in "Circles," Palmer immediately brought up "His Eye Is on the Sparrow." The gospel hymn, Palmer pointed out, is "as common in the Black Church as "Amazing Grace.""[52] Reappearing throughout this book, the hymn's thematic content recalls the Sermon on the Mount, in which Jesus tells the crowd gathered around him to look at the sparrows in the air who neither sow nor reap yet still feed and fly. Aren't you, Jesus asks his listeners, worth more than they? And won't God take care of you, too? So don't worry, he says, have faith.[53] As in Jesus's sermon, the birds in "His Eye Is on the Sparrow" assure the listener that it's all in God's hands: if the smallest of his creatures are numbered, then the people are, too. The hymn promises protection for everyone—birds and people, singers and listeners. When he was on the Vee-Jay label in the mid-1960s, Preston recorded an instrumental version of "His Eye Is on the Sparrow" in a conventional gospel arrangement,[54] and he continued to perform the song in later decades using the traditional vocal arrangement of earlier gospel artists, such as Mahalia Jackson. Preston's birds are much like Bob Marley's title characters in "Three Little Birds,"[55] creatures of flight who have learned to trust in a higher power.

Even when he was appealing strongly to a crossover pop audience, Preston addressed social justice issues important to the Black community. The circles of his song might also correspond to persistent injustice that continues even when gains are made elsewhere. In "Will It Go Round in Circles," Preston's speaker sings of nonlinear songs and stories without melodies or morals, a lack of clean resolutions or clear lessons. In the logic of the verse-chorus relationship, the song and the story are synonymous with each other, a reminder of Cooke's arrangement of "Nearer to Thee."[56] If they are the "it" that goes round in circles, they are also relational to the bird of the chorus. Read in the context of the civil rights movement, Preston's song knows about persistent injustice in America, especially in a post-1960s era without a linear path to equality. The speaker admits that the "bad guy" will "win every once in a while," a crucial and still-relevant insight with roots in a deep well of shared knowledge, reflective of other contemporary expressions of Afro-Atlantic flight.

In "Will It Go Round in Circles," Preston's bird song and story have uncertain outcomes because life is outside any individual's control. Accepting this as an undeniable truth can actually lead to agency. As Toni Morrison wrote in *Song of Solomon*, "If you surrendered to the air, you could *ride* it."[57] Preston recognizes—in a pop song no less—that sometimes stories don't have the endings we want, that cruel, destructive people can and do win. Dr. Jenkins's sermons at Victory Baptist have a similar philosophical bent. In January 2020, he preached that "sometimes you have to swallow some bitter."[58] Like Preston's songs, Dr. Jenkins's sermons often look plainly at injustice and hardship while encouraging congregants "to hold on to God's trusting hand," a message that folks in the Black Church have long been using to sustain themselves in the United States.

As is characteristic of Preston's gospel-infused music, the listener is constructed as a participant, lifted by the joyful noise. Shaped by the encouraging words of his church, Preston sang with faith and optimism to his friends, mentioned in the second line of "Circles." In this way, Preston is also the bird, meeting people where they are without judgment. As Palmer recollected, "[Preston] always said, 'Music is my life,' so maybe he could've meant, 'Let the music be my voice. I don't need words for you to understand it.'"[59]

Giving Thanks and Credit

Preston's career embodied the motto of Victory Baptist Church, "To serve the present age—my calling to fulfill," and his music offers clear examples of transatlantic flight, specifically musical conversations between Black musicians and the Beatles. Preston collaborated with the band while it was still together, and then he did the same individually with Harrison, Lennon, and Starr after the Beatles broke up; he covered their music throughout his career and composed original songs with intertextual references to the band's music. Preston was one of the very first Apple Corps artists signed to the Beatles' new label. Even with all this active production, collaboration, and compositional autonomy, Preston's claim to fame in the Beatles' story is often reduced to his effect on a single event: the cheer his presence brought to the grumpy Beatles in January 1969. This is a nearly slanderous diminishment of Preston. As we have shown, his musical contributions are much more complex, though complicated no doubt by his own humility.

Preston always expressed gratitude for his work with the Beatles. In the original liner notes to *That's the Way God Planned It*, Preston previews what became the lyrics of "Music Is My Life," adding, "I may not be the best around but I'm surely not the worst," before giving credit to God and then to the Beatles and Apple.[60] Preston often talked about the "hope" he took from the Beatles' determination to succeed with Apple.[61] After Harrison's death in 2001, Preston said, "The Beatles did treat me as a member of the group. And that was a great honour, you know?"[62] In many ways, Preston's continual credit-giving is the antithesis to McCartney's credit-taking.

Because he worked with earlier innovators of popular music—such as Little Richard and Ray Charles—Preston's oeuvre is a visible and aural link between the Beatles and their Black heroes. Although Preston's legacy is visible when you trace his path into collaborations with other white artists, such as the Stones, we can find his lesser-known contributions to popular music by understanding his influence on other Black artists. In this view, he becomes the one to watch, distinctive and thus imitable in his own right, so we continue to follow the musical flight of the blackbird to another "Blackbird" cover that drew direct and specific inspiration from Billy Preston.

CHAPTER 9

Y'all Ready, Girls?

"Blackbird" Soars in San Francisco with Sylvester, Two Tons O' Fun, and the Band

"Listen," Sylvester James Jr. began, "the first time I heard this song was in the Sixties. And it was done by the Beatles."[1] "The who?" answered Izora Armstead,[2] one half of the singing duo Sylvester dubbed Two Tons O' Fun, whose other half was Martha Wash. Together, they backed the lead singer at the end of the 1970s. Izora's feigned ignorance prompted Sylvester's slightly exaggerated repetition, *the Beatles.* "Oh" was Izora's understated response. Sylvester teased more clues equally unimpressive to Izora, Martha, and the rest of the band. Suggesting the song was about "animals" and more specifically "birds," he asked for some sound effects but rejected them as sounding like seagulls. Sylvester then announced that they were playing "Blackbird," repeating the title to distinguish the two words. He rallied Wash, Armstead, and the other backing singers with "Y'all ready, girls?" Izora came along reluctantly—"I guess so"—but they sound anything but reluctant when their voices join and take flight on the stage of the San Francisco War Memorial Opera House in 1979.[3]

With this take on "Blackbird," Sylvester, the gay Black disco queen, out-fabuloused the Fabs. His rendition appeared near the beginning of a now legendary three-and-a-half-hour performance. Recorded live and soon released on the album *Living Proof* (1979), "Blackbird" became a gospel-disco-call-and-response number. In fact, the arrangement of "Blackbird" intentionally called back to Billy Preston, the foundation for the song's glittering—soaring—makeover.

During the groundbreaking show, Sylvester and many of the artists in his band brought gospel backgrounds to "Blackbird." The previous chapter argued that Billy Preston's version roots "Blackbird" in the context of Flying Africans themes and other sensibilities cultivated in the Black Church. Here, we show how Sylvester and his collaborators continue to build this home for the Beatles song, drawing on Preston for inspiration. Interviews with two of those present on stage, Wash and Eric Robinson, revealed these Preston dynamics. They each offered valuable insight into gospel, especially as it informed Sylvester's and their takes on "Blackbird." Wash's familiarity with the Beatles, particularly her affinity for McCartney, adds yet another layer of intertextuality to the performance, which preceded the flight-oriented songs she still sings today.

Meet Sylvester

Sylvester emerged from a musical church background in Los Angeles similar to Preston's, who was almost a year to the day older than Sylvester. Both musicians consistently credited maternal family influences. As Wash recalled, Sylvester "was very, very close to his grandmother." Wash also suggested Sylvester and Preston knew each other from Los Angeles–area gospel workshops when they were young.[4] But Sylvester's path diverged from Preston's more mainstream trajectory. Even though a gospel sensibility informed his music, Sylvester left the Pentecostal church and found a new spiritual home in the San Francisco countercultural scene.

Sylvester emerged in the Cockettes, "a multiracial drag ensemble composed of members of various genders and sexual orientations," who "became synonymous with San Francisco counterculture and paved the way for the growing gay liberation movement."[5] Continuing to be "as outrageous and in-your-face and radically flamboyant as possible," Sylvester later fronted and recorded with the Hot Band.[6] Sylvester's career did not really take off, though, until he signed with Fantasy Records under the wing of producer Harvey Fuqua. Fuqua, Berry Gordy's brother-in-law, applied Motown polish to Sylvester's studio recordings, which Wash referenced in our interview: "[Fuqua] was right there with Berry and Smokey and all of them."[7] With Fuqua, Sylvester had two major 1978 hits, "Dance (Disco Heat)" and "You Make Me Feel (Mighty Real)," along with the successful 1979 album *Stars*.

Sylvester's pop success began with "You Make Me Feel (Mighty Real)," a disco anthem announcing Sylvester's bold gender and sexual claims. As Wash explained, "Sylvester was an activist and an openly gay Black man during the time when that was not really appreciated. You know, in the entertainment business you had to hide. He wasn't going to do that. He said, 'You accept me as I am or don't accept me at all. And that's okay.'"[8] In performances and interviews Sylvester exemplified gender fluidity as an "everyday choice" as well as a rhetorical strategy.[9] In addition to his playfulness with clothes and makeup, Sylvester's ability to sing falsetto meant that his voice traversed genders in song, fluidity visually embodied in live performances and music videos.[10]

Sylvester adored costuming and costume changes as Wash remembered,[11] and the 1979 *Living Proof* show that includes "Blackbird" was no exception. On the album's cover, he appears short-haired and boyish, dressed in purple trousers with matching tie, pouring a glass of champagne while surrounded by soon-to-be audience members. This corresponds with his "butch" look: "To Sylvester, butch was and always would be no less ephemeral and put-on than feminine drag—though for him, at least a bit less fun. Butchness might occasionally be a useful strategy. If people needed to see a man, he might be willing to be one for a while; if they needed to see a woman, he might bring her out."[12] The *Living Proof* album displays this contrast: the gatefold reveals Sylvester onstage in full-on diva look—gown and turban—flanked by Wash and Armstead, who wear white gowns that recall the gospel background all three shared.

Meet Martha Wash

Growing up in San Francisco in the 1960s, Martha Wash's family soundtracked their weekend household cleaning with gospel music, an experience familiar to many Black American religious households. Martha's secret radio-listening, though, afforded her exposure to many different genres of pop music—including the Beatles. A constant in Wash's career is her own "meshing" of genres, particularly the reconciliation of gospel music with other pop genres. She often tells a story about her first voice teacher, who encouraged her to stop singing gospel:

MW: My father worked for this woman who was a music teacher. He asked her if she would give me some music lessons, vocal lessons. She agreed, and I started going to her home and we were just really kind of getting into it—we were in the beginning stages of me learning arias.

And then she told me, "I want you to stop, if you can, I want you to stop singing gospel music, because it's very, very hard on the throat."

I said, "Mrs. Korenburg! I really can't do that because [*Wash begins to laugh*] because I teach the youth choir at my church. And I sing in the senior choir, the community choir. So I can't really do that!"

She said, "Well, okay. Can you not sing it as *hard*?" I said, "Okay, I can try that!" You know *that* didn't work because I was still in high school and singing in the school choir, too. I mean, you know . . . [*trails off and pauses, implying not singing hard was simply impossible*]

[Mrs. Korenburg] worked with me maybe six more months before she passed away. She was elderly, but she was still giving voice lessons. She passed away, and I never did continue on with [classical training]. But I *enjoyed* it, you know, I enjoyed it because it was something, again, something *different*. And in high school with my music teacher, one of the semesters he was teaching baroque music, which I liked as well! I like choral music, I love the sound of that as well.[13]

When she mentions baroque music, Wash offers another intersection with Simone and McCartney, who were both struck by Bach in particular.

Like Preston and Sylvester, Wash credits the very beginning of her singing journey to maternal influences, especially her mother, who "loved to sing and who also sang in the church choir":

MW: On the weekend, we were around the house cleaning. My mother had music on and what she had on was gospel music. And that was the *only* music that I listened to growing up as a child. I grew up listening to Mahalia Jackson and Clara Ward and the Roberta Martin Singers and the Staples Singers and all those gospel artists of that time.

But as I got older and became a teenager, I got a transistor radio. And what I would do is put it [*starts to laugh*] under my pillow at night! So, as a teenager, I was listening to all of the Motown people and the rock bands that were out at that time. But Lord, there were so many of them, Creedence Clearwater, Rare Earth. And the station—it was a Black station—would play different types of music at the same time, different genres of music. Plus! I learned about different types of music watching TV. I liked big band music: Tommy Dorsey, Glenn Miller, Duke Ellington. But gospel music was the root of my musical background because that is really what I could listen to the most.[14]

Wash mentioned the convergence of Motown and rock 'n' roll on one Black radio station, which led to the question: what about the Beatles?

MW: I remember as a kid when the Beatles first came over here. Maybe fifth grade, maybe fourth grade, something like that? And I used to watch them on the *Ed Sullivan Show*. I always thought [*starts to laugh*] Paul was the cutest.

I always thought Paul was the cutest one. [*still laughing*] I didn't become one of their "regular" fans who collected all their memorabilia and all that other kind of stuff. But I had a few pictures of Paul here and there. Growing up, I couldn't—I *definitely* could not—put them on my wall. My mother was not having that!

I *did* like their music; it was another form of music that I grew up listening to as a teenager. You know, their sound informed everything. And it was also different from what I was hearing. As time went on and I got a little bit older, I could understand [the Beatles' musical innovation] a little bit better. They were using elements from our American artists very well and meshing [those influences] with their sound. So, you know, it was all good to me.[15]

Along with her hidden pictures of Paul, Wash also kept secret music, using her book bag to sneak in 45s, which, she pointed out, were smaller than LPs and thus easier to hide.

Wash's musical education in the church also facilitated future collaborations, such as with Izora Armstead, her partner in Two Tons O' Fun with Sylvester and later in the Weather Girls:

MW: Izora's church and my church were right next door to each other. I went to St. Bula, Church of God in Christ. And she went to St. Mark's Baptist Church. The only thing that separated our churches was a little, small walkway and sometimes, on Sundays, if both of our windows were open, we could see each other's services going on.

But I didn't really know her then. I was still a little bit too young to know her then. But when I got to high school, I was almost ready to graduate, and I started singing in the Voices of Victory Community Choir. She was singing in a different community choir, the San Francisco Inspirational Choir. So, on every third Sunday, we would have what they call a "Third Sunday Musical," where all these different choirs would come in fellowship at a particular church and have a meeting. And that's how I got to know Izora. My former manager put us together in a gospel group called the "NOW Singers," which meant the "News of the World."

With her upbringing in "a very strict religious household" and musical advancement in the church, it's not surprising Wash was a particular fan of Billy Preston.[16]

It was through Preston, in fact, that Wash first encountered Sylvester. She told several stories that form a bridge from Preston to Sylvester to Izora, leading right to "Blackbird" in 1979. The gospel thread runs through these experiences:

MW: I'm going to insert Billy Preston in this whole conversation that we're getting ready to have.

Now, I have always, *always* been a big fan of Billy Preston. You know how some people like certain musical instruments? Well, I've always been a lover of a good piano player, good keyboard player, always. (And I like a good guitarist, too.) I won't say I'm a pianist, but I can play piano a little bit. And I used to play for the youth choir in my church. So, I always followed Billy's career, his albums, and all that stuff. In my mind [right now], I'm looking at a 45 of Billy when he was on Apple doing "That's the Way God Planned It."

So now fast-forward. I think it was at the Berkeley Community Theater in Berkeley, California. I was going to see Billy Preston. He was doing a show there, and I went to see his show. [*pauses, takes a breath*] There was an opening act. [*another pause*] It was Sylvester.

[*starts to laugh*] I did not know who Sylvester was! I'd never heard of him! But I was going to see Billy. So, I watched the opening act. And when he [Sylvester] started singing and performing, I said to myself, *Who is this guy? Who is he?* Seriously. I said, Oh, my *God*. I had never seen anything like him before. Seriously.

I enjoyed his show. [*pauses*] But I wanted to see Billy Preston! [*laughing*] Okay, Sylvester goes off, you know, he finishes his set and Billy comes on, and I'm having myself a good time.[17]

Fast-forward again, maybe, two years later? I get a phone call from a dear friend of mine. She is a vocalist, and she said that they were holding auditions for singers on this particular day. I went to the address, which is not far from where I was working at the time, and it was in a basement of a house. I walked in.

And there was Sylvester.

He was holding auditions for a new band and singer. And there were two thin, white girls who had just finished auditioning for him. When I walked in, I met him, and then I said, "I came to audition for you," really not knowing *what* was goin' on!

So, I audition for Sylvester. The funny thing was, the keyboard player, Phillip, was a guy that I knew. We grew up in church together. He played for his father's church, and we had known the family for years. And I said, "What are you doing here?!" He said, "I'm playing for him!" I said okay! So, Phillip played for me while I auditioned—and I can't even remember what the hell I sang. [*laughing*]

[*after pausing to think*] I can't even remember what I sang. It could have been a gospel song, I'm not even sure. More than likely. And when I finished, the girls were still standing there. He told them they could leave. And then he started talking to me, and I told him that I knew Phillip, and we were longtime friends, and grew up in church and stuff together.

And then Sylvester asked me, did I know anybody else as large as I was who could sing? And I said yes.

KK: How did that make you feel when he said that?

MW: Well, [*slight pause*] I didn't trip on it. I did not—well, 'cause I *was* large! You know, I was definitely larger than the other two girls, so I really didn't trip on it. I was trying to get a *gig*, you know?!

So, I brought in Izora, and Sylvester was working on some music. He was going into the studio within the next week. And that's how we went over to his other keyboard player, who lived in Sausalito. Sylvester had a Volkswagen Beetle at the time. And we, all three of us, crammed into that Beetle and drove across the Golden Gate Bridge, and we were singing songs on the radio. [*laughing*]

KK: Do you remember any of the songs?

MW: Nope! None. We were probably singin' some gospel songs as well, to get the harmonies and figuring out placement and all that other kind of stuff. Because Izora and I, we sang together, so we *knew* each other. We knew how to fall in and harmonize on the drop of a dime.

And that's really how it all started.

KK: It sounds like a classic "beginning of a band" story, all that youthful hopefulness and excitement.

MW: Well, for me, yeah! James Wirrick, the lead guitarist, and I were the two youngest ones in the group. Sylvester and Izora were older—Izora was the oldest of everybody. But I was . . . maybe twenty-one? Twenty-two? So this was all new for me although I had been singing in groups and choirs. But *this* was—this was a new professional career! I was getting *paid* to be a background singer.

And it's funny because Sylvester, he really never put us in a corner. He always had us up front with him, I'll say that.[18]

The observation is poignant: later, in the 1990s, when Wash sang backing vocals for Black Box and C+C Music Factory, she was uncredited, and her presence was visually erased in one music video:

MW: I was just thinking while I was talking . . . yeah, he kind of kept us there, up there with him. There were naturally times when we were off or together one side of him or stepped back from the front. But a lot of times we were singing right up there with him.

KK: Were you usually singing the soprano part?

MW: Yes.

KK: And then Izora would sing alto?

MW: Right.

KK: And then Sylvester would sort of do his vocal twirls in between?

MW: Well, it all depended. Usually, I would sing the top part, Sylvester would sing the middle part, and Izora would sing the bottom part. That's usually how it worked. Depending on the song and the arrangement [*starts to laugh*] sometimes I was on the bottom, sometimes Izora was in the middle, and Sylvester's on the top! But for the most part, usually I sang the top, he sang the middle, and Izora sang the bottom.

KK: How did your mom feel about your career, especially as you were starting as a twenty-one-year-old?

MW: She didn't like it. My parents, they did not care for it. "Look, Mom," I said. "Mom, I will always be singing gospel music in one form or way. But this is something *different* that I want to do. It doesn't mean that I've given up gospel music completely. I never will because that's my foundation as far as music is concerned. So, don't worry about that." And they wound up being fans.

My parents would, depending on where it was, come to the show. They came to the *Living Proof* show at the Opera House. They came to a few of our shows—and they never said anything else [in disapproval].[19]

Living Proof: Martha Wash on "Blackbird" (1979)

The irreverent banter before Sylvester's performance of "Blackbird" at the San Francisco War Memorial Opera House in 1979 was, according to Wash, "spontaneous." She explained, "Nothing was scripted that night except maybe the order of the show! We were kind of like that, you know, just conversations.

And you're listening in on that conversation!"[20] The singers were irreverent toward the Beatles, but they were very serious about the worth of the song—made clear by the vocal power they unleash on "Blackbird." After the first verse, Sylvester asks the sold-out crowd, "Did y'all get the message?"[21] Sylvester functions as musical and spiritual leader, leading his band and singers and directing the audience to witness the bird-themed song's transcendent flight, if only for that moment in time.

As the show's third song, following an overture medley and "Body Strong," "Blackbird" helped establish the intimate dynamics between performers and audience.[22] This San Francisco audience had just experienced the loss of Harvey Milk, the first openly gay man to hold public office in California. The song does call attention to Blackness through the image of the "black bird," but in this context the song is about rising in other ways, too. The Opera House had, in fact, served as one site for Milk's memorial. Sylvester's show, then, became a rallying point, a place for many different kinds of San Franciscans to gather:

MW: That was a really great night, a really great night. Naturally, we were *never* invited back, but it was a great night! That was a great night for San Francisco, too. You know, I think we were the second *band* to ever play at the Opera House; the first one was the Pointer Sisters.

And [the *Living Proof* performance] was really newsworthy. I mean that place was just overflowing with people. And I think what was so amazing was that it hit every demographic, every race, and all, *all* the different genders you can think of. Everybody came to have a really good time and that's really what it was. And then every kind of dress that you wanted to see (and some you couldn't think of) was there that night. It was really a magical, magical night.

KK: Elsewhere you've said there were women in ball gowns, and there were men with backless—

MW: Somebody had their ass out. And I went okay, alrighty. Again, anything that you could imagine and probably stuff that you never *would* imagine. Because everybody wanted to be *seen* and they wanted to see the show.

KK: You've also mentioned that the space was very, very loud and that it kind of shook?

MW: Yes. Sylvester's producer at the time, Harvey Fuqua, was up in the balcony, I guess the top balcony. And he said that balcony shook so bad it almost felt like an earthquake and, you know, San Francisco is known for earthquakes. That didn't include downstairs, but he said it felt like an earthquake up there. And I guess that's probably another one of the reasons why they didn't invite us back!

KK: Speaking of the balcony, during more of the spoken-word parts of "Blackbird," at one point Sylvester says something about it being darker up there and asks if they know what he's talking about.

MW: Yes. Because well, naturally the lights were down on everything. And at one point in the show, [Sylvester] said, "Turn up the lights" (I think that was on "You Are My Friend"), so he could see the audience, as much of the audience as possible, who had been singing to him.[23]

Sylvester sang many more songs that evening, but the Beatles' song is emblematic of the performance; the light and dark motifs even characterize the lighting of the show itself. Sylvester and his ensemble reveal the song's capacity to address transcendent flight that is both individually and socially desired, both particularly and broadly applicable. As a gay, Black man in drag, Sylvester's very presence in that opera house is an illustration of the song's promise of rising during a dark night. The following day, then-mayor Dianne Feinstein presented him with a key to the city.

Wash's summation of Sylvester and the band's "Blackbird" gestures toward the changeable, uplifting nature of "Blackbird":

MW: I've always liked [our] version as well. I think because of the tempo of it. The symbol of it. I liked it. You know, the original version is slower, slightly slower. And maybe more melodic, in fact, than our version. But our version really gets you moving.

Wash surmised that Sylvester's arrangement of "Blackbird" was done by keys player and soon-to-be musical director Eric Robinson, who also sang on the aforementioned "You Are My Friend."[24] Wash reached out to Robinson, who then provided us with more details that confirm the song's special place in music history.

Living Proof: Eric Robinson on "Blackbird" (1979)

Eric Robinson's "inspiration for music" started in the Church of God in Christ and Pentecostal churches.[25] Like Sylvester, Wash, Preston, and others in this book, Robinson went on from church beginnings to a career with number 1 pop hits and an impressive roster of collaborators. At fifteen, Eric left Indianapolis, running away to Los Angeles where he first toured with Bobby Womack and eventually R&B singer and pianist D. J. Rodgers. A not-yet-sixteen-year-old Robinson then signed a seven-year songwriting contract with Motown when the studio was still in the early days of its California residency.[26] Robinson wrote and played piano for such artists as Jermaine Jackson, Smokey Robinson, and Rose (Stone) Banks (aka "Sister Rose," sister of Sly Stone); he also played piano and organ for Little Richard's and the Reverend James Cleveland's respective gospel shows.[27]

Robinson and frequent collaborator Victor Osborn cowrote the aforementioned "Dance (Disco Heat)," a number 1 hit for Sylvester. On the heels of the song's success at the end of 1978, Sylvester invited Robinson on the road once he returned from touring with Natalie Cole. While they were preparing and selecting songs to perform, Robinson recalled having seen Sylvester perform "Blackbird" years back at a club on Sunset Boulevard.[28] For Robinson, the performance served as a "template or blueprint, a memory of the arrangement that remained in my mind all that time."[29]

Robinson's memory motivated him to recommend "Blackbird" for Sylvester's touring repertoire, but Sylvester didn't remember it. "Did I do that song?" he asked. It was then up to Robinson to re-create the arrangement: "I remembered the *bounce* of the rhythm. So, I added the piano riff." In our interview, Robinson sang the riff, adding, "That was a Billy Preston thing." He went on, elaborating: "That was a Billy Preston piano riff because I *love* Billy Preston. Anyone would listen to any Billy Preston record and hear that riff. [*sings it again*] You know what I mean, that little riff? I took that, and I embellished it."[30]

For Sylvester's "Blackbird," Robinson drew on Preston to "reinvent a similar music vibe from memory." From there, Sylvester arranged the vocals and Robinson completed the arrangement for the rest of the band. Robinson, still in his late teens in 1979, enthusiastically remembers the *Living Proof* concert in which "Blackbird" was a standout:

ER: We didn't have the embellishment [of "Blackbird"] as a part of the song in the show. Sylvester did that spontaneously. [Prior to the San Francisco performance,] I used to do that riff maybe three or four times. [*sings the entire introductory riff, leading to "Bla-a-a-a-ckbirr-rrd fly"*] And we went off. But! In the live show, he had it going on for about—what felt like a lifetime! [*laughs*] And listen to the record, it goes on for about two or three minutes. He talks, and it's just me on the piano still playing that same riff.

I had never played "Blackbird" like that before because Sylvester had never asked me to, ever. It was so spontaneous and, therefore, I didn't solo. I didn't go hardly beyond that riff because I was really nervous. And it was *live*! [*laughs*] I thought, what if I try to embellish this riff and mess it up? So, if anyone is wondering, that's why I play that stuff to that riff![31]

Robinson's arrangement was critical to the performance of "Blackbird": the "Billy Preston piano riff" allowed Robinson to vamp the song's opening phrase and follow Sylvester for cues. The stability of the repetitive riff enabled tremendous vocal flourishes while the rest of the singers and musicians answered Sylvester's calls throughout the song, too.

Echoing Wash's recollections, Robinson talked about facilitating onstage improvisation: "I knew the gospel and/or blues responses to ad-libs and spontaneity."[32] Following the *Living Proof* show in San Francisco, Robinson became Sylvester's musical director after a particularly well-received London show:

ER: When we went on tour, I watched Sylvester. Anytime Sylvester started to embellish or ad-lib, I'd anticipate that crescendo and direct the band to a well-played accent to any song in any show. That, coupled with positive newspaper reviews of Sylvester and the Two Tons O' Fun tour, caused me to be named the musical director.

I got the position because of my gospel training, and in gospel music we work together. We work with the singers. We can always tell when the singer's getting ready to go for a big note that's never been practiced before. We can feel the buildup, and we can build up from the keyboard, and then we can drop the keyboard. [*Robinson demonstrates and sings a call and response that relates the effect of the singer's buildup on the audience*] The audience gets the reward of a well-coordinated band and vocals that increase in intensity and excitement—similar to the experience of watching fireworks. This is also the effect achieved by a gospel minister, who propels the congregation to a peak of adulation, similar to a crowd's response to goals scored in a sports game.[33]

The topic of gospel ensemble work, especially how a keys player watches, follows, and responds, brought us back to Preston. Robinson recalled meeting up with him in Hollywood clubs: "We would end the night playing piano in random people's homes, which was fun and inspiring." Robinson also remembered visiting "Billy's ranch on one occasion with D. J. Rogers; we heard music of various artists, as well as Billy's future projects—all very exciting times."[34]

Soaring: Wash and Robinson Today

Sylvester died from AIDS-related complications in 1988, and Wash has been a longtime advocate in HIV/AIDS activism and LGBTQ+ rights. "[Members of this community have] always been my biggest fans," Wash said. "And it really started with singing with Sylvester."[35] After leaving Sylvester's flanks, Martha and Izora formed the Weather Girls, famously looking up into the sky and proclaiming, "It's raining men!" in the music video for that 1982 hit song.[36] Punctuated with hallelujahs that evoke the duo's musical background in the church, "It's Raining Men" is an uplifting manifesto promising relief from atmospheric pressure. The chorus forecasts the abundance of men descending from the sky like studly, less tragic Icaruses or fallen angels. One verse credits mother nature with teaching angels to fly, relating her to a "single woman" (like the one in "Lady Madonna") who carries the burden alone.

The Weather Girls also recorded tunes composed by Robinson following his work with Sylvester. In the 1980s, Robinson himself released two albums, *Walk in the Light* and, as Eric & the Good Good Feeling, *Funky*. During that decade, Robinson relocated to London—"imported," as he puts it—by Frank Collins who had recently formed the funk band Kokomo. There, Robinson witnessed Whitney Houston's performance of a song he wrote, "Wonderful Counselor," whose inspirations are both spiritual and secular (specifically, the 1975 film *Tommy*, featuring the Who). Houston later performed the song with Cissy and Gary Houston at the 1988 American Music Awards. Robinson, still based in London, is currently working on his soon-to-be-launched label, Mosound Music Ltd.[37]

Now a two-time Grammy nominee, Wash has also launched her own label, Purple Rose Records, allowing her to "do whatever kind of music I want, when I want."[38] But this wasn't always the case. After "It's Raining Men," ubiquitous in 1980s aerobics studios and gay dance clubs, Wash became even more associated with dance music. In zeitgeist-shaping vocals of the 1990s, Wash commanded dancers to move in "Strike It Up" and "Gonna Make You Sweat (Everybody Dance Now)." But these contributions to massive hits by Black Box and C+C Music Factory were initially uncredited; C+C also hired a model to lip sync in Wash's place in their popular MTV video. Like the title character of "Blackbird," Wash emerged from darkness imposed on her: flying into the light, she initiated industry-changing litigation that transformed the way vocalists and musicians' contributions would be credited on records.[39]

Wash now shares the spotlight with Norma Jean Wright (formerly of Chic) and Linda Clifford; together, they make up the First Ladies of Disco, a trio that records, tours, and performs together.[40]

MW: We've come together as a group and we've been doing this a little more than five years now. We've recorded two singles. The last one came out last year [2019] called, "Don't Stop Me Now."

She explains this song's relevance to the First Ladies of Disco:

MW: We're *all* of a particular age. We've been around since the disco era and before, some of us, you know. So, we're three ladies that are still very relevant in our music and performing and things like that. And it's been, it's been really, really great! [*laughing*] Except when [the pandemic] started and we had *just* performed at the Orleans Casino in February![41]

The "first lady" designation calls back to their gospel foundation: in Black churches, the pastor's wife is frequently referred to as the first lady, a sign of respect and honor. In relation to Wash, Wright, and Clifford, the designation signals their contributions to a major pop genre that was historically subject to racist, sexist, and homophobic denigration. At the same time, the first-lady moniker also elevates the genre, recognizing its significant foundations in the Black Church.

Spearheading the legacy project, Wash is now the one flanked by Wright and Clifford, rallying them with the kind of invocation Sylvester used for "Two Tons O' Fun": "Y'all ready, girls?" We saw this firsthand at the First Ladies of Disco's last show of their 2022 Retro Music Box Tour in Houston on October 29 at Zilkha Hall. As they perform, these First Ladies energetically stake a claim for their contributions and ongoing relevance to popular music, sampling their hits and sharing a few stories about their experiences in the music industry while giving credit to former collaborators. They seek to lift up their audiences, encouraging them to dance to the gospel-infused pop. One of the bandmembers even introduces the show as "going to church." Sylvester's presence is palpable, especially when Wash performs a cover of his "You Make Me Feel (Mighty Real)."

Wash's show samples a diverse array of music from the ladies' pasts, often bridging songs together into medleys. The song choices reflect Wash's present disposition, a resistance to being "pigeonholed into one kind of music," an attitude that recalls her diverse listening experiences as a girl.[42] This eclecticism is also expressed on her 2020 album *Love and Conflict*, which she characterized as "a musical journey that goes all the way back to the '60s psychedelic sound" and "continues on, into blues rock and then a little pop and then the little hint of gospel music and then a little hint of country, [all] with modern-day lyrics."[43]

Produced by Sami Basbous, whom Wash credits for the album's scope, *Love and Conflict* dropped in January 2020. This was months prior to the full onset of the pandemic, followed by summer protests related to George Floyd's 2020 murder by police in Minneapolis. As protests escalated, Wash released a Black Lives Matter–themed video for one of the record's new songs, "Soaring Free."[44] In the gospel-forward number, Wash sings, "Trails don't turn always right / But I will keep on moving." Wash's powerhouse voice is like a hand offered to the listener, who is encouraged to "hold on" in order to soar free. Like Preston's "Will It Go Round in Circles," Wash's song recognizes the hardships that motivate the need to fly away and locate a haven—and how important it is for a community to support this flight.

When she was still a bourgeoning musician, Wash admired Preston (and still does); he was a point of connection between Wash and Sylvester. That triangulation is mirrored in Robinson's arrangement of "Blackbird." Sylvester and his ensemble's landmark performance offered solace during a dark period in San Francisco's history. Aided by Wash, Robinson, and the other musicians and singers, Sylvester, with his bold expressions related to gender and sexuality, served as a spiritual guide for the audience in 1979. In the War Memorial Opera House, his "Blackbird" initiated a homebound flight during which he and the audience sang together. The Preston dynamics also demonstrate how covers of "Blackbird" can exist in conversation with one another as much as they do with the Beatles. The same is true for other bird and flight-oriented songs by some of the twentieth century's most influential Black artists, who call back to one another just as they call back to the Beatles.

CHAPTER 10

I Was Just Seeing Myself Singing

Bettye LaVette on Interpreting the Beatles and Singing a Bridge of Blackbirds

Looking svelte and chic in her black sleeveless pantsuit, Bettye LaVette stepped out of the darkness of a freezing night in January 2018 and became the blackbird singing into the light. In a black-box theater in San Antonio, the show had barely begun when LaVette hit pause to give instructions to the technicians running the board. LaVette, a veteran performer, knew exactly how she wanted the light, advising on adjustments with her characteristic mix of sass, cool, and good humor. As an aside she explained to the crowd, "A lot of people don't know how to light Black skin. They make you look purple!"[1] LaVette then sang into the light that she'd set right, filling the space with her music and stories. Throughout the show, LaVette was alone onstage but for her keyboard player. She perched on a stool, the corrected spotlight illuminating her in the intimate space, whose acoustics allowed for all the nuances of LaVette's dynamic voice. The sold-out show was not as full as it should have been that night; because of icy weather, less than a quarter of the ticketholders had come out. Still, LaVette performed for the audience of fifty-eight as if we were packed into stadium seats at the Hollywood Bowl, the venue where she first sang "Blackbird" in 2010.

During the 2018 San Antonio performance, LaVette prefaced "Blackbird" by making a persuasive case for her interpretation: "Nobody had broached the song from the perspective of the person that it's about. And the song is about . . . me. So, I thought, I'm going to broach it."[2] She began to sing in her soul-stirring style, and suddenly the song was brand new. Lavette's first-person "Blackbird" is about teaching herself to fly with broken wings and waiting all her life for *this* moment—despite all the heartache and struggle it took to get there.

When she claims the song is "about" her, LaVette Signifies on McCartney's stories about the song. To this point, we have shown how McCartney stepped into a profound narrative trope and artistic tradition in Black music that features birds and flight. By isolating an inspirational Black woman, he also unknowingly recalled Florence Mills, who has an original claim on the blackbird as a symbol of equal rights in twentieth-century popular song. Nina Simone also dubbed herself the "blackbird" of the music industry in the early 1960s. In fact, soon after "Blackbird" was released in 1968, McCartney did name a particular Black woman, Diana Ross, in the first known documentation of his civil rights–themed "Blackbird" story; she seems to have rejected the blackbird application (according to McCartney's conversation with Donovan) even though she later used a sparrow to emblematize her career. The Ross connection will become further ironic given LaVette's stories about the Supreme.

McCartney may not realize his musical bridge of Black women—but LaVette recognizes hers.

In 2020, LaVette released a studio version of her interpretation of the Beatles' song, which is the last track on the Grammy-nominated album *Blackbirds*. When she sings "to be free," LaVette's album concludes with the musical equivalent of opening a door and stepping into the light. The eight tracks preceding "Blackbird" are interpretations of songs popularized by Black women, Nina Simone among them, along with Dinah Washington, Billie Holiday, Ruth Brown, Della Reese, Sharon Robinson, and others. These are LaVette's "bridges," as she characterized them throughout our interview, Black American women singers, rhythm and blues forerunners who paved the way for her—and today's generation, too.[3] The Beatles' song is the exception on the record; with it, LaVette harnesses the blackbird metaphor to serve both the album's purpose and her story. In doing so, she also calls back to Black American women and the many other singers and musicians who have correlated themselves with blackbirds and, more broadly, tapped the trope of Flying Africans.

Meet Bettye LaVette

"Buzzard luck" is the bird-themed refrain LaVette uses repeatedly in her memoir for all her missed chances and bad fortune, and that phrase points to the context necessary for appreciating her "Blackbird" and its application to her career.[4] LaVette had an early hit with the single "My Man—He's a Loving Man," which reached number 7 on the rhythm and blues chart in 1962. Back then, she was a sixteen-year-old up-and-comer on Atlantic Records, a Detroiter hanging out with members of the Motown stable and others in that musical town. But her next single didn't do as well, and she ended up in Jerry Wexler's New York office breaking up with Atlantic (for the first time) after he encouraged her to work with Burt Bacharach, whom she considered too "fluffy." She performed another charting hit, "Let Me Down Easy" on the Calla label, for television viewers on an episode of ABC's *Shindig!* on June 9, 1965.[5] That success, though, wasn't the kickstart to her career that she wanted, a stop in a start-stop pattern that would replay itself again and again. Even though she never achieved the popular success of many of her Motor City peers, LaVette has never stopped working as a singer, always persevering through label disappointments and other letdowns. As she puts it, "More than simply loving music, I *am* music. Chapter by chapter, music is what drives my story forward."[6]

Unlike many of her contemporaries, LaVette's soulfulness does not derive from vocal training in the Black Church. Before her Louisiana-born parents relocated to Detroit, her musical education began in front of her family's "blues-blasting jukebox." Their communion was the "booze and barbeque sandwiches" they sold out of their Muskegon, Michigan, home, which gospel acts like the Dixie Hummingbirds frequented so as not to be spotted at public bars. Once in Detroit, LaVette (then Betty Jo Haskins) attended Catholic school (the choice of her "wine-loving Catholic" mother, who saw this education as a vehicle for "social mobility"), where she backtalked the nuns who wanted to cultivate her singing talent. After having a baby at fourteen, LaVette started public school, but those days were short-lived once she discovered the Detroit club scene that launched her singing career.[7] She later moved between New York City and Los Angeles, but Detroit has stayed ever in LaVette's heart.[8]

LaVette inhabits the songs she interprets. She finds the character in the lyrics much as an actor does with a script. This approach was fostered by her longtime mentor (and at-times manager) Jim Lewis, to whom she dedicated *Blackbirds* in 2020. Her theatrical disposition was further honed during forays into stage performance. At thirty, she learned to tap, which she called "one of the hardest things I've ever done," for a part in *Bubbling Brown Sugar*, revived on Broadway in 1976 and an "established hit" when she began touring with the company in 1977.[9] This revue was, in fact, a revival of a Harlem Renaissance–era musical (which had featured Duke Ellington and Count Basie among others), recalling the very genre and type of show that saw Florence Mills performing as the blackbird.[10] As we mentioned in the introduction,

LaVette's point-of-view shift in "Blackbird" also recalls another Detroit colleague, one whose church beginnings certainly were foundational. Aretha Franklin famously sang the Beatles' "Eleanor Rigby" in first person, becoming the title character and voicing her loneliness. With a similar shift in lyrical perspective, LaVette's song can be heard as calling back to Mills singing as the blackbird and Franklin singing as Eleanor Rigby.

LaVette's life has been full of rising and falling cycles. She now talks about being in her "fifth career."[11] Though each of LaVette's descents presented difficult challenges, each renewal brought more recognition, such as singing with Jon Bon Jovi for US president Barack Obama's inauguration in January 2009, the same month LaVette performed at the Kennedy Center Honors in celebration of the Who. The latter performance underscores her ongoing engagements with British Invasion artists, evidenced by her album *Interpretations: The British Songbook* (2014). It was, after all, English Northern Soul record collectors whose interest in LaVette helped spur one of her resurgences in the late 1980s and 1990s.

LaVette affectionately describes the "Northern Soul nuts" as the "hardcore R&B fans who respond to the funkier side of Motown. They pride themselves on loving the Detroit music and singers from the sixties who have gone unnoticed. The more obscure the better. Since no one was more obscure than I was, I became a Northern Soul sweetheart." What LaVette encountered among these fans, in addition to their deep admiration for her music, was knowledge of her story. To Northern Soul fans, especially deejay-turned-producer Ian Levine who came to Detroit in the late 1980s to "reclaim Gordy's empire," LaVette was a star—and their recognition finally made her feel like one. Hers was the music Northern Soul fans celebrated in clubs where deejays spun "old soul sounds and new frantic beats" to keep dancers going all night. An illustration of the transatlantic conversation between British and Black American music, this is another example of LaVette finding light to sing into. As she, ever the darkness-transcending blackbird, puts it, "The hustle never stops. When it does, you're either comatose or dead."[12]

LaVette in 2020

Laughing throughout our interview—which took place during a pandemic when it was hard to laugh—LaVette's joie de vivre was contagious. Her optimism isn't rooted in vague positivity or the charmed life of a star, but in a sense of humor about her experiences. On August 17, 2020, our phone call was one of several interviews the seventy-four-year-old singer gave that day.[13] But LaVette took her time, energetically telling (often-hilarious) story after story populated by some of the most well-known artists of the 1960s. She had recently won a Blues Music Award for "Soul Blues Female Artist of Year," and she was inducted into the Blues Hall of Fame. LaVette's stirring take on "Strange Fruit" had also been released months earlier, ahead of the album's impending August 28 drop date.

LaVette asked her label, Verve, to distribute her take on "Strange Fruit" in June as a gesture of solidarity with the Black Lives Matter movement, whose demonstrations intensified following the murder of George Floyd by Minneapolis police.[14] That song, with its antagonizing crows, responded poignantly to the present moment. But LaVette sensed an unusual reversal, seeing the application of other songs on her new album, too:

BL: "Strange Fruit" and *Blackbirds* became timely—in a week! You know, this is the first time the *world* has moved to match the music. Usually something happens and we write music about it. This here is what's *happening* in real time, and *Blackbirds* and "Strange Fruit" are just—what's happening! Unfortunately . . . that's what's happening.[15]

In order to hear the better future LaVette sees on the horizon, the past must be remembered and its relevance recognized. She maps this territory in the songs she selected for *Blackbirds*, a record whose concept is rooted in the title character of the Beatles' song.

"Blackbird" (Take 1): LaVette, the Hollywood Bowl, and the Beatles

Over the years, LaVette has habitually pointed out that she does not "cover" songs. She *interprets*[16] them—a distinction made clear with "Blackbird."

BL: He [McCartney] is singing about me. So that made it easy to interpret. And so many people here don't realize that the Brits call their women "birds." I've been so surprised how many people thought he was actually talking about a *birrrd*. [*laughing*][17]

Here, LaVette riffs on the explanation McCartney introduced during his Driving tours at the very beginning of the twenty-first century. LaVette continued, highlighting her own experience with "Blackbird" in live performance:

BL: The first time I performed ["Blackbird"] was at the Hollywood Bowl [in 2010]. And to be standing there with thirty-two violins at the Hollywood Bowl—I'd starved half to death just blocks from there when I lived in LA. And I'm here at the *Hollywood Bowl* doing a tribute to the Beatles with thirty-two strings. And that was, just, all my life I've waited for *this* moment.

KK: Do you remember hearing "Blackbird" in the '60s?

BL: I never heard the song before I did it at the Hollywood Bowl.

LaVette's memory of struggling in LA helps explain why her phrasing characterizes the dark night as cold rather than black. LaVette goes on to explain the integral role her current manager (and husband), Kevin Kiley, who is also a musicologist, plays in her selection and interpretation process:

BL: We were trying to find tunes, and for each one of these albums that I've done, he always gives me about one hundred tunes. And I pick the ones that I want to do out of that. And when we got ready to do this [Beatles] tribute [at the Hollywood Bowl], it was the same thing. And I picked the ones that I like.

    And it occurred to me, [McCartney's] singing about a Black girl. And I said, I definitely want to do this. And at the time, I didn't know that any other women had done it. I [thought] it would be kind of unique—since Paul wrote the tune, and I'm who he's talking about—for me to do it.

KK: When Kevin presents you with songs, does that mean he gives you the lyrics and—

BL: He plays a song for me. And if I *like* it, he prints up the lyrics for me. I'm always attracted to melodies, so ofttimes when I get the lyrics, they don't live up to the melody, and I just refuse to sing stupid songs. But ofttimes I'll find a melody that I just *love*, but the lyrics don't go anywhere and aren't saying anything, and I have to let it go.[18]

In addition to "Blackbird," the 2010 Hollywood Bowl set featured other Beatles tunes: "Here, There, and Everywhere,"[19] the Chuck Berry–influenced "Come Together," along with "We Can Work It Out," whose Stevie Wonder rendition might be as popular as the Beatles' version. LaVette's innovative take on "The Word" also appears on her *Interpretations* record.

    LaVette's recollections about recording *Interpretations* are a reminder that she's no stranger to songs by British Invasion artists: Even so, transforming songs everyone knows so well is no simple process.

BL: When we did the Who thing, "[Love,] Reign o'er Me," at the Kennedy Center Honors [in 2009], I was *sooo* low when I went into the rehearsal. I didn't like the song. I had never heard of it before. Once again, my husband, it's his favorite group, so he whips out all these *Who* songs. And I decided to do that one, and I . . . I didn't want to do it.

So when we came into the rehearsal, I said, [*pauses*] "I can't sing this song like this." And the music director, Rob Mathis, who went on to produce that next album, *Interpretations*, he said, "Well, how do you want it to go?" So I said, "Can everybody just not play nothing?" And I just sung it for him *a cappella*. And he said, "Come back tomorrow or later on this evening as soon as I get it finished." And he wrote that arrangement for me.

And so when it [the performance] started, Pete Townsend and— what's the other child's name?

KK: Roger Daltrey?

BL: Yes. I don't think they even knew what it *was* because it's so *different* from the intro.[20]

Backstage after the show, Daltrey and Townsend (visibly moved to tears during LaVette's performance) bowed down to LaVette, getting on one knee to show their admiration. LaVette's stunning Kennedy Center performance was a showstopper, personally meaningful to LaVette because she was in the company of contemporaries Barbra Streisand (an honoree) and Aretha Franklin, who, along with Beyoncé, was also performing that night.

Even before Kiley's influence on LaVette's song selection, LaVette was performing Beatles songs, including "Eleanor Rigby":

BL: "Eleanor Rigby" has actually been in my shows since . . . I think Ray Charles was the first to cover it. So since whatever year that was [1968], it's been in and out of my show for all of those years. Because my music director [Rudy Robinson], the one that lasted thirty years, he did this little arrangement based on the Ray Charles arrangement. But over the years, it became more and more—me. Like I wanted it to be. And it is still in all of my duo shows [when LaVette is accompanied by a keyboard player].[21]

Prior to the Beatles' official breakup, LaVette also recorded "With a Little Help from My Friends" for Karen, an imprint of Atlantic, in 1969 during her second go-around with that label. LaVette remembered recording the song on the recommendation of her aforementioned mentor-manager Jim Lewis, whose support she—young, stubborn, and fiercely independent—often resisted. It took her a while to see the wisdom of his advice, which often related to song selection and other strategies to garner wider appeal:

BL: Jim said, "Well, these guys [the Beatles] seem to be becoming very popular." And my band at the time was like seventeen, eighteen, nineteen [years old]. They were all over the Beatles and Sly and the Family Stone, and they were bringing these songs to rehearsal. We were doing something at the Art Institute in Detroit. I did "Fool on the Hill," "Something," "Yesterday," and "With a Little Help from My Friends."

LaVette continues remembering Lewis's influence:

BL: Jim would go into a record shop, he'd say, "Give me everything that came out this week." You couldn't do that now. And he would come out and he would listen to them and pick out whichever ones.

 You know, I started to, as I grew, I started to listen to [the Beatles] songs more closely and find my way into them. And they're just excellent songwriters.

KK: You mentioned it's the melody that leads you to a song.

BL: It's the melody. And it *has* to be the lyrics. I'm somebody's grandmother. I can't just stand up there and say nonsense, which is why it's so hard for me to do contemporary music because it's based mostly on whatever the hook is. And I need a *story*.[22]

When LaVette becomes the blackbird, you hear the story of her arrival, especially at the Hollywood Bowl. But this account of a rising up is much more than one person's flight.

LaVette's Sparrow and Blackbirds on Verve

Blackbirds follows LaVette's all-Dylan record, *Things Have Changed* (2018), which was also produced by Steve Jordan on the Verve label. LaVette and Dylan share a penchant for irony. But when it comes to delivery, LaVette's dynamic emotional register topples Dylan's characteristic remove, especially when she sings biting lines like "I'm in love with a man that don't even appeal to me." LaVette is known for her ability to vacillate between vulnerability and bravado, weariness and energy, restraint and dramatic outpouring—sometimes all within the space of one song.

LaVette's 2005 take on Dolly Parton's "Little Sparrow" is a good example of the interpreter's emotional range, especially as it comes through in a bird song. "Little Sparrow" is one of the relatively few times LaVette has interpreted a "woman's" song prior to *Blackbirds*. Along with "Tiny Sparrow," discussed in chapter 7, "Little Sparrow" is another name for the Appalachian folk song "Come All You Fair and Tender Ladies" (Roud 451). LaVette's interpretation via Parton is, then, situated in a legacy of women singers if we consider Aretha's performance of "Tiny Sparrow" in 1964 and the tune's folk history as a song directed to women. Parton's arrangement of "Little Sparrow" accentuates the bird motif by focusing on the chorus, which begins the song. The first verses call to the maidens, and the third verse shifts into a first-person point of view. The speaker imagines what would happen if she were the sparrow, a comparison device that accentuates the warning she gives fellow maidens to watch out for the kind of men who crush birds. Parton's speaker then claims she is not the sparrow, but, rather, "the broken dream / Of a cold false-hearted lover / And his evil cunning scheme."

As the song's troubadour in the banjo-fiddle tune, Parton sings as if blinking away tears, determined to share the song's lessons with other maidens.[23] When LaVette delivers these lines, though, she does so in a musically darker atmosphere driven by a melodic, dominant bass that announces its presence forcefully. She performs the brokenness with her voice, repeating lines that intensify her desperate commitment, as the fluttering and wronged sparrow, to look her false lover in the eye. Working in the blues tradition, LaVette's delivery makes clearer the correlation between singer and bird: the crushed sparrow and the broken dream are really one in the same, the abused products of a mean man—or the larger construct for which he and his betrayal stand.[24]

"Little Sparrow" is, however, an exception when it comes to LaVette's song selection: as her Dylan record illustrates, prior to *Blackbirds*, LaVette has more consistently gravitated toward songs popularized by men:

BL: Heretofore most of the things I've recorded have been men's songs. I've not liked the approach that women—generally, if you synopsize women's songs, they're "he hurt me, I loved him, and I wish I could leave." [*laughs*] I like to do songs from the men's perspective, which doesn't contain that.

But *these* particular women [interpreted on *Blackbirds*], they are the rhythm and blues people that I came across on. And I wanted these young women today to know that *I'm* the bridge they're coming across on. And it did not start with Donna Summer![25]

Blackbirds is the personal and collective musical journey of Bettye LaVette and the women whose songs she vocalizes with sass and soul. All the tracks on *Blackbirds* dwell in feeling, sometimes recognizing the consequences of broken or unfulfilled promises, as in "Blues for the Weepers." In a virtual performance she released a week prior to the album, "One More Song" also became a meta-commentary on live music and other communal experiences lost to the pandemic.[26] During a time when intimacy had to be imagined for many people isolated due to COVID-19 restrictions, LaVette voiced connection. Her interpretation of Lillian "Lil" Green's 1940 "Romance in the Dark" takes the listener into the bedroom, especially because LaVette slows down the phrasing to accentuate certain images. That song, also done by Billie Holliday and Dinah Washington, is more evidence of what LaVette means by "bridges" constituting Black women:

BL: [I thought that *Blackbirds* as] the title for the album will be great because it was about these Black women, the bridges that I came across on. These were the first rhythm and blues singers. And right now, they're being so marginalized.[27]

With *Blackbirds*, LaVette recognizes the Black American women who opened the door for future generations. Her commitment to this legacy echoes her struggle to become what she imagined for herself, a goal she is now achieving on the Verve label.

Blackbirds, like the all-Dylan record, was produced by Jordan for Verve:

BL: It's been such a joy—and a salvation as far as I'm concerned—working with Steve Jordan because I haven't had a Black producer for a *verrrry* long time. So [before him] I've had to bring people *around* to my way of thinking, like on the *Interpretations* album. They [the session musicians] were a studio full of white guys who grew up with these songs, who've played these licks a million times. When I got to the studio, immediately I said, "Forget about 'em. I don't wanna hear anything that I recognize. You've got the *notes* there in front of you. I'm going to sing the words, you play those *notes*—do not play those licks on that record."

KK: Was it hard for them to do that?

BL: I'm sure it was. I'm sure it was hard for them to rethink. And that [rethinking] is what Steve has been able to do for me. What Steve is doing is writing arrangements, [it's like he's] arranging Doris Day tunes for James Brown! He can hear it like that because he grew up the same way I did. So he understands *exactly* what I'm talking about. I don't have to *bring* him around to it. He understands *that's* what I was talking about.

The subject of recording on Verve brings LaVette back to her manager, Jim Lewis:

BL: Jim thought the sun rose and set with Norman Granz, who developed Verve. If Jim was not dead, [he'd be so thrilled] this would kill him! [*laughs*] This would just kill him, that I had sung *these tunes*—and on *Verve*?! So I'm just so glad to have been able to—to do it. He always knew that I could sing these songs. And I learned them and rehearsed them [back then], but I didn't want to sing 'em. I was seventeen, shit, I didn't want to sing those "save your love" [songs] or none of that! I said [to Jim], "You just want me to sound old because you're *old*." [*laughs*]

KK: After Jim, how did your singing keep developing? Did it change when you did the Broadway tour?

BL: Oh absolutely! Most people don't realize what it means to be directed. To be told how many steps to take, when to turn, whatever. Then you incorporate that into *you*. I am always aware of where the camera is, where the audience is. And it made me look different than just the chick who sung in a bar. You know, I had been singing when I did *Bubbling Brown Sugar* at least twenty years. But I had never been directed or any kind of staging or sung without a microphone [in my hand]. [In the stage production] the microphone was connected to me, which meant I had to learn to do more things with my hand because I didn't have a microphone in it. And, so, it made me look completely different as an entertainer than any of my contemporaries.

KK: That sense of drama really comes through in your performances now.

BL: I know what you mean. Oh, it has to *become*, it's what Jim kept trying to instill in me: it's not that your name is Bettye LaVette—you *are* Bettye LaVette. You have to, no matter how big or small you think that is, everything that you do has to—I didn't understand, Katie, I didn't understand anything he was saying! Nothing. It was boring and it was getting on my *nerves*. Oh my goodness!!! [*laughing*]

Jim made the woman you see before you today. I mean every detail, everything about this artist he made because all I was was a little girl, as he called me, "a little girl with a big booty, a small waist, and a big voice," but I was far from being what he wanted me to be.[28]

LaVette talked about learning to "become" Bettye LaVette, which still means staying in shape, the same size 6 she has always been (even though she does enjoy her champagne), as well as styling herself. She adapts her look according to the record—for example, adopting a dramatic gold aesthetic for the Dylan album. But as her stories about her mentor-manager Lewis illustrate, LaVette's career has not been easy; this was due, in part, to her own stubborn streak and sense of independence—neither of which she has given up.

LaVette on Lynch, Badalamenti, and the Solo Beatles (and Keith Richards)

LaVette is not embittered by her struggles, a truth that comes across in her interpretation of a tune that Nina Simone released in 1967. "I Hold No Grudge" is another *Blackbirds* song that was released ahead of the album during the spring of 2020—right as the United States and many other parts of the world were locking down due to the pandemic. As the album's opener, "I Hold No Grudge" becomes an invitation even though LaVette's voice makes it clear that acceptance is hard-won. The theme is certainly relevant to LaVette's history and all the almost-hits and other chances that didn't work out. In 2020, a message about moving past grudges was also broadly applicable given the widespread uncertainty about the pandemic's consequences. Ironically, "I Hold No Grudge" also brings up yet more Beatles' connections occasioned by concerts hosted by filmmaker David Lynch.

For more than a decade, LaVette has been involved in Lynch-sponsored concerts because the filmmaker is a particular fan of hers. At one of Lynch's "private parties," LaVette performed her interpretation of Harrison's "Isn't It a Pity," a song Simone memorably covered in 1972. Lynch's longtime composer Angelo Badalamenti then suggested that LaVette record "I Hold No Grudge," which the composer had cowritten when he was producing Simone. LaVette wasn't then familiar with Badalamenti:

BL: I thought he must be a saint because his name is so *mellifluous*. [*laughs*] [He introduced himself] and said, "I loved your performance."

In fact, LaVette had "I Hold No Grudge" in mind since the 1970s when she heard it in a Black beauty parlor, but she was waiting for a label who would be "receptive to this." Many years later, that turned out to be Verve, the label on which "most of these people [interpreted on *Blackbirds*] recorded." After she sent Badalamenti her recording, he praised her interpretation, adding that Simone would be proud, too.[29]

Lynch's own association with the surviving Beatles is due, in part, to their shared interest in Transcendental Meditation (TM), a practice that involves repeating a personal mantra. On separate occasions, Lynch and the Beatles received their official mantras from the founder of TM, the Maharishi Mahesh Yogi. Remembering that the Maharishi's 1968 Rishikesh retreat is one motivational setting for McCartney's "Blackbird" adds even more irony to LaVette's playful dig at TM:

BL: I love David, I've done lots of performances for him. I think the only reason I don't see more of him now is because I refuse to meditate. I said, "I'm too goddamn broke to meditate! I don't need to close my eyes and go over nothing. I need to try to find out what works and do that over again. I don't need to keep saying shit over and over!" [*laughing*][30]

LaVette has taken on the Beatles at other Lynch-sponsored events, such as Starr's "It Don't Come Easy," another from her *Interpretations* album and one well suited to the history of her career—much more than Starr's charmed life as a Beatle. At Lynch's 2014 birthday concert, held at the El Rey Theatre in Los Angeles, Starr was also honored, receiving the Lifetime of Peace and Love Award from Lynch's foundation. With Starr in the audience, LaVette schooled members of his All-Starr Band on one of the former Beatle's most well-known solo numbers. For example, LaVette turned toward guitarist Steve Lukather (of Toto) and sings, "You wanna sing the blues, you gonna have to pay some dues"[31] with her typical mixture of cheek and seriousness.

Starr's "It Don't Come Easy" provides a logic for what became his Peace and Love motto, and he always highlights those concepts with corresponding hand gestures in live performance. LaVette's interpretation discards the clichéd talk of peace and puts the emphasis on love as the thing that doesn't come easy. LaVette picks up on one reference to the speaker's love "growing" in Starr's version, often using variations of that word instead of "come" or "coming." She also draws out another line about what hinders love: all she wants is trust, but the fact that she's explaining that illustrates why it's difficult for her love to grow. Throughout the song, LaVette is both exasperated and committed, the language of growth positioning her as a kind of farmer who shows up every day to labor in a field that may or may not yield a harvest; just like a gardener, though, LaVette knows about nature's uncertainty. She is steady in the face of inevitable struggle, advising the messy addressee of the song, who is variously thrashing and traipsing, to calm down. As with "Blackbird," altering lyrics is about shifting perspective: she locates songs' meanings for today, not yesterday—not even that of the 1960s, which should have been her decade and wasn't.

"It Don't Come Easy" is a song about singing the blues, but LaVette found its blues register. During a cutaway interview with Lynch (added to a video of the performance), Ringo fumbled for the right words: "Bettye LaVette! Bettye LaVette took *my* song and turned it comp—into something else, which was so incredible, where she took that song into her own personality and life." Starr continued, "It's like something I wrote in like, 1893, when I was Blind Lemon Clubfoot."[32] The compliment recognizes LaVette's reinvasion of the British Invasion, a phenomenon indebted to Black Americans, like Starr's other hero, Lightnin' Hopkins. LaVette also praised Starr for his down-to-earth manner and sense of humor:

BL: Ringo has been so sweet. . . . We get along, I mean, completely. At the performance we did at Radio City Music Hall [in 2009], the day before we had a soundcheck and a press conference with the world press. And I knew that he was kind of famous for holding up the peace sign. So I held it up—I held my fingers behind his head! He said, "You aren't supposed to do that unless you're somebody's drunken uncle!" [*laughs*].

This 2009 concert was a multi-artist performance benefiting the David Lynch Foundation. McCartney was also on the roster.

KK: How was McCartney to be around?
BL: [McCartney] wasn't as friendly [as Starr]. I mean, he was like your general entertainer friendly. But Ringo immediately acts like he's known you forever. It was the same way with Keith Richards.
      Keith walked in the studio that morning. I had a coffee cup of champagne. And he had a coffee cup of whatever he was doing. He had a joint in his hand, and I had a vaporizer in mine. We sat on the couch and *talked*. And I told him, I said, "You know, if we had known each other in the '60s, we would have gotten into *trouble*." . . . At one point he told me,

[*does an imitation*] "You know, I'm um, I'm um, I'm known as a star." I
say, "You're just a millionaire fucking guitar player to me!"

LaVette checked Richards with her typical quick-witted backtalk, but in our
interview she expressed her gratitude to him for endorsing her work. As with
Ringo's Blind Lemon joke, such recognition acknowledges and continues to
participate in the ongoing transatlantic conversation between British and
Black American music:

BL: It was wonderful. I was so grateful to [Richards] for doing that for me.
       You know, to be able to put his name on the front of the album. I was
       so grateful.

LaVette is referring to Richards's support of *Interpretations*, along with his
written endorsement of her memoir. Richards also played guitar on multiple
tracks of LaVette's Dylan record, *Things Have Changed*. Not everyone LaVette
interprets is always so publicly supportive. She often tells a story about the
time Dylan approached her when they were both coming out of dressing
rooms. She said, "Hey, Robert Dylan!"; he gave her a kiss on the mouth and
walked away without saying a word.

BL: Bless his heart. And I haven't been able to get anything out of him since.
KK: I wondered if he had said anything about *Things Have Changed*.
BL: You know what, my husband told me I have to stop talking about it
       'cause he [Dylan] is so greatly *loved*. But I think that if I were powerful
       enough to just say someone's name and help them, I would say it.
          You know, you [Dylan] ain't gotta pay no bills, don't gotta pro-
       mote nothing. Just say the name. And I know he's been asked about it
       [LaVette's *Things Have Changed*]. I know that. You know, so if he just
       said my name, that would help me so much. So, my husband says that
       I said I sound bitter. I said, "Well, I am bitter. Shit! I'm not pretending
       to be bitter, I'm bitter!" [*laughs*]
          His son [musician Jakob Dylan] came to see me at the City Winery
       [in New York City].
KK: How was he?
BL: Oh, he was so *sweet*. He told me *he* loved it [*Things Have Changed*]. He
       came to see me! And I said, "What do you think your dad thinks about
       the album?" He said, "Who the hell knows?" [*laughs*] Everybody in the
       dressing room cracked up![33]

LaVette's insight into Dylan's lack of public support underscores a disposition that became even more apparent at the end of the interview, one that involves her consideration of her former Detroit colleagues and the city's current aspiring (and struggling) musicians. Even though LaVette remembers the slights and disappointments, she perseveres—and offers her hand to others, the ones who came before, alongside, and after her.

"Blackbird" (Take 2): LaVette as the Blackbird in Detroit

When Starr described LaVette's take on his song, he noticed how she makes songs relevant to herself by inhabiting their stories; in doing so, she expands the songs by opening up their meaning. Singing "Blackbird" in first person, LaVette stakes a claim for her consistently overlooked work in a musical career that began contemporaneously with the Beatles when LaVette was an up-and-comer in Detroit—another setting she has imagined for "Blackbird."

In an article that appeared prior to our interview, LaVette mentioned that McCartney was singing about a girl in a park.[34] At the end of our conversation, she more specifically situated "Blackbird" in Detroit with a reference to herself at Belle Isle, an actual park in the city. She alluded to the multitudes of meaning that "people" have attached to the song following McCartney's bird-as-girl story, as well as the agency she asserts over the interpretive process:

BL: I've heard several stories [about "Blackbird"] now because, after I knew I was going to do the tune, people were offering stories. So, these are the stories that people said, and I just liked that one better than the rest of them:

      [McCartney] was going through the park to smoke a joint and the girl was standing on the thing singing. And there was a park in Detroit called Belle Isle, which is where we all hung around when I was younger. I was just seeing myself standing up on a picnic table at Belle Isle—at night—with some of my friends hanging out and singing a song.

      That's just a story I chose to like. . . . I guess the man's saying, "Go ahead, take my damn song, change the history of it and everything!"

KK   You turn the song around when you sing it through the first-person point of view. It's like you've turned a camera around.

BL: I think it's about me. That's what I would have written about if I could write songs. And, so, it was just as if I told [McCartney] how I was longing to do this and how I wanted to fly and how everybody in Detroit was flying all around me. I think this is what he would have written and given to me.

Or—or!—I choose to think that! [*laughing*] That's the story I've decided to tell *me*. [*still laughing*]³⁵

In her recognition that there are many stories about this song, LaVette expresses a metatextual awareness about "Blackbird." She has chosen the *story* she likes, illustrating once again how she inhabits songs while expanding their application. And the story she likes has meaningful implications when it comes to Detroit's special role in the history of popular music.

LaVette situates "Blackbird" in the context of a musical journey that started in Detroit, but she doesn't hear a lonely blackbird; she imagines friends gathered at the park. The communal orientation is consistent with other memories of that city in the 1960s, when it was a hub for recording:

BL: There was so much going on in Detroit. When people say, "How did you, at sixteen years old, get started?" I say, "Are you joking?! In Detroit in 1962?" My neighbors were producers. It was nothing to get into show business. Maybe to get something that *worked* or to get it outside of Michigan, Ohio, and Illinois. But to record was not a big deal.³⁶

The Detroit scene was formatively shaped by Motown founder and producer Berry Gordy and his so-called stable of artists, which included Diana Ross.

In making the connection between "Blackbird" and Detroit, LaVette, in fact, Signifies on McCartney's first recorded story about the racial dynamics of "Blackbird." During his conversation with Donovan following the *White Album*'s release, McCartney mentioned Ross and the "offense" (perhaps playful, perhaps not) she took to "Blackbird."³⁷ This Supreme had the success that LaVette wanted but for which she wouldn't sacrifice her independent spirit. In the 1960s, LaVette relished occasions when she got to witness Ross being taken down a notch, such as when Motown songwriter Brian Holland's wife initiated a physical altercation with the Supreme, who was sitting with Holland:³⁸

BL: I see now, in retrospect, that a great deal of it was just jealousy. Diane *embraced* sophistication so much quicker than the rest of us did. We wanted to still be, like, a little *thuggish* and a little *girlish*, a little *trash-ish*, a little *star-ish*. And Diane just wanted to be a *star*. [*laughs*] And she stepped right on into it.

LaVette went on, explaining how quickly Ross "embraced whatever Berry Gordy [was picking up] in Hollywood or wherever he would go."[39] If we take McCartney at his word during the Donovan conversation, Ross seems to have rejected the association between the blackbird and herself (or other Black people) in the late 1960s. In a fascinating twist, LaVette has embraced that very bird, whose struggle to fly is much more applicable to LaVette's career than to Ross's.

LaVette continued reflecting on the musical history of Detroit, remembering the effect of Gordy moving the label to Los Angeles:

BL: Oh, my God, Detroit was devastated. . . . That's why I only hire Detroit musicians. It's a little more costly 'cause I have to pay to go fly up there and rehearse. Or fly all of them here. But I don't hire anybody but Detroit musicians. That city gave me, made me who I am.[40]

LaVette then spoke about her still-living contemporaries in Detroit, such as the last surviving member of the Four Tops, Duke Fakir, talking about how he and others need to be interviewed and written about while they're still alive. It was clear that, for LaVette, success doesn't mean forgetting the community, her birdsong the call that lifts up others, too.

When LaVette sings of herself as the blackbird coming out of the darkness and into the light, she realizes the song's personal application and expansive potential. By buttressing "his" meaning for the blackbird as a Black girl or woman, she Signifies on McCartney's song and his stories about "Blackbird" being motivated by the US civil rights movement. At the same time, LaVette flies out of the former Beatle's reach and becomes the blackbird who could never belong to him.

Twenty-First-Century "Blackbird" in Paul McCartney's Legend, for #BlackLivesMatter, and into Transoceanic Flightpaths

When the usually optimistic Beatle characterized night as death in "Blackbird," he offered up a profound, malleable image. More than five decades later, the song is still being used by McCartney and transformed by others. The history and legacy of "Blackbird" are much richer and more complicated than McCartney's legend about the song being inspired by a Black woman or civil rights, especially because the blackbird is a symbol whose meaning Black artists have continually freed from racist cages. Recognizing this complexity tells a more complete truth about a dark past that must be reckoned with for there to be any hope of the bright someday imagined in the lyrics of McCartney's song.

McCartney's last US concert dates of his Freshen Up Tour took place in summer 2019, prior to a polarizing US presidential election and the COVID-19 pandemic, which halted live performances. In these shows, "Blackbird" was a call to recognize what was broken and which US citizens were still not allowed to fly freely, especially in public spaces. The latter was made clear a year later when Christian Cooper, a "Black birder," was subject to racial profiling in New York City's Central Park. A white woman who refused to leash her dog called the police and claimed that an "African American man" was intimidating her. The incident received national attention, putting a spotlight on Cooper's birdwatching. In 2023 Cooper wrote an essay explaining the origins of his interest in birds, citing a red-winged blackbird as his "spark bird—the birding community's term for the bird that ignited my interest in all things feathered." A Mother Nature's son, his insight is reminiscent of both McCartney and R. H. Harris: "Over the years, the red-winged blackbird's raucous territorial cry would become like the voice of a familiar friend. To this day, that sound—which signals the males' return after being away all winter—is, for me, the first harbinger of spring."[1] The red-winged blackbird is the exact variety that flew over the little blackbird Florence Mills's Harlem funeral, and its connection to Cooper underscores the tensions between caged and liberated inherent in bird imagery explored throughout this book ironically motivated by McCartney's stories.

Like a returning blackbird, McCartney resumed touring with his Got Back Tour in the spring of 2022 and repeated the version of the "Blackbird" story cited in our introductory chapter. Yet, as Walter Benjamin said, "the finest stories are characterized by the lack of explanation."[2] McCartney's repetition asserts ownership of the song, doing the opposite of what "bird whisperer"[3] Toni Morrison recommended when she invoked the image of a bird in her 1993 Nobel Prize for Literature speech. For her, a bird is a metaphor for language: although the writer may worry about the "consequences" of her language, the bird's existence is now in others' hands. By retelling a story that gives himself credit, McCartney limits the song; Morrison characterizes that kind of discourse as "unyielding language content to admire its own paralysis."[4]

McCartney now insists that "Blackbird" was *always* intended to serve the cause of civil rights, but Black people in the Americas have long had their own songs of hope, especially those featuring flight. Perhaps, though, McCartney's "Blackbird" legend is a case of "story-truth" being "truer sometimes than happening-truth," as Tim O'Brien says in *The Things They Carried.*[5] Truer truth may apply to McCartney's desires for the song to comfort, figured as hope for Black people treated unjustly. There are very few Black people in the audience of his US shows, though. The mostly white crowd is comforted to know the song they've loved for all these years was progressive all along, and hasn't the nation come so far since the 1960s? Whether we take McCartney at his word or read him symptomatically, it seems undeniable that McCartney *wants* his song to heal, regardless of what the facts tell us about the song's actual history.

Another "Blackbird" Flies in 2021: Marilyn McCoo and Billy Davis Jr.

O'Brien's insight into story and truth also applies to Bettye LaVette, the Black American singer who took McCartney up on his blackbird-equals-Black-girl explanation, turning the song into her very own anthem. After LaVette released "Blackbird" in 2020 on *Blackbirds*, yet another interpretation of the song appeared in 2021, one that used McCartney's storytelling as a launch-pad, too.

Former Fifth Dimension members and Grammy winners Marilyn McCoo and Billy Davis Jr. released their version of "Blackbird" as a single two months ahead of their album *Blackbird: Lennon*-McCartney *Icons*. McCoo and Davis are earnest about their symbolism, but their use of the blackbird still Signifies on the Beatles. Like LaVette did the year before, McCoo and Davis gathered their new recordings under the wing of the blackbird, the central image they wanted listeners to key in on, as evidenced by the album's (now-defunct) website, IAmaBlackbird.com. The pair actively marketed their record, positioning it as a "help" for all victims while also making #BlackLivesMatter messaging primary, a double-voiced call that includes but also defines.

Along with remembering Black victims of racial violence, "Blackbird" became a vehicle for McCoo and Davis to tell their own story. At the music video's midway point, images of McCoo and Davis appear, as well as a replica of a 1977 newspaper clipping about a cross-burning in the yard of their home.[6] When McCoo and Davis use the blackbird to highlight injustice and as an appeal for equality, they recall Florence Mills, who, in the early 1920s, implored white people in the audience to understand her plea while also signaling her commitment to the uplift of Black audience members. McCoo and Davis's history of crossover appeal—they were the first Black couple to host a variety show on ABC—furthers their association with Mills. But the idea that nonthreatening Black entertainers' appeals to white audiences are still necessary almost one hundred years later is a profound illustration of America's inability to address its inequities and history of racism.

The "blackbirds" that McCoo and Davis sing about are specifically identified as Black people, especially young people: "When a blackbird leaves our mother's nest, one day, it will not return. In 2021, mothers throughout our country live in the fear that our blackbirds may prematurely not be able to return to the nest of home, because of bigotry and violence. . . . Blackbird is dedicated to the life and humanity of every blackbird, whether living now or lost in battle."[7] McCoo and Davis reinforced the parent-child dynamics when they explained the anthemic qualities of the song in the context of the 1960s:

> We must never forget that Blackbird was written following the 16th Street Baptist Church in Birmingham, Alabama being bombed . . . which killed four babies, Cynthia, Addie Mae, Carole and Carol Denise. The song, and the entire album, is about Civil Rights, which are human rights. We needed to use our art as activism and let everyone know: we can all be blackbirds for each other, and wage a peaceful war for every human being to be treated with fairness, dignity, and the right to live without a daily fear of harassment and even death. Blackbird is an expression of the reality we are living today.[8]

Like LaVette, McCoo and Davis provide a support beam to McCartney's civil rights explanation with a historical event McCartney has never mentioned in his "Blackbird" prefaces.

McCoo and Davis Signify on "Blackbird" to remember the Birmingham church bombing, the very tragedy that Simone identified as the awakening of her civil rights consciousness.[9] McCoo and Davis connect the image of the blackbird to the four girls, now memorialized in bronze statues on a street corner across from their rebuilt church. One of the girls looks as if she has lifted off into the sky with her arms outstretched overhead, her fingers reaching toward a small flock of birds. These birds appear to be both assisting her flight and motivating her touch. The other girls are figured next to her in a row; together, they form a line of succession, all on their way up. When McCoo and Davis explain their "Blackbird" in relation to these memorialized girls, the couple's song becomes even more reflective of Afro-Atlantic flight and the trope of Flying Africans: flight is an escape from cruelty and oppression on earth, though sometimes that new life is death.

As we have shown throughout this book, songs and stories of flight have been circulating for hundreds of years in arts of the African Diaspora. The trope of Flying Africans was here before McCartney, and it is here still. The metaphor's power resides in its history: flying responds to slavery and its consequences, and the polysemous uses and symbolism of black-colored birds are contingent on transatlantic musical conversations. These are dialogues McCartney is certainly part of, but they are much richer and more complicated than the stories he continues to tell about "Blackbird." As ways that cultures express truth, myths and legends are important, to be sure, but they are best when they open up expanses, as McCoo and Davis have done, rather than close them down.

"(Sittin' On) The Dock of the Bay": Transoceanic Flightpaths with Otis Redding and Yoko Ono

On the *White Album*, "Blackbird" includes birdsong sound effects added in postproduction, "including a warbling blackbird from the Abbey Road effects library."[10] A bird species' particular noises, whether quacking, honking, or chirping, are a means of identifying the bird, an aural naming and recognition within a song. In Black music, birdsong can express a key motif in the trope of Flying Africans, the connection between uttering the specialized noises and the ability to fly away from a coercive culture that denies freedom. This effect can be achieved through birdsong and corresponding birdcalls—even when birds seem to be otherwise absent (i.e., unmentioned in the lyrics). A perfect example is Otis Redding's "(Sittin' On) The Dock of the Bay," a song whose speaker has traveled two thousand miles from Georgia to face the Pacific each day—from sunup to sundown—in seagull-ridden San Francisco.

Redding didn't live to see how successful his song, cowritten with Steve Cropper, would be. It was released on Stax in early 1968, but Redding died in a plane crash on December 10, 1967. When it comes to 1960s hits with longevity, "(Sittin' On) The Dock of the Bay" rivals the most popular Beatles' songs. The speaker recounts his earlier cross-country movement, immediately recalling the Great Migration, which witnessed Black Americans traveling from the southern United States in two general directions: northward and westward. We mentioned Billy Preston's family's movement from Houston to Los Angeles during the 1940s as part of this phenomenon, also visualized in artist Jacob Lawrence's *Great Migration* series, one panel of which features luggage-bound Black people heading westward while blackbirds fly against a blue sky. In Redding's song, seagull sound effects offer a comparable complement.

Fulfilling Redding's plans for the song after he died, Cropper added the sounds of the seagulls and the waves; the significance of these effects becomes even more apparent after we consider the lyrics. They tread widely applicable territory, particularly the heartbreaking predicament of leaving home, as well as the beloved American directive to "Go west, young man," the c advice credited to nineteenth-century publisher Horace Greeley. But the speaker in Redding's song doesn't find in California the golden fruits of labor. Instead, he refuses to work. "(Sittin' On) The Dock of the Bay" depicts a Diasporic westward journey, but of a particular kind: one of refusal or resistance.

The speaker in "(Sittin' On) The Dock of the Bay" has reached his destination and is looking out over the Pacific Ocean, where every day he sees the ships coming and going. As he watches life swirl 'round him, this speaker recalls the one in the Beatles' "Good Morning Good Morning," a song we earlier connected to "The Red Rooster."[11] The Beatles song begins with a cock-a-doodle-doo, the brass section's trumpeter, and concludes with clucking, the bird noises bracketing verses of domestic and professional discontent. Lennon's speaker's psychic paralysis is eventually interrupted when he encounters some sexual excitement (away from home), but, bored by the day's routine, he's not easily roused. None of these connections are coincidental: when working on "(Sittin' On) The Dock of the Bay," Redding took direct inspiration from *Sgt. Pepper's Lonely Hearts Club Band*, especially in his experiments with tape loops.[12]

The sound effects of seagulls and waves create complementary imagery in the aural mise-en-scène: they, just like the ships, engage in a circular coming and going. Seagulls, waves, and ships are linked, their continuous action a contrast to the isolated, stationary speaker, who is unable to meet others' demands. When introducing his theory of the Black Atlantic, Paul Gilroy argues, "Ships immediately focus attention on the middle passage, on the various projects for redemptive return to an African homeland, on the circulation of ideas and activists as well as the movement of key cultural and political artefacts: tracts, books, gramophone records, choirs."[13] But Redding's speaker isn't gazing into the Atlantic—this is the Pacific, the peaceful ocean. Perhaps, like George Clinton's spaceship, the seagulls' flight offers an alternative for transcendence in a new place over a different ocean.[14] The lonely speaker, though, sings and whistles by himself. Whistling can be thought of as an attempt at returning birdcall to the seagull, but the speaker does not imagine flight or any other kind of movement. Rather than a fairy-tale transformation, Redding and Cropper offer perspective and specificity. Their speaker sees what he sees and dwells in the moment created through his sight and the things around him. Here we have a modernist approach to the Flying Africans trope.

And yet perhaps this meditative repose is itself resistance or at least refusal. We see such stances in literature from Melville to Beckett to Ellison, the lack of motion an antithesis to the constant movement demanded by the modernity, epitomized by ships (carrying goods from one globalized port to another) and seagulls (scavengers who are, let's face it, always looking for the next score).

Thinking again about the Beatles' *Pepper* as inspiring Redding, Harrison's "Within You Without You" comes into play. Motivated by the songwriter's deepening investment in Indian music and spirituality, this song articulates a philosophical view of the self and what flows in, through, and around the individual, who is "really only very small." Obviously, this is not a particularly Western outlook, and it is certainly not very American. Redding's song likewise cuts against the American notion of self-improvement, bound up in that go-west myth, impossible to separate from Manifest Destiny and all its consequences.

In this way, the dialogue between the Beatles and Redding necessitates a transpacific and transoceanic perspective that takes multiple geographical intersections into account. The same can be said if we consider bird and sky imagery in Lennon's solo work, putting our understanding of his indebtedness to Black music in conversation with the influence of Lennon's wife and collaborator Yoko Ono. With over sixty years of song content, Macca has certainly proven himself the birdman, but John frequently associated his speakers and song objects with birds and other sky-bound entities, often drawing himself and Yoko (and sometimes their son Sean) sitting on clouds.[15] As if to punctuate how he perceived them, Lennon's last book of nonsense writing is titled *Skywriting by Word of Mouth*, posthumously published in 1986.

When asked about her sky-themed art installations and comparable initiatives, Ono has often remembered the firebombing she witnessed in Japan during World War II, experiences that shaped her anti-war stance.[16] After her family's home was destroyed, they were displaced and hunger was constant: "In those days, I just looked at the sky, and it was so beautiful. And there was not many beautiful things in my life except the sky. And the sky was always changing, bright, beautiful. And so I really fell in love with the sky at the time."[17] The sky has remained a persistent inspiration and setting in her avant-garde work, which also included collaborations with Black jazz musicians like Ornette Coleman (they performed together at the Royal Albert Hall in 1968 when Lennon and the other Beatles were in India). Indeed, the lonely stasis with which Ono characterizes her childhood sky-gazing, including her detached observations of the firebombing itself, evokes a similar stillness found in Redding's song.

Given the popularity of the Beatles-inspired "(Sittin' On) The Dock of the Bay," it's possible the Redding song motivated engineers to consult the studio's library of sound effects to use on McCartney's "Blackbird." Within the recording of "Blackbird," then, actual birdsong answers McCartney. This call and response is another metaphor, one characterizing the formative, responsive presence of Black music in the Beatles' oeuvre. The metaphor also characterizes interpretations of "Blackbird" and reworkings of other Beatles tunes, as well as the stories that Black artists tell about these songs.

McCartney is not the only one with stories of a blackbird. There are many of them, and they keep being told. The tales, the songs, the birds—they make circles, and circle back, calling to one another across and within the transatlantic flights that characterize the history of Black music and the Beatles. As Cooper, the Black birder, puts it, "[Birds] can fly. We see them launch themselves effortlessly up into a medium with no boundaries while we remain earthbound, and we are inspired to dream. Imagine watching land and sea unfold beneath you not through the windows of an airplane but under your own power."[18]

Notes

INTRODUCTION

1. Bettye LaVette, interview by Katie Kapurch, August 17, 2020; see also chapter 10, below.

2. Paul McCartney, Austin City Limits Festival, Zilker Park, Austin, October 5, 2018.

3. Franklin, LaVette's contemporary and fellow Detroiter, also motivated McCartney's composition of "Let It Be," which Aretha then covered. See Sheffield, "Why Nobody Sang the Beatles."

4. Southern, *Music of Black Americans*, 521.

5. The early Beatles tend to get the most attention for their indebtedness to Black artists because of their output. Prior to 1966, the Beatles covered formative influences and contemporaries, including Chuck Berry, Little Richard, Arthur Alexander, Barrett Strong, the Isley Brothers, and Smokey Robinson and the Miracles—in addition to girl groups discussed in chapter 7, below—on singles and LPs. The band's middle period is often seen as a transitional moment on their way to high art, but Everett makes a compelling case for how the Beatles remained indebted to Motown, Atlantic, and Stax on *Revolver* (1966). As Everett concludes, an earlier discourse on musical transformation—from music for dancing to music for thinking—may have motivated subsequent critics to underplay the ongoing conversation between Black Americans and the Beatles. Everett, "Detroit and Memphis," 39. In his analysis of the *Rubber Soul* and *Revolver*-era Beatles, Hamilton similarly recognizes that "a moment long heard as the Beatles turning away from pop into the avant-garde of (white) rock was still marked by a deep engagement with contemporary black music, particularly that which was coming out of Detroit." Music writers, not the musicians themselves, obscured this dialogue. Hamilton, *Just Around Midnight*, 129.

6. In a 1989 C-SPAN interview, Proctor explained what happened: "I took the Four Seasons and Frankie Valli to London and made a trade with EMI Records in London to trade the Four Seasons records for the Beatles, who at the time were unknown. . . . It's a wonderful coup, except I have to say that I didn't think too much of it at the time because I only signed them to 30 sides and said, well, you know, we don't want to take any chances on this unknown. And so we had the first 30 sides of the Beatles records in America on the Vee-Jay label." "Life and Career of Barbara Proctor," March 31, 1989, C-SPAN video, 00:59:44, https://www.c-span.org/video/?6903-1/life-career-barbara-proctor.

7. For more on the history of the Beatles on Vee-Jay, see Spizer, *Beatles* and *Songs*.

8. "Life and Career of Barbara Proctor."

9. The pre-fame-Beatles-loved-Black-music narrative was generally unquestioned by those music critics who themselves shaped the historical record, framing the Beatles' borrowing as a beneficent cultural contribution to the United States. Elijah Wald calls this an "odd twist": "Many writers have described the British Invasion as a discovery of black music, applauding the Beatles, Stones, and Animals for introducing European Americans to African-American masters from Muddy Waters and Howlin' Wolf to Bo Diddley and Chuck Berry." The effect, Wald argues, is to relegate Black artists to the past, "the roots of rock 'n' roll rather than as part of its evolving present," even though "until the mid-1960s, white and black rock 'n' roll styles had evolved more or less in tandem." Wald, *How the Beatles*, 239. Ornette Coleman's biographer also

notes, "Some musicians called the Beatles' 1964 arrival in town 'the beginning of the end' for jazz. Slowly, but surely, club clienteles were shrinking, leaving owners unwilling to book risky music." Golia, *Ornette Coleman*, 137.

10. Clinton, *Brothas*, 47, 81.

11. LaVette, interview by Kapurch.

12. Calling back is a vehicle of remembering: Frederick "Douglass insisted on remembrance before any action: 'Perhaps there is too much past. But remember that all the present rests on all the past. Remember is as good a word as forget.'" Blight, *Frederick Douglass*, 679.

13. For an example of how deeply McCartney's interpretation is entrenched in pop culture, see the 2022 film *Glass Onion: A Knives Out Mystery*, which includes a character singing "Blackbird" near the film's beginning. Both film critics and social media users interpreted the presence of the song as a clue related to the film's Black women characters, one of whom is murdered. Her twin solves the mystery of her sister's death with the help of the franchise's detective, bringing truth out of darkness and into the light.

14. Miles, *Paul McCartney*, 485–86.

15. Lennon and McCartney likely did this at the prompting of Beatles' roadie and long-time assistant Mal Evans, who was working on a visual representation of the *White Album* in 1968. Kenneth Womack, interview by Katie Kapurch, November 8, 2022.

16. McCartney, *Lyrics*, 538; Beatles, *The Beatles*.

17. According to the foremost scholar of birds in ancient literature, Jeremy Mynott, English children "must learn to distinguish a robin, gull, duck, and pigeon (probably also an owl and a penguin, though they may never actually see one) well before they know the different kinds of trees, cars, or fish that there are." Mynott, *Birdscapes*, 56.

18. McCartney, *Lyrics*, 371.

19. "Blackbird by Bobby McFerrin," January 5, 2008, YouTube video, 00:02:44, https://youtu.be/37DHXrFfwrE.

20. "Bobby."

21. McFerrin discussed faith and his father, Robert McFerrin Sr., in Moring, "Bobby." McFerrin Sr. also sang the role of Porgy as performed by Sidney Poitier in the film *Porgy and Bess* (1959).

22. Tony "Gilly" Gilbert, who witnessed Marley composing "Three Little Birds," remembered the music and lyrics coming "together in a flow": "Bob got inspired by a lot of things around him, he observed life. I remember the three little birds. They were pretty birds, canaries, who would come by the windowsill at Hope Road." Quoted in Goldman, *Book of Exodus*, 241. Wailer Peter Tosh "was also a lover of birds; he kept a single blue and white parakeet that was given the freedom of his yard." Grant, *Natural Mystics*, 251.

23. Singer Marcia Griffiths also remembered the song as Marley's "official" dedication to herself and the other backing singers known as the I-Threes: "After the song was written, Bob would always refer to us as the Three Little Birds. . . . It was more or less expressing how we all came together, when he says, 'Rise up this morning, smile with the rising sun.' We loved it. Even when we were recording it, we know it was our song." Quoted in Goldman, *Book of Exodus*, 241. The multiplicity of origin stories parallels "the extent to which as early as 1971 the Wailers' biography was already subject to the old Jamaican adage: 'There is no such thing as facts, only versions.'" Grant, *Natural Mystics*, 194. On "versioning" in song, see also Kun, *Audiotopia*, 127.

24. Goldman, *Book of Exodus*, 241.

25. As testament to their pop functions, both "Don't Worry Be Happy" and "Three Little Birds" have been used to serve purposes distended from their composers. George H. W. Bush's 1988 presidential campaign appropriated "Don't Worry Be Happy"; McFerrin was vocal about his disapproval of his song's unlicensed use and refused to perform it. Although not unlicensed, Marley's song has been used for commercials, such as for the Sandals

resorts. It also became an unofficial anthem of Liverpool Football Club.

26. Paul McCartney, interview by Chris Douridas, *New Ground*, KCRW, May 25, 2002, audio, 02:00:00, https://www.kcrw.com/music/shows/chris-douridas/paul-mccartney; see also McCartney, *Lyrics*, 47–48.

27. Haefeli, *Paul* McCartney. This documentary supports the concert story, including a very brief cutaway dissolve of a Black woman fan singing "Blackbird" after McCartney's performance.

28. See Kapurch and Smith, "Blackbird Singing" and "Blackbird Fly," which consider the evolution of McCartney's "Blackbird" stories, arguing they are evidence of post-racial sentiment. In the twenty-first century, McCartney retroactively constructed himself as a civil rights activist in 1968, a romantic move in line with his colorblind rhetoric in the 1980s. We also find that his "Blackbird" stories took a turn in the second decade of the 2000s, illustrating his recognition that the civil rights movement and racism are not relegated to the past.

29. McCartney, *Lyrics*, 47.

30. Runtagh, "Beatles' Revelatory White Album."

31. Brothers, *Help!*, 285.

32. Everett explains that the "treble/bass counterpoint . . . may be a reference to the G-major outer-voice parallel tenths in the best known minuet from the Anna Magdalena collection." Everett, *Beatles as Musicians: Revolver*, 347. Brothers sees a "connection to [Ferdinando] Sor's *Study*, No. 19, opus 60 in G major (the same key as *Blackbird*)." Brothers, *Help!*, 341.

33. Miles, *Paul* McCartney, 485.

34. McCartney, *Lyrics*, 47.

35. See chapter 7, below.

36. Brothers, *Help!*, 342.

37. Gates and Tatar, *Annotated African American Folktales*, 70.

38. Colbert, *Black Movements*, 24.

39. Commander, *Afro-Atlantic Flight*, 7.

40. For a discussion of post–civil rights flight rhetoric, see Commander, *Afro-Atlantic Flight*; and Colbert, *Black Movements*.

41. Quoted in Heilbut, *Gospel Sound*, 79.

42. Ibid., 80.

43. Anthony Heilbut, CD liner notes to *Father and Sons*, 1.

44. Ibid.

45. Heilbut, *Gospel Sound*, 81.

46. Ibid., 79.

47. In lyrics, birdspeak functions as "aural imagery," which indicates "literary representations of sound—dialogue, music, screams, cries, laughter, and extraverbal sounds, as well as a full range of ambient sounds—that activate a reader's 'inner hearing.' Aural imagery implies both the literary representation of sound and the transmission of it." Stoever, *Sonic Color Line*, 286.

48. "When one text Signifies on another text, by tropological revision or repetition and difference, the double-voiced utterance allows us to chart discrete formal relationships in Afro-American literary history. Signifyin(g), then, is a metaphor for textual revision." Gates, *Signifying Monkey*, 96.

49. Ibid., 57–59.

50. Ibid., 58.

51. "The Signifying Monkey is the figure of a black rhetoric in the Afro-American speech community. He exists to embody the figures of speech characteristic to the black vernacular. He is the principle of self-consciousness in the black vernacular, the meta-figure itself." Ibid., 59.

52. Ibid., 56.

53. Ibid. This is not unlike the canonical literature Harold Bloom cites to theorize "the anxiety of influence," which is itself one of Gates's acknowledged precursors for his own remix of a theory. Ibid., 57.

54. Ibid.

55. Moore, "Donald Glover Calls Migos."

56. This is consistent with the "fluid" nature of the Flying Africans trope, "a recurrent pattern of imagery that is more vast and less knowable in oral genres, such as narratives, songs, and jokes." Smith Storey, "Flying."

57. Revision speaks to something larger: "Zora Neale Hurston has argued that the Afro-American is an 'appropriative' creature,

that 'while he lives and moves in the midst of a white civilization, everything he touches is re-interpreted for his own use.'" Quoted in Awkward, "Appropriative Gestures," 336. For more on Black artists' interpretations of white artists' songs, see Kun, who builds on Baker to theorize a "de-minstrilizing mask" that "is not meant to obscure, but to advertise: 'It distinguishes rather than conceals.'" Kun, *Audiotopia*, 142.

58. See discussion of sound and echo in Weheliye, *Phonographies*, 103.

59. Commander offers "Afro-Atlantic" "to account for the flows of a diversity of African-descended peoples" in a flight-focused study oriented toward "Black American cultural productions and migrations." Commander, *Afro-Atlantic Flight*, 5.

60. Gilroy, *Black Atlantic*, 15.

61. About "Black music's obstinate and consistent commitment to the idea of a better future," Gilroy says, "The power of music in developing black struggles by communicating information, organising consciousness, and testing out or deploying the forms of subjectivity, which are required by political agency, whether individual or collective, defensive or transformational, demands attention to both the formal attributes of this expressive culture and its distinctive moral basis. . . . This musical culture supplies a great deal of courage required to go on living in the present." Ibid., 36. Weheliye also argues, "Sound occupies a privileged place [in Black cultural production] precisely because it manages to augment an inferior black subjectivity—a subjectivity created by racist ideologies and practices in the field of vision—establishing venues for the constitution of new modes of existence." Weheliye, *Phonographies*, 50.

62. Gilroy, *Black Atlantic*, 19.

63. Wynter, *Critical Race Theory*, 62.

64. Sharpe quoted in ibid.

65. Ibid., 62.

66. Wynter, *Critical Race Theory*, 63–62.

67. Ibid., 64–65.

68. Ibid., 62–64.

69. Commander, *Afro-Atlantic*, 5.

70. See Shilliam, *Black Pacific*.

71. Palmer, *Deep Blues*, 41.

72. Gates finds these rhetorical features in his discussion of "sampling," which he argues has "less to do with signifying upon chart toppers than recovering signal formal elements in both well-known, canonical R&B or soul songs and in forgotten singles, often (but not always) the songs that nobody quite remembers or even heard the first time around." Gates, *Signifying Monkey*, xxxii.

73. Recall, for example, Sam Cooke and the Soul Stirrers' "Nearer to Thee." Gates also calls attention to the association between story and song in the subtitle of his 2021 study *The Black Church: This Is Our Story, This Is Our Song.*

74. Walter Everett and Katie Kapurch touch on Sheila E's 2017 version of "Blackbird" in their analysis of her take on "Come Together," a remix on which Ringo Starr collaborated. Everett and Kapurch, "Come Together." Other notable recent covers of "Blackbird" include Emma Stevens's 2019 performance, in which she sang the song in Mi'kmaq; the video, which enjoyed viral fame, raised awareness for challenges facing her Indigenous culture.

75. Everett includes numerous examples of the Beatles' indebtedness to specific Black musicians in his song-by-song, two-volume study, *The Beatles as Musicians*. For analyses specific to the Beatles mid-1960s dialogue with Motown and other Black labels, see Everett, "Detroit and Memphis"; and Hamilton, *Just Around Midnight*. See also multiple references to the Beatles' appeal among members of the Black Rock Coalition in Mahon, *Right to Rock*.

For a discussion of McCartney's solo collaborations with Stevie Wonder and Michael Jackson, see Kapurch and Smith, "Blackbird Singing." We argue these evidence post-racial romanticism in the 1980s. A solo McCartney also took conscious inspiration from Nigerian artist Fela Kuti, New Orleans musician Professor Longhair, as well as Jamaican musicians during his family's sojourns to the country in the 1970s, inspiration-taking that warrants more study.

To date, most analyses that explore Black musicians' responses to the Beatles focus on Danger Mouse's *Grey Album*. See Gunderson, "Danger," for a reading of this record, which mashes up songs from the Beatles' *White Album* and Jay-Z's *Black Album*. Ironically, "Blackbird" is not one of the *White Album* songs treated on the *Grey Album*.

CHAPTER I

1. Quoted in Murrow and Friendly, *Satchmo*.

2. "'Flee as a Bird' achieved the widest acceptance, undoubtedly due to the beautiful 'Spanish melody' to which the text was set. As Judith Tick describes it, the tune 'had enough integral shape to withstand its adoption in a variety of styles, running the gamut from keyboard variation to gospel hymn.' . . . Although often played as a dirge (it still is a jazz funeral standard of New Orleans brass bands), it also belonged to the repertoire of the Fisk Jubilee Singers and the Whitman Sisters. It has been recorded by both Winton Marsalis and Louis Armstrong." Woodard, "Flee as a Bird," 80–81.

3. Armstrong quoted in Murrow and Friendly, *Satchmo*.

4. See Brothers, *Louis Armstrong's New Orleans*.

5. Angela Davis locates the potency of double-voicedness in musical speech and speechified music in "a cultural tradition rooted in West African histories in which the communicative power of music is grounded in and enhanced by its 'musical' structure, and in which the communicative power of music is grounded in and enhanced by its relation to speech. It is within such a context that different meanings are not necessarily mutually exclusive, that 'sad' lyrics become 'happy,' depending on their musical context." Davis, *Blues Legacies*, 174. We can see this legacy in the Beatles song "Help!," in which the desperation in Lennon's lyrics is transformed in the upbeat musical setting.

6. Gates and Tatar, *Annotated African American Folktales*, 70.

7. Defining features include "strained vocal production indicat[ing] heightened emotions, precise synchrony between body and music, bending pitch, blue notes, hard initial attack, and the fixed and variable format for organizing rhythm." Brothers, *Help!*, xii.

8. Ibid., xii–xiii.

9. Ibid., xii–xiii.

10. Quoted in ibid., 233.

11. Brothers, *Help!*, 209.

12. See Lewisohn, *Tune In* (unless otherwise specified, this and all subsequent citations refer to the 2013 Crown edition).

13. Wenner, *Lennon*, 20.

14. Qtd in ibid.

15. Ibid.

16. Ibid.

17. Brothers, *Help!*, xiii.

18. Dargan, *Lining Out the Word*, 160.

19. Ibid.

20. Mundy, *Animal Musicalities*, 19.

21. Ibid., 22.

22. Hamilton, *People Could Fly*, 2.

23. Smith Storey, "Flying Words."

24. See Thompson, *Flash of the Spirit*, 44–47.

25. Smith Storey, "Flying Words."

26. "The primacy of nonmaterial transactions in the African's initial negotiations of slavery and the slave trade led to a privileging of the roles and figures of medicine men, griots, conjurers, priests, and priestesses. The emphasis on spiritual leadership (and leadings of the spirit) was embodied in at least one form as the founding institution of African American group life—the church." Baker, "Theoretical Returns," 421.

27. Colbert, *Black Movements*, 23.

28. The "three primordial freedoms, those which for most of human history were simply assumed," are "the freedom to move, the freedom to disobey and the freedom to create or transform social relationships. . . . Unlike free people, slaves cannot have friends

because they cannot make commitments or promises. The freedom to make promises is about the most basic and minimal of element of our third freedom, much as physically running away from a difficult situation is the most basic element of the first." Graeber and Wengrow, *Dawn of Everything*, 426.

29. The correlation between a voice, the mind, and bird imagery has sacred provenance in rituals associated with the Yoruba healing deity Osanyin: "Certain groups in Nigerian Yorubaland allege that the sound of Osanyin's voice relates 'to a little bird that represents him.' According to this tradition, this bird not only speaks when the deity is consulted, but also lives in the sacred calabash of Osanyin kept on his alter. Voice-throwing and bird imagery are integral to the cult of Osanyin. . . . The association of a bird with the head or mind of a person is revealed during the initiation of a person into the service of Yoruba gods in Cuba and Cuban-influenced portions of Miami and New York City. The full ceremony includes one of the most impressive reinstatements of the literature of Osanyin on New World soil." Thompson, *Flash of the Spirit*, 44–47.

30. Colbert, *Black Movements*, 23.

31. "The metaphorical and symbolic understandings of flying Africans rely on a cultural way of knowing—a worldview—that is specific to enslaved Africans and their progeny throughout the Americas." Young, "All God's Children," 55.

32. For more on Raven as trickster and shapeshifter, especially in Indigenous myths from the Pacific Northwest, see Radin, *Trickster*; and Swanton, *Tlingit Myths*, the latter of which is an anthropological study conducted in the beginning of the twentieth century.

33. Mynott, *Birds in the Ancient World*, 5–6.

34. Birds are symbols of hope, strength, and protection in Abrahamic religious traditions, but winged deliverance is not limited to Judaism, Christianity, and Islam. From the Greek Hermes to the Hindu Garuda to the Egyptian Thoth to the Chinese Fenghuang to the Native American Raven to the Aztecs'

eagle, winged deities and other avian figures mediate between worlds and other gods, serve as harbingers of news, facilitate rescue, and protect against death. See ibid., 330–31.

35. Gates and Tatar, *Annotated African American Folktales*, 67; see also Smith Storey, "Flying Words," for the significance of the buzzard and language in the trope of Flying Africans.

36. Gates and Tatar, *Annotated African American Folktales*, 71.

37. Ibid.

38. Ibid., 68.

39. Colbert, *Black Movements*, 23.

40. Ibid., 26.

41. Smith Storey, "Flying Words."

42. Commander, *Afro-Atlantic Flight*, 4–5.

43. Ibid.

44. Smith Storey, "Flying Words."

45. Gates and Tatar, *Annotated African American Folktales*, 65.

46. Ibid.

47. Ibid., 73, 75, 67.

48. Ibid., 67.

49. Smith Storey, "Flying Words," as summarized by Gates and Tatar, *Annotated African American Folktales*, 69 (emphasis ours).

50. Gates and Tatar, *Annotated African American Folktales*, 68.

51. Ibid., 67; Smith Storey, "Flying Words." For more on the documentation of Flying Africans tales and other folkloric accounts, see Young, "All God's Children Had Wings."

52. McDaniel, "Flying Africans," 28–30.

53. "Returns to the imagined beginning are radical in their rejection of the reality that has been constructed for Afro-Atlantic peoples, as 'there is no future in the New World . . . death is the only future.' Death in this sense denotes the condition of literal lifelessness, social exclusion, constant fear of violence, and unwarranted retributions for simply being Black that render the possibility of social life nearly unfeasible." Commander, *Afro-Atlantic Flight*, 53. On the subject of

Black death, see also Wilderson, *Afropessimism*, 224–25.

54. Gates and Tatar, *Annotated African American Folktales*, 68.

55. Vega-González, "Broken Wings," 76–77.

56. Morrison, *Song of Solomon*, 323; quoted in Gates and Tatar, *Annotated African American Folktales*, 72. For an analysis of Morrison's novel in relation to Icarus, see also Young, "All God's Children Had Wings," 62–64; and Colbert, *Black Movements*, 41–47.

57. Quoted in Gates and Tatar, *Annotated African American Folktales*, 68, 72.

58. Ibid., 68.

59. Gates and Tatar, *Annotated African American Folktales*, 67.

60. Dargan, *Lining Out the Word*, 153.

61. "The eschatological aspect of freedom in black Christianity is the most difficult to grasp. . . . It is a hope-laden articulation of the tragic quality of everyday life of a culturally degraded, politically oppressed and racially coerced labor force. Black Christian eschatology is anchored in the tragic realism of the Old Testament wisdom literature and the proclamation of a coming kingdom by Jesus Christ. Anthropologists have observed that there is a relative absence of tragic themes in the ancient oral narratives of West Africa. Is it no accident that the black understanding of the gospel stresses this novel motif, the utterly tragic character of life and history?" West, *Cornel West Reader*, 437.

62. Gates and Tatar, *Annotated African American Folktales*, 79.

63. Heilbut, *Gospel Sound*, xx. Theorizing Flying Africans, Jason R. Young explains the comingling of African culture and Christian belief: "Enslaved men and women maintained aspects of African ritual practice that continue to give meaning to their lives, while adopting religious practices that carried the mark of their new lives in the Americas. The result was a worldview densely populated with people and spirits who played persistent, active roles in the lives of enslaved men and women." Young, "All God's Children Had Wings," 61.

64. Heilbut, *Gospel Sound*, xx–xxi.

65. Dargan, *Lining Out the Word*, 1–2, 7–8.

66. Ibid., 1.

67. Ibid., 96.

68. Ibid., 102.

69. "The vocal techniques concentrated in Dr. Watts hymn singing have been replicated in every major genre of black music produced from 1800 to 1970." Ibid., 9.

70. Quoted in Work, *American Negro Songs*, 129.

71. Smith Storey, "Flying Words."

72. Work, *American Negro Songs*, 129.

73. For an introduction to Dekker, see Alleyne, *Encyclopedia of Reggae*, 64–65.

74. Quoted in CD liner notes to Swan Silvertones, *Amen, Amen, Amen*.

75. Quoted in Pareles, "Swans' Gospel Messages."

76. Ibid.

77. Roud Folk Song Index are provided throughout this book whenever a folk song with that designation is introduced. The database can be consulted online at https://www.vwml.org/component/content/article/20-vwml-site/vwml-help-pages/256-roud-index-guide.

78. Zolten, "Oh Mary Don't You Weep."

79. Gates and Tatar, *Annotated African American Folktales*, 78.

80. McDaniel, "Flying," 34.

81. Ibid., 35.

82. Quoted in Gates and Tatar, *Annotated African American Folktales*, 78.

83. Work, *American Negro Songs*, 180.

84. Solomon and Solomon, *Honey*, 69.

85. Death's summoning line is the title of the Del Vikings' "Come and Go with Me," the song Lennon was singing (and improvising) when McCartney first saw him performing with the Quarry Men at the Woolton village fete in 1957.

86. Solomon and Solomon, *Honey*, 69.

87. Heilbut, *Fan Who Knew Too Much*, 70.

88. Solomon and Solomon, *Honey*, 69.

89. Ibid. See also the discussion of shoes as a symbol of freedom among enslaved people in Dargan, *Lining Out the Word*, 178–79.

90. Salvatore, "'Eagle Stirrith Her Nest.'"

91. Franklin, "Eagle Stirreth Her Nest."

92. Quoted in Werner, *Higher Ground*, 27.

93. Franklin, "Eagle Stirreth Her Nest."

94. Ibid.

95. "The sermon climaxes in a frenzy of moans wrapped around the most basic promise of the gospel vision: 'One of these days, my soul will take wings. . . . A few more days. O Lord.'" Werner, *Higher Ground*, 26.

96. The Black Church "is the major institution created, sustained, and controlled by black people themselves. . . . The profound insights *and* petty blindnesses, immeasurable depths *and* immobilizing faults, incalculable richness *and* parochial impoverishment of that complex hybrid people called Afro-Americans surface most clearly in the black church." West, *Cornel West Reader*, 426.

97. Gates, *Black Church*, 2.

98. Colbert, *Black Movements*, 52.

99. Ibid., 140.

100. Youngquist, *Pure Solar World*, 196. The opening of *Mothership Connection* pays "homage to Sun Ra, togged in fur cape and platform shoes," and Sun Ra later paid tribute to Clinton on his 1979 LP *On Jupiter*: "Clinton may take Sun Ra's music places it doesn't usually go, but Sun Ra takes it back and launches funk into outerspace." Ibid., 247–48.

101. Clinton, *Brothas*, 140.

102. Ken McLeod quoted in Colbert, *Black Movements*, 51.

103. Colbert, *Black Movements*, 53–54.

104. See Work, *American Negro Songs*, 148.

105. Vincent, *Funk*, 254.

106. Clinton, *Brothas*, 81, 47, 79.

107. Ibid., 81.

108. Ibid.

109. Ibid.

110. The authors are grateful to Tim Kinley, P-Funk archivist and historian, for assistance with details related to the timing of this tour and Clinton's recollections.

CHAPTER 2

1. Jackson, *Beatles*; for McCartney's solo bird branding, see Kapurch, *Disney*.

2. We use the term "British" here and elsewhere to characterize folk arts—especially those featuring birds—that circulate in and between England, Ireland, Scotland, and Wales.

3. Brown, "Negro Folk Expression," 53.

4. Robbins, *Secular Lyrics*, 43–45; Perkins, "Medieval Carol Survival," 235.

5. Perkins, "Medieval Carol Survival," 237, 240.

6. Robbins, *Secular Lyrics*, 45.

7. Coletta, *Biosemiotic Literary Criticism*, 244.

8. *OED Online*, s.v. "bird, n.," accessed January 16, 2023, https://www-oed-com .ezproxy.spl.org/view/Entry/19327?.

9. See chapter 10, below.

10. Roberts, *Heavy Words*, 23–26.

11. See Opie and Opie, *Oxford Dictionary of Nursery Rhymes*.

12. Bryan, *History of English Balladry*, 125.

13. Perkins, "Medieval Carol Survival," 235–36.

14. The song "evolved in two separate directions . . . developing two distinct sets of regional characteristics" according to "the lines of westward migration: in the North from New England to Iowa and in the South from North Carolina to Missouri." Ibid., 239.

15. Ibid., 239–40.

16. See chapter 4, below.

17. "In the Fifties, a version of the song called 'As I Roved Out' provided the title for the first folk music series on the BBC. Paul McCartney heard it being such in Liverpool in 1960, which inspired him to rewrite it in a modern context as 'I Saw Her Standing There.'" Schofield, *Fairport by Fairport*, 395.

18. Quoted in ibid.

19. Palmer, *Deep Blues*, 41.

20. Quoted in Wenner, *Lennon*, 140.

21. See both of Everett's *Beatles as Musicians* volumes.

22. Alleyne, Everett, and Kapurch, "Billy Preston."

23. Ibid.

24. NPR Music, "Rhiannon Giddens: Tiny Desk (Home) Concert," May 28, 2020, YouTube video, 00:20:15, https://youtu.be /h4lul94cSi8.

25. The wings of the title character of Giddens's "Black as Crow" appear on the album's cover. When Giddens previewed an earlier illustrated version of the record's cover, she explained bird imagery in relation to the album's concept: "When we considered the artwork around our album, we thought of birds migrating and yet always returning home. We thought of flying to be reunited with those loved and lost. And we thought of the transformation and change we have seen in the last year." Rhiannon Giddens. Facebook post. *Facebook*. April 2, 2021.

26. NPR Music, "Rhiannon Giddens."

27. "In the Dogon, Yoruba, and other West African cultural traditions, the process of nommo—naming things, forces, and modes—is a means of establishing magical (or, in the case of the blues, aesthetic) control over the object of the naming process. Through the blues, menacing problems are ferreted out from the isolated individual experiences and restructured as problems shared by the community. As shared problems, threats can be met and addressed within a public and collective context." Davis, *Blues Legacies*, 33.

28. Mahar, *Behind the Burnt Cork Mask*, 233.

29. This legacy is further complicated by the performance of blackface by Black performers, but we can readily see the racist implications of certain performances by white men. See also Lott, *Love and Theft*; Taylor and Austen, *Darkest America*.

30. Mahar, *Behind the Burnt Cork Mask*, 21.

31. The page also claims that Emmett performed the song (whose title phrase only "appears in the first verse") with "'unprecedented success . . . both in Europe and America.'" Ibid., 373.

32. Quoted in Als, "Toni Morrison's Profound and Unrelenting Vision."

33. See chapter 3, below.

34. Gates, *Signifying Monkey*, 57; see overview in our introduction, above.

35. See Mynott, *Birds in the Ancient World*.

36. Robbins, *Secular Lyrics*, 41–42.

37. For the Beatles' indebtedness to the British Romantic literary imagination, see Schneider, *Long and Winding Road*.

38. Line 43 in Coleridge's "The Nightingale, a Conversational Poem," in Wordsworth and Coleridge, *Lyrical Ballads*.

39. Goldblatt, *Mad Day Out*.

40. Referencing *Prometheus Unbound* and another bird poem, "To a Skylark," Paul Youngquist posits Percy Shelley as "a revealing precursor to Sun Ra at the level of poetic language." Youngquist, *Pure Solar World*, 77–78.

41. See table in Alleyne, Everett, and Kapurch, "Billy Preston."

42. Beatles, *Beatles Anthology*, 136.

43. In addition to "Lady Madonna," Fats Domino included another Lennon-McCartney tune centered on a woman, "Lovely Rita," on the 1968 record *Fats Is Back*.

44. Quoted in Womack, *Beatles Encyclopedia*, 271.

45. Opie and Opie, *Oxford Dictionary of Nursery Rhymes*, 365.

46. Ibid., 122–24.

47. Beatles, *Beatles Anthology*, 27.

48. McCartney released his take on "I'm in Love Again" in 1991.

49. Opie and Opie, *Oxford Dictionary of Nursery Rhymes*, 185.

50. Ibid.

51. See chapter 5, below.

52. Opie and Opie, *Oxford Dictionary of Nursery Rhymes*, 471–72; Roberts, *Heavy Words*, 30–32.

53. More support for this reading is found in the colloquial use of "blackbirds" for black-wearing monks—who were affected when Henry VIII closed the monasteries and persecuted Catholics. Ibid.

54. Roberts, *Heavy Words*, 31.

55. Opie and Opie, *Oxford Dictionary of Nursery Rhymes*, 471; Roberts, *Heavy Words*, 32.

56. Quoted in Lewisohn, *Tune In*, 423.

57. MacDonald, *Revolution*, loc. 5506.

58. Opie and Opie, *Oxford Dictionary of Nursery Rhymes*, 173.

59. McCartney, *Lyrics*, 371.

60. Ibid.

61. Ibid., 47.

62. Rice, *Captain Sir Richard Francis Burton*, 460.

63. Jeff Place, CD liner notes to Lead Belly, *Smithsonian Folkways Collection*, 59; see also 42.

64. Christian, "African-Centered Approach," 292–95. See also Tibbles, *Liverpool*; Richardson, Schwarz, and Tibbles, *Liverpool*.

65. See Lewisohn's *Tune In* for detailed genealogies for the individual Beatles, whose largely Anglo-Irish and working-class roots shaped their ethnic identities.

66. Quoted in Wenner, *Lennon*, 146.

67. Christian, "African-Centered Approach," 293. "Black folk from the 18th Century landed at British ports, such as London, Bristol, and Liverpool, as enslaved property to be bought and sold in British slave auctions. . . . They also arrived in Britain to become domestic servants to sea captains, wealthy merchants, and members of the British aristocracy. . . . Other Black settlers, such as sons of African dignitaries or the offspring of White masters from Caribbean plantations, came to be educated. Some of these forced settlers were to become major players in the fight for abolition." Ibid., 292–93.

68. "The 20th Century has witnessed a catalog of horrific racism that has beset the Black community in Liverpool." Ibid., 294–95.

69. "The term was associated in particular with the sugar cane industry. It originated in Australia, where *blackbird* is a slang term for indigenous peoples." Gates and Tatar, *Annotated African American Folktales*, 81.

70. When theorizing the Flying Africans trope, Smith Storey also mentions a slave ship, the *Young Hero*, originating in Liverpool; records from the ship's doctor document the horrific events, specifically "the captain's decision to decapitate a corpse to prevent slaves from committing suicide." As Smith Storey explains, "Other eighteenth-century pamphlets suggest dismemberment as a solution for repeated slave suicides, as several writers reported that Africans would not kill themselves if they thought they would return to Africa with a maimed body. Around this issue anyway, the Overseer figures demonstrate some understanding of the African's concept of death." Smith Storey, "Flying Words."

71. Sherwood, "Perfidious Albion," 175–76.

72. In 1860, the USS *Saratoga* surveilled and intercepted the *Nightingale*, catching the crew in the act of boarding victims in Angola. The *Nightingale*'s Captain Bowen ("Prince of Slavers") escaped, and the ship was then forced to return survivors to Monrovia before returning to New York, whose court barely punished the crew's remaining leaders. Ibid., 175–76.

73. Ibid., 176.

74. In Ovid's *Metamorphoses*, the gods turn Philomela and her sister Procne into a nightingale and a sparrow, respectively, while they run away from Procne's husband, Tereus, who is turned into a hoopoe. Tereus had earlier raped Philomela and cut out her tongue to silence her. To expose his cruelty, Philomela then wove the assault into a tapestry, whose revelation motivated Procne to punish Tereus by feeding his own son to him; hence the chase that turned all three into birds.

75. Stoever, *Sonic Color Line*, 121.

76. Ibid., 118.

77. Chybowski, "Becoming the 'Black Swan,'" 125.

78. Ibid., 125–26.

79. Ibid., 135.

80. Stoever, *Sonic Color Line*, 112.

81. Ibid.

82. Quoted in ibid., 127.

83. Ibid., 127.

84. Quoted in ibid.

85. Lott, *Love and Theft*, 243–44.

86. Quoted in Blight, *Frederick Douglass*, 317.

87. See Simpson, "Blackface Othellos."

88. Morrison, "Race," 795.

89. Ibid., 800–801.

90. Ibid., 783–84.

CHAPTER 3

1. Quoted in Egan, *Florence Mills*, 3.

2. Doktor, "Finding Florence Mills," 453.

3. Egan, *Florence Mills*, 2.

4. On the subject of Black uplift, Adair notes Mills's frequent references to racism in interviews, as well as her monetary donations and volunteer work that benefited Harlem-based charities, including "the Speedwell Society for abandoned and convalescent children, the women's auxiliary of the Urban League, and the YWCA." Adair makes an important distinction relevant to the subject of Black uplift as it was defined at the beginning of the twentieth century: "Mills did not conform to the pressure to perform in mediums deemed dignified by the black elite, such as dramatic theater or literature. It is important to stress, that by not conforming to African American bourgeois ideas of advantageous black creative production, Mills challenged the notion that racial uplift could only be attained through forms of cultural performance determined legitimate by the black political elite" ("Respectable Vamp," 10).

5. "One ever feels his two-ness,—an American, a Negro; two souls, two thoughts, two unreconciled strivings; two warring ideals in one dark body, whose dogged strength alone keeps it from being torn asunder." Du Bois, *Souls of Black Folk*, 2.

6. "She could be whimsical, she could be almost grotesque; but she had the good taste that never allowed her to be coarse. She could be *risqué*, she could be seductive; but it was impossible for her to be vulgar, for she possessed a naiveté that was alchemic." James Weldon Johnson quoted in Doktor, "Finding Florence Mills," 462.

7. Ibid., 457.

8. Adair, "Respectable Vamp," 15–16: *Shuffle Along* was progressive in content and form; however, the show also contained many sexist racial politics prevalent in the African American theater during the early twentieth century. The producers of the show were notorious for only casting lighter-skinned, slim African American women and there were references in the show that asserted that lighter-skinned African American women were more desirable than darker-skinned African American women. Additionally, production photographs and sheet music cover art featured only light-skinned African American women. Florence Mills was considered a talented performer, but she was not the producers' first choice to play Ruth Little. Mills had a darker skin complexion than the producers' first choice, Gertrude Sanders. One of the shows' songs, "If You Haven't Been Vamped by a Brown Skin, You Haven't Been Vamped at All," alludes to the perceived sexual skill of darker-skinned African American women.

9. Egan, *Florence Mills*, 70.

10. Ibid.; see also 107–8.

11. Ibid., 1.

12. Adair, "Respectable Vamp," 14. Adair situates Mills's Broadway performances in vaudeville, "reveal[ing] the ways she made use of the cultural economies of vaudeville to resist dominant constructions of race and gender" and showing how "Florence Mills manipulated white American and

European desires to consume slave culture and expanded economic and cultural possibilities for African American women entertainers" (8).

13. Egan, *Florence Mills*, 119.

14. Ibid., 111–12.

15. Ibid., 107.

16. Ibid., 113.

17. Doktor, "Finding Florence Mills," 453.

18. Quoted in Adair, "Respectable Vamp," 18.

19. Quoted in Doktor, "Finding Florence Mills," 453.

20. Ibid.

21. Doktor, "Finding Florence Mills," 453.

22. Maeterlinck, *Blue Bird*.

23. Quoted in Egan, *Florence Mills*, 271.

24. Ibid., 235.

25. Mills, "Dramatis Personae."

26. Adair, "Respectable Vamp," 18.

27. Doktor, "Finding Florence Mills," 457.

28. Ibid., 451. Doktor's analysis of *Levee Land* is instructive and relevant: "In [the] final section, what sometimes sounds like a chamber ensemble in *Levee Land* becomes an all-out jazz band, and Mills sings a repeated strain, mimicking caricatures of each instrument in the band—her voice personifying the very sounds that caused her [character] to stray from her god. She sings about the 'sob and cry' of the fiddles, the 'plunk plunk and brunk' of the banjo, and the 'sob and moan' of the trombone as the instruments solo. Given what critics say about her uncanny ability to entertain, it is likely she played this instrument imitation to the hilt, manipulating her timbre in divergent ways to sound like a saxophone or banjo or male preacher. By the third repetition of the stanza, Mills sings forte over the full ensemble and the rhythm section's dense texture" (465). The modernist jazz aesthetic, required by the composition and actualized by Mills, anticipates the vocal arrangement Bobby McFerrin brought to the Beatles' "Blackbird" in the 1980s.

29. In one review, "Mills was described as 'a fascinating creature to look at with the skinny legs and body of some athletic boys thirteen or fourteen, black smoothed bobbed hair and a large, very large Negro mouth.' The commentator's use of the word 'creature' in reference to Mills exemplifies twentieth century constructions of African Americans as animalistic. The comparison of Mills to adolescent boys illuminates the hyper-sexual focus on Mills' body. The comments are not surprising given the context of early twentieth century primitivism but they highlight some of the obstacles Mills had to negotiate." Adair, "Respectable Vamp," 11.

30. Egan, *Florence Mills*, 168.

31. Quoted in Egan, *Florence Mills*, 190.

32. Adair, "Respectable Vamp," 11.

33. Quoted in Egan, *Florence Mills*, 190.

34. See Dirix, "Birds of Paradise."

35. W. E. B. Du Bois, letter to Florence Mills, May 10, 1925. I am grateful to public historian Erica Buddington, who circulated this letter through her Twitter account (@ericabuddington) on June 11, 2021.

36. A recent online discussion responding to Buddington's Twitter post (see above) critiqued Du Bois's gesture as objectifying and manipulative. The debate raises a broader subject concerning Mills's interaction with Black intellectuals and other elites of her time. Both Du Bois and his contemporary Alain Locke defined Black uplift through a politics of respectability, encouraging Black participation in drama and literature, that is, serious art forms. Even though they were critical of other Black artists who performed comedy and "lesser" art forms, both Du Bois and Locke approved of and supported Mills. So, Mills was navigating their aesthetic judgement, no doubt inflected with gendered and sexual objectification, but their support also testifies to her musical skill and complex performances; her very public commitments to Black community organizations and vocal criticism of racism in the United States also ingratiated her to them. See Doktor, "Finding Florence Mills"; Adair, "Respectable Vamp."

37. Doktor, "Finding Florence Mills," 452–53.

38. See the subtitle of Egan's biography, *Harlem Jazz Queen*, which argues for an appreciation of Mills as a jazz singer "based on her nonverbal, instrumental singing." Egan, *Florence Mills*, 267.

39. Ibid., 270.

40. Mills, "Dramatis Personae."

41. Doktor, "Finding Florence Mills," 452.

42. Mills's expressed comfort with the British public speaks to Cornel West's analysis of double consciousness in Du Bois's *The Souls of Black Folk*: "For Du Bois, the dialectic of black self-recognition oscillated between being *in* America but not *of* it, from being black natives to black aliens. Yet Du Bois overlooked the broader dialectic of being American yet feeling European, of being provincial but yearning for British cosmopolitanism." West, *Cornel West Reader*, 58.

43. Ward, "Music," 61.

44. Taylor and Austen, *Darkest America*, 43.

45. Lewisohn, *Tune In*, 25, 46–47, 290.

46. Mills, "Dramatis Personae."

47. Egan, *Florence Mills*, 175.

48. Ibid., 206–7.

49. Ibid., 267, 206.

50. Quoted in ibid., 235.

51. Egan, *Florence Mills*, 285.

52. Giddens, *Visions of Jazz*, 110.

53. Egan, *Florence Mills*, xvii–xviii.

54. See "Florence Mills," July 29, 2014, YouTube video, 00:02:10, https://youtu.be/PcjpX8yynJw; see also BWW Desk, "Tony Nominee."

55. Egan, *Florence Mills*, 113.

56. Ibid., 126–27.

57. See Brothers, *Louis Armstrong's New Orleans*.

58. Mack, *Pie, Pie Blackbird*.

59. See chapter 2, above, for this nursery rhyme in relation to the Beatles.

60. Egan, *Florence Mills*, 55, 72, 90.

61. Mills's performance of the song was significant because it marked "the first time a song declaring romantic love between an African American man and woman was performed on stage for an interracial audience." Adair, "Respectable Vamp," 15.

62. Norman, *Shout!*, 86.

63. Jasen, *Century of American Popular Music*, 30.

64. McCartney, CD liner notes to *Kisses on the Bottom*.

65. Ibid.

66. The Beatles did not have much to do with the film's production, but an allusion to "Bye Bye Blackbird" appears in *Yellow Submarine* when the Chief Blue Meanie admits that his "cousin is the bluebird of happiness." Dunning, *Yellow*.

67. Everett, *Beatles as Musicians: Revolver*, 112–13, 189–90.

68. McCartney, CD liner notes to *Kisses on the Bottom*.

69. *James Paul McCartney TV Special* (1973) included in McCartney and Wings, *Red Rose Speedway*.

70. *Paul McCartney and Wings Fly South*; *Paul McCartney and Wings: Rockshow*.

71. Quoted in Laurent, *King*, 36.

72. See Davis, *Blues Legacies*, 83–84.

73. Wolfe and Lornell, *Life*, 244.

74. Lead Belly, *Smithsonian Folkways Collection*.

75. This song is credited to Simone along with Jackie Alper and Ron Vander Groef.

76. Simone, *Nina Simone in Concert*.

77. Adler, "Letter from Selma."

78. Quoted in Zolten, *Great God A'mighty*, 20.

79. Ibid., 20–21.

80. Ibid., 21.

81. See also discussion of Black Swan Records in Davis, *Blues Legacies*, 152.

CHAPTER 4

1. John Reynolds quotes Harrison in the 2015 Smithsonian tribute film *Legend of Lead Belly* directed by Alan Ravenscroft.

2. Lead Belly preferred the two-name spelling, although he was commonly known by "Leadbelly" in the twentieth century. For more on Lead Belly's name, see Robert

Santelli, CD liner notes to Lead Belly, *Smith-sonian Folkways Collection*.

3. Wolfe and Lornell, *Life*, 7.

4. Ibid., 262–63.

5. Lomax, "15A."

6. The song opens, "Twas on one Sunday morning," which is reflected in "Grey Goose," whose first line always references the morning of Sunday or Monday. The first verse tells of an angel descending from heaven (winged flight) to remove the stone in front of Jesus's tomb. The subsequent verses recount the actions of pairs who bear witness to the "empty tomb": John and Peter, who "came a-running," and Mary and Martha, "who came a-weeping." The last line of the song ends abruptly, "And lo! their Lord had gone," an awestruck revelation at Jesus's departure, quite similar to beholding the unbreakable grey goose's flight. Quoted in Work, *American Negro Songs*, 101.

7. Werner, *Change Is Gonna Come*, 29.

8. Quoted in Lomax, "15A."

9. See chapter 1, above.

10. Gates and Tatar, *Annotated African American Folktales*, 73.

11. See Thorsteinson, "From Escape to Ascension."

12. Smith Storey, "Flying Words," as summarized by Gates and Tatar, *Annotated African American Folktales*, 69 (emphasis ours).

13. Smith Storey, "Flying Words."

14. Smith Storey, "Flying Words," as summarized by Gates and Tatar, *Annotated African American Folktales*, 69.

15. Ibid.

16. Ibid.

17. When they printed what they titled "De Grey Goose" in *American Ballads and Folk Songs* in 1934, the Lomaxes classified the song as a "reel," generally a dance song, but defined in that book with the racist subtitle "Songs 'ob de Wor'ly N––.'" Lomax and Lomax, *American Ballads*, 236.

18. Place, CD liner notes to Lead Belly, *Smithsonian Folkways Collection*, 51.

19. Szwed, *Man*, 41.

20. Lomax, "Negro Material."

21. Ibid. The top of the next page of Alan Lomax's manuscript reads, "This is the text of The Blue Goose," underneath which Lomax only provides an overview ("one couplet to every page of brilliant illustration") and an example of a lyric ("he was six weeks a falling"). Each word is on its own line and the vertical column reveals the formal structure throughout the song: for each of the goose's six-week actions, the respective line is six words. In addition to a doodle, Lomax also included the words of the response, "Lawd! Lawd! Lawd!" The next page is headed with "Ladies and gentleman," followed by a list of other songs that include "Little John Henry" and "Pick a Bale o' Cotton."

22. Lomax and Baker, "Grey Goose."

23. Lomax, "15A."

24. Lomax and Lomax, *American Ballads*, 252.

25. Lomax, "15A."

26. Lomax, "Sugarland, Texas."

27. Ibid.

28. See, for example, the cover art and sheet music for the 1844 "De Ole Grey Goose" in the Library of Congress holdings. Reps, *De Ole Grey Goose*.

29. Ibid.

30. Agnew, *Entertainment in the Old West*, 34.

31. See Szwed, *Man*.

32. Lomax, "15A."

33. Ibid.

34. Wolfe and Lornell, *Life*, 296.

35. Szwed, *Man*, 44.

36. Ibid., 44–45, 48; Wolfe and Lornell, *Life*, 100.

37. Szwed, *Man*, 45.

38. Wolfe and Lornell, *Life*, 265.

39. Place, CD liner notes to Lead Belly, *Smithsonian Folkways Collection*, 19; see also Wolfe and Lornell, *Life*.

40. Szwed, *Man*, 45.

41. Quoted in Santelli, CD liner notes to Lead Belly, *Smithsonian Folkways Collection*, 15.

42. Wolfe and Lornell, *Life*, 195.

43. Weheliye, *Phonographies*, 70. Mahon's insight into authenticity is also

relevant to presentism here: "Although concepts of black authenticity have changed over time, they are embedded in a vision of black identity as an essence, a static category that transcends time and space." Mahon, *Right to Rock*, 11.

44. Alan Lomax reflected, "Without the violent past, the white audience never would have noticed him." Quoted in Wolfe and Lornell, *Life*, 197.

45. Ravenscroft, *Legend of Lead Belly*. "The reverberations begin with [Richard] Wright's challenges to John Lomax's packaging of Lead Belly as a 'to-be lynched' body, a calculated visual stunt turning the sonic color line into a tripwire, with Lead Belly's voice signalling the robustness of the black masculine threat for the white Northern listening ear and viscerally conditioning how black male voices would be incorporated into the nation during the Great Depression's racial upheaval." Stoever, *Sonic Color Line*, 192; see also 193–206.

46. "Leadbelly," *March of Time*.

47. Wolfe and Lornell, *Life*, 166–67; see also Szwed, *Man*, 60.

48. Szwed, *Man*, 60.

49. Ibid., 59.

50. Szwed, *Alan Lomax*, 60.

51. Contemporary reviews "give a sexual charge to the notion of enchantment, simultaneously hypermasculinizing Lead Belly and feminizing him as a seductress." Stoever, *Sonic Color Line*, 203.

52. Wolfe and Lornell, *Life*, 197.

53. Place, CD liner notes to Lead Belly, *Smithsonian Folkways Collection*, 21.

54. Wolfe and Lornell, *Life*, 212.

55. Ibid., 221.

56. Place, CD liner notes to Lead Belly, *Smithsonian Folkways Collection*, 22.

57. Wolfe and Lornell, *Life*, 221.

58. Ibid., 222.

59. Lead Belly, *Shout On*.

60. Bragg, *Roots*, 15.

61. Lead Belly, *Where Did You Sleep Last Night*.

62. "Leadbelly," *March of Time*.

63. Wolfe and Lornell, *Life*, 256.

64. Lead Belly, *Sings for Children*.

65. For more on the history of the Soundie and the medium's representation of Black Americans, see Delson, *Soundies*.

66. Sloan and Chang, *Three Songs*.

67. Bing Crosby was rumored to play John Lomax. Wolfe and Lornell, *Life*, 234.

68. These materials "languished for nearly two decades" until Seeger acquired them. Ibid., 235.

69. To perform "Cotton," Lead Belly wore a straw hat and light-colored clothes; he was filmed outdoors against a blue sky evocative of an open field. For "Hammer," Lead Belly wore a denim work shirt and bandana around his neck—but red curtains of a playhouse or movie theater form the backdrop. These staged settings now read as metacommentary, calling attention to the performance itself. Seeger positioned "Grey Goose" in the middle of these two songs, presenting the "real" Lead Belly of the 1940s, when he was known to wear fashionable tailored suits accompanied by beautiful ties and handkerchiefs. See also Ravenscroft, *Legend of Lead Belly*; and Wolfe and Lornell, *Life*.

70. Quoted in Fitzpatrick, "Lead Belly."

71. Quoted in Santelli, CD liner notes to Lead Belly, *Smithsonian Folkways Collection*, 15.

72. Beatles, *Beatles Anthology*, 30.

73. Ibid., 28.

74. Ibid., 14.

75. "Ex-Beatle," 62.

76. "Musical cousins to the more literary 'beatniks,' 'traddies' tended to be openly intellectual, politically liberal, and musically snobbish. Trad as a form boasted a strangely nostalgic emphasis on what were considered to be the original, or traditional, roots of American jazz music, specifically the acoustic, duple-meter-driven New Orleans jazz combo." Hamilton, *Just Around Midnight*, 105.

77. "Authenticity is far from natural; instead, prevailing views of what is authentic become naturalized." Mahon, *Right to Rock*, 10.

78. "The teddy boys were . . . able to reconcile a worldview marked by ethnic nationalism, a desire to 'keep Britain white,' with an enthusiasm for a music that was neither white nor British. This move . . . positions the teddy boys as among the earliest in a long line of white rock and roll fans who have violently mined the music for racialized fantasies of hypermasculinity while strategically ignoring any real connection to black people." Hamilton, *Just Around Midnight*, 104.

79. Bragg, *Roots*, 153.

80. Ibid., 155.

81. Ibid., 17.

82. "Donegan delivered 'Rock Island Line' as a rollicking yarn ('Now this here's the story . . .'), relating the rolling tale of a train driver who fools a tollgate-keeper on the railroad running down into New Orleans. One hearing was enough to engross British teenagers—boys especially—and sales began to pick up speed the same way Donegan's voice gradually accelerated through the two-and-a-half-minute recording." Lewisohn, *Tune In*, 85–86.

83. Bragg, *Roots*, 155. Lewisohn also explains, "The timely coincidence that the word 'rock' was in its title was enough to open certain ears, but it was the acoustic guitar sound on 'Rock Island Line' that had the greatest impact. . . . 'Rock Island Line' made a particular splash in Liverpool, where it spent two weeks in the 'Top 3.'" Lewisohn, *Tune In*, 86.

84. "'Rock Island Line' was never a huge hit—it spent five weeks in the top ten and peaked at 9—but it hung around the chart for six months, during which time John Lennon, who never had much money, managed to buy or steal it. George Harrison also bought it—the first record he did get." Lewisohn, *Tune In*, 86.

85. Womack, *Beatles Encyclopedia*, 334.

86. "While Donegan would always be its revered figurehead, the number of participants would soon be counted in tens of thousands." Lewisohn, *Tune In*, 96.

87. Bragg, *Roots*, 288.

88. The railroad's logic has merged with (and diverged from) flight, expressed in fictional flying trains, some taking their inspiration from actual trains like the *Midnight Special*. Zabel, *(Underground) Railroad*, 37.

89. Beatles, *Beatles Anthology*, 20.

90. Bragg, *Roots*, 14.

91. See chapter 2, above.

92. Alleyne, Everett, and Kapurch, "Billy Preston."

93. Bragg, *Roots*, xiv.

94. Ibid.

95. John Bealle, CD liner notes to *Bullfrog Jumped*.

96. Ibid.

97. Lomax, Jackson, and Futch, "Go Tell Aunt Tabby."

98. In 1925, Dorothy Scarborough argued against what she (anachronistically) calls a "Yankee" origin of "Go Tell" and argued for an African American origin in the South, specifically Texas. She also highlighted the persistent features of "Go Tell": "The owner of the unfortunate goose appears diversely as Aunt Nancy, Aunt Abby, and so on, but the goose remains constant, always old and always grey, and its sad fate ever the same." Scarborough, *On the Trail*, 195.

99. Noticing the recurring "religious symbolism," the editors of *Folk Songs of the Catskills* point to the "Lookit over Yonder" and consider the transgression of the preacher, along with the "Lord, Lord, Lord" lament, as evidence for a connection between the "Go Tell" song cycle and the "Grey Goose" that Lead Belly recorded. Cazden, Haufrecht, and Studer, *Folk Songs*, 555.

100. Davies, *Beatles Lyrics*, 283.

101. Everett, *Beatles as Musicians: Revolver*, 46.

102. See chapter 2, above.

103. This has happened so many times over the course of McCartney's six-decades-plus career that cataloging it requires separate investigation. See Kapurch, *Disney Plus Beatles*.

104. Womack, "Paul McCartney's Spectacular Return."

105. Quoted in Marchese, "Paul McCartney."

106. "Lead Belly Book Inspired Keith Richards' 'Goodnight Irene' Cover," September 19, 2015, YouTube video, 00:02:39, https://youtu.be/6gVyjRiFFQg. Incidentally, Richards's *Crosseyed Heart* was produced with Steve Jordan, who also produced Bettye LaVette's *Blackbirds*; see chapter 10, below.

107. Quoted in Marchese, "Paul McCartney."

108. See also McCartney, *Lyrics*, 810–11.

109. Lead Belly, *Leadbelly*. "The blues never remain fixed on one perspective, but rather different songs—sometimes the same song—explore experiences from various vantage points. This feature of the blues, the aesthetic incorporation of several perspectives and dimensions, may be interpreted as reflective of West African philosophical outlooks and representational strategies." Davis, *Blues*, 49.

110. This is not to say that Lennon got this directly from Lead Belly; the 1949 recording wasn't circulated until 1973 when Playboy issued the record based on one audience member's magnetic wire recording. Place, CD liner notes to Lead Belly, *Smithsonian Folkways Collection*, 25.

111. McCartney, *Lyrics*, 811.

CHAPTER 5

1. Quoted in Lewisohn, *Tune In*, 90.

2. "Ex-Beatle," 61.

3. McCartney, *Lyrics*, 47.

4. For more on this reference, see chapter 7, below.

5. Le Gendre, *Don't Stop the Carnival*, 213.

6. Calypso was shaped and nourished by Carnival, the Mardi Gras celebration born out of Roman Catholic colonization. The genre's defining rhythms derive from the West African Kaiso and Canboulay music brought over by enslaved Africans forced to work on French sugar plantation owners in the seventeenth century. See Cowley, *Carnival*; Paquet, Saunders, and Stuempfle, *Music, Memory, Resistance*.

7. McCartney, foreword, xi.

8. Kilmister, *Lemmy*, 28.

9. See, for example, descriptions of the 1958 Notting Hill race riots in Hamilton, *Just Around Midnight*, 101–5.

10. See discussion of Trads and Teds in chapter 4, above.

11. Bedford, *Fab One Hundred and Four*, 28.

12. For more on Signifyin(g) in calypso as it relates to the Beatles, see Alleyne, Everett, and Kapurch, "Billy Preston."

13. For an introduction to the history of the Windrush generation, see Phillips and Phillips, *Windrush*.

14. McGrath, "Phillips."

15. Ibid.

16. Lewisohn, *Tune In*, 86.

17. McGrath, "Phillips." See also Le Gendre, *Don't Stop the Carnival*, 212–15.

18. Lewisohn, *Tune In*, 174.

19. Ibid., 175.

20. Bedford, *Fab One Hundred and Four*, 380. The Shades were backed by the Beatles a couple more times that year and signed with Beatles manager Brian Epstein. Ankrah's introduction to Lennon and McCartney happened backstage at a Little Richard concert at the Tower Ballroom in 1962 when the Beatles opened for their idol. Ibid., 379–80.

21. Brothers, *Help!*, 201.

22. McGrath, "Liverpool's Black Community."

23. McGrath, "Phillips" and "Where You Once Belonged," 16–17. Henry, in "The Man Who Put the Beat in the Beatles," groups Harrison into "Woodbine's Boys," but the nickname usually applies to Lennon and McCartney alone.

24. Quoted in ibid.

25. See Alibhai-Brown and McGrath, "Lord Woodbine"; and Rand, "Windrush."

26. McGrath, "Phillips."

27. Alibhai-Brown and McGrath, "Lord Woodbine."

28. Quoted in ibid.

29. Ibid.; for more firsthand accounts, see also Bedford, *Fab*.

30. Alibhai-Brown and McGrath, "Lord."

31. Quoted in Henry, "Man Who Put the Beat."

32. Ibid.

33. Alibhai-Brown and McGrath, "Lord Woodbine."

34. McGrath, "Liverpool's Black Community."

35. Lewisohn, *Tune In*, 283.

36. Quoted in Jones, "At Home."

37. Quoted in Henry, "Man Who Put the Beat."

38. That form, Everett notes, was "standardized around the rural Mississippi delta by the 1920s and given a more sophisticated, urban treatment in Chicago by the 1930s." Everett, *Beatles as Musicians: The Quarry Men*, 54.

39. Beatles, *Beatles Anthology*, 44.

40. Ibid.

41. The aforementioned steel pannist Gobin clued Woodbine into the Hamburg scene and its potential for profits. See McGrath, "Phillips"; and Bedford, *Fab One Hundred and Four*, 212–13, 284.

42. Beatles, *Beatles Anthology*, 45.

43. Quoted in Henry, "Man Who Put the Beat."

44. Henry, "Man Who Put the Beat."

45. Alibhai-Brown and McGrath, "Lord Woodbine."

46. Quoted in Henry, "Man Who Put the Beat."

47. See Phillips and Phillips, *Windrush*; Gentleman, *Windrush Betrayal*; Grant, *Homecoming*.

48. McGrath, "Phillips."

49. Both McGrath and Bedford confirmed this lack of documentation in personal communications with Katie Kapurch in 2020.

50. One of these clubs was the Pink Flamingo. Le Gendre, *Don't Stop the Carnival*, 212.

51. Quoted in Bedford, *Fab One Hundred and Four*, 216.

52. Le Gendre, *Don't Stop the Carnival*, 215.

53. Quoted in Bedford, *Fab One Hundred and Four*, 216.

54. Le Gendre, *Don't Stop the Carnival*, 160.

55. "Carnival, key manifestation of the humanity of the people of Trinidad, in all its irreverence, resistance, passion and wit, is the great stage for calypso. Any true calypso singer, whether accompanying themselves on guitar or backed by a percussionist or band, has to be able to prove their worth in the heat of that cauldron of knowing and opinionated listeners." Ibid., 162.

56. Birnbaum, *Before Elvis*, 374.

57. Bedford, *Fab One Hundred and Four*, 216.

58. "The whole point of calypso, and what it shares with the blues in America, is that it is a form of discourse as applicable to the ravages of a hurricane or the wreckage of infidelity as it is the brutality of the police or the beauty of a sporting event." Le Gendre, *Don't Stop the Carnival*, 162.

59. Hanly, *Produced by George Martin*.

60. "A Book at Bedtime," *Monty Python's Flying Circus*, season 3, episode 12, aired January 11, 1973, on BBC1.

61. For more on the reggae-inspired Paul and Linda McCartney tracks in the 1970s, see Alleyne, "White Reggae," 22–23.

62. McCartney and Wings, *Red Rose Speedway*.

63. See Grant, *Homecoming*.

64. Quoted in Henry, "Man Who Put the Beat."

65. Lewisohn, *Tune In* (extended special ed.), 797–98; McGrath, "Where You Once Belonged," 17.

66. Lewisohn, *Tune In*, 115–16.

67. Thompson, *Reggae*, 152.

68. Ibid.

69. Lewisohn, *Tune In*, 152.

70. Lennon, *In His Own Right*, 50–51.

71. Alleyne's contribution to Alleyne, Everett, and Kapurch, "Billy Preston."

72. Lewisohn, *Tune In* (extended special ed.), 797.

73. Quoted in McGrath, "Where You Once Belonged'," 16–17. Everett also reproduces this quote and mentions "Ask Me Why." Everett, *Beatles as Musicians: The Quarry Men*, 127. Elsewhere, Everett hears the "Latin rhythm" on "Ask Me Why," but in his analysis of the song's musical features he does make specific connections to calypso. Ibid., 136; see also 233, 271.

74. Lennon and Ono, *Milk and Honey*.

75. Lennon and Ono, *Double Fantasy*.

76. Rand, "Eccentric Legend."

77. Offering proof of this when the sculpture was reerected after a refurbishment in 2015, Woodbine's daughter, Carol Phillips, produced the miniature mock-up that Dooley had given her father. Ibid.

78. Lennon, *Plastic Ono Band*.

79. See chapter 2, above.

80. "Mud Is All You Need to Repair Paul."

81. Le Gendre, *Don't Stop*, 214.

82. McGrath, "Liverpool's Black Community." For more Beatles and Liverpool-centric studies of Lord Woodbine and other Black musicians' influence on the band, see McGrath, "Liverpool's Black Community" and "Where You Once Belonged"; Bedford, *Fab*; and Hogan, *Beat Makers*. Lord Woodbine is also discussed briefly in an expansive study of Black music in Britain from the Tudor era to the 1960s; see Le Gendre, *Don't Stop*, 212–15.

CHAPTER 6

1. The association between black-colored birds and sorrow has precedent, specifically the nursery rhyme "One for Sorrow" and a ballad that dates to the year 1500, "Crow and Pie." See chapter 7, below, which positions these songs in relation to the folk revival that preceded the Beatles' 1968 "Blackbird."

2. Assumptions about the nightingale's sadness stem largely (but not singularly) from the Greek myth of Philomela. See Mynott, *Birds in the Ancient World*, 172, 279, 410.

3. See chapter 1, above.

4. Quoted in Light, *What Happened*, 32.

5. Simone, *I Put a Spell on You*, 41–42.

6. Ibid., 23.

7. Ibid., 19.

8. Quoted in Cohodas, *Princess Noire*, 136.

9. Simone, *I Put a Spell on You*, 89.

10. "By 1964 a new body of freedom or protest songs . . . written by artists such as Nina Simone, Curtis Mayfield, James Collier, and others came to reflect [serve] as documentation of the evolving political identity of young black America. It is through works such as 'Mississippi Goddamn,' 'Keep on Pushing,' and 'Burn, Baby, Burn' that one can chronicle the growing anger that exploded in 1964 and '65, with rioting in major cities across the country, and in '66 with Stokely Carmichael's shouts of 'Black Power.'" Kernodle, "I Wish I Knew," 296.

11. Simon, *I Put a Spell on You*, 90.

12. Ibid., 98–100.

13. "The voice in the song could be interpreted as an external voice of a racist person or as an internal voice, which most likely resulted from internalization of racist affliction. Simone's lyrics speak to [Black people] who have struggled with feeling caged up, and who feel that equality and liberty in America will never be realized." Bratcher, *Words and Songs*, 84.

14. Simone, *I Put a Spell on You*, 88.

15. Simone's pessimism in this song recalls Wilderson's theory of "Afropessimism": "'Mad at the world' is Black folks at their best." Wilderson, *Afropessimism*, 40.

16. This, Everett notices, is similar to what occurs "just before every time the title is sung in 'Mr. Moonlight,'" released in 1962 by Piano Red (as Dr. Feelgood and the Interns) and covered by the Beatles in 1964. Walter Everett, personal communication with Katie Kapurch, December 24, 2020.

17. Ibid.

18. Everett, *Beatles as Musicians: Revolver*, 190.

19. Everett, *Beatles as Musicians: The Quarry Men*, 326.

20. Quoted in Cohodas, *Princess Noire*, 143.

21. See chapter 2, above.

22. See chapter 3, above.

23. "The source of creativity in 'Revolution (Parts 1 & 2)' comes from Simone's realization that the ideas of Black separatism and Black Power empower her and other Black people. As she is empowered, she then pours her empowerment into her music, for it is her way to instill pride in Black folk." Bratcher, *Words and Songs*, 167.

24. Talking about his civil rights symbolism in one 2005 interview, McCartney explained that he was addressing a "Black woman" in the segregated southern United States: "You were only waiting for this moment to arise, you know, you're finally getting your rights." "Paul McCartney—Blackbird (The Beatles): The Story Behind the Song," December 4, 2017, YouTube video, 00:05:11, https://youtu.be/BpWHJkEosAA.

25. See Roessner, "We All Want." Roessner makes a compelling case for Lennon's use of pastiche and parody as postmodern techniques that facilitate a political critique, but our analysis here is concerned with how Simone heard the song, an interpretation available in her response.

26. Everett, *Beatles as Musicians: Revolver*, 173.

27. Ibid.

28. Simone, *I Put a Spell on You*, 100.

29. Smith Storey, "Flying Words," as summarized by Gates and Tatar, *Annotated African American Folktales*, 69.

30. Thompson, *Summer of Soul*.

31. See chapter 1, above.

32. "To Love Somebody" was the title track of a 1969 Simone album that includes parts 1 and 2 of her "Revolution," along with covers of other male artists of that generation, such as Bob Dylan and Leonard Cohen.

33. Wenner, *Lennon*, 82.

34. Quoted in Eldridge, "Nina Simone," 5.

35. Quoted in Angelou, "High."

36. See Simone, *I Put a Spell on You*, 101, 135, 141.

37. See chapter 3, above, for an introduction to blackbird-bluebird dynamics in American popular song.

38. Quoted in Cohodas, *Princess Noire*, 315.

39. See chapter 3, above.

40. See Simone, *I Put a Spell on You*.

41. Ibid., 158.

42. Quoted in Garbus, *What Happened*.

43. Angelou, "Nina Simone," 132–34.

44. See chapter 1, above.

45. Commander, *Afro-Atlantic Flight*, 56.

46. Ibid., 57.

47. In 1969, a lesser-known work of poetry, Carolyn Rodgers's *Songs of a Blackbird*, was also published. Like Angelou's novel, Rodgers's collection was shaped by and contributed to the Black Arts Movement, a New York–based collective that also included James Baldwin and other major figures circa 1965 to 1975. Also like Angelou, Rodgers positions her authorship in relation to the subject position of the bird. See Mitchell and Davis, *Encyclopedia*, 267.

48. Dunbar, *Lyrics*, 102.

49. "Alicia Keys: Blackbird (Piano & I: AOL Sessions +1)," July 1, 2011, YouTube video, 00:03:37, https://youtu.be/JrTbf_ws9Is.

50. See the introduction, above, and chapters 7 and 10, below.

51. Quoted in Dean, "Gay Fiction Author."

52. Duplechan, *Blackbird*, 105–6.

53. Ibid., 106.

54. *Blackbird* is the prequel to *Eight Days a Week* (1985), another novel whose title references the Beatles. More can be said about Black Americans' allusions to the Beatles in fiction. James Baldwin, for example, represented remixing in *Just Above My Head*: "Jimmy begins improvising on the piano, around "Here Comes the Sun," blending it with "Oh Happy Day," and threatening, generally, to work himself up into a fine camp-meeting frenzy. It sounds very clear and beautiful, in my empty house, on this

chilly, sunlit Sunday." Baldwin, *Later Novels*, 984.

55. Nelson, "Artist."

56. Ibid.

CHAPTER 7

1. See reference to Dargan in chapter 1, above.

2. Boyd, *Wonderful*, 198.

3. In English balladry, a "minstrel ballad" refers to songs by professional singers known as "minstrels," whose speakers often insert themselves and their lessons; minstrel ballads are delineated from folk ballads, which derive from the oral tradition. The genres did, however, influence each other, which is exactly what Child's reference to the "popular features" indicates in the case of "Crow and Pie." Frances James Child quoted in Atkinson, *English Traditional Ballad*, 75.

4. In addition to Roud Folk Song Index classifications, the Child Ballads numerical designations indicate a song's existence in the folklorist Frances James Child's documentation (see above).

5. See chapter 1, above, for a discussion of Reverend Franklin's sermon. The 2021 season of the series *Genius* (National Geographic) incorporates avian imagery into characters' dialogue to represent the conflicts facing Aretha Franklin, alluding to her iconic takes on bird songs like "Skylark," "Tiny Sparrow," and "Mockingbird." In a scene in which Franklin and Dr. Martin Luther King Jr. share a private conversation, she confesses to feeling like "a bird with a broken wing." Perhaps screenwriter Suzan-Lori Parks is referencing the Dunbar bruised-wing image that Maya Angelou recalls in *I Know Why the Caged Bird Sings*. That intertextual association comes through when Franklin is compared to a caged bird in a subsequent episode, in which the comparison is used to characterize her career's oversight by her father; in this case, the irony relates to the escaping bird of his famous sermon.

6. Cross, *Room Full of Mirrors*, 306.

7. Ibid., 339.

8. Ibid., 82. Birds also show up in seemingly coincidental ways in Hendrix's biography: for example, the Velvetones, Hendrix's "first significant band," had a "steady weeknight gig at Birdland, the legendary club at Madison and Twenty-second Street" in Seattle. Ibid., 68. Also, in the 2017 documentary *Betty: They Say I'm Different*, Betty Davis mentions the "crow" she sees in Jimi Hendrix. The "Funk Queen" and former wife of Miles Davis is another mid-century Black American artist for whom birds, particularly crows, are instructive and emblematic.

9. "Beatle Blind Date."

10. One "progression comes untransposed from Jimi Hendrix's first single, 'Hey Joe,' a favorite of McCartney's, released on December 23, 1966, and performed on 'Top of the Pops' on the night the Beatles recorded the track." Everett, *Beatles as Musicians: Revolver*, 118.

11. Ibid., 101.

12. Ibid., 93.

13. Quoted in Cross, *Room Full of Mirrors*, 206.

14. Ibid., 206, 60.

15. Miles, *Paul*, 485.

16. "Jimi Hendrix Cleared of Blame."

17. In 1962, McCartney learned Little Richard's preshow ritual of steaming his head under a towel, from which he would emerge and proclaim, "I can't help it cos I'm so beautiful" ("Paul on Little Richard").

18. Cross, *Room Full of Mirrors*, 53–54.

19. Miles, *Paul McCartney*, 201.

20. See both of Everett's *Beatles as Musicians* volumes.

21. McCartney, "Paul on Little Richard."

22. Lewisohn, *Tune In*, 102.

23. White, *Life and Times*, 91.

24. Quoted in Dalton, "Little Richard." When Little Richard attributes his talent to divine gift and "magic," he is participating in the discursive tradition theorized by Yvonne P. Chireau: "The creations that black people have woven into their quest for spiritual empowerment and meaning." Chireau

explains, "African American 'religion' is not always distinct from what others call 'magic.' Instead these are complementary categories, and they have historically exhibited complementary forms in African American culture" (*Black Magic*, 2, 7). These insights are also applicable to Preston's rhetoric of gratitude in the next chapter.

25. McCartney, *My Long and Winding Road*, 118.

26. Miles, *Paul* McCartney, 485.

27. MacDonald, *Revolution*, loc. 5425

28. Quoted in Bose, *Across the Universe*, 223–24.

29. Ibid., 229.

30. Kevin Howlett, "Track by Track," CD liner notes to the Beatles, *The Beatles*.

31. Pattie Boyd, interview by Katie Kapurch, July 15, 2019. To be clear, Boyd did not dispute McCartney's civil rights explanation. She brought up "Blackbird" when asked which songs made her think of Rishikesh.

32. Lewisohn, *Complete Beatles*, 282.

33. Everett, *Beatles as Musicians: Revolver*, 190; see also 46.

34. See chapter 4, above.

35. Everett, *Beatles as Musicians: Revolver*, 177.

36. Runtagh, "Beatles' Revelatory White Album."

37. Margo Stevens quoted in Norman, *Shout!*, 385.

38. Howlett, "Track by Track."

39. Lewisohn, "Double Lives."

40. "Paul McCartney Is Interviewed."

41. See chapter 3, above.

42. Davies, *Beatles Lyrics*, 284.

43. Ibid., 283.

44. Beatles, *No. 3 Abbey Road NW8*.

45. McCartney, *Lyrics*, 48. See also Kreps, "Paul McCartney Meets Women."

46. See Lewisohn, *Tune In*.

47. McCartney, *Lyrics*, 48.

48. Jackson, *Beatles*; see also Alleyne, Everett, and Kapurch, "Billy Preston."

49. See chapter 6, above.

50. Adding to the "many blackbirds" Donovan mentions, on September 6, 1969,

that a short Apple-produced film featuring Mary Hopkin—and including her mentor, McCartney—was aired on ITV following a children's television program called *Magpie*. Lewisohn, *Complete Beatles*, 298.

51. Letts, CD liner notes to *Don Letts Presents the Mighty Trojan Sound*, 3.

52. Greene, *Travels*, 92.

53. Procter, *Dwelling Places*, 5.

54. Procter, *Writing Black Britain*, 96.

55. In that film, Dr. Kitty Oliver speaks poignantly about what the Beatles' choice meant to her as a Black girl growing up in segregated Florida. Although they took a definitive public stance, the Beatles weren't active in the process that led up to the performance because they left concert contracts and their logistics decisions to manager Brian Epstein. See Gunderson, *Some Fun Tonight*.

56. Quoted in Cleave, "Paul," 76.

57. Ibid.

58. Church Gibson, "Deification," 101–2.

59. Kapurch, "Beatles," 144–46. For more on the Shirelles and other girl groups' influences on the Beatles, see Bradby, "She"; Warwick, *Girl Groups*; Warwick, "You're Going to Lose That Girl"; Kapurch, "Crying."

60. On *Please Please Me*, the Beatles covered "Chains" (the Cookies), "Boys" (the Shirelles), and "Baby It's You" (the Shirelles); on *With the Beatles*, they covered "Please Mr. Postman" (the Marvelettes) and "Devil in Her Heart" (title changed from "Devil in His Heart" by the Donays).

61. Mahon, *Black Diamond*, loc. 2382.

62. Spizer, *Beatles*, 175; Mahon, *Black Diamond*, loc. 2365.

63. Hamilton, *Just Around Midnight*, 124.

64. Mahon, *Black Diamond*, loc. 2363.

65. For the Shirelles and other girl groups' influences on and interactions with the Beatles, see Warwick, *Girl Groups*; Bradby, "She Told Me"; Mahon, *Black Diamond*; and Kapurch, "Crying" and "Beatles."

66. Everett, *Beatles as Musicians: Quarry Men*, 127; Mahon, *Black Diamond*, loc. 2360.

67. Mahon, *Black Diamond*, loc. 2365.

68. For more on Motown's shaping of and responses to the Beatles, see Hamilton, *Just Around Midnight*.

69. Mahon, *Black Diamond*, loc. 2152. As Mahon elsewhere explains, "The 1964 arrival of the Beatles upended the short-lived period of racial integration on the charts, as the extraordinary success of the British group ushered in a phalanx of white artists from the United Kingdom. The Detroit-based Motown label, whose owner Berry Gordy made a concerted effort to produce music performed by African Americans with crossover appeal, had a steady stream of hits throughout the decade, but black artists who were not part of the Motown empire were displaced from the pop charts" (loc. 402).

70. For other examples, see Hamilton, who cites a well-wishing note sent to the Beatles and signed by Marvin Gaye, Stevie Wonder, and Smokey Robinson. In it, Motown also proposed they record together, "for an album like 'Friends across the sea.'" Ibid., 124.

71. Quoted in "The Supremes' Mary Wilson."

72. Quoted in Cutler, "Reflections."

73. See Warwick, *Girl Groups*.

74. Spector, *Be My Baby*, 78.

75. Ibid., 76–91.

76. Quoted in Miles, *Paul* McCartney, 485.

77. Ross, *Secrets*, 150.

78. Alleyne's contribution to Alleyne, Everett, and Kapurch, "Billy Preston."

79. Miles, *Paul* McCartney, 419; Lewisohn, "Double Lives"; Everett, *Beatles as Musicians:* Revolver, 188–89.

80. Turner, *Beatles*, loc. 932.

81. McCartney may not have understood the radically collective context he encountered: "a mode of musical presentation in which everyone involved is considered a 'performer'—or perhaps in which no one, the song leader included, is considered a 'performer'—and one in which the producer of the music plays a privileged role in calling forth the responses of the audience." Davis, *Blues Legacies*, 362.

82. Smith Storey, "Flying Words."

83. The "ob la di, ob la da" phrase is reminiscent of a musical phrase associated with the buzzard named Yank'o. See chapter 1, above.

84. Lewisohn, "Double Lives"; see also Everett, *Beatles as Musicians:* Revolver, 188–89.

85. Miles, *Paul* McCartney, 419.

86. Turner, *Beatles*.

87. Van Buskirk, "Video: Paul McCartney."

88. Davies, *Beatles Lyrics*, 283.

89. Bugliosi, *Helter Skelter*, 301.

90. Ibid., 301, 312, 324.

91. Beatles, *Beatles Anthology*, 311.

92. Stubbs, "Paul McCartney."

93. See Kapurch and Smith, "Blackbird Singing," 62.

94. Quoted in Leroux, "Ramsey's Rhythms."

95. Quoted in Lewis, "'Butt-Shakers."

96. Ibid.

97. Isolation is again what Franklin empathizes with when she considers the title character of "Lady Madonna," a single mother struggling to make it all work. That theme applied to the US television show *Grace Under Fire*, which used Franklin's cover as its theme song during the first season it aired on ABC in 1993. Transforming the Fats Domino–inspired boogie woogie into an even funkier groove, Franklin's delivery encourages listeners to imagine Lady Madonna as a single Black mother, the kind of woman becoming a favorite punching bag for conservative politicians like Ronald Reagan, who was instrumental in the racist construction of the "welfare queen." Although *Grace Under Fire* featured a working-class white woman in the lead, the presence of Franklin's song pointed to the previous decade's racialized discourse on single mothers.

CHAPTER 8

1. Robert Palmer, interview by Katie Kapurch, August 24, 2019.

2. In 1969, Preston picked up a Fender Bass VI for "Old Brown Shoe" when he was

recording with the Beatles. In a moment captured on film, Preston turns toward the camera while Paul McCartney holds George Harrison's Telecaster guitar. Jackson, *Beatles*.

3. Palmer, interview by Kapurch.

4. See Gates, *Black Church*.

5. Beatles, *Beatles: Get Back*, 131; Palmer, interview by Kapurch.

6. Brothers, *Help!*, 300.

7. According to Preston, his authorship of this song came as a surprise to McCartney. "Billy Preston: 'John Was the Boss Beatle,'" October 29, 2008, YouTube video, 00:08:59, https://youtu.be/GHwyU6yOY3A.

8. Palmer, interview by Kapurch.

9. Rev. Dr. W. Edward Jenkins, Victory Baptist Church, Los Angeles, January 12, 2020.

10. Quoted in Jackson-Fossett, "Legendary Musician."

11. *Burt Sugarman's "The Midnight Special."*

12. Cole, *Nat King Cole Show*.

13. Werner, *Higher Ground*, 7.

14. Rev. Dr. W. Edward Jenkins, interview by Katie Kapurch and Jon Marc Smith, June 12, 2022; see also "Victory Baptist Church History."

15. Johnnie Pearl Knox, interview by Katie Kapurch, January 12, 2020; Jenkins, interview Katie Kapurch, January 12, 2020; see also "Victory Baptist Church History."

16. McDonald, interview by Katie Kapurch, August 23, 2019.

17. Knox, interview by Kapurch.

18. Ibid.

19. Matthew 3:14.

20. Preston, *Kids & Me*.

21. Luke 3:21–23.

22. "Billy Preston: 'John Was the Boss Beatle.'"

23. Ibid.

24. Jackson, *Beatles*.

25. Beatles, *Beatles Anthology*, 319.

26. Pareles, "Billy Preston."

27. Beatles, *Beatles Anthology*, 319.

28. Palmer, interview by Kapurch.

29. Alleyne, Everett, and Kapurch, "Billy Preston."

30. Ibid.; see also Everett, *Beatles as Musicians: The Quarry Men*, 29.

31. Beatles, *Beatles Anthology*, 318.

32. Jackson, *Beatles*.

33. Everett's contribution to Alleyne, Everett, and Kapurch, "Billy Preston."

34. Beatles, *Beatles: Get Back*, 126.

35. Werner, *Change Is Gonna Come*, 43.

36. Beatles, *Beatles: Get Back*, 139.

37. Boyd, interview by Kapurch.

38. Derek Taylor, LP liner notes to Preston, *That's the Way*.

39. Quoted in Andy Davis, CD liner notes to Preston, *Encouraging Words*.

40. Andy Davis, CD liner notes to Preston, *Encouraging Words*.

41. "Billy Preston: 'John Was the Boss Beatle.'"

42. Sean Ross, CD liner notes to Billy Preston, *Ultimate Collection*, 2.

43. McDonald, interview by Kapurch.

44. Ibid.

45. David T. Walker, personal communication with Katie Kapurch, October 5, 2019.

46. Quoted in Gates, *Black Church*, 35.

47. McDonald, interview by Kapurch.

48. Kimberley Jenkins, interview by Katie Kapurch and Jon Marc Smith, June 12, 2022.

49. John Tobler, CD liner notes to Preston, *I Wrote a Simple Song / Music Is My Life*.

50. Ross, CD liner notes to Billy Preston, *Ultimate Collection*, 3.

51. Palmer, interview by Kapurch.

52. Ibid.

53. Matthew 5–7.

54. Palmer, interview by Kapurch.

55. See the introduction, above.

56. Ibid.

57. Morrison, *Song of Solomon*, 337; quoted in Gates and Tatar, *Annotated African American Folktales*, 65.

58. Rev. Dr. W. Edward Jenkins, Victory Baptist Church, Los Angeles, January 12, 2020.

59. Palmer, interview by Kapurch.

60. Quoted in Taylor, LP liner notes to *That's the Way.*

61. "Billy Preston: Los Angeles July '96!!!," October 29, 2008, YouTube video, 00:09:37, https://youtu.be/7Dxv0RA0rwU.

62. Quoted in Betts, *Motown*, loc. 13672.

CHAPTER 9

1. Sylvester, *Living Proof.*

2. Ibid. There are no audio-visual recordings of this iconic performance, but Wash confirmed it was Izora who pretended like she didn't recognize the Beatles. Martha Wash, interview by Katie Kapurch, April 21, 2020.

3. Sylvester, *Living Proof.*

4. Wash, interview by Kapurch.

5. "Cockettes." One member of the Cockettes described them as "a hippie glitter genderfuck troupe." Quoted in Gamson, *Fabulous*, 41. Sometimes accessorizing with feathers (which Sylvester continued to do, especially with boas), the band's name is another reminder that the bird symbolism can be sexually evocative, too.

6. Kerry Hatch (Hot Band bandmember) quoted in Gamson, *Fabulous*, 91. As Gamson explains, "Sylvester and the five longhaired straight white boys . . . were something of an odd match" even though "the new Hot Band could play." Ibid.

7. Wash, interview by Kapurch.

8. Ibid.

9. Gamson, *Fabulous*, 158–59.

10. Describing Sylvester at the beginning of the 1970s, Gamson explains his appeal: "A black man reviving music from another era in white gowns and high voice, singing of lovin' dat man of his: it would be difficult to create a more fitting star for San Francisco." Ibid., 68.

11. Wash, interview by Kapurch.

12. Gamson, *Fabulous*, 158.

13. Wash, interview by Kapurch.

14. Ibid.

15. Ibid.

16. Ibid.

17. "Sylvester and the Hot Band opened a lot of other people's's shows, but almost never headlined. They were something like gregarious, gorgeous, bridesmaids at the wrong wedding: you loved them to death, but you weren't quite sure what they were doing there." Gamson, *Fabulous*, 100.

18. Wash, interview by Kapurch.

19. Ibid.

20. Ibid.

21. Sylvester, *Living Proof.*

22. "A relationship of identity is enacted in the way that the performer dissolves into the crowd. Together, they collaborate in a creative process governed by formal and informal, democratic rules." Gilroy, *Black Atlantic*, 200.

23. Wash, interview by Kapurch.

24. Ibid.

25. Robinson, personal correspondence with Katie Kapurch, March 28, 2022:

> My career in music started with singing taught by my mother and Dr. Roscoe Poland at age 4; babysitters then taught piano until age 7. Valda Hudson schooled me in jazz and classical piano lessons, and my accomplished Uncle Jimmy Halliburton rehearsed and accompanied me in Classical, Negro Spirituals and Gospel music from age 7 to 10. By 10, I was composing songs and was given the title of national pianist with the Thomas A. Dorsey convention of Gospel Choirs and Choruses. We travelled devoutly to many cities performing and listening to gospel's greatest artists including Shirley Caesar, Rev. James Cleveland, Mighty Clouds of Joy, Mattie Moss Clark and many others.

26. Along with cowriter Victor Osborn, Robinson was signed to Motown by Jeffrey Bowen and Berry Gordy IV. Eric Robinson, interview by Katie Kapurch, November 24, 2020.

27. Ibid.

28. Ibid. Gamson's biography lists the Beatles' "Blackbird" among songs Sylvester

played with Sylvester and the Hot Band in San Francisco and Los Angeles. Gamson, *Fabulous*, 91.

29. Robinson, personal correspondence with Kapurch; Robinson, interview by Kapurch.

30. Robinson, interview by Kapurch.

31. Ibid.

32. Ibid.

33. Robinson, personal correspondence with Kapurch; Robinson, interview by Kapurch.

34. Ibid. Robinson was also "acquainted with Kenny Lupper, one of Preston's protégés," whose gospel album Robinson calls "fantastic": "I admired Lupper's Hammond organ skills. He also played organ on the Aretha Franklin and Reverend James Cleveland album [*Amazing Grace*]." Robinson, personal correspondence with Kapurch.

35. Wash, interview by Kapurch.

36. "The Weather Girls: It's Raining Men (Video)," February 7, 2013, YouTube video, 00:04:54, https://youtu.be/I5aZJBLAu1E.

37. Robinson, interview by Kapurch; Robinson, personal correspondence with Kapurch.

38. Wash, interview by Kapurch.

39. Ibid.

40. The First Ladies of Disco's name was inspired by James Arena's 2013 book of the same name.

41. Wash, interview by Kapurch.

42. Ibid.

43. Ibid.

44. Martha Wash, Facebook post, June 7, 2020, https://facebook.com/themarthawash/posts/3071955822886957/.

CHAPTER 10

1. Bettye LaVette, Carlos Alvarez Studio Theater, San Antonio, January 11, 2018.

2. The wording quoted here is from a filmed 2017 Nashville concert, but she used a nearly identical preface in the 2018 San Antonio show cited above. Bettye LaVette, Americana Music Festival, Twelfth

and Porter, Nashville, September 16, 2017. "Bettye LaVette 'Blackbird' Song by John Lennon / Paul McCartney (Nashville, 16 September 2017)," September 17, 2017, YouTube video, 00:04:12, https://youtu.be/OSgTAK-mH84.

3. LaVette, interview by Kapurch. LaVette's use of the bridge metaphor to explain the women to whom she is paying homage on *Blackbirds* recalls Baldwin's use of the word in *Just Above My Head*: "Our suffering is our bridge to one another. Everyone must cross this bridge, or die while he still lives." Baldwin, *Later Novels*, 611.

4. LaVette, *Woman Like Me*. David Freeland also subtitled the chapter featuring his interview with LaVette "Buzzard Luck"; see *Ladies of Soul*, 79,

5. Preston performed on this episode, too, singing "Baby Face," a song he sang on stage throughout his career.

6. LaVette, *Woman Like Me*, 53–54, 60, 89, 171.

7. Ibid., 5–6, 13, 15–21.

8. LaVette, interview by Kapurch.

9. LaVette, *Woman Like Me*, 86–90, 135, 148–49.

10. See chapter 3, above.

11. Gonyea and Watters, "My Fifth Career."

12. LaVette, *Woman Like Me*, 186–90.

13. LaVette, interview by Kapurch.

14. See Doyle, "Bettye LaVette."

15. LaVette, interview by Kapurch.

16. LaVette's approach to music as interpretation resembles "polyphonic" strategies in literature authored by African American women: "Recursive structures accomplish a blend between figurative processes that are reflective (like a mirror) and symbolic processes whose depth and resonance make them reflexive. This combination results in texts that are at once emblematic of the culture they describe as well as interpretive of this culture." Holloway, "Revision," 388.

17. LaVette, interview by Kapurch.

18. Ibid.

19. The Beatles' "Here, There, and Everywhere" is significant to this book, carrying

the memory of "Bye Bye Blackbird." The Beatles' here-there-everywhere phrasing also appears in Nina Simone's "Fodder in Her Wings"; see chapters 3 and 5, above.

20. LaVette, interview by Kapurch.

21. Ibid.

22. Ibid.

23. Parton, "Little Sparrow."

24. LaVette, "Little Sparrow."

25. LaVette, interview by Kapurch.

26. Bettye LaVette, "Bettye LaVette: One More Song (Live Session)," July 24, 2020, YouTube video, 00:05:16, https://youtu.be /Uylu4zSLWOk.

27. LaVette, interview by Kapurch.

28. Ibid.

29. Ibid.

30. Ibid.

31. "Bettye LaVette–It Don't Come Easy–2014," July 7, 2020, YouTube video, 00:06:21, https://youtu.be/1EGcAUh42TE.

32. "Ringo Tells David Lynch His Reaction to Bettye LaVette's Performance of It Don't Come Easy," December 5, 2015, YouTube video, https://youtu.be/Gmet-zL_gE4.

33. LaVette, interview by Kapurch.

34. Deusner, "On 'Blackbirds.'"

35. LaVette, interview by Kapurch.

36. Ibid.

37. See chapter 7, above.

38. LaVette, Woman Like Me, 81–82.

39. LaVette, interview by Kapurch.

40. Ibid.

CONCLUSION

1. Cooper, "Three Years."

2. See the discussion of Benjamin's insight in Fields and Fields, Racecraft, 180–81.

3. Guzman, "Remembering."

4. Morrison, "Nobel Lecture."

5. O'Brien, Things, 171.

6. Marilyn McCoo and Billy Davis Jr., "Marilyn McCoo & Billy Davis Jr.–"Blackbird" Beatles Cover (Official Video)," YouTube, April 17, 2021, https://youtu.be/ZEgRI mwoW_Y.

7. Quoted in "Music Icons."

8. Ibid.

9. See chapter 6, above.

10. MacDonald, Revolution, 292. The "added bird calls . . . function remarkably well in the G-major context." Everett, Beatles as Musicians: Revolver, 190.

11. See chapter 1, above.

12. Miller, "Inside Otis Redding's Final Masterpiece"; for more on Redding and the Beatles, see also Riley, "Drive My Car."

13. Gilroy, Black Atlantic, 4; quoted in Colbert, Black Movements, 52.

14. See chapter 1, above.

15. Gutterman, John Lennon.

16. Graham, "Why Yoko Ono."

17. "Yoko Ono. To See the Sky. 2015."

18. Cooper, "Three Years."

Bibliography

PRINT AND AUDIOVISUAL MATERIALS

Adair, Zakiya R. "Respectable Vamp: A Black Feminist Analysis of Florence Mills' Career in Early Vaudeville Theater." *Journal of African American Studies* 17 (2013): 7–21.

Adler, Renata. "Letter from Selma." *New Yorker*, April 2, 1965. https://www.new yorker.com/magazine/1965/04/10/let ter-from-selma.

Agnew, Jeremy. *Entertainment in the Old West: Theater, Music, Circuses, Medicine Shows, Prizefighting, and Other Popular Amusements.* Jefferson, NC: McFarland, 2011.

Alibhai-Brown, Yasmin, and McGrath, James. "Lord Woodbine: The Forgotten Sixth Beatle." *The Independent*, October 23, 2011. https://www.indepen dent.co.uk/arts-entertainment/music /features/lord-woodbine-forgotten-sixth -beatle-2015140.html.

Alleyne, Mike. *The Encyclopedia of Reggae: The Golden Age of Roots Reggae.* New York: Sterling, 2012.

——. "White Reggae: Cultural Dilution in the Record Industry." *Popular Music and Society* 24, no. 1 (2000): 15–30.

Alleyne, Mike, Walter Everett, and Katie Kapurch. "Billy Preston and the Beatles *Get Back*: Black Music and the Wisdom of Wordplay and Wit." In *The Beatles and Humor*, edited by Katie Kapurch, Richard Mills, and Matthias Heyman. New York: Bloomsbury Academic, forthcoming.

Als, Hilton. "Toni Morrison's Profound and Unrelenting Vision." *New Yorker*, January 27, 2020. https://www.newyorker .com/magazine/2020/02/03/toni-mor risons-profound-and-unrelenting-vision.

Amazing Grace. Directed by Alan Elliott and Sydney Pollack. New York: Neon, 2018.

Angelou, Maya. *I Know Why the Caged Bird Sings.* 1969. Reprint, New York: Ballantine, 2009.

——. "Nina Simone: High Priestess of Soul." *Redbook*, November 1970, 132–34.

Atkinson, David. *The English Traditional Ballad: Theory, Method, and Practice.* London: Routledge, 2017.

Awkward, Michael. "Appropriative Gestures: Theory and Afro-American Literary Criticism." 1988. Reprinted in *African American Literary Theory: A Reader*, edited by Winston Napier, 331–47. New York: New York University Press, 2000.

Baker, Houston A., Jr. "Theoretical Returns." 1991. Reprinted in *African American Literary Theory: A Reader*, edited by Winston Napier, 421–42. New York: New York University Press, 2000.

Baldwin, James. *Later Novels.* Edited by Darryl Pinckney. New York: Library of America, 2015.

"Beatle Blind Date: Paul McCartney Reviews the New Pop Singles." *Melody Maker*, February 25, 1967.

Beatles. *The Beatles Anthology.* San Francisco: Chronicle, 2000.

——. *The Beatles: Get Back.* London and New York: Apple / Callaway, 2021.

——, dirs. *Magical Mystery Tour.* 1967. Reissue, Apple, 2012.

Bedford, David. *Fab One Hundred and Four.* Deerfield, IL: Dalton Watson, 2013.

Betts, Graham. *Motown Encyclopedia.* N.p.: AC Publishing, 2014. Kindle.

Birnbaum, Larry. *Before Elvis: The Prehistory of Rock 'n' Roll.* Lanham, MD: Scarecrow Press, 2013.

Blight, David W. *Frederick Douglass: Prophet of Freedom*. New York: Simon & Schuster, 2018.

"Bobby McFerrin's Improv-Inspired 'Vocabularies.'" *NPR*, April 9, 2010. https://www.npr.org/2010/04/09/125725036/bobby-mcferrins-improv-inspired-vocabularies.

Bose, Ajoy. *Across the Universe: The Beatles in India*. Haryana: Penguin, 2018.

Boyd, Pattie, with Penny Junor. *Wonderful Tonight: George Harrison, Eric Clapton, and Me*. New York: Three Rivers Press, 2007.

Bradby, Barbara. "She Told Me What to Say: The Beatles and Girl-Group Discourse." *Popular Music and Society* 28, no. 3 (2005): 359–90.

Bragg, Billy. *Roots, Radicals and Rockers: How Skiffle Changed the World*. London: Faber & Faber, 2017.

Bratcher, Melanie E. *Words and Songs of Bessie Smith, Billie Holiday, and Nina Simone*. New York: Routledge, 2007.

Brothers, Thomas. *Help! The Beatles, Duke Ellington, and the Magic of Collaboration*. New York: Norton, 2018.

———. *Louis Armstrong's New Orleans*. New York: Norton, 2006.

Brown, Sterling. "Negro Folk Expression: Spirituals, Seculars, Ballads and Work Songs." *Phylon* 14, no. 1 (1953): 45–61.

Bryan, Frank Egbert. *A History of English Balladry and Other Studies*. Boston: Gorham Press, 1913.

Bugliosi, Vincent, with Curt Gentry. *Helter Skelter: The True Story of the Manson Murders*. 1974. Reprint, New York: Norton, 1994.

Burns, Ken, dir. *Country Music*. Walpole, NH: Florentine Films, 2019.

BWW Desk. "Tony Nominee Jonelle Allen Plays Florence Mills in BLACKBIRD This Halloween at Saddleback College" *Broadway World*, October 30, 2015. https://www.broadwayworld.com/los-angeles/article/Tony-Nominee-Jonelle-Allen-to-Portray-Florence-Mills-in-BLACKBIRD-This-Halloween-at-Saddleback-College-20151029.

Cassells, Cyrus. *The Gospel According to Wild Indigo*. Carbondale: Southern Illinois University Press, 2018.

Cazden, Norman, Herbert Haufrecht, and Norman Studer, eds. *Folk Songs of the Catskills*. Albany: State University of New York Press, 1982.

Chireau, Yvonne P. *Black Magic: Religion and the African American Conjuring Tradition*. Berkeley: University of California Press, 2003.

Christian, Mark. "An African-Centered Approach to the Black British Experience: With Special Reference to Liverpool." *Journal of Black Studies* 28, no. 3 (1998): 291–308.

Church Gibson, Pamela. "The Deification of the Dolly Bird: Selling Swinging London, Fuelling Feminism." *Journal for the Study of British Cultures* 14, no. 2 (2007): 99–111.

Chybowski, Julia J. "Becoming the 'Black Swan' in Mid-Nineteenth-Century America: Elizabeth Taylor Greenfield's Early Life and Debut Concert Tour." *Journal of the American Musicological Society* 67, no. 1 (2014): 125–65.

Cleave, Maureen. "Paul." *Datebook* 5, no. 8 (September 1966): 71–72, 74–76.

Clinton, George, with Ben Greenman. *Brothas Be, Yo Like George, Ain't That Funkin' Kinda Hard on You? A Memoir*. New York: Atria Books, 2014.

"The Cockettes." Harvard Library, n.d. https://library.harvard.edu/collections/cockettes.

Cohodas, Nadine. *Princess Noire: The Tumultuous Reign of Nina Simone*. Chapel Hill: University of North Carolina Press, 2010.

Colbert, Soyica Diggs. *Black Movements: Performance and Cultural Politics*. New Brunswick, NJ: Rutgers University Press, 2017.

Cole, Nat King (host). *The Nat King Cole Show*. Performances by Cornel Wilde, Peggy King, Michel Ray, and Billy

Preston. NBC, November 5, 1957.
Paley Center for Media. https://www
.paleycenter.org/collection/item/?q=
about&p=760&item=B:61988.

Coletta, W. John. *Biosemiotic Literary Criticism: Genesis and Prospectus*. Cham: Springer, 2021.

Commander, Michelle D. *Afro-Atlantic Flight: Speculative Returns and the Black Fantastic*. Durham, NC: Duke University Press, 2017.

Cooper, Christian. "Three Years After a Fateful Day in Central Park, Birding Continues to Change." *New York Times*, May 26, 2023.

Cornelius, Don (host). *Soul Train*. Performances by Billy Preston, Rufus, George McCrae, and Franklin Ajaye. September 7, 1974.

Cowley, John. *Carnival, Canboulay and Calypso: Traditions in the Making*. Cambridge: Cambridge University Press, 1996.

Cox, Philip, dir. *Betty: They Say I'm Different*. New York: Monoduo, 2017.

Cross, Charles R. *Room Full of Mirrors: A Biography of Jimi Hendrix*. New York: Hachette Books, 2005.

Cutler, Jacqueline. "Reflections on Supremes Fashion and History." *New York Daily News*, September 7, 2019.

Dalton, David. "Little Richard: Child of God." *Rolling Stone*, May 28, 1970. https:// www.rollingstone.com/music/music -features/little-richard-child-of-god-2 -177027/.

Dargan, William T. *Lining Out the Word: Dr. Watts Hymn Singing in the Music of Black Americans*. Berkeley: University of California Press, 2006.

Davies, Hunter, ed. *The Beatles Lyrics*. New York: Little, Brown, 2014.

Davis, Angela Y. *Blues Legacies and Black Feminism*. New York: Vintage, 1998.

Dean, Will. "Gay Fiction Author Larry Duplechan: No More Novels to Write." *Desert Sun*, April 10, 2015. https:// www.desertsun.com/story/news/2015 /04/10/blackbird-novel-larry-duplechan /25607507/.

Delson, Susan. *Soundies and the Changing Image of Black Americans on Screen: One Dime at a Time*. Bloomington: Indiana University Press, 2021.

Deusner, Stephen. "On 'Blackbirds,' Bettye LaVette Honors Black Women Who Inspire Her (Part 2 of 2)." *Bluegrass Situation*, August 21, 2020. https:// thebluegrasssituation.com/read/on -blackbirds-bettye-lavette-honors-black -women-who-inspire-her-part-2-of-2/.

Dirix, Emmanuelle. "Birds of Paradise: Feathers, Fetishism and Costume in Classical Hollywood." *Film, Fashion and Consumption* 3, no. 1 (2014): 15–29.

Doktor, Stephanie. "Finding Florence Mills: The Voice of the Harlem Jazz Queen in the Compositions of William Grant Still and Edmund Thornton Jenkins." *Journal of the Society for American Music* 14, no. 4 (2020): 451–79.

Doyle, Patrick. "Bettye LaVette on Why She's Singing 'Strange Fruit' Now." *Rolling Stone*, June 19, 2020. https:// www.rollingstone.com/music/music -features/bettye-lavette-strange-fruit -interview-1017853/.

Du Bois, W. E. B. *The Souls of Black Folk*. 1903. Reprint, New York: Dover, 2016.

Dunbar, Paul Laurence. *Lyrics of the Hearthside*. New York: Dodd, Mead, 1899.

Dunning, George, dir. *Yellow Submarine*. Beverly Hills, CA: United Artists, 1968.

Duplechan, Larry. *Blackbird*. 1986. Reprint, Vancouver: Arsenal Pulp Press, 2006.

Egan, Bill. *Florence Mills: Harlem Jazz Queen*. Lanham, MD: Scarecrow Press, 2004.

Eldridge, Royston. "Nina Simone: Nina's the Medium for the Message." *Melody Maker*, April 19, 1969.

Everett, Walter. *The Beatles as Musicians: The Quarry Men Through* Rubber Soul. Oxford: Oxford University Press, 2001.

——. *The Beatles as Musicians:* Revolver *Through the* Anthology. Oxford: Oxford University Press, 1999.

——. "Detroit and Memphis: The Soul of *Revolver*." In "*Every Sound There Is*": *The Beatles'* Revolver *and the Transformation of Rock and Roll*, edited by Russell Reising, 25–57. London: Ashgate, 2002.

Everett, Walter, and Katie Kapurch. "Come Together." In *Analyzing Recorded Music: Collected Perspectives*, edited by William Moylan, Lori Burns, and Mike Alleyne, 127–43. New York: Routledge, 2022.

"Ex-Beatle Tells How Black Stars Changed His Life." *Jet*, October 26, 1972.

Fields, Karen E., and Barbara J. Fields. *Racecraft: The Soul of Inequality in American Life*. London: Version, 2014.

Fitzpatrick, Richard. "Lead Belly Has Inspired a Music Generation." *Irish Examiner*, June 10, 2015. https://www.irishexaminer.com/lifestyle/arid-20335558.html.

Freeland, David. *Ladies of Soul*. Jackson: University of Mississippi Press, 2001.

Gamson, Joshua. *The Fabulous Sylvester: The Legend, the Music, the Seventies in San Francisco*. New York: Picador, 2005.

Garbus, Liz, dir. *What Happened, Miss Simone?* Netflix, 2015.

Gates, Henry Louis, Jr. *The Black Church: This Is Our Story, This Is Our Song*. New York: Penguin, 2021.

——. *The Signifying Monkey: A Theory of African-American Literary Criticism*. 1988. Reprint, Oxford: Oxford University Press, 2014.

Gates, Henry Louis, Jr. and Maria Tatar, eds. *The Annotated African American Folktales*. New York: Norton, 2018.

Gentleman, Amelia. *The Windrush Betrayal: Exposing the Hostile Environment*. London: Guardian Faber, 2019.

Giddens, Gary. *Visions of Jazz: The First Century*. Oxford: Oxford University Press, 1998.

Gilroy, Paul. *The Black Atlantic: Modernity and Double Consciousness*. Cambridge, MA: Harvard University Press, 1993.

Glass Onion: A Knives Out Mystery. Directed by Rian Johnson. Los Angeles: T-Street Productions, 2022.

Goldblatt, Stephen. *Mad Day Out*. San Francisco: Fotovision, 2010.

Goldman, Vivien. *The Book of Exodus: The Making and Meaning of Bob Marley and the Wailers' Album of the Century*. New York: Three Rivers Press, 2006.

Golia, Maria. *Ornette Coleman: The Territory and the Adventure*. London: Reaktion, 2020.

Gonyea, Don, and Gemma Watters. "'My Fifth Career': Bettye LaVette Reinvents Bob Dylan for Herself." *All Things Considered: NPR*, May 19, 2018, https://www.npr.org/2018/05/19/612088231/my-fifth-career-bettye-lavette-reinvents-bob-dylan-for-herself.

Graeber, David, and David Wengrow. *The Dawn of Everything: A New History of Humanity*. New York: Farrar, Straus and Giroux, 2021.

Graham, Whitney. "Why Yoko Ono Wants You to Look at the Sky for 24 Hours." *Getty*, June 17, 2021. https://www.getty.edu/news/why-yoko-ono-wants-you-to-look-at-the-sky-for-24-hours/.

Grant, Colin. *Homecoming: Voices of the Windrush Generation Hardcover*. New York: Random House, 2019.

——. *The Natural Mystics: Marley, Tosh, and Wailer*. New York: Norton, 2011.

Greene, Graham. *Travels with My Aunt*. New York: Penguin, 1969.

Gunderson, Chuck. *Some Fun Tonight! The Backstage Story of How the Beatles Rocked America—The Historic Tours 1964–1966*. San Francisco: Backbeat Books, 2016.

Gunderson, Philip A. "Danger Mouse's *Grey Album*, Mash-Ups, and the Age of Composition." *Postmodern Culture* Volume 15, Number 1, September 2004. Project MUSE, May 2, 2020.

Gutterman, Scott. *John Lennon: The Collected Artwork*. San Rafael, CA: Insight Editions, 2014.

Guzmán, Sandra. "Remembering Toni Morrison, the Bird Whisperer." *Audubon Magazine*, August 5, 2020. https://www.audubon.org/news/remembering-toni-morrison-bird-whisperer¶

Haefeli, Mark, dir. *Paul McCartney: Back in the U.S.; Concert Film*. Los Angeles: Capitol, 2002.

Hamilton, Jack. *Just Around Midnight: Rock and Roll and the Racial Imagination*. Cambridge, MA: Harvard University Press, 2016.

Hamilton, Virginia. *The People Could Fly: The Picture Book*. New York: Knopf, 2015.

Hanly, Francis, dir. *Produced by George Martin*. Parlophone/Capitol, 2001.

Heilbut, Anthony. *The Fan Who Knew Too Much: Aretha Franklin, the Rise of the Soap Opera, Children of the Gospel Church, and Other Meditations*. New York: Knopf, 2012.

——. *The Gospel Sound: Good News and Bad Times*. New York: Limelight, 1997.

Heinzerling, Zachary, dir. *McCartney 3, 2, 1*. 6 episodes. Santa Monica, CA: Hulu, 2021.

Henry, Tony. "The Man Who Put the Beat in the Beatles." *The Observer*, August 2, 1998. https://www.proquest.com/newspapers/man-who-put-beat-beatles-john-paul-george-he-was/docview/250395325/se-2.

Hogan, Anthony. *The Beat Makers: The Unsung Heroes of the Mersey Sound*. Gloucestershire: Amberley, 2017.

Holloway, Karla F. C. "Revision and (Re)membrance: A Theory of Literary Structures in Literature by African-American Women Writers." 1990. In *African American Literary Theory: A Reader*, edited by Winston Napier, 387–98. New York: New York University Press, 2000.

Howard, Ron, dir. *The Beatles: Eight Days a Week–The Touring Years*. Apple, 2016.

Jackson, Peter, dir. *The Beatles: Get Back*. 3 episodes. Burbank, CA: Disney+, 2021.

Jackson-Fossett, Cora. "Legendary Musician Rodena Preston Passes Away." *Los Angeles Sentinel*, September 17, 2017. https://lasentinel.net/legendary-musician-rodena-preston-passes-away.html

Jasen, David A. *A Century of American Popular Music*. New York: Routledge, 2013.

"Jimi Hendrix Cleared of Blame for UK Parakeet Release." *BBC News*, December 12, 2019. https://www.bbc.com/news/uk-england-50755015.

Jones, Dylan. "At Home with Paul McCartney: His Most Candid Interview Yet." *GQ*, August 4, 2020. https://www.gq-magazine.co.uk/culture/article/paul-mccartney-interview.

Kapurch, Katie. "The Beatles, Gender, and Sexuality." In *Fandom and the Beatles: The Act You've Known for All These Years*, edited by Kenneth Womack and Kit O'Toole, 139–66. Oxford: Oxford University Press, 2021.

——. "Crying, Waiting, Hoping: The Beatles, Girl Culture, and the Melodramatic Mode." In *New Critical Perspectives on the Beatles: Things We Said Today*, edited by Kenneth Womack and Katie Kapurch, 199–220. London: Palgrave Macmillan, 2016.

——. *Disney Plus Beatles*. New York: Bloomsbury, forthcoming.

Kapurch, Katie, and Jon Marc Smith. "Blackbird Fly: Paul McCartney's Legend, Billy Preston's Gospel, and Lead Belly's Blues." *Interdisciplinary Literary Studies* 22, no. 1 (2020): 5–30.

——. "Blackbird Singing: Paul McCartney's Romance of Racial Harmony and Post-Racial America." In *New Critical Perspectives on the Beatles: Things We Said Today*, edited by Kenneth Womack and Katie Kapurch, 51–74. New York: Palgrave Macmillan, 2016.

Kernodle, Tammy L. "'I Wish I Knew How It Would Feel to Be Free': Nina Simone and Redefining of the Freedom Song of the 1960s." *Journal of the Society for American Music* 2, no. 3 (2008): 295–317.

Kilmister, Lemmy, with Janiss Garza. *White Line Fever: The Autobiography.* New York: Citadel, 2002.

Kreps, Daniel. "Paul McCartney Meets Women Who Inspired Beatles' 'Blackbird.'" *Rolling Stone*, May 1, 2016. https://www.rollingstone.com/music /music-news/paul-mccartney-meets -women-who-inspired-beatles-black bird-57076/.

Kun, Josh. *Audiotopia: Music, Race, and America.* Berkeley: University of California Press, 2005.

Laurent, Sylvie. *King and the Other America: The Poor People's Campaign and the Quest for Economic Equality.* Oakland: University of California Press, 2018.

LaVette, Bettye, with David Ritz. *A Woman Like Me.* New York: Penguin, 2012.

"Leadbelly." In *March of Time*, vol. 1, no. 2, produced by Louis de Rochemont and his brother Richard de Rochemont. New York: Time Inc., 1935.

Le Gendre, Kevin. *Don't Stop the Carnival: Black Music in Britain.* Leeds: Peepal Tree Press, 2018.

Lennon, John. *In His Own Write.* 1964. Reprint, New York: Simon & Schuster, 2010.

———. *Skywriting by Word of Mouth.* New York: Harper and Row, 1986.

Leroux, Charles. "Ramsey's Rhythms." *Chicago Tribune*, February 4, 2007. https://www.chicagotribune.com/news /ct-xpm-2007-02-04-0702040496 -story.html.

Lester, Richard, dir. *A Hard Day's Night.* 1964. Reissue, New York: Criterion, 2014.

Lewis, John. "'Butt-Shakers and Toe-Tappers': Ramsey Lewis Brought Jazz to the People." *The Guardian*, September 14, 2022. https://www.theguardian .com/music/2022/sep/14/ramsey -lewis-butt-shakers-toe-tappers-jazz -people.

Lewisohn, Mark. *The Complete Beatles Chronicle.* London: Pyramid, 1992.

———. "Double Lives: Between the Beatles' Grooves." Keynote address, Monmouth University, November 10, 2019.

———. *Tune In: The Beatles; All These Years.* Vol. 1. New York: Crown, 2013.

———. *Tune In: The Beatles; All These Years.* Vol. 1. Extended special ed. New York: Little, Brown, 2013.

Light, Alan. *What Happened, Miss Simone? A Biography.* New York: Crown Archetype, 2016.

Lomax, Alan. "15A. THE GREY GOOSE. Sung by James (Iron Head) Baker and Group, Sugarland, Texas, 1934. Recorded by John A. and Alan Lomax." In *Afro-American Spirituals, Work Songs, and Ballads*, 1942. Archive of American Folk Song, Library of Congress Music Division. https://www.loc.gov/folklife /LP/AfroAmerSpirtualsL3_opt.pdf.

———. "Negro Material: The Story of the Mighty Blue Goose by Iron Head Assisted by Alan Lomax." 1933. Collected in *Writings, Baker, Iron Head, John A. Lomax and Alan Lomax Papers, 1907–1969*, by John A. Lomax and Alan Lomax. American Folklife Center, Library of Congress. https:// www.loc.gov/item/afc1933001_ms 383/.

Lomax, John A. "Sugarland, Texas." 1941. Collected in *Ballad Hunter*. American Folklife Center, Library of Congress. https://www.loc.gov/item/afc1941005 _ms095/.

Lomax, John A., and James Baker (Iron Head). "The Grey Goose." Recorded by John A Lomax, Central State Farm, Sugarland, Texas, 1933. American Folklife Center, Library of Congress. https://www.loc.gov/item/afc9999005 .674/.

Lomax, John A., Corine Jackson, and Hasel Futch. "Go Tell Aunt Tabby." Recorded by John A. Lomax and Ruby T. Lomax, Raiford, Florida, June 4, 1939. Audio recording. 00:02:07. https://www.loc.gov/item/lomaxbib000558/.

Lomax, John A., and Alan Lomax. *American Ballads and Folk Songs*. 1934. Reprint, New York: Dover, 1994.

——. *Negro Folk Songs as Sung by Lead Belly*. New York: Macmillan, 1936.

Lott, Eric. *Love and Theft: Blackface Minstrelsy and the American Working Class*. Oxford: Oxford University Press, 2013.

MacDonald, Ian. *Revolution in the Head: The Beatles' Records and the Sixties*. 3rd ed. Chicago Review Press, 2007. Kindle.

Mack, Roy, dir. *Pie, Pie Blackbird*. Burbank, CA: Warner Bros., 1932.

Maeterlinck, Maurice. *The Blue Bird: A Fairy Play in Six Acts*. 1908. Translated by Alexander Teixeira De Mattos in 1910. Reprint, Chapel Hill, NC: Project Gutenberg, 2013. https://www.gutenberg.org/files/8606/8606-h/8606-h.htm.

Mahar, William John. *Behind the Burnt Cork Mask: Early Blackface Minstrelsy and Antebellum American Popular Culture*. Urbana: University of Illinois Press, 1999.

Mahon, Maureen. *Black Diamond Queens: African American Women and Rock and Roll*. Durham, NC: Duke University Press, 2020. Kindle.

——. *Right to Rock: The Black Rock Coalition and the Cultural Politics of Race*. Durham, NC: Duke University Press, 2004.

Marchese, David. "Paul McCartney Is Still Trying to Figure Out Love." *New York Times*, November 30, 2020. https://www.nytimes.com/interactive/2020/11/30/magazine/paul-mccartney-interview.html.

McCartney, Angie. *My Long and Winding Road: My First 82.9 Years*. Wolverhampton: ROK Books, 2013.

McCartney, Paul. *Blackbird Singing: Poems and Lyrics, 1965–1999*. Edited by Adrian Mitchell. New York: Norton, 2001.

——. Foreword to *Liverpool: Wondrous Place: From the Cavern to the Capital of Culture*, by Paul DuNoyer, ix–xi. London: Virgin, 2007.

——. *The Lyrics: 1956 to the Present*. Edited by Paul Muldoon. New York: Liveright, 2021.

——. "Paul on Little Richard." May 10, 2020. https://www.paulmccartney.com/news-blogs/news/paul-on-little-richard.

McDaniel, Lorna. "The Flying Africans: Extent and Strength of the Myth in the Americas." *Nieuwe West-Indische Gids / New West Indian Guide* 64, nos. 1/2 (1990): 28–40.

McGrath, James. "Liverpool's Black Community and the Beatles: Black Liverpudlian Angles on the Beatles' History." *Soundscapes: A Journal on Media Culture* 12 (2010). https://www.icce.rug.nl/~soundscapes/VOLUME12/Interview_McGrath.shtml.

——. "Phillips, Harold Adolphus (1929–2000)." *Oxford Dictionary of National Biography*, October 4, 2012. https://doi.org/10.1093/ref:odnb/74400.

——. "'Where You Once Belonged': Class, Race and Liverpool Roots of Lennon and McCartney's Songs." *Popular Music History* 9, no. 1 (2014). https://doi.org/10.1558/pomh.v9i1.27616.

Miles, Barry. *Paul McCartney: Many Years from Now*. New York: Henry Holt, 1997.

Mills, Florence. "Dramatis Personae." Interview by Hannen Swaffer for the *Daily Express*. Reprinted in *The Crisis*, September 1927.

Miller, Stuart. "Inside Otis Redding's Final Masterpiece '(Sittin' On) The Dock of the Bay.'" *Rolling Stone*, December 10, 2017. https://www.rollingstone.com/music/music-features/inside-otis-reddings-final-masterpiece-sittin-on-the-dock-of-the-bay-122170/.

Mitchell, Verner D., and Cynthia Davis. *Encyclopedia of the Black Arts Movement.* Lanham, MD: Rowman & Littlefield, 2019.

Moore, Sam. "Donald Glover Calls Migos 'the Beatles of This Generation.'" *NME,* January 9, 2017. https://www.nme.com/news/music/donald-glover-migos-beatles-of-this-generation-1940450.

Moring, Mark. "Bobby McFerrin Gets Spirit-You-All." *Christianity Today,* July 29, 2013. https://www.christianitytoday.com/ct/2013/july-web-only/bobby-mcferrin-gets-spirit-you-all.html.

Morrison, Matthew D. "Race, Blacksound, and the (Re)Making of Musicological Discourse." *Journal of the American Musicological Society* 72, no. 3 (December 2019): 781–823.

Morrison, Toni. "Nobel Lecture." The Nobel Prize, December 7, 1993. https://www.nobelprize.org/prizes/literature/1993/morrison/lecture/.

———. *The Song of Solomon.* 1977. Reprint, New York: Vintage, 2004.

"Mud Is All You Need to Repair Paul." *Liverpool Echo,* September 16, 2005, updated May 8, 2013. https://www.liverpoolecho.co.uk/whats-on/music/mud-you-need-repair-paul-3527788.

Mundy, Rachel. *Animal Musicalities: Birds, Beasts, and Evolutionary Listening.* Middletown, CT: Wesleyan University Press, 2018.

Murrow, Edward R., and Fred W. Friendly, prods. *Satchmo the Great.* Beverly Hills, CA: United Artists, 1957.

"Music Icons Marilyn McCoo and Billy Davis Jr. Release Official Music Video of Single 'Blackbird.'" *Tennessee Tribune,* April 21, 2021. https://tntribune.com/music-icons-marilyn-mccoo-and-billy-davis-jr-release-official-music-video-of-single-blackbird/.

Mynott, Jeremy. *Birdscapes: Birds in Our Imagination and Experience.* Princeton, NJ: Princeton University Press, 2009.

———. *Birds in the Ancient World: Winged Words.* Oxford: Oxford University Press, 2018.

Nelson, Sabrina. "Artist Sabrina Nelson." *Detroit Performs,* May 20, 2020. https://www.detroitperforms.org/2020/05/sabrinanelson/.

Norman, Philip. *Shout! The Beatles in Their Generation.* London: Touchstone, 2005.

O'Brien, Tim. *The Things They Carried.* New York: Houghton Mifflin, 1990.

"One-Way Ticket: Jacob Lawrence's Migration Series and Other Visions of the Great Movement North." MoMA, April 3–September 7, 2015. https://www.moma.org/calendar/exhibitions/1495.

Opie, Peter, and Iona Opie, eds. *The Oxford Dictionary of Nursery Rhymes.* Oxford: Oxford University Press, 1997.

Palmer, Robert. *Deep Blues.* New York: Penguin, 1981.

Paquet, Sandra, Patricia J. Saunders, and Stephen Stuempfle, eds. *Music, Memory, Resistance: Calypso and the Caribbean Literary Imagination.* Kingston: Ian Randle, 2007.

Pareles, Jon. "Billy Preston, 59, Soul Musician, Is Dead; Renowned Keyboardist and Collaborator." *New York Times,* June 7, 2006. https://www.nytimes.com/2006/06/07/arts/07preston.html.

———. "Swans' Gospel Messages." *New York Times,* November 16, 1988.

Parks, Gordon, dir. *Leadbelly.* Hollywood, CA: Paramount Pictures, 1976.

Paul McCartney and Wings Fly South: Live in Melbourne 1975 [film]. N.p.: FAB Productions, 2010.

Paul McCartney and Wings: Rockshow (1976) [film]. New York: Eagle Rock Entertainment, 2014.

Perkins, George. "A Medieval Carol Survival: 'The Fox and the Goose.'" *Journal of American Folklore* 74, no. 293 (1961): 235–44.

Phillips, Michael G., and Phillips, Trevor. *Windrush: The Irresistible Rise of*

Multi-Racial Britain. London: Harper-
Collins, 1998.

Place, Jeff. *Lead Belly: The Smithsonian
Folkways Collection*. Washington DC:
Smithsonian Folkways Recordings,
2015. https://folkways-media.si.edu
/liner_notes/smithsonian_folkways
/SFW40201.pdf.

Procter, James. *Dwelling Places: Postwar
Black British Writing*. Manchester:
Manchester University Press, 2003.

——, ed. *Writing Black Britain, 1948–1998:
An Interdisciplinary Anthology*. Manchester: Manchester University Press,
2000.

Radin, Paul. *The Trickster: A Study in American Indian Mythology*. 2nd ed. New
York: Schocken, 1972.

Rand, Lisa. "The Eccentric Legend Behind
Liverpool's Famous 'Black Christ'
Sculpture." *Liverpool Echo*, January 17,
2020. https://www.liverpoolecho.co.uk
/news/liverpool-news/eccentric-legend
-behind-liverpools-famous-17560280.

——. "Windrush War Hero Who Smuggled
the Beatles George Harrison into Hamburg." *Liverpool Echo*, December 27,
2019. https://www.liverpoolecho.co
.uk/news/liverpool-news/windrush-war
-hero-who-smuggled-17399489.

Ravenscroft, Alan, dir. *Legend of Lead Belly*.
Washington, DC: Smithsonian, 2015.

Reps, Chas. *De Ole Grey Goose*. New York:
C. G. Christman, 1844. Notated music.
Music Division, Library of Congress.
https://www.loc.gov/item/sm1844
.390870/.

Rice, Edward. *Captain Sir Richard Francis
Burton: A Biography*. Cambridge, MA:
De Capo, 1990.

Richardson, David, Suzanne Schwarz, and
Anthony Tibbles, eds. *Liverpool and
Transatlantic Slavery*. Liverpool: Liver-
pool University Press, 2007.

Riley, Tim. "Drive My Car: 60s Soulsters
Embrace Lennon-McCartney." In
*Beatlestudies 3: Proceedings of the
Beatles 2000 Conference*, edited by
Yrjö Heinonen and Jyväskylän yliopisto,

15–24. Jyväskylä: University of Jyväskylä, Department of Music, 2000.

Robbins, Rossell Hope, ed. *Secular Lyrics
of the XIVth and XVth Centuries*. 1952.
Reprint, Oxford: Clarendon Press,
1955.

Roberts, Chris. *Heavy Words, Lightly
Thrown: The Reason Behind the
Rhyme*. New York: Gotham, 2005.

Roessner, Jeffrey. "We All Want to Change
the World: Postmodern Politics and
the Beatles' 'White Album.'" In *Reading
the Beatles: Cultural Studies, Literary Criticism, and the Fab Four*, edited
by Kenneth Womack and Todd Davies,
147–58. Albany: State University of
New York Press, 2006.

Ross, Diana, *Secrets of a Sparrow: Memoirs*. New York: Villard Books, 1993.

Runtagh, Jordan. "The Beatles' Revelatory White Album Demos: A Complete
Guide." *Rolling Stone*, May 29, 2018.
https://www.rollingstone.com/music
/music-lists/the-beatles-revelatory
-white-album-demos-a-complete-guide
-629178/blackbird-3-627800/.

Salvatore, Nick. "'The Eagle Stirrith Her
Nest': Reverend C. L. Franklin (1953)."
Library of Congress National Recording Registry, 2010. https://www.loc
.gov/static/programs/national-record
ing-preservation-board/documents
/TheEagleStirrethHerNest.pdf.

Santelli, Robert. Introduction. In *Lead Belly:
The Smithsonian Folkways Collection*,
11–15. Washington DC: Smithsonian
Folkways Recordings, 2015. https://
folkways-media.si.edu/liner_notes/sm
ithsonian_folkways/SFW40201.pdf.

Scarborough, Dorothy. *On the Trail of Negro
Folk-songs*. Cambridge, MA: Harvard
University Press, 1925.

Schneider, Matthew. *The Long and Winding
Road from Blake to the Beatles*. New
York: Palgrave Macmillan, 2008.

Schofield, Nigel. *Fairport by Fairport*. London: Essential Works, 2013.

Sgt. Pepper's Lonely Hearts Club Band. Directed by Michael Schultz. Universal City, CA: Universal, 1978.

Sheffield, Rob. "Why Nobody Sang the Beatles Like Aretha." *Rolling Stone*, August 16, 2018. https://www.rollingstone.com/music/music-features/aretha-franklin-beatles-eleanor-rigby-712267/.

Sherwood, Marika. "Perfidious Albion: Britain, the USA, and Slavery in the 1840s and 1860s." *Contributions in Black Studies* 13, no. 1 (1995): 174–200.

Shilliam, Robbie. *The Black Pacific: Anti-Colonial Struggles and Oceanic Connections.* London: Bloomsbury, 2015.

Simone, Nina, with Stephen Cleary. *I Put a Spell on You: The Autobiography of Nina Simone.* 1991. Reprint, Cambridge, MA: Da Capo Press, 2003.

Simpson, Erik. "Blackface Othellos and Irish Melodies: James Joyce's Minstrelsies." *ELH* 88, no. 3 (2021): 715–42.

Seeger, Pete, ed. *Three Songs by Leadbelly.* Directed by Blanding Sloan and Wah Mong Chang. Folklore Research Film, 1945.

Smith Storey, Olivia. "Flying Words: Contests of Orality and Literacy in the Trope of the Flying Africans." *Journal of Colonialism and Colonial History* 5, no. 3 (2004). http://www.doi.org/10.1353/cch.2004.0090.

Solomon, Olivia, and Jack Solomon. *Honey in the Rock: The Ruby Pickens Tartt Collection of Religious Folk Songs from Sumter County, Alabama.* Macon, GA: Mercer University Press, 2002.

Southern, Eileen. *The Music of Black Americans: A History.* 1971. Reprint, New York: Norton, 1997.

Spector, Ronnie, with Vince Waldron. *Be My Baby: How I Survived Mascara, Miniskirts, and Madness, or My Life as a Fabulous Ronette.* 1990. Reprint, Los Angeles: Words in Edgewise Books, 2015.

Spizer, Bruce. *The Beatles Are Coming: The Birth of Beatlemania in America.* New Orleans: 498 Productions, 2003.

——. *Songs, Pictures, and Stories of the Fabulous Beatles Records on Vee-Jay.* New Orleans: 498 Productions, 1998.

Stoever, Jennifer Lynn. *The Sonic Color Line: Race and the Cultural Politics of Listening.* New York: New York University Press, 2016.

Stubbs, Dan. "Paul McCartney: Fuh the Win." *NME*, September 14, 2018. https://www.nme.com/nme-big-read-paul-mccartney-beatles-brothers-arguing-thats-families.

"The Supremes' Mary Wilson Recalls Meeting the Beatles." *ABC News Radio*, February 5, 2014. http://abcnewsradioonline.com/music-news/2014/2/5/the-supremes-mary-wilson-recalls-meeting-the-beatles-we-aske.html.

Swanton, John. R. *Tlingit Myths and Texts.* Smithsonian Institution Ethnology, Bureau of Bulletins, vol. 39. Washington DC: US Government Printing Office, 1909.

Szwed, John. *Alan Lomax: The Man Who Recorded the World.* New York: Penguin, 2010.

Taylor, Yuval, and Jake Austen. *Darkest America: Black Minstrelsy from Slavery to Hip Hop.* New York: Norton, 2012.

Thompson, Ahmir "Questlove," dir. *Summer of Soul (. . . Or, When the Revolution Could Not Be Televised).* Searchlight Pictures / Hulu, 2021.

Thompson, Dave. *Reggae and Caribbean Music.* Enfield: Backbeat Books, 2002.

Thompson, Robert Farris. *Flash of the Spirit: African and Afro-American Art and Philosophy.* New York: Vintage, 1983.

Thorsteinson, Katherine. "From Escape to Ascension: The Effects of Aviation Technology on the Flying African Myth." *Criticism* 57, no. 2 (2015): 259–81.

Tibbles, Anthony. *Liverpool and the Slave Trade.* Liverpool: Liverpool University Press, 2018.

Turner, Steve. *The Beatles: The Stories Behind the Songs, 1967–70*. London: Carlton Books, 2009. Kindle.

Van Buskirk, Eliot. "Video: Paul McCartney and Youth Talk 'The Fireman.'" *Wired*, November 18, 2008. https://www.wired.com/2008/11/the-fireman/.

Vega-González, Susana. "Broken Wings of Freedom: Bird Imagery in Toni Morrison's Novels." *Revista de Estudios Norteamericanos*, no. 7 (2000): 75–84.

"Victory Baptist Church History." Victory Baptist Church of Los Angeles, n.d. https://www.victoryla.com/who-are-we/church-history/.

Vincent, Rickey. *Funk: The Music, the People, and the Rhythm of the One*. New York: St. Martin's Press, 2014.

Wald, Elijah. *How the Beatles Destroyed Rock 'n' Roll: An Alternative History of American Popular Music*. Oxford: Oxford University Press, 2009.

Ward, Brian. "Music, Musical Theater, and the Imagined South in Interwar Britain." *Journal of Southern History* 80, no. 1 (2014): 39–72.

Warwick, Jacqueline. *Girl Groups, Girl Culture: Popular Music and Identity in the 1960s*. New York: Routledge, 2013.

——. "You're Going to Lose That Girl: The Beatles and Girl Groups." In *Beatlestudies 3: Proceedings of the Beatles 2000 Conference*, edited by Yrjö Heinonen and Jyväskylän yliopisto, 161–67. Jyväskylä: University of Jyväskylä, Department of Music, 2000.

Watson, Renée. *Harlem's Little Blackbird: The Story of Florence Mills*. Illustrations by Christian Robinson. New York: Random House, 2012.

Weheliye, Alexander G. *Phonographies: Grooves in Sonic Afro-Modernity*. Durham, NC: Duke University Press, 2005.

Wenner, Jann. *Lennon Remembers*. 1971. Reprint, London: Verso, 2000.

Werner, Craig. *A Change Is Gonna Come: Music, Race, and the Soul of America*.

Ann Arbor: University of Michigan Press, 2006.

——. *Higher Ground: Stevie Wonder, Aretha Franklin, Curtis Mayfield, and the Rise and Fall of American Soul*. New York: Three Rivers Press, 2004.

West, Cornel. *The Cornel West Reader*. New York: Civitas, 1999.

White, Charles. *The Life and Times of Little Richard*. London: Omnibus, 2003.

Wilderson, Frank B., III. *Afropessimism*. New York: Liveright, 2020.

Wolfe, Charles, and Lornell, Kip. *The Life and Legend of Leadbelly*. 1992. Reprint, New York: Da Capo, 1999.

Womack, Kenneth. *The Beatles Encyclopedia: Everything Fab Four*. Santa Barbara, CA: Greenwood, 2016.

——. "Paul McCartney's Spectacular Return to Form: New Solo Album 'McCartney III' Sizzles and Soars." *Salon*, November 14, 2020. https://www.salon.com/2020/11/14/paul-mccartneys-spectacular-return-to-form-new-solo-album-mccartney-iii-sizzles-and-soars/.

Wonfor, Geoff, and Bob Smeaton, dirs. *The Beatles Anthology*. 1995. Reissue, London: Apple, 2003.

Woodard, Patricia. "'Flee as a Bird': Mary Dana Shindler's Legacy." *American Music* 26, no. 1 (2008): 74–103.

Wordsworth, William, and Samuel Taylor Coleridge. *Lyrical Ballads, with a Few Other Poems*. London, 1798. Project Gutenberg, 2021. https://www.gutenberg.org/files/9622/9622-h/9622-h.htm.

Work, John W. *American Negro Songs: 230 Folk Songs and Spirituals, Religious and Secular*. 1940. Reprint, Mineola, NY: Dover, 1988.

Wynter, Kevin. *Critical Race Theory and Jordan Peele's "Get Out."* New York: Bloomsbury Academic, 2022.

"Yoko Ono. *To See the Sky*. 2015." MoMA, May 17–September 7, 2015. https://www.moma.org/audio/playlist/15/377.

Young, Jason R. "All God's Children Had Wings: The Flying African in History,

Literature, and Lore." *Journal of Afri-
cana Religions* 5, no. 1 (2017): 50–70.
Youngquist, Paul. *A Pure Solar World: Sun
Ra and the Birth of Afrofuturism*. Aus-
tin: University of Texas Press, 2016.
Zabel, Darcy. *The (Underground) Railroad
in African American Literature*. New
York: Peter Lang, 2004.
Zolten, Jerry. *Great God A'mighty! The Dixie
Hummingbirds: Celebrating the Rise
of Soul Gospel Music*. Oxford: Oxford
University Press, 2003.
——. "'Oh Mary Don't You Weep': The Swan
Silvertones (1959)." Library of Con-
gress National Recording Registry,
2014. https://www.loc.gov/static/pro
grams/national-recording-preservation
-board/documents/OhMaryDontYou
Weep.pdf.

MUSICAL RECORDINGS

Armstrong, Louis. "Flee as a Bird." *Satchmo:
A Musical Autobiography of Louis Arm-
strong*. Decca, 1957.
——. "Hello, Dolly!" / "A Lot of Livin' to Do."
Kapp, 1964.
Beach Boys. "Caroline No." *Pet Sounds*.
Capitol, 1966.
Beatles. *Abbey Road*. Apple, 1969.
——. *Anthology 1*. Apple, 1995.
——. *Anthology 2*. Apple, 1996.
——. *The Beatles* [*The White Album*]. Apple,
1968. Reissue, Apple, 2018.
——. *Beatles for Sale*. Parlophone, 1964.
——. *The Complete Star Club Tapes, 1962*.
1F2, 2015.
——. "Free as a Bird" / "Christmas Time (Is
Here Again)." Apple, 1995.
——. "From Me to You" / "Thank You Girl."
Parlophone, 1963.
——. *Help!*. Parlophone, 1965.
——. "Help!" / "I'm Down." Parlophone,
1965.
——. "I Want to Hold Your Hand" / "I Saw
Her Standing There." Capitol, 1963.
——. "Lady Madonna" / "The Inner Light."
Parlophone/Capitol, 1968.
——. *Let It Be*. Apple, 1970.

——. *Live! At the Star-Club in Hamburg,
Germany, 1962*. Lingasong, 2006.
——. *Magical Mystery Tour*. Parlophone/
Capitol, 1967.
——. *No. 3 Abbey Road NW8* [unofficial
release]. Audifön, 1979.
——. *Please Please Me*. Parlophone, 1963.
——. *Revolver*. Parlophone/Capitol, 1966.
——. *Rubber Soul*. Parlophone/Capitol,
1965.
——. *Sgt. Pepper's Lonely Hearts Club
Band*. Parlophone/Capitol, 1967.
——. "She Loves You" / "I'll Get You." Parlo-
phone, 1963.
——. "Strawberry Fields Forever / Penny
Lane." Parlophone/Capitol, 1967.
——. "We Can Work It Out" / "Day Tripper."
Parlophone/Capitol, 1965.
——. *With the Beatles*. Parlophone, 1963.
Beatles, with Billy Preston. "Get Back" /
"Don't Let Me Down." Apple, 1969.
Belafonte, Harry. "Coconut Woman" /
"Island in the Sun." RCA, 1957.
——. "Don't Ever Love Me" / "Mama Look at
Bubu." RCA, 1957.
Berry, Chuck. "Maybellene" / "Wee Wee
Hours." Chess, 1955.
——. "Sweet Little Sixteen" / "Reelin And
Rocking." Chess, 1958. Brown, James.
"Say It Loud—I'm Black and I'm Proud."
King, 1968.
*Bullfrog Jumped: Children's Folksongs from
the Byron Arnold Collection* [compi-
lation]. Alabama Folklife Association,
2006.
Cantor, Eddie. "Bye Bye Blackbird." *The
Eddie Cantor Story (Songs by Eddie
Cantor from the Original Sound Track)*.
Capitol, 1953.
Charles, Ray. "Sticks and Stones" / "Wor-
ried Life Blues." ABC-Paramount,
1960.
——. *Volcanic Action of My Soul*. ABC/Tan-
gerine, 1971.
Cooke, Sam, with the Soul Stirrers. "Nearer
to Thee." *Sam Cooke with the Soul
Stirrers: The Complete Specialty
Recordings*. Specialty, 2002.
Cooke, Sam. *Night Beat*. RCA Victor, 1963.

Cookies. "Chains" / "Stranger in My Arms." Dimension, 1962.

Dekker, Desmond, and the Specials. "Wings of a Dove." *King of Kings*. Trojan Records, 1993.

Del-Vikings. "Come Go with Me" / "How Can I Find True Love." Fee Bee, 1957.

Domino, Fats [Antoine Dominique Domino Jr.]. *Fats Is Back*. Reprise, 1968.

——. "My Blue Heaven" / "I'm in Love Again." Imperial, 1956.

Donays. "Bad Boy" / "Devil in His Heart." Correc-Tone, 1962.

Donegan, Lonnie. "Does Your Chewing Gum Lose Its Flavour (On the Bedpost Overnight?)" / "Aunt Rhody (The Old Grey Goose)." Pye Nixa, 1959.

—— [Lonnie Donegan's Skiffle Group]. "Rock Island Line" / "John Henry." Decca, 1955.

Don Letts Presents the Mighty Trojan Sound [compilation]. Trojan, 2003.

Donovan. "The Magpie." *A Gift from a Flower to a Garden*. Epic, 1967.

Ellington, Duke, and His Cotton Club Orchestra. "Black Beauty" / "Jubilee Stomp." Victor, 1928.

Faithfull, Marianne. *Come My Way*. Decca. 1965.

——. *Marianne Faithfull*. Decca, 1965.

Father and Sons [compilation]. Spirit Feel, 1990.

Fireman [Paul McCartney]. *Electric Arguments*. One Little Indian / ATO, 2008.

Flamingos. "I Only Have Eyes for You" / "Goodnight Sweetheart." Bell Sound, 1959.

Franklin, Aretha. *Amazing Grace*. Atlantic, 1972.

——. "Eleanor Rigby"/ "It Ain't Fair." Atlantic, 1969.

——. *This Girl's in Love with You*. Atlantic, 1970.

——. "The Long and Winding Road." *Young, Gifted and Black*. Atlantic, 1972.

——. "Mockingbird." *Runnin' Out of Fools*. Columbia, 1965.

——. "Skylark." *Laughing on the Outside*. Columbia, 1963.

——. "Tiny Sparrow." 1964. *The Essential Aretha Franklin - The Columbia Years*. Columbia, 2010.

Franklin, Reverend C. L. "The Eagle Stirreth Her Nest." Chess, 1953.

Funkadelic. *Let's Take It to the Stage*. Westbound, 1975.

Giddens, Rhiannon, with Francesco Turrisi. *They're Calling Me Home*. Nonesuch, 2021.

Golden Gate Quartet. "Swing Down, Chariot." *Golden Gate Spirituals*. Columbia, 1947.

Hendrix, Jimi. *The Cry of Love*. Electric Lady, 1971.

Hendrix, Jimi [Jimi Hendrix Experience]. *Axis: Bold as Love*. Track/Reprise, 1967.

——. "Hey Joe" / "Stone Free." Polydor, 1966.

——. "Purple Haze" / "51st Anniversary." Track/Reprise, 1967.

Howlin' Wolf. "The Red Rooster" / "Shake for Me." Chess, 1961.

Johnson, Lonnie. "Blackbird Blues." 1927. *Volume One, 1925–1929*. Real Gone Jazz, 2017.

Keys, Alicia. *Songs in A Minor*. J, 2001.

Kitchener, Lord [Aldwyn Roberts]. *Calypsos Too Hot to Handle*. Vol. 1. Melodisc, 1955.

——. "Kitch (Small Comb, Scratch Me Head)." Melodisc, 1951.

——. "Festival of Britain" / "London Is the Place for Me." Melodisc, 1951.

——. "Take It Easy"/ "Redhead." Lyragon, 1953.

Kravitz, Lenny. "Fly Away." *5*. Virgin, 1998.

LaVette, Bettye. *Blackbirds*. Verve, 2020.

——. *Interpretations: The British Rock Songbook*. ANTI-, 2010.

——. "Let Me Down Easy" / "What I Don't Know Won't Hurt Me." Calla, 1965.

——. "A Little Help from My Friends" / "Hey Love." Karen (Atlantic), 1969.

——. "Little Sparrow." *I've Got My Own Hell to Raise*. ANTI-, 2005.

——. "My Man—He's a Lovin' Man" / "Shut Your Mouth." Atlantic, 1962.

——. *Things Have Changed*. Verve, 2018.

Lead Belly [Huddie Ledbetter]. *Leadbelly*. Playboy, 1973.

——. *Lead Belly Sings for Children*. Smithsonian Folkways, 1999.

——. *Negro Folk Songs for Young People*. Folkways, 1960.

——. *Shout On (Lead Belly Legacy Vol. 3)*. Smithsonian Folkways, 1998.

——. *The Smithsonian Folkways Collection*. Smithsonian Folkways, 2015.

——. *Where Did You Sleep Last Night (Lead Belly Legacy Vol. 1)*. Smithsonian Folkways, 1996.

Lennon, John. *John Lennon / Plastic Ono Band*. Apple, 1970.

Lennon, John, and Yoko Ono. *Double Fantasy*. Geffen/Capitol, 1980.

——. *Milk and Honey*. Polydor, 1984.

Lewis, Ramsey. *Mother Nature's Son*. Cadet, 1968.

Luboff, Norman [Norman Luboff Choir]. *Calypso Holiday*. Columbia, 1957.

Marley, Bob, and the Wailers. *Exodus*. Island, 1977.

——. "Wings of a Dove." *The Birth of a Legend*. Calla, 1976.

Marvelettes. "Please Mister Postman" / "So Long Baby." Tamla, 1961.

McCartney, Paul. *Back in the U.S.: Live 2002*. MPL Communications, 2002.

——. *Chaos and Creation in the Backyard*. Parlophone/Capitol, 2005.

——. *Driving Rain*. Parlophone, 2021.

——. *Egypt Station*. Capitol, 2018.

——. *Kisses on the Bottom*. Capitol, 2012.

——. *McCartney*. Apple, 1970.

——. *McCartney II*. Parlophone, 1980.

——. *McCartney III*. MPL Productions, 2020.

McCartney, Paul, and Wings. "Give Ireland Back to the Irish." Apple, 1972.

——. *London Town*. Parlophone, 1978.

——. *Red Rose Speedway*. 1973. Reissue, Capitol, 2018.

——. *Wings over America*. Capitol, 1976.

McCartney, Paul, featuring Stevie Wonder. "Ebony and Ivory" / "Rainclouds." Parlophone/EMI/Columbia, 1982.

McCoo, Marilyn, and Billy Davis Jr. *Blackbird: Lennon-McCartney Icons*. BMG, 2021.

McFerrin, Bobby. "Blackbird." *The Voice*. Elektra/Musician, 1984.

——. *Spirityouall*. Masterworks, 2013.

Mighty Sparrow [aka King Sparrow, né Slinger Francisco]. *King Sparrow's Calypso Carnival*. Cook, 1959.

Migos. "Birds." *No Label II*. Quality Control Music, 2014.

Mills Brothers. "Yellow Bird" / "Baby Clementine." Dot, 1958.

Murphy, Delia. "Down by the Glenside" / "If I Were a Blackbird." His Master's Voice, 1949.

——. "If I Were a Blackbird" / "Down by the Glenside." Regal Zonophone, 1940.

Nirvana. *MTV Unplugged in New York*. DGC, 1994.

——. *With the Lights Out*. DGC, 2004.

Paragons. *On the Beach with the Paragons*. Treasure Isle, 1967.

——. "Yellow Bird"/ "Black Bird Singing." Treasure Isle, 2011.

Paragons, featuring Roslyn Sweat. "Black Birds Singing" / "Always." Duke, 1973.

Parliament. *Funkentelechy vs. the Placebo Syndrome*. Casablanca, 1977.

——. "The Goose." Casablanca, 1974.

——. *Mothership Connection*. Def Jam West, 1975.

Parton, Dolly. "Little Sparrow." *Little Sparrow*. Sugar Hill / Blue Eye, 2001.

Penguins. "Hey Señorita" / "Earth Angel." Dootone, 1954.

Presley, Elvis. "Swing Down Sweet Chariot." *His Hand in Mine*. RCA Victor, 1960.

Preston, Billy. *Encouraging Words*. 1969. Reissue, Apple, 2010.

——. *I Wrote a Simple Song / Music Is My Life*. 1971. Reissue, BOGO, 2011.

——. *The Kids & Me*. A&M, 1974.

——. *Music Is My Life*. A&M, 1972.

——. *16 Yr. Old Soul*. Derby, 1963.

——. *That's the Way God Planned It*. Apple, 1969.

Prince [Prince Rogers Nelson] and the Revolution. "When Doves Cry." *Purple Rain*. Warner Bros., 1984.

Redding, Otis. "(Sittin' On) The Dock of the Bay"/ "My Sweet Lorene." Stax, 1968.

Richards, Keith. *Crosseyed Heart*. Republic, 2015.

Robinson, Eric [as Eric & the Good Good Feeling]. *Funky*. Equinox, 1989.

———. *Walk in the Light*. RCA Victor, 1982.

Shirelles. "Baby It's You" / "The Things I Want to Hear." Scepter, 1961.

———. "Will You Love Me Tomorrow" / "Boys." Scepter, 1960.

Simone, Nina. "Ain't Got No, I Got Life" / "Do What You Gotta Do." RCA, 1968.

———. *Fodder on My Wings*. 1982. Reissue, Verve, 2020.

———. "Four Women." *Wild Is the Wind*. Philips, 1965.

———. "Here Comes the Sun." *Here Comes the Sun*. RCA, 1971.

———. "Isn't It a Pity." *Emergency Ward*. RCA, 1972.

———. "I Wish I Knew How It Would Feel to Be Free." *Silk & Soul*. RCA, 1967.

———. "Little Liza Jane"/ "Blackbird." Colpix, 1963.

———. *Nina Simone at Carnegie Hall*. Colpix, 1963. Reissue, EMI, 2005.

———. *Nina Simone at the Village Gate*. Colpix, 1962.

———. *Nina Simone in Concert*. Philips, 1964.

———. *Nina Simone with Strings*. Colpix, 1966.

———. "Revolution." RCA, 1969.

———. "To Be Young, Gifted and Black." *Black Gold*. RCA, 1970.

———. *To Love Somebody*. RCA Victor, 1969.

Sremmurd, Rae, featuring Gucci Mane. "Black Beatles." Ear Drummers / Interscope, 2016.

Starr, Ringo. *Sentimental Journey*. Apple, 1970.

Supremes. "Where Did Our Love Go" / "He Means the World to Me." Motown, 1964.

Swan Silvertones. *Amen, Amen, Amen: The Essential Collection*. Rockbeat, 2015.

———. "Move Up"/ "Oh Mary Don't You Weep." Vee-Jay, 1958.

Sylvester [Sylvester James Jr.]. *Living Proof*. Fantasy, 1979.

———. *Stars*. Fantasy, 1979.

Sylvester [Sylvester James Jr.], with Two Tons O' Fun. "Dance (Disco Heat)." / "You Make Me Feel (Mighty Real)." Fantasy, 1978.

Taylor, Billy. "I Wish I Knew How It Would Feel to Be Free." Capitol, 1964.

Taylor, Eva, with Clarence Williams's Blue Five featuring Louis Armstrong and Sidney Bechet. "I'm a Little Blackbird Looking for a Bluebird" / "Mandy, Make Up Your Mind." Okeh, 1925.

Waller, Fats. "Bye-Bye Florence." *Fats Waller with Morris's Hot Babies: 1927, Volume 2*. RCA, 1972.

Wash, Martha. *Love and Conflict*. Purple Rose, 2021.

Weather Girls. "It's Raining Men." Columbia, 1982.

Wells, Mary. *Love Songs to the Beatles*. Twentieth Century–Fox, 1965.

Williams, Marion. "He's Watching Over You" / "Got on My Travelling Shoes." Savoy, n.d.

———. "Packin' Up" / "Through Eternity." Gospel, n.d.

Wills, Bob, and His Texas Playboys. "Ida Red" / "Carolina in the Morning." Vocalion, 1938.

———. "Ida Red Likes the Boogie" / "A King Without a Queen." MGM, 1949.

Index